(Preceding page)

The audience at the Théâtre des Funambules
(Children of Paradise).

Catherine Deneuve

Jeanne Moreau

Jean Gabin

Michèle Morgan

Jean-Paul Belmondo

Gérard Philipe

Jean Marais

Edwige Feuillère

THE GREAT
FRENCH
FILMS

James Reid Paris

Introduction by François Truffaut

THE CITADEL PRESS   SECAUCUS, N.J.

First edition
Copyright © 1983 by James Reid Paris
All rights reserved
Published by Citadel Press
A division of Lyle Stuart Inc.
120 Enterprise Ave., Secaucus, N.J. 07094
In Canada: Musson Book Company
A division of General Publishing Co. Limited
Don Mills, Ontario
Designed by Christopher Simon
Manufactured in the United States of America

Library of Congress Cataloging in Publication Data

Paris, James Reid.
  The great French films.
  Bibliography: p.
  1. Moving-pictures—France—Plots, themes, etc.
I. Title.
PN1993.5.F7P276   1983   791.43'75   83-1767
ISBN 0-8-065-0806-X

This book is dedicated to
Jean Cocteau
who remains with us . . . .

*"With the cinema, death is killed,
literature is killed, poetry is made to live a
direct life. Imagine what the cinema of
poets might be."*

—JEAN COCTEAU.

Jean Cocteau directing Mila Parély
during the filming of *Beauty and the Beast*.

ACKNOWLEDGMENTS

The author is immeasurably indebted to many friends who share his love of French cinema without whose unselfish and unstinting help *The Great French Films* could never have been realized. Accordingly, the author wishes to express his profound gratitude to all those grouped for the sake of convenience as follows:

For their loyal support, encouragement, valued professional advice, and—above all—friendship: Mme. Chantal (de Bonnafos) Lombardi, Professor Emerita at Seton Hall University; the film historian and writer William Pratt; Michel Zerbib (Michaël Zer Aviv), Television and Film Consultant, Services Culturels Français (Los Angeles); and the author's brother, William Paris.

For her initial response of total cooperation which helped launch my project as well as her long-term assistance: Mme. Catherine Verret, Déleguée des Etats-Unis at Unifrance Film (New York).

For their generous loan of many of the beautiful and rare stills used in this book: Services Culturels Français (New York)—and the kindness of Geneviève Hureau; Bob Harris at Images Film Archive, Inc.; Saul J. Turell and Virginia Martin at Janus Films; and Unifrance Film (New York)—and the gracious attention from Lyse A. Middleton.

For additional stills: Ciné-Images (Paris); Cinema 5; Elisabeth Coppens and the Cinémathèque Royale (Brussels); Museum of Modern Art / Film Stills Archive—and the most cooperative Mary Corliss; National Film Archive / Stills Library (British Film Institute); New Line Cinema; and Donald L. Velde, Inc. (New York). (The remaining stills, approximately half used in the book, come from the author's private collection.)

For making available screenings of very hard-to-see films for the author's research: William K. Everson; Ben Harrison, Director of the Essex-Hudson Film Center at the East Orange Public Library (New Jersey); M. Patrick Imhaus, Ministère des Relations Extérieures: Direction Générale des Relations Culturelles, Scientifiques et Techniques (Bureau du Cinéma, Paris); Mme. Armelle Maala of the Services Culturels Français (New York);

Mme. Anne-Marie Marotte at Facsea; and John Montague at New Yorker Films.

For both lending me exquisite stills and providing rare film screenings: David J. Grossman, Temple University Cinematheque (Philadelphia) and Bill Kenly of Paramount Pictures.

For their valuable holdings and courteous and efficient staff: 42nd Street Reading Room, New York Public Library; French Institute / Alliance Française; Research Center, Lincoln Center Library for the Performing Arts; Seton Hall University Library; Charles Silver and the Museum of Modern Art / Film Study Department; and the archives of Unifrance Film (Paris).

For supplying extremely useful information, these correspondents: The British Academy of Film and Television Arts, Kevin Brownlow, René Clément, Louis Malle, Alain Resnais, and S.E.D.I.F. (Société d'Exploitation et de Distribution de Films).

And for a variety of helpful reasons: Roger Blunck; David Boyle; Ben Cutler; Ellen Jo Emerson at Unifrance (New York); Steve Fagan at New World Pictures; Rose Gallo; Wojciech Karpiński; Arthur Kornfeld; Bert Marino; Robert Mazzocco; Armand Panigel; Angela Papallo; Robert Rappaport; Bernhard W. Scholz, Dean, Seton Hall University; Helen Scott; the Seton Hall University Research Council for their summer stipend; John Skillin; Julienne Slonin at Unifrance (New York); Phyllis Stock, Ph.D.; Brigitte Sys, Ira Tulipan—and my friends at the Writers Guild (New York).

The author expresses his gratitude to his editor, Mr. Allan J. Wilson, for his longstanding patience and understanding as well as to the talented and cooperative staff at Citadel, especially Carmela Cohen, Arthur Smith, and David Goodnough. The author is indebted to Mr. A. Christopher Simon for his beautiful book design.

And, finally, a special and heartfelt note of thanks to François Truffaut for his generous Introduction, enthusiastic support, terrific stills, and—above all—his wonderful films.

Gérard Philipe and Micheline Presle (*Devil in the Flesh*)

CONTENTS

Jean Renoir completing *Grand Illusion* (1937).

Jacques Becker

THE GREAT FRENCH FILMS

Carné's Team: Joseph Kosma (composer), Jacques Prévert (screenwriter), Marcel Carné (director), Jean Gabin (actor), and Alexandre Trauner (set designer) preparing *La Marie du Port* (1949).

Alain Resnais on the set of *Last Year at Marienbad* in 1960.

Louis Malle, Jeanne Moreau, and Louise de Vilmorin preparing *The Lovers*, released in 1958.

Jean-Luc Godard at the time of *Breathless* (1960).

René Clair

Robert Bresson

50 YEARS OF FRENCH CINEMA

by François Truffaut

This beautiful book, *The Great French Films,* presents a very interesting and representative sampling of French film production over a fifty-year period. In the course of my reading at no time did I have the temptation to question the selections of James Reid Paris or to contrast my own list of preferred films to his. What I find remarkable in the fan which he unfolds beneath our eyes is that he combines films which are familiar to the American public with others unseen in the United States for too long a time.

One must always keep in mind that the knowledge we have of a country's literature or cinema is closely dependent on the curiosity and zeal of publishers and film distributors. For example, Jean Grémillon's films are nearly as unknown in the United States as those of Frank Borzage in France.

In the American system, the true "father" of a film was for a long time (and perhaps is still today) the *producer.* When a major company produces a film, the artistic as well as physical ownership (rights not only to the work but to the negative also) is secured for an unlimited time. This explains why the American cinematographic heritage remains so enduring, well-protected, and efficiently distributed not only in the United States but throughout the world.

In the European system, more respectful of the author's rights, things are different. For example, a French producer buys the adaptation rights to a novel from a publisher for a period of fifteen years.

*A group of Art Houses—currently more than seven hundred in France—receiving certain tax breaks from the government to encourage the distribution of art, experimental, or repertory films.   —JRP.

François Truffaut directing *Day for Night.*

That same producer afterwards hires one or two screenwriters to adapt this novel and he obtains the rights to their work for, say, twelve years. Then he engages a director (considered by French law as one of the authors) from whom he secures the rights for twenty years.

If one can immediately see the advantages of this procedure for the artists, one can equally see the disadvantages when, twenty years after the film's release, *un circuit d'art et d'essai** wishes to give it a second life. The initial producer is always the film's owner, fifteen or twenty years after its début, but he no longer retains anything legally except the *physical film itself,* that is to say the various existing copies of it and the edited negative kept in storage. To obtain the rights *to distribute* the film anew, the producer must contact once more the book's author and publisher, the screenwriters, and the director—or their heirs—and determine a new apportionment of any possible profits. That is why certain French films are so difficult to see today, even in France, even on television, particularly those of Becker, Bresson, and Guitry.

More strongly still than by their legal and economic structures, American and French films are differentiated by their style.

The American cinema is a cinema of plot, the French cinema is a cinema of characterization. Because of that the silent cinema which was geared to the spirit of simplification has been less brilliant in France (with the prestigious exception of Abel Gance) than in America. Jean Renoir, René Clair, and Jacques Feyder with their penchant for nuance, had need of sound and dialogue to express themselves and that is why they are in full bloom in the sound era, which permitted them to present human beings in all their complexity. Another great difference between our two cinemas is that in

François Truffaut directing his first feature, *The Four Hundred Blows.*

France we had some very good *artists* but few good *craftsmen*. There existed in Hollywood the very thriving "B" movies, composed of *"films de commandes"** which were admirably executed and whose artistic importance was recently recognized—I am thinking here of the work of Allan Dwan, Raoul Walsh, William Wellman, Tay Garnett or Michael Curtiz. There was nothing similar to this in France, where the good films were made by the powerful and ambitious directors, with the exception perhaps of two names well represented here, Christian-Jacque and Julien Duvivier, two fine French *craftsmen* who could execute *"films de commandes"* well and who were admirers of the American cinema.

The history of the French sound movies opened with two great avant-garde films produced by a Maecenas, the Vicomte de Noailles: *L'Age d'Or* by Buñuel and Dali and *Le Sang d'un Poète (The Blood of a Poet)* by Jean Cocteau. Then came Jean Vigo; the two films that this young man of genius directed before his premature death at the age of 29—*Zéro de Conduite (Zero for Conduct)* and *L'Atalante*—suffice to make him the greatest director in the history of French cinema. In the course of my trips to the United States I have been happy to confirm that Jean Vigo's work, brief but inspired, is regularly shown there, at least on campuses.

*Movies "made to order,"—the term "Programmers" is a close approximation.   —JRP.

If the French critic before the war never doubted the worth of René Clair, Jacques Feyder or Marcel Carné, he was often condescending with regard to Abel Gance or Jean Renoir and deliberately scornful toward Marcel Pagnol and Sacha Guitry, both accused of making, not films, but "filmed theatre." After the war, the films of Bresson, Cocteau, and Ophüls were, in their turn, seriously underestimated, like those of Orson Welles in the United States.

It was against this anti-poetic attitude of the official critics that a group of young critics expressing themselves in the monthly review *Les Cahiers du Cinéma* protested at the beginning of the 1950's. They attacked those well-executed but impersonal films which were often adapted from great classical or modern novels (Stendhal, Dostoevsky, Gide, Zola, Colette, Simenon, etc.) but whose audacities were rendered banal by the adapters. These cold and dry productions were praised by the major newspapers who grouped them under the label "psychological realism" without seeing that it was a *simplified psychology* and a *deformed reality*. In this type of cinema the star was always prestigious, the supporting players were made to appear stupid or ridiculous, and, in films purporting to be about childhood, the kid was always relegated to the background and upstaged by the star.

The young critics asserted from the same impulse their hostility to all ideas of a school or all restrictive definitions of the cinema. They rejected totally (at times at the risk of committing some injustices in their turn) the idea of the *cinéma d'équipe,** replacing it with the concept of the *cinéma d'auteur.*† They affirmed that a good director is not necessarily a manipulator of crowds or a talented technician who converts the thoughts of another into images, but, rather, a strong personality expressing himself through the cinema.

In applying to the cinema a proclamation of the playwright Jean Giradoux, "There are no good plays, there are only good authors," I proposed at that time with my friends from the *Cahiers du Cinéma* a theory of *"la politique des auteurs"* which meant to rehabilitate those filmmakers who participated closely in the writing of the films which they

*"Team cinema," a movie resulting from the collaboration of different artisans, the traditional Hollywood studio system.   —JRP.

†An influential tenet formulated by Truffaut which emphasizes a more *personal* aspect of filmmaking by insisting, among other things, that a film always has one principal author, and that this author should be the film's director.—JRP.

directed, those who expressed themselves "in the first person": Cocteau, Tati, Becker, Bresson, Renoir, Pagnol, Guitry, and Ophüls.

Starting with 1959, these young critics went on in their turn to become directors, grouped in spite of themselves under the designation "New Wave". They endeavored to make personal and intimate films which appealed to their wishes. It obviously does not suit me to pass judgment on this group of which I have been a part and which holds me in solid bonds. In any event, one judges better from a distance and I am convinced that James Reid Paris and the American cinéphiles are better situated than we are to estimate and compare the French cinema of yesterday and today, the same as in certain periods we were able in France to discern, before you, the beauties contained in *Singin' in the Rain, Johnny Guitar* or *Kiss Me Deadly*.

Since he succeeds so well in describing the French films which he loves—and especially in describing them *before* judging them—I approve of this book of James Reid Paris and as I hold his work before me I feel myself in an euphoric state of friendly solidarity.

F.T.

6 February 1982. Paris.
(tr. Chantal de Bonnafos).

Abel Gance (in dark round hat with sunglasses) during the shooting of the Brienne snowball fight sequence for *Napoléon* at Briançon. The crew: Simon Fieldman, Technical Director; Jules Kruger, Cameraman (seated on the sled); and Alexandre Volkoff, Assistant Director, center.

Julien Duvivier, right, directing Fernandel in *The Man in the Raincoat (L'Homme à l'Imperméable)* (1950).

Jean Vigo, left, directing Dita Parlo and Jean Dasté on the set of *L'Atalante.*

François Truffaut with Jean Renoir.

regret the slight attention paid to many outstanding artists such as Jean Grémillon. In an Appendix I briefly discuss an additional fifty films which were award-winning and noteworthy.

By no means do I dare claim that *The Great French Films* is a definitive study. It is, hopefully, a useful introduction or, if you will, *"hors d'oeuvres,"* a sampling.

Unless otherwise specified, all dates refer to a film's release date, a book's publication date or year of theatrical presentation.

AUTHOR'S NOTE

In its long and fascinating history, French cinema has been justly celebrated and admired and has exerted a profound world-wide influence.

France was the first country to recognize and encourage the medium of films as an art form, "the seventh art," by her artists and intellectuals. "Long live the young Muse, cinema, for she possesses the mystery of a dream and allows the unreal to become real," wrote Jean Cocteau.

America as well as other countries came to expect something "special" from the best films that France exported: incomparable acting (Raimu, Harry Baur), brilliant and personal direction from masters with vision and genius (Jean Renoir), an honest depiction of life which other countries could only envy (Pagnol's *The Marseilles Trilogy*), an ever-renewing experimentation (the New Wave), and, above all, a hard-to-define but constant manifestation of the rare quality of "poetry" (Carné's *Children of Paradise*). Indeed British critic Roger Manvell stated: "No country has contributed more than France to the art of film."

The problem of selection for this book was formidable. Exigencies of space precluded the mention of the avant-garde as well as the animated and documentary features. Although France dominated the world film market until World War I, she only regained an international recognition with the advent of sound and I was forced to merely suggest the riches of her silent cinema—a period frequently disparaged by the French themselves and which is sorely in need of reevaluation. I have tried to chiefly stress the work of those directors whose reputations have extended far beyond France and

Isabelle Huppert (*The Lacemaker*).

Jean Marais and Josette Day (*Beauty and the Beast*)

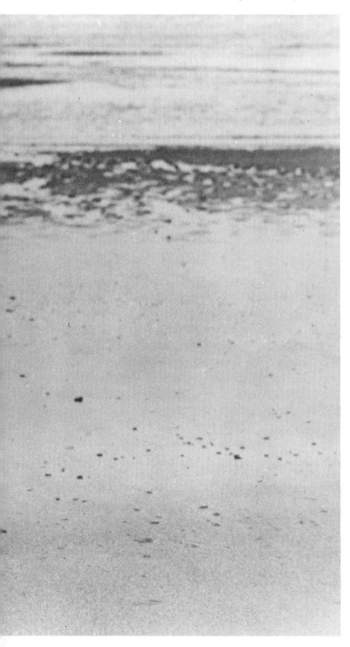

"Cinema is a flame in the shadows."

—ABEL GANCE.

"A film is not a dream that is told but one that we all dream together."

—JEAN COCTEAU.

NAPOLEON

(Napoléon Vu par Abel Gance)

WESTI (FROM INITIALS OF PRODUCERS WLADIMIR WENGEROFF AND HUGO STINNES) / SOCIÉTÉ GÉNÉRALE DES FILMS   1927

CREDITS

Screenplay and Direction: Abel Gance; *Photographers:* Jules Kruger, Léonce-Henry Burel, Joseph-Louis Mundviller, Roger Hubert, Emile Pierre and Lucas; *Assistant Directors:* Henry Krauss, Viacheslav Tourjansky, Henri Andréani, Alexandre Volkoff, Pierre Danis, and Marius Nalpas; *Editors:* Abel Gance with Marguerite Beaugé; *Music:* Arthur Honegger; *Running Time:* approximately 220 minutes (version shown at the Opéra premiere), *Paris Premiere:* April 7, 1927, at the Paris Opéra; *New York Premiere:* February 11, 1929; *16 mm. Rental Source:* Images.

CAST

Napoléon Bonaparte: Albert Dieudonné; *Joséphine de Beauharnais:* Gina Manès; *Napoléon as a Boy:* Vladimir Roudenko; *Georges Jacques Danton:* Alexandre Koubitzky; *Jean-Paul Marat:* Antonin Artaud; *Maximilien Robespierre:* Edmond van Daële; *Louis Saint-Just:* Abel Gance; *Tristan Fleuri:* Nicolas Koline; *Violine Fleuri:* Annabella; *Rouget de Lisle:* Harry Krimer; *Général Lazare Hoche:* Pierre Batcheff; *Paul Barras:* Max Maxudian; *Joseph Bonaparte:* Georges Lampin; *Pasquale Paoli:* Maurice Schutz; *Pozzo di Borgo:* Acho Chakatouny; *Antonio Salicetti:* Philippe Hériat; *Général Carteaux:* Léon Courtois; *Charlotte Corday:* Marguerite Gance; *La Bussière:* Jean d'Yd.

BACKGROUND

Abel Gance was born in Paris on October 25, 1889.

Portrait of *Napoléon*'s director Abel Gance as Saint-Just.

His family tried to pressure him to become a lawyer but in 1907 he ran off to Brussels to act in the theatre. In 1911 he formed his own production company, Le Film Français, and directed his first picture, *La Dique (ou Pour Sauver la Hollande)*. Gance made the powerful anti-war film *J'Accuse* (1919) followed by the ambitious melodrama *La Roue* (1922) with Séverin Mars. His imaginative and innovative technique of rapid cutting produced breathtaking effects. This seminal film was studied at the Moscow Academy as a model of montage.

In 1921 on a visit to America to launch *J'Accuse* Gance met D. W. Griffith and revealed to him his dream of making a film about Napoléon. The great American director confessed that he, too, was planning a work on the same subject but felt duty-bound to renounce his project in favor of the impressive young director of *J'Accuse*. Gance researched his subject exhaustively. The extensive scenario, which took him more than a year to complete, would represent a gigantic fresco of

19

Portrait of Albert Dieudonné as Napoléon Bonaparte.

"The Child is father of the Man"—the budding leader Napoléon (Vladimir Roudenko), hatless, head near the flag, wounded but undaunted, in the remarkable snowball fight scene at Brienne.

Napoléon's life broken up into six separate films. The first film would have three episodes: "The Youth of Bonaparte," "Bonaparte and the Revolution," and "The Italian Campaign." The five remaining films would be: *From Arcole to Marengo, From 18 Brumaire to Austerlitz, From Austerlitz to the Hundred Days, Waterloo,* and finally *Saint Helena**. Financing through the combined efforts of a German coal magnate and a Russian financier enabled Gance to begin the first film of his great project, which cost over 17 million francs (approximately $850,000).

Several actors were considered for the lead role, including the Russian tragedian Ivan Mosjoukine, before Gance was convinced that Albert Dieudonné was ideal for the part after first rejecting him because he was overweight. The actor dieted and won the role of a lifetime. Gance recruited the Russian tenor Alexandre Koubitzky for Danton and the lovely Annabella making her screen début as Violene and cast himself as the elegant Saint-Just.

*Gance's screenplay was subsequently used in Lupu Pick's *Napoléon auf St. Helena* (1929) with Werner Krauss in the title role.

At the Club des Cordeliers, Danton (Alexandre Koubitzky), in the pulpit, leads the crowd in the rousing "Marseillaise." Its author, Rouget de Lisle (Harry Krimer), stands to the left of the revolutionary figure.

Shooting began on January 17, 1925, at Billancourt, outside of Paris. The production encountred great setbacks and obstacles: Dieudonné almost drowned during the shooting in Corsica. Hugo Stinnes, the financier, died; then, six months into the filming, all credit was stopped. With about a fourth of the film shot, Gance, enormously in debt, tried desperately for six months to raise funding. Luckily another Russian financier, Jacques Grinieff, helped form a company, the Société Générale des Films, which enabled Gance to resume. But then during the filming of the battle scenes of Toulon some magnesium blew up, severely burning Gance and his crew. Covered with bandages, the indefatigible director was back at work eight days after the accident.

Locations were chosen where the events took place, including Napoléon's home in Corsica. Luckily, Gance documented on film (*Autour de Napoléon*) the making of his massive and technically innovative work-in-progress. We can understand how sincere were Gance's oft-quoted aims regarding *Napoléon:* "To make the spectator become an actor; to involve him at every level in the unfolding of the action; to sweep him away in the flow of pictures" when we see the camera mounted on a dolly, strapped to an operator's chest, tied to the

Fleeing his enemies in Corsica, Napoléon (Albert Dieudonné) hoists the tricolor in place of a missing sail and heads for France to meet his destiny. The start of the celebrated *"Double Tempête"* sequence.

saddle of a horse—even attached to a type of guillotine! etc.—all to create a dynamic and immediate experience for the enraptured viewer.*

Feeling, as he said: "The action *must* burst the restrictive limits of that mean little rectangle which is the ordinary cinema screen," Gance executed a brilliant idea he had been harboring for several years, namely filming the climatic "Entry into Italy" in a newly created wide-screen process which was termed "Polyvision" by music critic Emile Vuillermoz. André Debrie constructed an apparatus which consisted of three cameras mounted on top of each other set at different angles and controlled by a synchronized motor. Without having time to test the experimental camera, Gance went ahead and shot scenes of the French encampment in this new process. Gance shot the same scenes simultaneously in color and 3-D but later decided not to use them, fearing they would be too distracting for the viewer.

Finally, after nearly two years of shooting, the

*Striking production shots of *Napoléon* can be seen in film historian Kevin Brownlow's excellent documentary, *Abel Gance—the Charm of Dynamite* (1968), distributed in the U.S. by Images.

production stopped in August of 1926. The third episode was not completed; Napoléon's Italian campaign was simply highlighted in the concluding triptych. Then followed the torturous period of editing this most difficult film, which took Gance more than half a year; the resulting eyestrain caused him to suffer a detached retina. Thrilled with the possibilities of Polyvision, Gance edited two additional triptych sequences: the *"Double Tempête"* and the *"Bal des Victimes."* In screening the triptychs the curtains would part revealing two other full-sized screens on either side of the central screen on which would flash from three synchronized projectors a single, breathtaking panorama or three separate scenes which could be "orchestrated" in the editing. Gance exclaimed: "The theme, the story one is telling, is on the central screen. The story is prose, and the wings, the side screens, are poetry."

Napoléon was ready for its premiere. Although its hero is associated with an eagle, the film's strange fate of fame, neglect, near oblivion, then ultimate "resurrection" to fresh glory would seem to link it more appropriately with the phoenix.

SYNOPSIS

The first episode reveals Napoléon as an embryonic man of destiny. We encounter him as a boy (Vladimir Roudenko) at the military college of Brienne (circa 1780) demonstrating impressive leadership abilities during a snowball fight. A scullion, Tristan Fleuri (Nicolas Koline), admires the youth's pluck. When Napoléon's schoolmates set free his pet eagle, the angered youth retaliates by starting an animated fight in the dormitory. Later, his eagle returns to him, an omen linked indissolubly with his destiny.

The next and major episode treats Napoléon's relations with the French Revolution. It is Paris, 1789. To an impassioned crowd at the Club des Cordeliers, Danton (Alexandre Koubitzky) introduces "La Marseillaise" by Rouget de Lisle (Harry Krimer) which will be the official anthem of the Revolution. Lieutenant Bonaparte (Albert Dieudonné) thanks the composer. Napoléon meets Joséphine (Gina Manès) enroute to a palmist who informs her she will be queen.

Napoléon, now a captain, returns to his native Corsica in 1792. England and France are at war and he is angered to learn that the nationalist leader Paoli (Maurice Schutz) is preparing to turn the island over to the British. Napoléon tries to stir up sentiment for the Republic and a price is put on his head. Fleeing the enemy's troops on horseback, the outlaw-hero abducts the French flag from headquarters and escapes at Capitello in late May 1793 in a small boat. It lacks a sail and Napoléon resourcefully hoists the tricolor. As he combats a powerful tempest at sea we intercut to the stormy Convention in Paris where the radical Jacobins wrestle for power with the moderate Girondins.

Royalist Toulon is in revolt against the French government; England and other allied forces have sent troops and ships. The Revolution is endangered. The incompetent, soon-to-be-replaced Général Carteaux (Léon Courtois) commands the siege of the port in the fall of 1793 and sets up headquarters in an inn owned by Fleuri whose daughter Violine (Annabella) finds herself attracted to Napoléon. Now a major, Napoléon launches a bold artillery assault at night in torrential rain on the British fortress at Little Gibraltar. The British retreat; an exhausted hero sleeps on the ground watched over by his eagle of destiny.

Paris, 1794. The twelve-member Committee of Public Safety which includes Robespierre (Edmond van Daële) and Saint-Just (Abel Gance) perpetuates a Reign of Terror. Danton is guillotined; Napoléon declines an offer to command the Paris garrison and is arrested; even Joséphine is imprisoned. The excesses lead to the reaction of Thermidor (July 1794); Robespierre is overthrown and the Terror ends. Napoléon, released and now a general, draws up plans for an Italian Campaign but they are not adopted. When newly strengthened Royalist forces rise in revolt in Paris on 12 Vendémiaire (October 4, 1795), Constitutionalist Paul Barras (Max Maxudian) orders Napoléon to put it down. The Republic is thus saved; Bonaparte is famous. At the lavish *Bal des Victimes* he flirts with Joséphine.

Barras appoints Napoléon "Commander-in-Chief of the Army of Italy" in March 1796. Napoléon marries Joséphine, once the mistress of Barras. After a brief honeymoon he bids her farewell. Before departing for battle Napoléon enters the deserted convention hall to muster strength. The ghosts of Danton and other fallen leaders appear to press on him the need to be faithful to the ideals of the Revolution.

At the headquarters in Albenga, Napoléon confronts a demoralized army and instills in them his dream of glory. On April 11, 1796, he marches north into the Piedmont valley. There's a montage of the successful battle of Montenotte, ending with Napoléon's augural eagle soaring in the heavens.

COMMENTARY

In an edited print running approximately 220 minutes with two triptychs, *Napoléon* had a gala premiere at the Paris Opéra on April 7, 1927. The film received a standing ovation; Charles de Gaulle, attending with André Malraux, shouted "Bravo, tremendous, magnificent!" Henri-Georges Clouzot commented: "It is the most prestigious cinematographic evocation that we have seen yet." The complete film without triptychs, running nearly seven hours, was shown on successive evenings in separate installments. An abridged version played the smaller theatres.

The release of *The Jazz Singer* in October 1927 spelled the doom of silent cinema. Gance simply could not raise money to continue with his ambitious project. And Polyvision with its great cinematic potential—"I was convinced that Polyvision would be the cinema's new language," Gance said—this revolutionary innovation was quickly overlooked in the rush to sound.

Threatened by the talkie revolution and fearing the possibilities of a Polyvision one, M-G-M bought the American rights to *Napoléon* for $75,000 then distributed a truncated eight-reel version without the triptychs. The lackluster result made scant impression in the United States. (Forced to compete with the emerging popularity of television, the American film industry came up with the widescreen process known as Cinerama in 1952 with no mention made of Gance's trailblazing efforts.)

To survive, Gance directed a series of commercial films which did not enhance his reputation. Two significant exceptions were his impressive treatment of Beethoven's life, *Un Grand Amour de Beethoven* (1936), and his remake of *J'Accuse* (1937), a sincere effort to prevent WWII.

At the Office of Topography Napoléon (Albert Dieudonné) carefully maps a daring Italian campaign.

In 1935 Gance released *Napoléon Bonaparte*. Most of the footage came from the silent version, with added stereophonic sound *("la Perspective Sonore")*, another invention. At a bleak moment in 1952, fearing the world would never understand him and in a state of despair, "I flew into a rage," Gance said, "and threw most of the triptychs into the fire." To commemorate Napoléon's bicentennial in 1969, Minister for the Arts André Malraux awarded Gance a grant to prepare another treatment. The director shot new scenes with Albert Dieudonné, reedited earlier versions, and released the work,

23

Before his invasion of Piedmont in April 1796, Napoléon (Albert Dieudonné), now Commander-in-Chief, on horseback center triptych, reviews his ill-equipped army positioned in the Alps foothills near Albenga.

Only 27, at the outset of a military campaign destined to lead him to greatness, Napoléon (Albert Dieudonné), left triptych, surveys the encamped troops under his command. Another striking panoramic shot in Polyvision.

minus triptychs, as *Bonaparte et la Révolution* (1971).*

None of the later versions can compare with the original, however, and for rescuing and restoring the incredible silent classic current and future lovers of film are indebted to the persevering work of Kevin Brownlow. The first public screening of the restored *Napoléon* with the aged but undaunted director in attendance was held at the Telluride Film Festival in Colorado in September 1979. Several reels—including the two missing triptychs—are yet to be found; only a portion of the original Honegger music remains.

Napoléon, with a score by Carl Davis and projected at the correct speed of 20 fps (feet per second), premiered in London on November 30, 1980. It ran five hours and was an enormous success. Under the auspices of Francis Ford Coppola's Zoëtrope organization, *Napoléon*, projected at 24 fps and with some cuts, was shown at the

*Distributed here by Images.

Radio City Music Hall in New York on January 23, 1981. Carmine Coppola conducted a sixty-piece orchestra in a rousing score he composed for the film. The result was electrifying: a glorious standing ovation for what was for this viewer and undoubtedly thousands of others the most exciting cinematic experience of a lifetime. Gance's rediscovered masterpiece began a triumphal tour with live orchestra first throughout America, then Europe.

Besides having a masterly sense of composition, especially in long shots, Gance possessed a remarkable ability to make history come alive and to handle huge crowd scenes in a dynamic way. The passionate and innovative director made breathtaking use of hand-held cameras, rapid-fire cutting, multiple superimpositions, tracking shots—even an underwater camera enclosed in a metal cage to capture waves seen from the point of view of the waves! In employing these techniques with great skill, Gance achieved a camera mobility which was phenomenal.

The march into Northern Italy: The chanting "Beggars of Glory" ("*Les Mendiants de la Gloire*"), center triptych, follow their triumphant leader Napoléon (Albert Dieudonné), seen on horseback in both left and right triptychs.

Among the many striking scenes, one could mention the exciting pillow fight in the Brienne dormitory. All of a sudden the screen splits into four, then nine individual scenes, each of which shows separate action. Then additional shots are superimposed over each split image; the overall effect was to achieve, in the words of Gance, "an intense synthesis at the service of a paroxysm. The mirror screen was able to become a prism, a mosaic of light."

Unforgettable is the *"Double Tempête"* sequence in which Gance links Napoléon's battling a storm at sea with the tempestuous developments at the convention which recalls Victor Hugo's apt metaphor from *"Quatre-vingt-treize"*: "To be a member of the Convention was to be a wave in the ocean." The director realistically reconstructed the raging sea at the Billancourt studio; later in the convention hall he mounted his camera on a huge pendulum which swung over the extras' heads and which could simulate perfectly the vertiginous movement of waves. Then he brilliantly intercut shots between the two, accelerating the growing intensity of the "storms" via parallel editing and producing a frenzied climax of dazzling juxtaposition and rapid superimpositions. The *pièce de résistance* is, of course, the surviving eighteen-minute triptych of Napoléon's "Entry into Italy" which displays spectacular triple screen panoramas—Napoléon's ride on horseback from far right panel, across center, and onto left panel is marvellous—as well as split screens showing central action with contrapuntal lateral scenes. When Gance employs rapid superimpositions on the triple screen the effect is simply overwhelming. And for a stunning climax, during the panoramic shot of a soaring eagle, the left screen went blue, the center white, and the right red to form a gigantic tricolor.

Controversy abounds in Gance's fanciful treatment of history—dates, events, characterizations of actual figures were changed—and especially in his romanticized depiction of Napoléon as the heroic but ultimately unsuccessful standard-bearer of the goals of the French Revolution. For Gance, Napoléon was a Promethean figure, a sort of political artist. A personal vision, not an accurate biography, was his aim in the film. (The original title, *Napoléon Seen by Abel Gance,* indicates his approach.) *Napoléon,* then, with Albert Dieudonné's formidable presence, is more epic poem than history.

Director George Stevens said of *Napoléon:* "There has never been such vitality, such passion on the screen, before or since Gance," and critic Charles Champlin referred to it as "a film against which all the others have to be measured, now and forever." Gance's masterpiece is considered the greatest technical achievement of the silent film era.

Abel Gance received the Grand Prix National du Cinéma in 1974 in recognition of the total achievement of his career and an honorary César in 1981. The British Academy of Film and Television Arts bestowed on Gance their highest award, a Fellowship, in 1981. The great visionary director who described his unrealized projects as "cathedrals of light" died in Paris on November 10, 1981, at the age of 92.

25

A pensive Napoléon (Albert Dieudonné), center triptych, recalls the face of his beloved Joséphine (Gina Manès) which we see superimposed on scenes of the battle of Montenotte in the flanking triptychs.

THE PASSION OF JOAN OF ARC

(La Passion de Jeanne d'Arc)

SOCIÉTÉ GÉNÉRALE DES FILMS   1928

CREDITS

Screenplay, Direction, and Editing: Carl Th. Dreyer, screenplay based in part on a treatment by Joseph Delteil; *Photographer:* Rudolph Maté; *Assistant Directors:* Paul la Cour and Ralf Holm; *Music:* Victor Alix

and Léo Pouget; *Running Time:* 110 minutes; *Paris Premiere:* October 25, 1928; *New York Premiere:* March 28, 1929; *16 mm. Rental Source:* M.O.M.A.

CAST

Joan of Arc: Renée (Marie) Falconetti; *Bishop Pierre Cauchon:* Eugène Silvain; *Nicholas Loyseleur:* Maurice Schutz; *Jean Lemaître:* Michel Simon; *Jean Massieu:* Antonin Artaud; *Jean Beaupère:* Louis Ravet; *Jean d'Estivet:* André Berley; *Guillaume Erard:* Jean d'Yd.

BACKGROUND

Carl Theodor Dreyer was born in Copenhagen on February 3, 1889. His directorial career was launched with *The President (Praesidenten)* (1920). Due to the enormous popularity in France of his seventh feature, *Thou Shalt Honor Thy Wife (Du Skal Aere Din Hustru)* (1925), the Société Générale des Films offered him a contract to direct a film on a great French personage. Dreyer agreed to do Joan of Arc, who had been canonized in 1920. "I wanted to interpret a hymn to the triumph of the soul over life," Dreyer wrote.

For publicity reasons the popular author of *Vie de Jeanne d'Arc* (1925), Joseph Delteil, was credited as co-scenarist although the treatment he prepared was unsatisfactory to Dreyer who preferred instead to write his own based on Pierre Champion's 1921 text of the actual trial. The film was originally entitled *La Passion et la Mort de Jeanne d'Arc.*

Believing, as he wrote later, that "the artist should portray the *inner* and not the *outer* life," Dreyer sought what he termed "abstraction": "An artist shall abstract from reality in order to reinforce its spiritual content." As aids, the director wanted simplification, a paring away of "all elements that do not support his central idea," as well as the transformation of that idea into symbolism.

Dreyer daringly employed the Aristotelian unities to heighten his tragedy. He condensed Joan's long trial, spread out over three months and twenty-nine sessions, to one day, her last on earth, with just five interrogations. The locale was the one castle and environs; there were no distracting subplots.

Dreyer wanted sound for *The Passion of Joan of Arc,* but the necessary equipment was not available. Accorded a large budget—over seven million francs (approximately $350,000)—the film was naturally conceived for a popular, not an avant-garde,

After the gruelling second interrogation in her cell, soldiers place a straw crown and arrow on the prisoner Joan (Renée Falconetti), imitating the mockery of Christ.

audience. Although Lillian Gish had been initially considered for the lead, Dreyer found his ideal Joan in the person of Renée Falconetti, a young actress performing boulevard comedy. He sensed: "There was a soul behind that façade." Even though this would be her first and only screen appearance, she would be immortalized under Dreyer's direction. He recruited stage actors such as Eugène Silvain, doyen of the Comédie Française, yet would cast a major part solely on facial features—thus the Earl of Warwick was played by an anonymous café-keeper.

Set designers Hermann Warm and Jean Hugo erected a huge cement castle replete with drawbridge, towers, etc., between Montrouge and Petit Clamart, suburbs of Paris. Although very little can be glimpsed of this vast set, it helped create a sense of place for his actors. Dreyer ordered deep holes dug around it for low-angle filming. Interiors were economically shot at Billancourt in an empty automobile assembly plant which Dreyer rented. Shooting began in May 1927 and lasted almost to the end of the year. Unusual for its time, Dreyer shot in chronological order to permit him to gradually develop the emotional intensity he desired. Actors appeared without make-up so that every facial detail could be registered. In Dreyer's quest for perfection there were many rehearsals and retakes.

Fidelity to the official transcript suggested a film style to the director: "Each question, each answer, quite naturally called for a close-up. It was the only possibility." Dreyer's tone of "holy seriousness" inspired his outstanding cast and crew. Jacques Feyder said of this labor of devotion: "Dreyer has attained in this work the heights of power and emotion unequalled in cinema."

SYNOPSIS

Rouen. The Palais de Justice. May 30, 1431. Joan of Arc (Renée Falconetti), age nineteen, is to be tried for heresy and witchcraft. Inspired by her heavenly visions she had led troops and fought bravely against the English occupation forces in France but was captured by the Burgundians, British allies, and delivered to a court of ecclesiastics presided over by Bishop Cauchon (Eugène Silvain). The ultimate power belongs to the Earl of Warwick, who wants her killed.

The film opens in a large hall. Joan is brought in. Taunted for her mission, for her claims of seeing

A fearful Joan (Renée Falconetti) enters the torture chamber, the foreboding setting for her third interrogation.

Saint Michael, for her masculine attire, she holds to her faith and her hope of deliverance.

In her cell the oppressive cross-examination continues. She affirms her eventual release from prison "by means of a great victory!"

The third session occurs in the torture chamber. The judges try to inflict gnawing doubts in Joan by claiming her visions were Devil-inspired. Shown the various instruments of torture, the frightened girl faints.

In her cell, ill with fever, Joan is bled before the fourth hearing begins. The crafty Cauchon tempts her with the Eucharist—but first she must sign that confession. Mustering strength, she turns on her accusers.

A weak Joan is carried on a stretcher to the churchyard. If she refuses to sign the abjuration she will be burnt at the stake. Fearful of her life and anxious to be of further use to her king, she gives in.

In her cell, condemned to life imprisonment, her head is shaved. She spies a straw crown and realizes that through fear she has betrayed her God. Full of shame, she courageously recants her abjuration and understands that "the great victory" promised is her martyrdom, that her "release" is her death.

Joan is led to the stake. We witness the painful

27

spectacle of her agonizing death. "You have burnt a saint!" comes from the unruly crowd. Soldiers chase the mob from the castle.

COMMENTARY

The Passion of Joan of Arc had its world premiere in Copenhagen on April 21, 1928. After a press screening in Paris that June the Archbishop demanded many cuts. Without Dreyer's permission, the film was mutilated by the censors before it opened in October. (Eight months had to pass before an uncut version appeared.) The English censors banned it until late 1930. It was released untimely when talking pictures were the rage; showings were limited to art theatres and, although hailed critically as a masterpiece, it proved a commercial disaster. Then in the succeeding decades, as with many silent film classics, negatives were destroyed, and surviving prints were in several different versions.

In 1951 a negative was found which became the basis of the Lo Duca version distributed the next year with an added sound track of selections by J. S. Bach, Albinoni, Vivaldi, etc. However the director felt the original rhythm was distorted and he disowned this rendition. An effort is being made to restore the original version.

Dreyer makes each spectator feel a witness to Joan's harrowing ordeal by employing:

Subjective shots: the judges, shot at low angles, appear menacing and grotesque; Joan, shot from high angles, seems vulnerable and defenseless.

Frequent close-ups: "They make it possible for me," Dreyer said, "to bring the audience very near to the physical and mental torture that Joan suffered . . ."

Montage: there is a powerfully edited sequence in the torture chamber in which shots of sharp blades, spikes, etc., grow shorter and accelerate; the terrified girl is overwhelmed.

Cross cutting: shots of Joan at the stake are intercut with a mother nursing her child, soldiers swaying their maces, etc., to create memorable effects of poignancy and tension.

Mlle. Falconetti gave such an astonishing performance that many critics regard it as the finest by

At the stake where she is about to be burnt to death, an anguished Joan (Renée Falconetti) dressed in a penitent's gown finds solace in embracing the processional cross.

With another monk elevating a cross to comfort Joan in her agony, a sympathetic Massieu (Antonin Artaud), right, watches the death of a saint.

an actress in screen history. "She *lived* the part," Dreyer said. "There was something indefinable about her—something that was not of this world." A rhythmic editing style, striking lighting effects from the use of charcoal lamps, outstanding photography—"Maté . . . gave me what I wanted . . . realized mysticism" (Dreyer)—enhanced the film's artistic values. Although there were many screen treatments of Joan of Arc's life, none has surpassed the artistic integrity, power, and spiritual impact of Dreyer's masterpiece.

The uncompromising artist was only able to make five more features before he died in Copenhagen on March 20, 1968. "The cinema cannot do without art," he admonished.

The Passion of Joan of Arc is ageless, unforgettable, transcendent, a masterpiece of religious art. Critic Vernon Young aptly called it "the most intensive inquest of a human soul in the history of the motion picture."

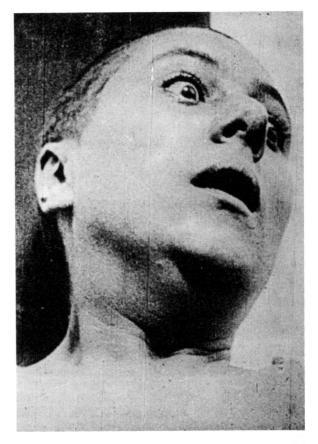

"Jesus!" screams Joan (Renée Falconetti) during her long and excruciating death throes. "In Falconetti . . . I found what I might, with very bold expression, allow myself to call 'the martyr's reincarnation.' "
—Carl Dreyer.

29

LE MILLION

SOCIÉTÉ DES FILMS SONORES TOBIS   1931

CREDITS

Screenplay: René Clair, based on the play by Georges Berr and Marcel Guillemaud (1910); *Director:* René Clair; *Photographers:* Georges Périnal and Georges Raulet; *Assistant Director:* Georges Lacombe; *Editor:* René Le Hénaff; *Music:* Armand Bernard, Philippe Parès, and Georges Van Parys; *Lyrics:* René Clair; *Running Time:* 91 minutes; *Paris Premiere:* April 15, 1931; *New York Premiere:* May 20, 1931; *16 mm. Rental Source:* Images.

Prosper (Louis Allibert), left, informs his friend Michel (René Lefèvre), right, surrounded by threatening creditors, that one of them has won the Dutch lottery.

CAST

Béatrice: Annabella; *Michel Bouflette:* René Lefèvre; *Vanda:* Vanda Gréville; *Crochard alias Père-La-Tulipe:* Paul Olivier; *Prosper Bénévant:* Louis Allibert; *Sopranelli:* Constantin Stroesco; *Mme. Ravellina:* Odette Talazac; *Stage Manager:* Pitouto; *Taxi Driver:* Raymond Cordy; *Grocer:* Jane Pierson; *Butcher:* André Michaud; *Conductor:* Armand Bernard.

BACKGROUND

René Clair was born René Chomette in Paris on November 11, 1898. He aspired to be a writer and began his career as a journalist. He started playing bit roles in films in 1920 and was a young leading man in several of Louis Feuillade's serials. To keep his family name unsullied for his literary career, he adopted the pseudonym "Clair" for his movie work. Clair was an assistant to director Jacques de Baroncelli in Belgium and directed his first film, *The Crazy Ray (Paris Qui Dort)* (1923), which was followed by the highly respected *Entr'acte* (1924), an avant-garde experimental short.

The brilliant farce, *The Italian Straw Hat (Un Chapeau de Paille d'Italie)* (1927), remains, however, Clair's best achievement in the silent period. In his work he wished to go back to the traditions of pre-World War I Paris and make comedies for the general public.

Clair thought the arrival of sound threatened to theatricalize a medium which was primarily visual.

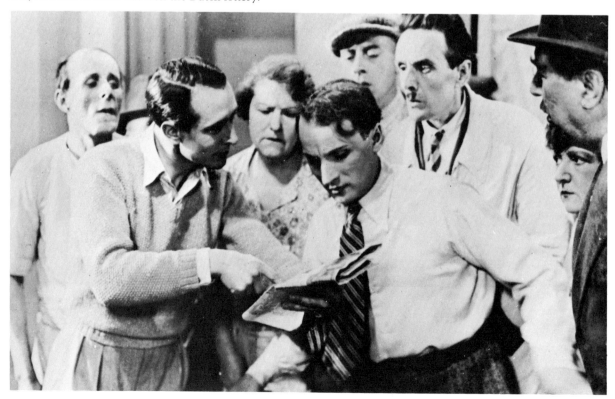

When he started experimenting with sound he was careful to let the images, not the dialogue, dominate. Although its use of sound was provisional, Clair's first talkie, *Under the Roofs of Paris (Sous les Toits de Paris* (1930), was an international hit. Clair began to work on his second and far superior talkie, *Le Million*—based on a twenty-year-old farce—in 1930. However, he soon realized that fidelity to the original would result in excessive dialogue, and dialogue, he felt, evoked the everyday world and inhibited a sense of fantasy. "I wanted an atmosphere of foolishness," Clair said, "and we decided it should not be realistic." He arrived at a solution: "I conceived that it would be possible to recapture the unreality of the light

Having invited all the tradespeople to his room to pay them, Michel (René Lefèvre) discovers he doesn't have the ticket but persuades them to stay there while he retrieves it.

Hiding behind the stage scenery, Michel (René Levèvre) and Béatrice (Annabella) are unhappy after a lover's quarrel.

comedy by replacing words with music and songs. From that moment on my work began to interest me."

Giving the farce a contemporary setting and retaining the characters and the idea of the lost lottery ticket from the play, René Clair shaped a new plot and contributed the hilarious opera sequence and many original and clever touches.

In addition Clair put some gauze between the actors and the sets which created an illusion of unreality although real objects could be seen behind it. Clair said: "I think it is one of the most

In *Les Bohémiens* the devoted lovers, sung by soprano Mme. Ravellina (Odette Talazac) and tenor Sopranelli (Constantin Stroesco), left, find their happiness in peril.

interesting experiments that has been made in sets—by my colleague [Lazare Meerson] and me." The film was shot at the Studio Tobis at Epinay-

31

sur-Seine. *Le Million* is a brilliant comedy which has not lost its freshness or appeal.

SYNOPSIS

It is Paris around 1930. Some neighbors trace the sounds of music at night to a loft where a party is in progress. They are told: It all began that morning. . . .

Michel (René Lefèvre), an impoverished artist, is besieged by his creditors who demand their money. In the same tenement, police chase Crochard (Paul Olivier), a thief a.k.a. Père-La-Tulipe, who takes refuge in the room of Béatrice (Annabella), the girl friend of Michel. Crochard puts on Michel's jacket left there to be sewn. When the cops barge in they see him playing the piano for a cooperative Béatrice and leave. Full of gratitude, Crochard promises to help the young lady if she is ever in need, then skips off wearing the garment.

Michel's sculptor buddy Prosper (Louis Allibert) informs Michel that he's won a million florins in the Dutch lottery. The delightfully surprised artist invites all the tradesmen to his loft for a party then remembers putting the ticket into his jacket. Crochard runs a second-hand store as a cover for his criminal activities. Tenor Sopranelli (Constantin Stroesco) enters and buys Michel's jacket as a costume for his performance that evening.

Michel summons Béatrice from her ballet class to get his ticket. She tells him about Crochard and eventually recalls his address. He rushes to the store and asks Crochard for the jacket. However, the police raid the place and arrest Michel whom they take to be the notorious thief. Crochard suspects something is valuable about the garment and makes plans to attend the opera that evening.

A greedy Prosper learns about the jacket from Michel then promptly refuses to identify his friend at the police station. However, the creditors identify the "millionaire" and he's released.

In Sopranelli's dressing room Prosper, his girl friend Vanda (Vanda Gréville), and Béatrice give it each a separate try but no one manages to get hold of the garment.

Béatrice catches Vanda on the make for Michel and gets jealous. Without dialogue, letting the words of the song plead his cause, Michel wins Béatrice back as they huddle behind scenery onstage throughout the opening number.

During the performance of the opera which follows, a riotous melee develops as Michel, Prosper, and Crochard's gang fight onstage over the

jacket. The battered garment lands on top of a taxi whose driver (Raymond Cordy) has been conveying Michel around all day. Michel and Béatrice enter it and when they discover the dangling jacket Crochard's gang intercepts it. The disconsolate pair return to the party in the loft.

Michel is about to confess the truth when Crochard enters in happy deus ex machina fashion and hands the jacket and then the ticket to the stunned man. All join hands in a merry song and dance.

COMMENTARY

Because the use of sound had yet to be solidified in convention, Clair was free to experiment. Discovering that he could utilize music in an innovative way to undermine an illusion of reality and to liberate a feeling of poetry, Clair achieved effects which were novel and delightful: a group of creditors surrounding Michel suddenly becomes a chorus and breaks into song. Internal thoughts such as Prosper's conflict over betraying Michel are rendered in a song sung by an offscreen chorus. Through the use of a variety of musical-theatrical forms such as operetta, ballet, musical comedy, and silent film comedy, Clair circumvented conventional dialogue and kept his fantasy aloft.

The successful *Le Million* abounds in many brilliant and often hilarious scenes.

The opera sequence is priceless. The fun starts with a ludicrous love duet between the great Sopranelli (of the New York Metropolitan to be sure) and Madame Ravellina, two superannuated ingénues each possessing an enormous girth with egos to match—she looking ridiculous in her Melisande-length pigtails and miles of tulle, he shorter and equally silly in his Bohemian ensemble. Their temperaments flare up but once the curtain rises they start an outpour of their eternal passion highlighted by cascading rose petals and end in a "romantic" embrace with the tenor barely managing to get his arm around her waist.

The merriment continues during the presentation of *Les Bohémiens* in which Sopranelli declaims his love and warns his rival to keep away from his beloved (Mme. Ravellina).

In the intermission a lady fan throws a bouquet which bops Sopranelli on the head. Gallantly he offers the tribute to the soprano but when the curtain falls he snatches it from her.

In the next act Sopranelli throws his jacket on the ground before he fights his rival. Michel and Prosper yank at either end, and when the tenor puts it on again he discovers that both sleeves have been ripped off!

The climax is reached when the ensuing mad scramble for Michel's jacket is seemingly transformed into a football game with lots of running and tackling accompanied by a loud roar as if at a stadium. This brilliant satire on opera certainly influenced the delightful antics of the Marx Brothers in Sam Wood's *A Night at the Opera* (1935).

Both Annabella and René Lefèvre are charming and convincing as the young lovers. The pace of this successful film never lets up. The timing, the tight structure built around the classic chase, the precision editing, the non-stop fun (Brava Ravellina! Bravo Sopranelli!) and Clair's brilliant style make *Le Million* his most highly regarded film and a timeless comic masterpiece. "From the point of view of invention," Clair said, "I suppose it's my most important contribution to the cinema."

Père-La-Tulipe (Paul Olivier), center, with glasses, produces the disputed jacket to a delighted Béatrice (Annabella) and a surprised Michel (René Lefèvre), then the lottery ticket to bring the events to a happy ending.

33

MARIUS

MARCEL PAGNOL / PARAMOUNT
PUBLIX CORPORATION   1931

CREDITS

Screenplay: Marcel Pagnol from his play; *Director:* Alexander Korda; *Photographer:* Ted Pahle; *Editor:* Roger Spiri-Mercanton; *Music:* Francis Gromon; *Running Time:* 130 minutes; *Paris Premiere:* September 18, 1931; *New York Premiere:* April 14, 1933; *16 mm. Rental Source:* Images.

CAST

César Olivier: Raimu; *Marius:* Pierre Fresnay; *Fanny:* Orane Demazis; *Honoré Panisse:* Fernand Charpin; *Honorine Cabanis:* Alida Rouffe; *M. Brun:* Robert Vattier; *Félix Escartefigue:* Paul Dullac; *Piquoiseau:* Alexandre Mihalesco; *Second Mate:* Edouard Delmont; *Stoker:* Maupi.

BACKGROUND

Marcel Pagnol was born in Aubagne near Marseilles on February 28, 1895, and had a long and successful career as a playwright, film producer and director, critic, memoirist, and novelist. He spent his first twenty-seven years in Marseilles, which became a boom town of the French Empire between the wars, and was to achieve international fame recording the rich spirit of its colorful and zestful inhabitants. After teaching English for some years—his father was a schoolteacher as well—he began to devote his full attention to writing when his plays became successful. The popular *Topaze* (1928) was to be filmed several times in France, England and America.

Marius, Pagnol's next play, was completed in

1928. It is interesting to note that it was a self-contained play and not written deliberately as the first part of what was eventually to become known as *The Marseilles Trilogy.*

Pagnol took for his hero a young Marseilles poet, Louis Brauquier, who had wanderlust. He offered the role of Panisse to Raimu (stage name of Jules Auguste César Muraire, born December 17, 1883) who had performed in music halls, made a couple of silent films prior to WWI, and had appeared in many plays. Raimu instinctively felt that César was the role he should play and ordered the playwright to expand the part. Pagnol acquiesced. The role of Marius was played by Pierre Fresnay, formerly associated with the Comédie Française, who prepared himself for the part by working for two weeks in a bar in Marseilles' Vieux-Port. *Marius* opened at the Théâtre de Paris on March 9, 1929,

Marius (Pierre Fresnay) is annoyed when he learns from Fanny (Orane Demazis) that he has a "rival" in Panisse.

34

Marius (Pierre Fresnay), thinking he's leaving that night for a long voyage, tries to express his affection for his father when César (Raimu) spontaneously displays his profound love for his son.

and was an enormous success, running for over one thousand performances in three continuous years.

When Paramount acquired the film rights in 1931, Pagnol demanded and received approval on the adaptation. Since the American film company could not send back its substantial French earnings, the "frozen francs" were generally used to make multilingual versions of American films for the European market at its subsidiary company, Paramount Publix Corporation, located outside of Paris at Joinville.

Alexander Korda (1893-1956) directed films in his native Hungary, then in Austria, Germany, and the U.S.A. before he was offered *Marius*, which became the first important film with which he was associated.

Korda assuaged all fears of Pagnol by agreeing to let the stage actors repeat their roles on film. Pagnol kept a careful eye on the proceedings and began his apprenticeship in film with this movie.

The great card scene: César (Raimu), left, tries to signal his partner Escartefigue (Paul Dullac), right, across the table while Panisse (Fernand Charpin) and M. Brun (Robert Vattier), back to camera, observe.

Korda was not happy with the set constructed in the studio and commissioned a superior replacement from his artist-brother, thereby launching Vincent Korda's long career as a leading art director in British cinema.

The film, shot simultaneously in German (Korda

35

directing), Swedish and Italian versions between June and August of 1931, became an enormous commercial success.

SYNOPSIS

Marius (Pierre Fresnay) is a young man working in the Bar de la Marine in Marseilles and secretly longing to run off to sea. His widowed father César (Raimu) berates his son's idleness and lack of concentration but underneath adores him. We meet César's delightful cronies: the rich sailmaker Panisse (Fernand Charpin), the ferry-boat captain and well-known cuckold Escartefigue (Paul Dullac), and the dandyish customs inspector from Lyons, M. Brun (Robert Vattier).

Although Marius loves Fanny (Orane Demazis), the young daughter of the portly fishwife Honorine (Alida Rouffe), he cannot make a commitment to her since he plans to sail away soon. When the middleaged widower Panisse proposes marriage to Fanny in the bar, Marius nonetheless loses his temper. Fanny whets his jealousy further in an attempt to move him to marry her. A local character Piquoiseau (Alexandre Mihalesco) tells Marius a berth might be available on a ship leaving that evening.

Honorine learns that her unhappy daughter is in love with the apparently unresponsive Marius and has no desire to marry Panisse. Honorine visits César. They discuss their children's problems and after some wrangling come to a settlement over the eventual dowry.

Fanny enters the bar at closing time, tells Marius she has refused Panisse's marriage offer, then blurts out her love for him. Marius reveals the truth: he has been thinking of escaping for a long time but only his love for her has kept him in Marseilles. When Piquoiseau appears to inform Marius that the man he was to replace has returned, the enamored couple retreat to his bedroom to spend the night. Some months pass. César is aware that his son is seeing a woman but he doesn't know who she is. Fanny makes plans for marriage and housekeeping with Marius, but his heart isn't in it.

One day Piquoiseau informs Marius that there's a berth for him on the *Malaisie* leaving the next morning. When Marius rejects the offer, Piquoiseau tells him that Fanny is ruining his life. Fanny overhears this exchange and realizes that she must sacrifice him so that he can fulfill his dreams. Honorine returns to her home early the next morning and discovers Marius asleep in Fanny's bedroom. Hysterical, she rushes to inform César, who is much more understanding about such matters. Honorine demands an immediate wedding.

César breakfasts with his son and quietly urges him to do the right thing by Fanny. Piquoiseau enters to announce the ship's approaching departure but the unhappy youth says he cannot go. Fanny senses that if he marries her he won't be happy and so she dissembles and tells Marius she was considering marrying Panisse. His money could help her mother.

An angry Marius believes her, grabs his bag, and dashes out. Fanny distracts César so that Marius can escape without being detected. César takes Fanny to his bedroom and discloses his plans for the couple. From the window a heartbroken Fanny sees the *Malaisie* sailing away and faints.

COMMENTARY

Marius is noted for its rich characterization far more than for its plot or theme. Pagnol was able to create a whole gallery of larger-than-life characters without patronizing or caricaturing them.

César is the most impressive figure. Hot-tempered, warmhearted, fiercely loyal, full of tenderness and understanding, this patriarch made immortal by Raimu endearingly typifies all humanity. With his expressive face, eloquent eyes, bear-like frame and grumbling, foghorn voice, Raimu projected into César much of his own inimitable personality. *Marius* marked the first great screen success of this instinctual actor.

Orane Demazis convinces us of her great capacity for love and of the essential nobility of her character. Pierre Fresnay is outstanding as the devoted son torn by deep conflicts. And Charpin is the perfect foil to Raimu, while all the supporting players are effective and memorable. Korda succeeded admirably in adapting the cast's stage performances to the subtler demands of the screen and evoking an authentic atmosphere which adds so much to the film's success.

Critics objected at the time to its relatively immobile camerawork and labelled *Marius* "canned theatre" (*"théâtre en conserve"*). The rush to film plays which resulted from the popular introduction of sound produced a spate of dull, static films. This phenomenon threatened to destroy the unique opportunities which cinema presented. However, the essential stage-bound aspect of *Marius's* direction and slow pacing are made acceptable to later viewers because of its fascinating performances.

Marius suffered some drawbacks initially in becoming known in America. A mediocre adaptation by Sidney Howard called *Marseilles* flopped on Broadway in 1930. And the film did not fare well when it was cut and first presented without English subtitles in New York in 1933. Considered "daring" due to its treatment of pre-marital sex, *Marius* was refused a certificate in England and only released there in 1949.

The film abounds in outstanding scenes and witty lines:

One recalls César giving a virtuoso demonstration to Marius on how to recover the last drop at the tip of a liqueur bottle or later telling his absent-minded son: "When they'll hold the stupid asses' dance you won't be in the orchestra."

The deeply moving evening scene when Marius, contemplating imminent departure, and César express their love for each other.

The great card game scene during which César attempts to cue his dull-witted partner Escartefigue on which card to play by clutching his chest and making references to his "heart" and then exclaims when he is found out that "If one cannot cheat with one's friends it's no longer worthwhile to play cards!"

Fortunately there was more to come concerning the delightful habitués of the Bar de la Marine.

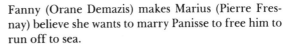

César (Raimu) quietly urges Marius (Pierre Fresnay) to marry Fanny: "Marius, honor is like a match: you can only use it once. . . ."

Fanny (Orane Demazis) makes Marius (Pierre Fresnay) believe she wants to marry Panisse to free him to run off to sea.

A NOUS LA LIBERTE

SOCIÉTÉ DES FILMS SONORES TOBIS   1931

CREDITS

Screenplay and Direction: René Clair; *Photographer:* Georges Périnal; *Assistant Directors:* Albert Valentin and Ary Sadoul; *Editor:* René Le Hénaff; *Music:* Georges Auric; *Lyrics:* René Clair; *Running Time:* 104 minutes; *Paris Premiere:* December 31, 1931; *New York Premiere:* May 17, 1932; *16 mm. Rental Source:* Images.

CAST

Emile: Henri Marchand; *Louis:* Raymond Cordy; *Jeanne:* Rolla France; *Paul Imaque, Jeanne's Uncle:* Paul Olivier; *Paul:* Jacques Shelly; *Foreman:* André Michaud; *Maud, Louis' Mistress:* Germaine Aussey; *Gigolo:* Alexandre d'Arcy; *Gangster Leader:* William Burke; *Speaker:* Vincent Hyspa; *Deaf Old Man:* Léon Lorin.

BACKGROUND

Thanks to the commercial success of *Le Million*, René Clair was allowed a large budget and given great artistic control over his next project, a satire on modern industrialized society whose provisional title, *Liberté Chérie*, would become *A Nous la Liberté*.

"The idea for *A Nous la Liberté* came to me," Clair said, "in an industrial suburb of Paris where I one day saw a few wildflowers growing against a background of smoking factory chimneys. The contrast triggered something off in me and the idea crystallized. I saw the picture exactly as it eventually turned out."

Concerning Emile, the film's protagonist, Clair remarked: "I visualize a dreamer, a romantic, a

vagabond, and I want to set him in my film against a background of tremendous mechanism." The gentle and innocent tramp was inspired by Chaplin.

The character of Louis was based on the remarkable career of Charles Pathé (1863-1957), the French industrialist who rose from terrible poverty to control an empire comprising the phonograph and film industries.

Clair for the first time voiced his views on society in the film: "I wanted to fight the machine which was enslaving man instead of contributing to his happiness." The film was, he maintained, "above all against the idea of the sanctity of work when it is uninteresting and non-individual." Clair observed: "We must work in order to live, but it is absurd to live merely in order to work. If work were intelligently organized, if machines worked for man instead of against him, this film would have no reason to exist."

So that it wouldn't appear to be a problem picture, he again resorted to the operetta format he had used before: "I thought that *A Nous la Liberté* risked being heavy if treated realistically," and added: "I thought that the bitter pill I had pre-

38

Ex-convict Louis (Raymond Cordy) at his music stall in a flea market. The humble beginning of the future industrialist.

pared would be more easily swallowed when coated with diverting music."

Shooting was completed by November 1931 at the Studio Tobis. *A Nous la Liberté* proved to be Clair's most ambitious and provocative film.

SYNOPSIS

Emile (Henri Marchand) and Louis (Raymond Cordy) are buddies in prison and plot an escape. Only Louis succeeds and in rapid fashion rises from running a second-hand music stall in a flea market to managing the vast enterprise of "Louis Records." Ironically, he escaped prison but is now enslaved by his work.

By this time Emile is free but soon gets arrested for vagrancy. Despondent, he tries to hang himself but the bars give way and Emile climbs out to freedom. He is attracted to Jeanne (Rolla France), a young woman he spots who is zealously guarded by her uncle (Paul Olivier). Both work at Louis' factory. Emile manages to get a job there and pursues Jeanne. He encounters a suspicious Louis who first threatens him with a revolver then proffers money to bribe him. Emile is disheartened, Louis realizes

Emile (Henri Marchand) attempts suicide when he's arrested again but the bars give way and he finds himself free.

The happy reunion of Louis (Raymond Cordy) with his old prison buddy Emile (Henri Marchand).

he's misjudging him, and the two embrace in friendship. Later an ex-convict sees Emile leaving Louis' mansion.

When Louis discovers Emile is in love with Jeanne he uses his influence with the uncle to arrange a match. Gangsters invade the tycoon's

39

home. The Leader (William Burke) demands blackmail and threatens to expose Louis. Emile learns that his beloved is actually in love with a fellow worker, Paul (Jacques Shelly.)

Louis maneuvers the gangsters into an office at the factory, then locks them in. He empties the cash from a safe into a suitcase and meets Emile evading suspicious policemen. The gangsters get free and one steals the suitcase. The police grab him just as he's about to escape and the suitcase is abandoned on the roof. The police arrest the gangsters but the Leader will have his vengenance by producing evidence about Louis' past.

The next day is the opening of the new, fully automated phonograph factory. In the crowd Louis recognizes the police inspector and realizes that his number is up. A strong wind arises and soon banknotes from the opened suitcase start flying around the courtyard. The officials can restrain themselves no longer and in the ensuing skirmish for the money Louis puts on a worker's uniform and escapes with Emile.

While the workers loaf, fish, and dance (Jeanne and Paul among them), Emile and Louis head for the open road and freedom.

COMMENTARY

A Nous la Liberté was cited as "Most Amusing Film" by public referendum at the 1932 Venice Biennial.

René Clair achieved his satirical aims brilliantly in his film by clever visual means. When Emile is arrested for vagrancy we cut to a classroom where children learn by rote the axiom which will control their lives: "Work is compulsory because work is freedom." Then when he later goes to work at Louis' factory he encounters an assembly line and the rigid regimentation which he knew before in prison—there are even numbers on the uniform as in jail. Thus, with similar camera angles and precise editing, the juxtaposition of the modern factory with the traditional prison underscores the former as tyrannical and dehumanizing and exposes the lie "Work is freedom."

Clair satirized greed too. When Louis realizes the truth of their relationship, he flings a wad of notes on the floor near his mistress. She feigns indifference but when the footman makes a grab for them she pounces on the money first. This foreshadows the delightful climax when the officials in top hats, models of respectability and dignity, reveal their true natures when they scramble for banknotes tossed by the wind.

Louis the Industrialist (Raymond Cordy) at the pinnacle of his career, making a speech at the opening of his new automated factory.

With its witty echoes of silent screen comedy, its contemporary satiric relevancy, its sparse use of dialogue, its natural acting, and its delightfully appropriate and lilting music by George Auric, *A Nous la Liberté* should have been a hit but wasn't. However it eventually gained a reputation as a classic.

The Communists perceived "anarchist tendencies" in the film, while Hungary, sensitive to its "subversive" nature, banned it, feeling it constituted "an instrument of dangerous propaganda for the social order and peace among the classes."

Lazare Meerson's futuristic and deliberately inhuman sets earned him an Academy Award nomination (1931-32) for Art Direction, marking the first time a French film was thus honored by the Hollywood Academy of Motion Picture Arts and Sciences.

When Chaplin's *Modern Times* (1936) appeared one could see the influence of Clair's film, particularly in the scenes when the assembly line progression goes haywire. The Nazi-dominated Tobis company, partly in an attempt to discredit Chaplin for his alleged "Jewish extraction," wanted to instigate a suit for plagiarism and tried unsuccessfully to enlist Clair's support. Clair countered: "We are all tributaries of a man whom I admire and if he was inspired by my film, this is a great honor for me." The lawsuit was withdrawn.

Feeling that some of the operetta touches were too old-fashioned, Clair re-edited the film in 1951. The utopian vision of automation may strike us today as naive and dated. Nonetheless we must admire Clair's acuity in depicting his contemporary machine age as a deplorable state of servitude which produces automatons and acknowledge that the film expresses a statement which is universal and timeless, namely that the human spirit must be free. In 1971 Clair commented that he was glad he created *A Nous la Liberté:* "It's all about the unrest of young people and I'm very pleased to have made a 'hippie' movie over forty years ago."

René Clair continued his distinguished career with work in England, then in Hollywood during the war years, and finally back in France. Evident throughout is the "Clair touch"—a personal blend of sophisticated wit, intelligence, fantasy, and delicate comedy. Clair has written: "To laugh is to dream, to laugh is to be free, to laugh is to take revenge, to laugh is to possess everything we lack in reality."

René Clair was received into the Académie Française on May 10, 1962, with this praise: "You have fully satisfied those who demand of a visual art that it enrich their knowledge of man."

His remarkable reflections on film, *Cinema Yesterday and Today (Cinéma d'Hier, Cinéma d'Aujourd'hui,* Paris, 1970) was published in New York in 1972. In 1980 René Clair was awarded the Grand Prix National du Cinéma. The highly respected and influential filmmaker died in his home in Neuilly, a Paris suburb, on March 15, 1981.

All dignity is thrown to the wind as the officials at the ceremony scramble for the falling banknotes.

41

Lamy; *Music:* Vincent Scotto; *Running Time:* 142 minutes; *Paris Premiere:* October 8, 1932; *New York Premiere:* February 12, 1948; *16 mm. Rental Source:* Images.

CAST

César Olivier: Raimu; *Fanny:* Orane Demazis; *Marius:* Pierre Fresnay; *Honoré Panisse:* Fernard Charpin; *Honorine Cabanis:* Alida Rouffe; *M. Brun:* Robert Vattier; *Félix Escartefigue:* Auguste Mouriès; *Aunt Claudine Foulon:* Milly Mathis; *Chauffeur:* Maupi; *Dr. Félicien Venelle:* Edouard Delmont.

BACKGROUND

After adapting *Marius* for the screen, Marcel Pagnol prepared a sequel which, like its predecessor, was first written and performed as a play. *Fanny,* dedicated to Orane Demazis who continued to play the heroine, opened at the Théâtre de Paris on December 5, 1931. Since Raimu had had a temporary falling out with Pagnol, the role of César was played by the great Harry Baur. With the

FANNY

LES FILMS MARCEL PAGNOL/ESTABLISSEMENTS BRAUNBERGER-RICHEBÉ   1932

CREDITS

Screenplay: Marcel Pagnol from his play; *Director* Marc Allégret; *Photographers:* Nicolas Toporkoff, André Dantan, Roger Hubert, Georges Benoit, and Coutelain; *Assistant Directors:* Yves Allégret, Pierre Prévert, and Eli Lotar; *Editor:* Raymond

Pretending to be indifferent, César (Raimu) has Fanny (Orane Demazis) read the long-awaited letter from his absent son.

Reconciled to the marriage between Fanny (Orane Demazis) and Panisse (Fernand Charpin), César (Raimu) foresees his future wealthy grandson smoking cigars as big as his arm.

exceptions of Pierre Fresnay and Alida Rouffe, the rest of the cast was the same as in the film *Marius*. The play was enormously successful.

When Paramount at Joinville was preparing the first film version of Pagnol's *Topaze* (shot in 1932), the playwright was offended when, without any consultation, a writer was brought in to rewrite the dialogue. Pagnol saw that the only way to have complete control over his work was to make his own films. The first step was to enter into partnership with a distributing company. Next, Marc Allégret was hired as a director for *Fanny*, Pagnol's inaugural effort as an independent producer. Marc Allégret (1900-73) had a long career in French cinema and like several of his contemporaries is best remembered for work done in the 1930's (such as *Entrée des Artistes* 1938). A fine discoverer of talent, Allégret helped launch the careers of Jean-Pierre Aumont, Michèle Morgan, Gérard Philipe, and Brigitte Bardot among others.

Pagnol reassembled the cast of *Marius* in order to preserve the sense of continuity in the sequel. (Paul Dullac was replaced by Auguste Mouriès, however.) Interiors were shot at the Billancourt studios; exteriors in the Marseilles area.

During the filming of *Fanny* (June-July 1932)

Pagnol was continuing his apprenticeship in film, learning how to deal with the many technical problems of production and increasing his involvement in the film's direction, all of which would help him in the near future. Great care was taken to make *Fanny* faithful to the spirit of its predecessor and it, too, proved an outstanding success.

SYNOPSIS

As the *Malaisie* departs with Marius (Pierre Fresnay), his father César (Raimu) carries Fanny (Orane Demazis), who had fainted in his bedroom when her lover left, to her mother Honorine (Alida Rouffe). Fanny revives and tells César that Marius has gone; his longing for the sea was slowly killing him. César is deeply hurt. Almost a month passes without a word from his son, but César feigns indifference. Finally a letter arrives.

The widowed sailmaker Panisse (Fernand Charpin) visits Honorine and once more repeats his request for the hand of Fanny. Fanny, discovering she is pregnant, prays for the return of Marius so that he can marry her in time. When Honorine learns about Fanny's condition she is hysterical and orders her out of the house. Fanny faints and she is immediately solicitous. Honorine tells her to marry the wealthy Panisse but Fanny would prefer to wait for Marius. However, Honorine insists that she save the family honor and Fanny agrees.

She visits Panisse and decides to tell him the truth. She is surprised to learn that he is not upset but actually overjoyed at the prospect of fatherhood. His marriage was childless and he had

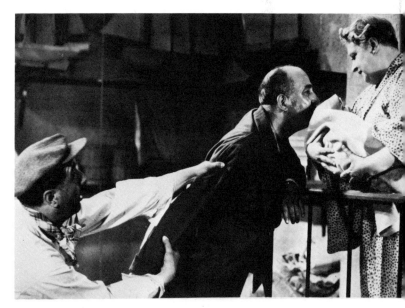

The great moment arrives: César (Raimu) restrains the ecstatic Panisse (Fernand Charpin) as he sees his son held by Honorine (Alida Rouffe).

desired a son desperately for thirty years. He will marry her but asks that the identity of the baby's father be kept hidden.

César enters to inform Panisse that Marius will return in a little more than two years. When he learns that Panisse is going to marry Fanny he starts quarreling with him since he expects Marius to marry her. As their testy passions mount and violence seems imminent, Fanny appears from the next room and confirms the news.

César misunderstands and thinks Fanny is marrying Panisse for his money. Then, learning of her pregnancy, he acquiesces but expresses hurt that they will steal his grandchild. Only when they propose to make him godfather and agree to naming the boy "César-Marius Panisse" is César placated.

The couple marry. Easter morning a joyful Panisse learns he has a son. A year passes during which César hasn't told Marius about his baby.

Marius returns on a brief leave and embraces his father. While Panisse takes a business trip to Paris, Marius visits Fanny who tells him her husband is sleeping in the next room. Marius reveals that he was homesick for his father and for Marseilles. He is upset that Fanny didn't wait for him.

A friend, Escartefigue (Auguste Mouriès), arrives with flowers which Panisse sent from the station. An angry Marius catching Fanny in a lie has guessed that the child is his. Soon both reveal their undying love for the other and when Marius kisses her passionately César appears and breaks up their embrace. He tells Marius not to deceive Panisse. Then Panisse arrives—he changed his mind about going to Paris. This is the moment he has dreaded: Marius returning and demanding his son.

In the ensuing powerful confrontation Panisse refuses to surrender the child and Marius realizes that although she loves him Fanny would never go off without the baby. Drawing on her great strength of character, Fanny bravely tells Marius that the child is not morally his, that because of his extraordinary care and devotion Panisse is the actual father now. She honestly declares her love for Marius. César steps in and with great parental authority orders Marius away from the household. It is the best solution, however painful. Marius departs hastily and a devastated Fanny weeps unconsolably.

COMMENTARY

As with *Marius* the great strength in *Fanny* lies in its fascinating characterization. These lovable and believable characters could immediately arouse our interest and sympathy with their simple, appealing humanity.

Raimu, of course, continued to dominate the work, this *"force de la nature"* who was catapulted into stardom relatively late in his career. Pagnol described him as having a "benign patriarchal countenance" which "belies his gruff manner and demonstrates that if he barks he has no bite."

Each of the memorable characters has great scenes in which he or she dominates:

César's hilarious commentary on Marius's long-anticipated letter which Fanny reads to him followed by his response, dictated to her, full of fatherly advice and concern.

Panisse's graceful acceptance of the pregnant Fanny as his wife since it will mean the joyful realization of his lifelong dream of parenthood.

Fanny's sudden nobility when she defends her husband's parental claim on Marius's son.

For such wonderful acting and moving incidents we can easily pass over the film's shortcomings as cinema. Though Allégret tried to "open up" the play with occasional tracking shots, the film, consisting chiefly of medium shots and long takes, maintains an atmosphere of "canned theatre." Pagnol was to defend his cinematic practice: "The talking film is the art of printing, fixing, and propagating theatre." This view would be challenged by René Clair and others but it is consistent with a playwright who values the importance of dialogue above everything else.

Fanny was remade in foreign countries: in Italy as *Fanny*, directed by Mario Almirante (1933), and in Germany as *Zum Schwarzen Walfisch* (1934), with Emil Jannings as César. When M-G-M bought the remake rights to *Fanny* the distribution of the original film was held up in America for sixteen years. Their version, laundered, sentimentalized, and called *Port of Seven Seas*, was released in 1938. With its casting of Wallace Beery, Maureen O'Sullivan and Cora Witherspoon the result was more mulligan stew than genuine bouillabaisse. Notable only was Frank Morgan as Panisse.

The great theme in *The Marseilles Trilogy*, so evident here in *Fanny*, is its celebration of parental love. The strong bond between César and Marius is mirrored by the powerful bond between Panisse and his son, especially when Marius appears on the scene to threaten it.

One more chapter has to be written in this unforgettable saga which will reunite the lovers and bring *The Marseilles Trilogy* to a satisfactory conclusion.

The climactic scene: Marius (Pierre Fresnay), right, returns to claim his beloved Fanny (Orane Demazis) and confronts Panisse (Fernand Charpin) and César (Raimu).

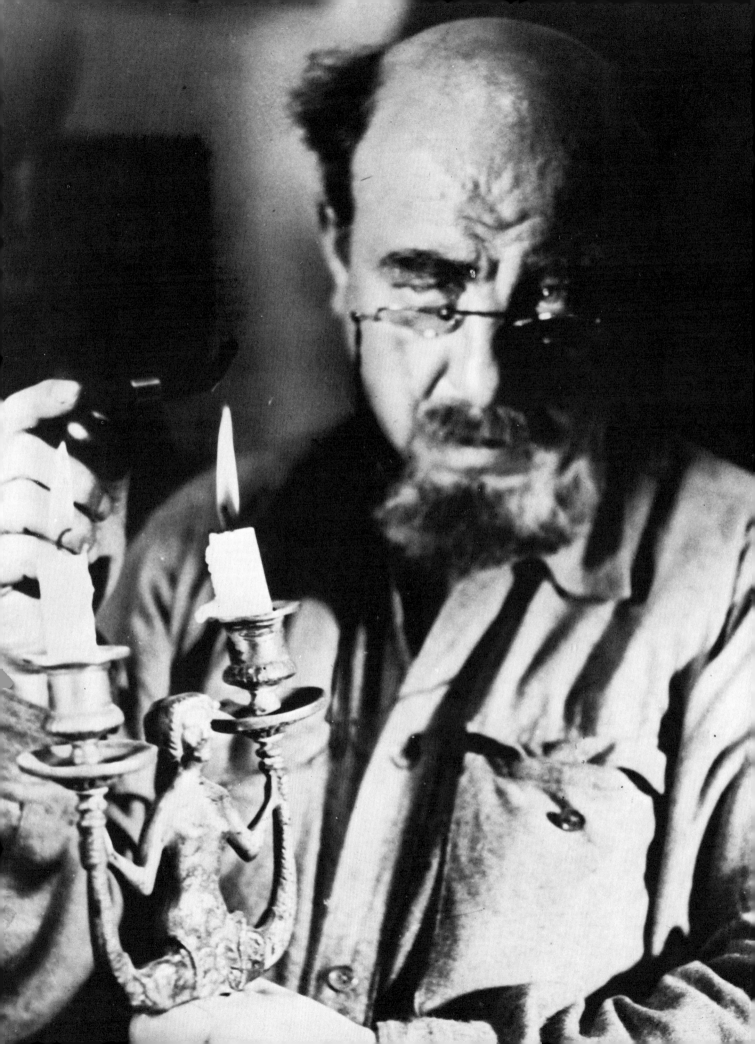

POIL DE CAROTTE

FILMS LEGRAND MAJESTIC/LES FILMS
MARCEL VANDAL-CHARLES DELAC   1932

Poil de Carotte (Robert Lynen) attempts to console his mother (Catherine Fonteney) after her husband humiliates her, but he is rebuffed.

CREDITS

Screenplay: Julien Duvivier, based on the collection of stories by Jules Renard (1894), published in New York, 1967; *Director:* Julien Duvivier; *Photographer:* Armand Thirard; *Assistant Director:* Jean-Paul Le Chanois; *Editor:* Marthe Poncin; *Music:* Alexandre Tansman; *Running Time:* 80 minutes; *Paris Premiere:* October 13, 1932; *New York Premiere:* May 25, 1933; *16 mm. Rental Source:* Em Gee Film Library.

CAST

M. Lepic: Harry Baur; *Poil de Carotte:* Robert Lynen; *Mme. Lepic:* Catherine Fonteney; *Uncle:* Louis Gouthier; *Ernestine Lepic:* Simone Aubry; *Félix Lepic:* Maxime Fromiot; *Mathilde:* Colette Segall; *Honorine:* Mme. Marty; *Annette:* Christiane Dor.

BACKGROUND

Julien Duvivier was born in Lille (Nord) on October 8, 1896, and had a long and distinguished career as a French film director—he occasionally shot films outside of France. At first he tried acting, then became an assistant director to the celebrated Antoine, founder of the significant and influential Théâtre Libre, who advised him to try his hand at film making. Among Duvivier's output of silent films was a version of *Poil de Carotte*, adapted by Jacques Feyder and the director, released in 1925. After completing three talkies, Duvivier decided to remake the Renard classic in what was to become his favorite film, *Poil de Carotte.*

Jules Renard had published his astringent, chiefly autobiographical stories of an unloved red-haired boy in 1894. It became enormously popular and was successfully presented on the stage in 1900 (the American adaptation of the one-act play was called *Carrots* and Ethel Barrymore appeared in it on Broadway in 1902) and subsequently had several film treatments.

Renard wrote the work to satisfy a grudge against his mother and to restore the truth about childhood. Instead of depicting the child as a "beautiful angel" as had previous writers, he wished to bring to light the bad instincts of the child ("the little animal") which he often hid. Realistic, scathing, and ringing with honesty, the book has become a French classic.

Duvivier gave a narrative structure leading up to a climax to a work which was chiefly a collection of deftly told anecdotes. He softened the harshness of the book, compressed the action to one summer vacation and added plot elements from a Renard play, *La Bigote* (1909). Duvivier assembled a brilliant cast. The great Harry Baur, soon a rival with Raimu for the rank of greatest French screen actor of his day, was wisely chosen to play the father. Although Baur (born April 12, 1880) had appeared in a few silent films, his real film career began with sound. Duvivier's *David Golder* (1931) was his and the director's first talking picture.

47

(Opposite Page) Portrait of the great Harry Baur as M. Lepic.

M. Lepic (Harry Baur) demands that his wife (Catherine Fonteney) leave their son alone.

Catherine Fonteney of the Comédie Française had the role of the neurotic, spiteful mother.

Duvivier found his central character walking down a Parisian boulevard with his American mother. Eleven-year-old Robert Lynen was totally convincing and natural in this, his first film role as the pathetic and unforgettable "Poil de Carotte." The film was shot at the Pathé-Nathan Studios at Joinville.

SYNOPSIS

Returning to his village in the province of Nièvre for his summer vacation is Poil de Carotte (Robert Lynen), a boy around twelve years old. His father, M. Lepic (Harry Baur), has not spoken to his shrewish wife (Catherine Fonteney) for many years. Generally treated with indifference by his father, Poil de Carotte is the object of his mother's never-abating hatred and derision. While she spoils the first son Félix (Maxime Fromiot) and her daughter Ernestine (Simone Aubry), she persecutes the red-haired boy unmercifully. He performs all the odious chores and is ordered to close up the chicken coop, a frightening experience since he's terrified of the dark. Only Annette (Christine Dor), the new maid, befriends the lonely and mistreated lad.

Mme. Lepic forces Poil de Carotte to feign indif-

ference to his father's invitation to go hunting and does everything possible to prevent any friendship between the two. A happy visit to the farm of his uncle (Louis Gouthier) is interrupted by a summons to return home. Angry and frustrated, the boy vents his rage by whipping the horse to breakneck speed. Annette warns M. Lepic that sometimes unhappy children commit suicide.

The father slowly comes round to the boy. When ordered to go to the store by his mother, Poil de Carotte bravely refuses. M. Lepic stands up for him and orders Félix to go. A defeated Mme. Lepic is hysterical. When she falsely accuses the child of stealing some household money his father orders her to leave him alone.

M. Lepic is running for mayor. While Poil de Carotte dresses to meet his dad at City Hall, the vengeful mother locks him in his room. He sneaks out the window and greets his newly victorious father, but M. Lepic is so busy with his well-wishing friends he ignores his son. Feeling rejected, Poil de Carotte runs off.

Thinking that he'll always be lonely and unhappy, he makes up his mind to take his life. He meets his little friend Mathilde (Colette Segall) and tells her his plans. She of course is too young to understand. Poil de Carotte heads to the barn to hang himself.

At the reception for the new mayor Mathilde innocently repeats her friend's suicide threat to the uncle who, worried, tells M. Lepic. The father rushes to the barn just in time to prevent his son from hanging himself.

In a moving reconciliation scene, M. Lepic tells

Poil de Carotte (Robert Lynen) bids farewell to his "wife" Mathilde (Colette Segall) before attempting suicide.

48

the boy that he was a late and unwanted child. Stirred to a renewed love and interest in his son, he calls him by his rightful name "François." The radiant boy has found protection and love at last.

COMMENTARY

One of the remarkable qualities of this moving film in addition to Thirard's fine photography is its realistic depiction of childhood. At a time when Hollywood presented Jackie Cooper and other child actors in heavily sentimentalized films or else displayed a tendency to make the children appear "cute" by spouting adult remarks, *Poil de Carotte* (as well as *La Maternelle* and others) portrayed children in a totally natural manner, not idealized and problem-free as adults might fancy them. As a result, children seemed honest, complex, and, above all, real and believable.

Skillfully directed by Duvivier, the young Robert Lynen gave a memorable performance as the skinny, deprived Poil de Carotte, starving for affection but who is as mischievous and bighearted as any normal boy. Lynen had an instant appeal and could easily arouse poignant reactions in the viewer.

Robert Lynen (1921-1944) had a brief, tragedy-stalked life. Raised in terrible poverty, he lived with his family on the outskirts of Paris in a tent. After his screen earnings enabled them to move to a better home, his artist-father took his life. Although Robert made eleven films (1932-39), his most significant screen role was that of Poil de Carotte. As a member of the Maquis, the French underground in WWII, he was captured and shot by the Nazis in 1944.

Harry Baur had such forceful personality and talent that a few gestures could reveal the character he was playing, even the person's thoughts. His M. Lepic was one of an outstanding gallery of screen characterizations renowned for their range and depth. A great stage and screen actor, Baur too met a tragic death in the war. Denounced as a "Jew" and a "communist," he was tortured by the Gestapo and died shortly afterward on April 8, 1943. It is believed that the real reason for his treatment was his refusal to reveal information concerning the Resistance, to which he belonged. Mme. Fonteney was effective as the vicious Mme. Lepic, never going into excess or caricature.

There are many subtle touches in the film. M. Lepic notices that there is no photo of his youngest son among the collection on the mantlepiece. The

M. Lepic (Harry Baur) reaches out to befriend his unhappy son (Robert Lynen) whom he has rescued from hanging.

sum of Poil de Carotte's neglect is contained in that small detail.

A memorable sequence is the lyrical "wedding" scene in which a garlanded Poil de Carotte and his "bride" Mathilde march barefooted and dignified through the fields near a brook while his uncle sings and accompanies the charming processional with music from his hand-organ. Even the animals join in the chorus, a moment of operetta à la René Clair. There is not one false note in the fluid and careful direction of Duvivier. Low angle shots from the child's level emphasize the overpowering tyranny of the mother.

Slight in plot but rich in characterization, *Poil de Carotte* was a critical and popular success, running for more than a year in Paris alone. Initially banned in England by the Board of Film Censors, it was subsequently licensed for adults. Although acclaimed for its artistry there (as well as in America where it was known for a while as *The Red-Head)*, it was nevertheless considered a frank and daring film and forbidden to child viewers in both countries.

Poil de Carotte marked the beginning of Duvivier's great, international career. Although the film was remade several times (by Paul Mesnier in 1951; by Henri Graziani in 1973), it is the delicate and poetic Duvivier version of 1932 which is best remembered and which has endured as a film classic.

ZERO FOR CONDUCT

(Zéro de Conduite)

ARGUI FILMS   1933

In the No Smōking section of the train Bruel (Constantin Goldstein-Kehler) and Caussat (Louis Lefèvre), returning from vacation, enjoy their cigars.

CREDITS

Screenplay, Director, Editor: Jean Vigo; *Photographer:* Boris Kaufman; *Assistant Directors:* Albert Riéra, Henri Storck, and Pierre Merle; *Music:* Maurice Jaubert; *Lyrics:* Charles Goldblatt; *Running Time:* 43-45 minutes (existing versions); *Paris Premiere:* November 1945; *New York Premiere:* June 21, 1947; *16 mm. Rental Source:* Images.

CAST

Caussat: Louis Lefèvre; *Colin:* Gilbert Pruchon; *Tabard:* Gérard de Bédarieux; *Bruel:* Constantin Goldstein-Kehler; *Huguet:* Jean Dasté; *M. Parrain, known as Pète-Sec (Dry-Fart):* Robert Le Flon; *The Principal:* Delphin; *M. Santt, Assistant Principal, known as Bec de Gaz (Gas-Snout):* Du Verron [Blanchar]; *The Chemistry Teacher:* Léon Larive; *The Priest:* Henri Storck; *Police Commissioner:* Louis de Gonzague-Frick; *Guardian's Daughter:* Michèle Fayard.

BACKGROUND

Although Jean Vigo's life was brief (1905-34) and his output unavoidably small (two shorts, two fea-

The extraordinary slow-motion processional sequence in the boys' dormitory after the uprising.

The new teacher Huguet (Jean Dasté) amuses the kids during recess by doing his Chaplin walk. Tabard (Gérard de Bédarieux) is the second boy from the left.

tures), he holds the honored position of being one of the major film directors of all time ("one of the very few real originals who have ever worked on film"—critic James Agee).

Vigo was born in Paris on April 26, 1905. His father, who referred to himself as Miguel Almereyda, was a militant anarchist who was found strangled in prison in 1917 when Jean was twelve. The boy had adored him and one can trace Almereyda's spirit in the future director's denouncement of authority and celebration of liberty in his films. A present from his father-in-law enabled Vigo to make his first film, a short which was the innovative social documentary, *A Propos de Nice* (1930), with the Russian émigré Boris Kaufman as cameraman.

After running a film club in Nice and shooting a commissioned short about Jean Taris, the swimming champion *(Taris, 1931)*, Vigo met Jacques-Louis Nounez, a businessman. Nounez wanted to create films of medium length, on a limited budget, without stars or name directors. After abandoning several projects, Vigo received permission from Nounez to make a film about children which was tentatively called *Les Cancres (The Dunces)*. Vigo was granted total freedom to make his film provided it

was kept within a modest budget. Interiors were shot at the G.F.F.A. (Gaumont-Franco-Film-Aubert) Studios in Paris from December 24, 1932, to January 7, 1933. Exteriors were shot at Saint-Cloud and the Belleville–la Villette railway station, January 10-22, 1933. The work, done at breakneck speed, frequently necessitating single takes, and threatened by the bad health of the young director, became, miraculously, the classic *Zero for Conduct*.

SYNOPSIS

Vacation over, two boys, Caussat (Louis Lefèvre) and Bruel (Constantin Goldstein-Kehler), amuse themselves on the train taking them back to their provincial school.

With the exception of Huguet (Jean Dasté), who is a regular guy with the kids, the other teachers at the school are repressive and creepy while the pompous and platitudinous principal (Delphin) is a bearded dwarf. Punishment for the slightest infraction of the rules results in a "zero for conduct" which means detention on Sunday.

The principal fiercely disapproves of the close friendship between Bruel and Tabard (Gérard de Bédarieux), a new boy in class who is very shy and lonely. Events build up to an open rebellion by the students: The kids protest the unvarying beans served them in the dining-hall. Tabard curses his fat and repulsive chemistry teacher (Léon Larive) who fondles him. Forced to apologize publicly in front of the principal and his class, Tabard bursts out again with, "I say . . . shit on you!"

The revolt begins in the dormitory with Tabard reading a proclamation denouncing the administration and exhorting open rebellion. In the ensuing frenzy, kids overturn beds, an enormous pillow fight begins, and, for climax, there's a stunning dream-like parade of jubilant boys.

The following day is the Commemoration Day ceremonies with a priest and invited officials in attendance. The figures of authority are juxtaposed with a row of large dummies. The four leaders: Caussat, Tabard, Bruel, and Colin (Gilbert Pruchon), who have hid out in the attic, start pelting the guests below with old books, chamber pots, and stones thrown from the rooftops. Huguet urges them on and encourages the other pupils to join in. The officials take refuge as the four victorious revolutionaries climb up on a roof exulting in their freedom.

COMMENTARY

After a private screening on April 7, 1933, to an invited audience, *Zero for Conduct* aroused much controversy. Before beginning a commercial run, the film was banned by the Board of Censors that August. It is felt that at the time the government feared the film "might create disturbances and hinder the maintenance of order." Being the son of the well-known anarchist Almereyda did not help the young director either.

Though circulated in a limited way through French film clubs and released in Belgium, *Zero for Conduct* had to wait for the Liberation to enter into general distribution in France after a twelve-year ban. It received enthusiastic acclaim finally. In 1946 the Museum of Modern Art screened it and it began a commercial run in New York (a brief scene involving adolescent nudity was ordered deleted by the state censors, however, and was not restored until 1962) paired with *L'Atalante* the following year. Gradually, the director's work became internationally known and celebrated.

An autobiography, an attack on the French educational system, a psychological study of the young, a film of social revolt, *Zero for Conduct* is, above all, a poetical evocation of childhood. Since the forces of authority in the adult world conspire to inhibit the children and suppress their beautiful, wild spirit, Vigo cleverly depicts the "guardians of morality," not as they appear in normal life, but as they seem to the eyes of children or at least to the satirical vision of the director. Thus realism gives way to poetry and such hilarious caricatures result as the snoop, "Gas-Snout" ("a tiptoeing lobster dressed in an undertaker's suit"—Agee), and, of course, the principal with his inflated rhetoric, midget body, weak, shrill voice, and ridiculous beard—through satiric diminution rendered immortally absurd. Whereas the kids are alive and vital, most of the adults are mere puppets. Granted, the children are idealized, but that was part of Vigo's aim: childhood should command respect and awe.

There are strong political implications here: Society, like school, which is a microcosm of it, is run by a powerful minority forcing its will on the weak majority. However, the message is that the weak *can* unite to successfully overthrow their overbearing oppressors.

The rebellion and ultimate victory at the end of the film echo the sentiments of the anarchist movement. Even Tabard's insolent retort, "I say . . . shit on you!," had political significance: In 1912 when Gustave Hervé, a colleague of Vigo's father, left prison a few months before his long sentence was up, he was in terrible health, felt he owed nothing to the minister who got him released, and wanted to express this publicly. Almereyda obliged him by composing a banner headline in the radical newspaper *La Guerre Socialist* with that startling challenge printed without asterisks: "I say SHIT on you!" No wonder the government was nervous over the film.

Zero for Conduct was an intensely personal film, the author releasing the long-stored memories of his unhappy childhood. The sensitive Tabard represents the young Vigo in the film.

Viewers cannot fail to be thrilled with the dormitory revolt scene which moves from a realistic plane to a lyrical outburst on a surrealistic level when the ecstatic boys—carrying paper lanterns, the air thick with pillow feathers—stage a dazzling processional projected in slow motion accompanied by Jaubert's spooky music. Vigo evokes the rich visual dream world of the children's subconscious minds imaginatively on the screen. It is truly a brilliant, unforgettable experience.

The film's lack of clear continuity resulting in a rather "jumpy" narrative (which was to influence the New Wave movement some twenty-five years later) was unintended by Vigo. Finding that he shot much more than the agreed upon length, he could choose those scenes—regardless of their merit—which told a logical, coherent story or select the most "genuine" sequences without bothering about

Commemoration Day: the Principal (Delphin), front row on left, the Police Commissioner (Louis de Gonzague-Frick) and other "dignitaries" assemble to review the festivities.

the missing connections. With the instinct of a poet, Vigo decided on the latter and opted for a stylistic unity based on an inner logic. We the viewers must fill in the gaps.

Vigo makes use of cinematic references: Jean Dasté does a turn as Chaplin; the pillow fight scene in the dormitory is straight out of Gance's *Napoléon;* the brief animated cartoon in a study hall sequence recalls the work of Emile Cohl, etc. Vigo uses sparse, simple dialogue and makes his points chiefly by purely visual means.

Zero for Conduct is not unflawed: the low level of the sound quality and the "loose ends" effect resulting from the lack of a finished script are some faults which have been pointed out, but they do not detract from the imagination and vitality of the work.

In spite of the fact that no complete, unmultilated version of the film survives, *Zero for Conduct* is one of the great seminal, liberating, and influential films of all time. Lindsay Anderson's story of a rebellious boys' school in England, *If* (1968), which contains strong political overtones, is one example of Vigo's abiding presence.

Zero for Conduct remains a fresh discovery for each succeeding generation of lovers of film.

On the rooftop the four triumphant revolutionaries bound to freedom at the film's end. From top to bottom: Bruel (Constantin Goldstein-Kehler), Caussat (Louis Lefèvre), Tabard (Gérard de Bédarieux), and Colin (Gilbert Pruchon).

L'ATALANTE

ARGUI FILMS   1934

CREDITS

Screenplay: Jean Vigo and Albert Riéra, based on an original scenario by Jean Guinée [R. de Guichen]; *Director:* Jean Vigo; *Photographer:* Boris Kaufman;

Assistant Directors: Albert Riéra, Charles Goldblatt, and Pierre Merle; *Editor:* Louis Chavance; *Music:* Maurice Jaubert; *Lyrics:* Charles Goldblatt; *Running Time:* 89 minutes; *Paris Premiere:* September 13, 1934 (as *Le Chaland Qui Passe*); *New York Premiere:* June 21, 1947; *16 mm. Rental Source:* Images.

CAST

Père Jules: Michel Simon; *Jean:* Jean Dasté; *Juliette:* Dita Parlo; *The Peddler:* Gilles Margaritis; *Cabin Boy;* Louis Lefèvre; *Juliette's Mother:* Fanny Clar; *Juliette's Father;* Raphaël Diligent; *Office Manager:* Maurice Gilles; *The Best Man:* René Bleck; *The Thief:* Charles Goldblatt; *Extras at Station:* Jacques and Pierre Prévert.

BACKGROUND

It is to his credit that after the banning of *Zero for Conduct*, producer Jacques-Louis Nounez gave another project to Jean Vigo to film in spite of being warned against underwriting the cost of "subver-

sive" activities. The story Vigo was assigned was called *L'Atalante,* a rather ordinary account of the marriage of a young barge captain and a country girl. Vigo used this simply as a point of departure in which to develop rich characterization and to invest it with his personal magic. For the first time he had a large budget for a full-length feature and well-known actors: Michel Simon, who was active in French cinema since the silent period and more recently had worked with Jean Renoir in *La Chienne* (1931) and *Boudu Saved from Drowning (Boudu Sauvé des Eaux)* (1932), and Dita Parlo, who had made films in Germany, Hollywood, and France. Vigo recruited Jean Dasté and Louis Lefèvre, who had appeared in *Zero for Conduct.*

Interiors were shot at G.F.F.A. (Gaumont-Franco-Film Aubert) studios. Exteriors included Conflans-Saint-Honorine, the village of Maurecourt (Seine-et-Oise), Le Havre, and various canals. "We were intoxicated by the admirable landscape of the Parisian canals and developed the action against a backdrop of locks, steep banks, cabarets, and waste ground," Vigo wrote, and his assistant Riéra noted that "his [Vigo's] overflowing imagination permitted him to improvise with astounding facility. It wasn't the words that inspired him, but faces, objects, landscapes."

After almost four months of exhaustive shooting, from November 15, 1933 to the end of February 1934, with Vigo constantly struggling with bad health, *L'Atalante* was completed. Unfortunately it was to be his final masterpiece.

SYNOPSIS

Jean (Jean Dasté), the young captain of the barge *L'Atalante,* marries Juliette (Dita Parlo), a village girl who has never left home before, and together with the colorful sailor Père Jules (Michel Simon) and cabin boy (Louis Lefèvre) sail away.

Juliette becomes bored with the housekeeping routine on the barge and being left alone much at night, and longs to see the sights of Paris. The lovers quarrel. The eccentric Père Jules befriends Juliette and shows her his room full of cats and exotic, often bizarre, souvenirs.

Jean reluctantly agrees to accompany his wife to Paris but Père Jules announces he wants to see a doctor, so the captain stays and guards the barge. The next day Jean takes Juliette to a cabaret where a sprightful peddler (Gilles Margaritis) flirts with her. Full of jealousy and anger, Jean leaves his wife on the barge and takes off with the crew. The

peddler appears, offers Juliette a musical salute, and details the wonders of Paris. Jean returns and throws him off the barge.

As Jean sulks and paces the deck, a restless Juliette below decides to slip off to see Paris briefly. A sullen Jean discovers his wife is gone and gives orders to depart immediately without her. When Juliette returns to the dock she realizes that *L'Atalante* has left. A thief steals her purse which prevents her from catching up with the barge at its next stop.

Then we see individual scenes of the unhappy, separated lovers, lonely, sleepless, and erotically tormented. Père Jules has to cover for the distraught captain when reports arise complaining of his inefficiency. The determined sailor decides to find Juliette so that Jean can function again.

At Le Havre Père Jules discovers Juliette work-

Boris Kaufman's striking nocturnal shot of an apprehensive wife (Dita Parlo) at the front of the barge *L'Atalante.*

55

ing as a cashier in a record shop and brings her back to the barge. A poignant reconciliation is effected and *L'Atalante* continues on its way.

COMMENTARY

After several cuts recommended by the editor, *L'Atalante* was privately screened on April 25, 1934, for the company representatives, cinema owners, and distributors. Despite some critical praise the film in its present condition was considered commercially worthless. Gaumont, the distributors, inserted a popular song, "Le Chaland Qui Passe" ("The Passing Barge"), by Cesare Andrea Bixio, intermittently throughout Jaubert's wonderful score, amputated the film drastically, and left only a few scenes intact. The revised film, retitled *Le Chaland Qui Passe*, opened in mid-September 1934 and was a box office disaster provoking hisses from the audience.

Following a bedridden period of seven months, suffering from the wasting rheumatic septicaemia, Jean Vigo died in his Paris home on October 5, 1934, shortly after the fiasco of his final effort. In Paris on October 30, 1940, the film was finally re-released under its original title with Jaubert's music restored and a few missing scenes included.

An attempt was made in 1950 by P. E. Sallès Gomès and critic Panfilo Colaprete to reconstruct a version which approximated the original *L'Atalante*. As with *Zero for Conduct* there does not exist a complete, uncut version of the film as Vigo had created it, but hopes to make this an eventual possibility have not been abandoned.

L'Atalante is full of scenes of rare beauty and unforgettable poetry:

The opening dreamlike sequence of the silent wedding couple walking arm in arm through the town, across fields and down paths to the barge is arresting and haunting.

The scene in which Père Jules shows Juliette the treasures in his room achieves a startling, grotesque affect when we suddenly come upon a jar containing a pair of severed hands, the sole remains of his friend.

Memorable too is the scene in which Jean dives into the water searching for an image of his sorely missed wife—earlier in the film Juliette had told

At the Aux Quatre Nations cabaret, the lively peddler (Gilles Margaritis), right, dances with Juliette (Dita Parlo) to the growing annoyance of her husband Jean (Jean Dasté), left.

him if you open your eyes under water you will be able to see your beloved—and beholds a superimposition of her, smiling and floating in her wedding dress. This exquisite moment is surrealistic and illustrates the luminous world of the imagination. Working as a poet, Vigo employs suchlike dream-imagery when realism proves inadequate.

Also powerful is the parallel montage of the parted lovers—he on the barge and she in Paris—as they undress, and go to bed followed by dissolves of each agonizing with insomnia and longing. Their movements are synchronous to suggest that they are a unit.

Although both Jean Dasté and Dita Parlo are perfect in their parts, convincing and appealing, it is Michel Simon who dominates *L'Atalante* with a performance that is a tour de force as Père Jules, a great character role which is undoubtedly his finest screen achievement. Simon based his interpretation on an extraordinary man he once knew who was known as Father Isaac. Jean Renoir paid Simon a great compliment when he said that he was one of those "who have been invented solely to allow us to make great films."

Boris Kaufman achieved some remarkable photographic effects, particularly in scenes of the actors on the deck of the mist-laden or fog-engulfed barge. Although he went on to a famous career in Hollywood working with Elia Kazan and Sidney Lumet among others, he felt nostalgia for his period of collaboration with Vigo and said he lost "a cinematographic paradise." Vigo, he observed, "used everything around him: the sun, the moon, snow, night. Instead of fighting unfavorable conditions, he made them play a part."

Jaubert's score provides an extraordinary accompaniment to the film's mood. The most renowned composer of French film music in the 1930's was killed in action in WWII.

As in *Zero for Conduct* there are some gaps in the continuity of *L'Atalante* which create an unclear effect and indicate technical inexperience, but a unity of style and atmosphere—and the presence of genius—compensate for any flaw.

Although Vigo's death was a great loss to French cinema we should be grateful for the brilliant work he managed to create in his brief and trouble-strewn life. After viewing *L'Atalante*, critic Elie Faure defined "the very spirit of Vigo's work" as "almost violent, certainly tormented, feverish, overflowing with ideas and truculent fantasy, with virulent, even demonic romanticism that still remains humanistic." The influential and exquisite

L'Atalante demonstrates that Vigo had a genius to create genuine poetry out of the ordinary lives of simple people.

In France, starting in 1952, there has been an annual "Prix Vigo" awarded to new directors who show quality and an independence of spirit.

Père Jules (Michel Simon), center, has the cabin boy (Louis Lefèvre) get the phonograph in an attempt to cheer up the disconsolate captain (Jean Dasté).

In a Le Havre record shop, Père Jules (Michel Simon) discovers a delighted Juliette (Dita Parlo).

CARNIVAL IN FLANDERS

(La Kermesse Héroïque)

SOCIÉTÉ DES FILMS SONORES TOBIS   1935

CREDITS

Scenario: Charles Spaak and Jacques Feyder, based on a story by Charles Spaak; *Dialogue:* Bernard Zimmer (French version); *Director:* Jacques Feyder; *Photographer:* Harry Stradling; *Assistant Directors:* Marcel Carné and Charles Barrois; *Editor:* Jacques Brillouin; *Music:* Louis Beydts; *Running Time:* 115 minutes; *American Version:* 92 minutes. ; *Paris Premiere:* December 1, 1935; *New York Premiere:* September 22, 1936; *16 mm. Rental Sources:* Corinth.

CAST

Mme. Burgomaster (Cornélia): Françoise Rosay; *The Burgomaster:* André Alerme; *The Duke d'Olivarès:* Jean Murat; *Chaplain:* Louis Jouvet; *Siska:* Micheline Cheirel; *Breughel:* Bernard Lancret; *The Fish-Wife:* Lyne Clévers; *The Baker's Wife:* Maryse Wendling; *The Inn-Keeper's Wife:* Ginette Gaubert; *Captain:* Alexandre d'Arcy; *The Dwarf:* Delphin; *The Butcher:* Alfred Adam; *Fishmonger:* Arthur Devère; *2nd Spanish Lieutenant:* Claude Sainval.

BACKGROUND

Jacques Frédérix was born on July 21, 1885, in the Brussels suburb of Ixelles. When he decided to enter the theater instead of the military, his father forbade his use of the family name. As Jacques Feyder, the young Belgian came to Paris in 1911 and acted in a Méliès film as well as serials by Louis Feuillade. He became an assistant director to Gas-

58

Lazare Meerson's striking and meticulous recreation of the Flemish village of Boom.

59

ton Ravel and, when the director was mobilized in the war, completed for him *Monsieur Pinson, Policier* (1916). He married the great French actress Françoise Rosay in 1917 and she subsequently was his leading lady in many of his films. His Zola adaptation, *Thérèse Raquin* (1928), regarded as his best silent film, is now considered lost.

After his contemporary political satire, *Les Nouveaux Messieurs* (1928) was temporarily banned by the French government, a discouraged Feyder left for Hollywood in 1928. There, at M-G-M he directed Garbo's last silent film, *The Kiss* (1929), as well as the German and Swedish versions of her first talkie, *Anna Christie* (1930). Disillusioned and feeling unfulfilled, Feyder returned to France in 1933 and directed *Le Grand Jeu* (1934) and *Pension Mimosas* (1935) before he began his greatest film, *Carnival in Flanders.*

"After *Pension Mimosas,*" Feyder wrote, "I had the ambition to . . . relax myself with the amusement of a farce." Remembering the trouble which accompanied *Les Nouveaux Messieurs,* he wished to film an uncontroversial historical subject "far removed from actuality." He turned to a story which the celebrated screen writer Charles Spaak had written ten years earlier. The project had been turned down formerly since producers felt that the public wasn't interested in costume pictures.

Feyder assembled his gifted collaborators, to whom he always acknowledged his indebtedness, and began work on the expensive film which was first titled, *Les Six Bourgeois d'Alost.* He went to the paintings of the old Flemish and Dutch masters of the sixteenth and seventeenth centuries for inspiration. Then the distinguished set designer Lazare Meerson spent six months in various libraries and museums steeping himself in detail before building an authentic reproduction of Boom, a large village in the province of Antwerp. It took three months to recreate this village at Epinay-sur-Seine and real cement, steel, and plaster were used instead of the traditional papier-mâché and cardboard.

Film designer Léon Barsacq commented on Meerson's achievement: "The exterior sets are an undeniable triumph. In a limited space, Meerson succeeded in building a kind of synthesis of a Flemish town with its canal, belfry, city gates, middle-class houses with stepped gables, and shops overflowing with food and lengths of cloth."

Jean Murat replaced Jules Berry originally considered for the role of the Duke, and Louis Jouvet played the friar, a part intended for Michel Simon.

Françoise Rosay starred in both the French and German version *(Die Klugen Frauen)*, which Feyder also directed. The film was shot between June and September 1935.

"Although the Charles Spaak story . . . could have happened in no other period save that boisterous one of the Flemish renaissance when Flanders was under the heel of Philip of Spain," Feyder wrote, "my chief concern is how successful we have been in imparting to the film's humor an ageless quality that will make its satire as applicable to our own time as it was then." Feyder succeeded admirably, creating a brilliant work as fresh and lively now as it was to his contemporaries.

Portrait of Françoise Rosay in her best-remembered role, that of Cornélia, Mme. Burgomaster. Georges K. Benda's beautiful dress was inspired by a Frans Hals portrait.

60

SYNOPSIS

On the morning of September 17, 1616, the village of Boom prepares for its annual carnival. Jean Breughel (Bernard Lancret), a young painter, is in love with Siska (Micheline Cheirel), the pretty daughter of the Bourgomaster (André Alerme) and his wife Cornélia (Françoise Rosay). Siska's father insists she marry the butcher (Alfred Adam) with whom he's made a business deal. Cornélia sides with her daughter.

An envoy from the King of Spain* rides into the village furiously, informing the city fathers by note that a battalion is to be quartered in Boom for the night. The aldermen are petrified with fear, as they recall previous Spanish pillage and atrocities. The Burgomaster devises a stratagem. He will feign death and the Spanish troops will respect the village's mourning accordingly. When Cornélia tries to learn her husband's plans, she is told that these matters do not concern women. The citizens are ordered not to show resistance to the soldiers. The high-spirited and vigorous Cornélia is disgusted with the men's cowardice and rallies the women around her. We've accepted the domination of men for too long, she asserts. Let's give an example of how women will save Boom by their energy, resolution, and courage. . . .

*The King referred to is Philip II of Spain (1527-98) although the action is set in the year 1616.

Cornélia leads a welcoming committee to greet the approaching Duke d'Olivarès (Jean Murat) and his men. The Duke sympathizes with the "loss" of Boom's Burgomaster but the horses need rest. He promises to leave at dawn. The leaders are billeted among the friendly hostesses. Cornélia maneuvers a flirtatious Duke into commanding the wedding of Jean and Siska.

After a memorable night, the soldiers depart having been "entertained" in every way. As the Duke passes, Cornélia, watching from a balcony, waves discreetly to him. She restores her husband's maculine pride by telling the joyous crowd that only the Burgomaster's heroism saved Boom and accorded the city a tax exemption for a year. The Duke does things well, a pleased Burgomaster tells Cornélia, who smiles enigmatically, caressing a necklace which the handsome officer gave her.

COMMENTARY

Ultranationalists in Belgium and Holland saw in this "uncontroversial" film an attack on Flemish honor and in theaters in major cities there were noisy demonstrations and arrests, release of rats

The welcoming committee offers wine to the arriving Spaniards: The Baker's Wife (Maryse Wendling), the Captain (Alexandre d'Arcy), the Duke (Jean Murat), the Chaplain (Louis Jouvet), the Innkeeper's Wife (Ginette Gaubert), Mme. Burgomaster (Françoise Rosay), 2nd Spanish Lt. (Claude Sainval) and Dwarf (Delphin).

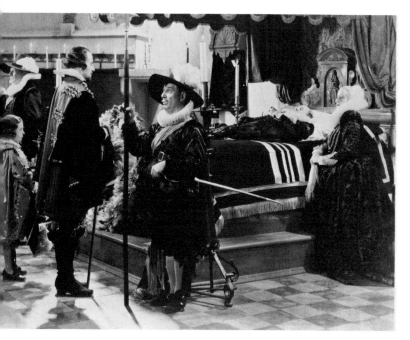

The Duke (Jean Murat) and Dwarf (Delphin) pay their respects to the "dead" Burgomaster (André Alerme). The Fishmonger (Arthur Devère) and the Burgomaster's "widow" (Françoise Rosay) are by the bier.

and stink bombs, and destruction of seats. The film was even accused of being Nazi-inspired!

Nonetheless, *Carnival in Flanders* became an enormous hit, receiving the Grand Prix du Cinèma Français for 1935 as well as the prize for "Best Direction" (German version) at the Venice International Exposition in 1936. It won the New York Film Critics Award for "Best Foreign Film" (1936). Many critics referred to the film as a "living museum" in which the paintings of Breughel, Hals, Memling, Vermeer and others came to life vividly and memorably.

When war broke out, Goebbels banned the film. Unfortunately during the Occupation there was talk that Feyder deliberately tried to show that resistance was futile and "collaboration" was the best policy. The director stated that it was not his wish to hold up for derision the heroic resistance which the Belgians were noted for, but simply "to popularize and spread throughout the world the prestigious art of the great painters of my native country."

Carnival in Flanders is a classically structured film employing the unities of time, place, and action. The plot can be seen as a variant of Aristophanes' *Lysistrata*. In the classic Greek comedy the Athenian and Spartan women band together and deny sex to their husbands until peace is restored; here, however, the ladies of Boom unite and agree to bestow their favors on the invaders to prevent bloodshed and plunder.

Françoise Rosay—vivacious, charming, and delightful in this, her best-remembered role—dominates the film. The great Louis Jouvet is deliciously droll and deadpan as a worldly monk. André Alerme—short, hotheaded, and pompous—is a perfect foil for Mme. Rosay. Strutting about in baggy pantaloons, he resembles a peevish penguin. Witty dialogue, rapid pacing, impressive sets and costumes contributed to the film's triumphant success.

Feyder's last years were marred by poor health and vain attempts to reestablish his critical reputation. The brilliant craftsman ("He was for me an incomparable master"—Charles Spaak), died in Geneva during the night of May 24, 1948.

An expensive musical comedy version of *Carnival in Flanders* was badly received on Broadway in 1953 and closed quickly.

Carnival in Flanders remains Feyder's masterpiece, a gem. Film historian Charles Ford paid it the ultimate accolade by declaring that it is one film which would seem impossible to remake.

A suspicious Burgomaster (André Alerme) is disconcerted to find his wife (Françoise Rosay) not in the arms of the Duke but alone with their baby.

A DAY IN THE COUNTRY

(Une Partie de Campagne)

FILMS DU PANTHÉON 1936 (Year of Production)

CREDITS

Screenplay: Jean Renoir, based on the story by Guy de Maupassant (1881), known in English as "A Country Excursion"; *Director:* Jean Renoir; *Photographer:* Claude Renoir; *Assistant Directors:* Jacques Becker, Jacques B. Brunius, Henri Cartier-Bresson, Claude Heymann, Yves Allégret, and Luchino Visconti;* *Editor:* Marguerite Renoir (Final version: Marinette Cadix); *Music:* Joseph Kosma, Song hummed by Germaine Montero; *Running Time:* 40 minutes; *Paris Premiere:* May 8, 1946; *New York Premiere:* December 12, 1950, included in *Ways of Love; 16 mm. Rental Source:* Facsea.

CAST

Henriette Dufour: Sylvia Bataille; *Henri:* Georges Saint-Saëns (Georges Darnoux); *Rodolphe:* Jacques Borel (Jacques B. Brunius); *Mme. Dufour:* Jane Marken; *M. Dufour:* André Gabriello; *Anatole:* Paul Temps; *Grandmother:* Gabrielle Fontan; *Père Poulain, the Innkeeper:* Jean Renoir; *The Waitress:* Marguerite Renoir; *The Old Priest:* Peirre Lestringuez; *Young Seminarian:* Jacques Becker; *Boy Fishing:* Alain Renoir.

BACKGROUND

Jean Renoir, who had been regarded in his later years as the world's greatest living film director, was

*The last three assistants are thought to have worked only briefly on the film.

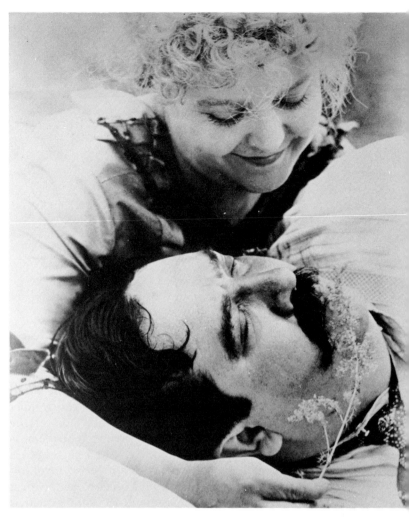

Mme. Dufour (Jane Marken) feels amorous after dining in the country, but her husband Cyprien (André Gabriello) prefers to take a nap instead.

born in Paris on September 15, 1894, the second son of Pierre August Renoir, the great French Impressionist painter (1841-1919). After being seriously wounded in the trenches during WWI, the young Jean discovered the cinema during his convalescence. He began his career as a ceramist, then made figurines for experimental movies. This led to scriptwriting and in 1924 he directed his first film, *La Fille de l'Eau*, starring his first wife, Catherine Hessling. Renoir acknowledged the influences of American film on him: "Chaplin, Stroheim, and Griffith were my masters." He considered *Nana* (1926) the most important of his eight silent films. *La Chienne* (1931) was a powerful early talkie, followed by such memorable films as *Boudu Saved from Drowning (Boudu Sauvé des Eaux)* (1932), *Toni* (1934) (a significant precursor to the Italian neo-realist movement), and *The Crime of M. Lange (Le Crime de M. Lange)* (1935).

After making *People of France (La Vie Est à Nous)*

63

After they row to his favorite spot on the island, Henriette (Sylvia Bataille) finds herself drawn to the serious Henri (Georges Darnoux).

(1936) as a collective enterprise to aid the Front Populaire, Renoir decided to shoot a short, quiet period film based on Maupassant's story, "Une Partie de Compagne." Renoir wrote: "The theme is so important that it could very well have been a full-length film. A tale of disappointed love, followed by a ruined life could furnish matter for a long novel. But Maupassant gives us the essentials in a few pages, and it was the transposition to the screen of these bare bones of a big story that attracted me."

For exteriors he selected the Loing River, near Montigny, and Marlotte, the village where his father had painted as well as the locale of his first film. "The great reason for choosing these exteriors," Renoir said, "was that I knew them absolutely; I knew at what time the light would be directed agreeably at which group of trees. I knew the smallest details of that countryside."

Although *A Day in the Country* flows with much ease and grace, its history was long and complicated with even a stormy episode in America. Exterior shooting began on July 15, 1936, and was supposed to last a week. "My script was designed for fine weather," Renoir said, "and I wrote it with scenes of brilliant sunshine in mind." However, it turned out to be an extremely rainy summer and the director wisely took advantage of it and revised his scenario accordingly. Renoir said later "I believe that without the rain, the end of the film would not have a certain tragic side which finally became the essence of the film."

64

A Dionysian moment: the prancing "satyr" Rodolphe (Jacques B. Brunius) pursues a not unwilling Mme. Dufour (Jane Marken).

By early September the production ran over budget, the crew was tense, the weather impossible. Renoir tried several times to raise money in Paris but to no avail. Producer Pierre Braunberger halted proceedings and the director began work on *The Lower Depths (Les Bas-Fonds)*. Braunberger thought the footage could be turned into a full-length film and had Jacques Prévert prepare a rewrite. However, Renoir's dissatisfaction with the new script and his busy schedule prevented him from any further work on the film. Without his realizing it, *A Day in the Country* was actually finished and perfect.

There remained two unshot scenes: the Dufours leaving their Paris shop for their excursion and, following Maupassant's ending, Henri's subsequent visit there where he learns that Henriette has married Anatole. Braunberger hit upon the idea of replacing these scenes with explanatory titles. However, the one print prepared was destroyed by the Nazis, but fortunately Henri Langlois had saved the unedited negative. Later, with Renoir's approval from America, Marguerite Renoir began to re-edit the film. Joseph Kosma contributed his moving score and the work was finally released some ten years after it had been shot.

SYNOPSIS

In the summer of 1860 Parisian shopkeeper M. Dufour (André Gabriello) takes his family and his insipid future son-in-law Anatole (Paul Temps) to the country for a day's outing. At the inn where they stop, two young men, the high-spirited Ro-

dolphe (Jacques B. Brunius) and his serious friend Henri (Georges Darnoux), discover the attractive Dufour daughter Henriette (Sylvia Bataille). Rodolphe is all for a seduction attempt, but Henri warns, ironically as it turns out, that if she fell for him, this one-day escapade would ruin her life.

After the Dufours eat, Rodolphe invites the ladies for a ride in the fellows' two rowboats. To distract the men, he produces fishing rods which they accept eagerly. Henri dashes ahead and intercepts Henriette, leaving the mother for Rodolphe. In the rowboat Henri offers to date the sensitive young girl but she replies that her father wouldn't allow it.

On an island Henri leads the timid girl to a place under a tree to observe a nightingale calling for its mate while Rodolphe sports with Mme. Dufour (Jane Marken) elsewhere. Henri tries to kiss Henriette but she resists him at first, then surrenders to his ardor. Rain falls and time passes.

Some years later a solitary Henri rows to the locale and encounters Henriette whose boring husband Anatole naps nearby. In their short meeting each reveals how indelible and precious their brief interlude had been. While a pensive Henri looks up at the nightingale, the unhappy wife rows her husband back.

COMMENTARY

Inspired by the success of the British-made anthology films based on Maugham's short stories, *Quartet* (1948) and *Trio* (1950), Joseph Burstyn compiled three unreleased films, *A Day in the Country*, Pagnol's *Jofroi* (1934), and Rossellini's *The Miracle (Il Miracolo)* (1948), to make up *Ways of Love*, which opened in New York in 1950. Immediately the Rossellini segment aroused controversy. The film was picketed, denounced as "blasphemous" and its license was revoked in N.Y. State on the grounds that it was "sacrilegious." In spite of its stormy reception, *Ways of Love* was selected by the N.Y. Films Critics as the "Best Foreign Film" of 1950. The case went to the U.S. Supreme Court which ruled in its favor. One result of the uproar was that the Renoir film was largely ignored. Now, by itself, we can discover anew the beauties of this undeservedly neglected gem.

There are many exquisite moments in the successful and popular *A Day in the Country*. There is a memorable scene when Henriette, awakening to the beauty of nature, asks her mother if she had ever felt these strange, tender stirrings within her. The older woman agrees but adds she is now more "reasonable." "One of the most beautiful sequences in all of cinema," critic André Bazin writes, "is the moment . . . when Sylvia Bataille is about to accept the advances of Georges Darnoux. . . . We are ready to laugh, when suddenly the laugh catches in our throat. With . . . [her] incredible glance, the world begins to spin and love bursts forth like a long-stifled cry. . . . I can think of no other director, except perhaps Chaplin, who is capable of evoking such a wrenching bit of truth from a face, from an expression."

Then there is the epilogue, Renoir's brilliant addition, which is striking for its economy and poignancy. My tenderest memories are here, Henri

With all the surging desire of her adolescence, Henriette (Sylvia Bataille) submits to the passionate advances of Henri (Georges Darnoux).

tells Henriette, who, holding back her tears, answers that she thinks of this place every night. A touching scene that is delicate and powerful as it calmly suggests a love that was thwarted.

Pictorially the film is rich as Renoir captures the beautiful, impressionistic world of his father. When Henriette joyously propels her swing, Renoir evokes his father's painting "La Balançoire" ("The Swing")(1876) among others. We should acknowledge Claude Renoir's superlatively photographed rain sequence which follows the couple's lovemaking and suggests, in critic Pierre Leprohon's words, "a sense of abandonment and flight." He concludes, *A Day in the Country* may not be Renoir's greatest film, but it may be most dear to those who admire him, because it seems the one closest to his heart, and to ours."

"The Sundays are now as sad as the Mondays. . . ." An unhappy Henriette (Sylvia Bataille) helps her prosaic husband Anatole (Paul Temps) into his jacket on the site where she had earlier experienced rapturous but fleeting love.

CESAR

LA SOCIÉTÉ DES FILMS MARCEL
PAGNOL   1936

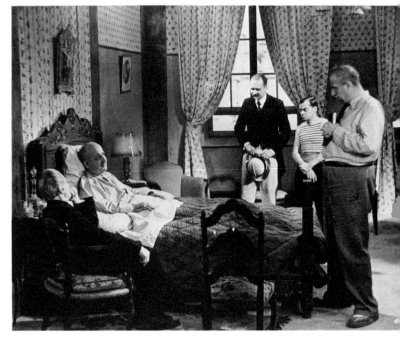

Friends gather around the bedside of the dying Panisse (Fernand Charpin): the priest Elzéar (Thommeray), M. Brun (Robert Vattier), the Chauffeur (Maupi), and César (Raimu).

CREDITS

Screenplay and Direction: Marcel Pagnol; *Photographer:* Willy; *Assistant Director:* Pierre Méré; *Editors:* Suzanne de Troeye and Jeanette Ginestet; *Music:* Vincent Scotto; *Running Time:* 160 minutes; *Paris Premiere:* November 18, 1936*; *New York Premiere:* October 27, 1948; *16 mm. Rental Source:* Images.

CAST

César Olivier: Raimu; *Marius:* Pierre Fresnay; *Fanny:* Orane Demazis; *Honoré Panisse:* Fernand Charpin; *Césariot:* André Fouché; *Honorine Cabinis:* Alida Rouffe; *Aunt Claudine:* Milly Mathis; *M. Brun:* Robert Vattier; *Félix Escartefigue:* Paul Dullac; *Chauffeur:* Maupi; *Dr. Félicien Venelle:* Edouard Delmont; *Fernand:* Doumel; *The Priest Elzéar:* Thommeray; *Pierre Dromard:* Robert Bassac.

BACKGROUND

After the successful release of the movie *Fanny* Marcel Pagnol started his own film production company, Les Auteurs Associés, in 1933. Thenceforth Pagnol would be totally free to chose his own subjects and realize his projects without anyone's interference or control.

The studio was based in Marseilles. Pagnol bought and installed his own equipment and acquired a number of theaters in the area to serve as outlets for his films. At this point in his life he

*Trade screening date; public presentation came shortly afterwards.

Fanny (Orane Demazis) reveals to her son Césariot (André Fouché) the truth about his parentage.

Césariot (André Fouché) learns about his father from César (Raimu), who is both his godfather and grandfather.

finally committed himself to a career as a filmmaker. In 1934 Pagnol directed his first film, *Le Gendre de Monsieur Poirier*, followed by *Jofroi*, which marks the beginning of his significant collaboration with the writer Jean Giono. He also produced the important neo-realistic film, *Toni*, directed by Jean Renoir. That same year (1934) the company's name was changed to La Société des Films Marcel Pagnol.

Pagnol was to serve as an inspiration and model to those filmmakers discouraged by the predominantly commercial concerns of the large organizations. After directing *Angèle* (1934) with Fernandel and several other works including his first personal version of *Topaze* (1936), Pagnol set about bringing to a happy conclusion the fates of Marius and Fanny.

César was written directly for the screen. Again, for the sake of unity and continuity the famous cast was reassembled for the film, which was made between May and August of 1936. Interiors were shot at the Studios Pagnol; exteriors were shot in Marseilles, the coast of Les Lecques, and Toulon. *César's* success was guaranteed.

SYNOPSIS

Years have passed since the action of *Fanny*. The son of Marius (Pierre Fresnay) and Fanny (Orane Demazis), called Césariot (André Fouché), is now eighteen years old and a student. The aging man

he believes is his father, Panisse (Fernand Charpin), has had a heart attack.

The film opens with César (Raimu), the longtime friend of Panisse and father of Marius, summoning the priest (Thommeray) to the bedside of the supposedly dying man. Fanny learns that Panisse will pull through for now but will not live to Christmas. The priest insists that Panisse inform his son who his real father is, but Panisse cannot bring himself to do this. Some time later Panisse dies and is sorely missed by his friends.

Fanny finally tells her son, now twenty, about his parentage. The self-righteous, rigid son is shocked. She confesses her intense love for Marius whom she has not seen in many years. Césariot reveals to César, whom he had always supposed was just his godfather, what he has discovered and learns the whereabouts of Marius as well as an account of the alleged dubious activities of the estranged son.

Under the pretense of visiting a friend, Césariot sails off to find his father, who works in a garage in Toulon. Without revealing his identity he meets and befriends Marius. However, Fernand (Doumel), the owner of the garage, is put off by the youth's bearing and plays a joke on him by trying to get him involved in some "opium smuggling" with Marius and his "gang."

Césariot falls for the lies and, embittered, returns home. Since his alibi, Dromard (Robert Bassac), had come visiting him in the meantime, Césariot is exposed and tells the truth about his vacation to his family. Césariot angrily denounces Marius as a scoundrel but Fanny, always loyal, defends him.

Fernand visits the Bar de la Marine and, realizing that Césariot is the son of Marius, confesses his lies and tells the youth that Marius is in town. Césariot meets Marius and discloses that Fanny is his mother. Reconciled with his father after their misunderstanding, the young man takes him to meet César and Fanny. In a long confrontation scene Marius defends himself of all the charges against him acquired over the years and attacks the group for making him an exile from his family and his son.

Each character tries to justify his actions, though Marius feels that Fanny's sacrifice was unnecessary. He leaves after telling Césariot that the two of them can go fishing anytime he wishes. Some time later Marius opens a marine motor business near Marseilles while Césariot has gone off to do his military duty.

Fanny visits Marius at his home. The two have an intimate conversation outdoors. Although he still

Césariot (André Fouché) returns from visiting Marius and sees his alibi exposed by Fanny (Orane Demazis) while Aunt Claudine (Milly Mathis), Honorine (Alida Rouffe), far right, and César (Raimu) look on.

loves her, his pride would keep him from marrying her and taking Panisse's money. Also there is now a difference in class at this point, an added conflict. Fanny tells him that she loves only him. César appears, steals the key to Marius's car to prevent him from leaving, and tries to play Cupid to the now middleaged lovers. He informs them that Césariot told him he approves of his mother's remarriage with Marius and walks off, content to see Marius and Fanny finally reconciled and happy.

COMMENTARY

César continues the same enchanting characterization which made the earlier two parts of the trilogy so memorable. In no way is it a letdown as it reunites the long-separated lovers.

César has lively music by Vincent Scotto and abounds with typical fine scenes:

As Panisse is attended to by the priest, César speculates amusingly on what sort of God is awaiting the dying man.

There's a beautiful moment in an ensuing card game when César stares at Panisse's empty chair—the whole sense of loss is exquisitely conveyed.

In the confrontation scene near the end, Marius reveals how he has kept an eye on his father via a friend who visited César's bar regularly. "How many people has he given hell to in five minutes?" Marius would ask his informant, and when he

The long-separated lovers Marius (Pierre Fresnay) and Fanny (Orane Demazis) are finally reunited.

heard there were two, or three, or four he knew that his father was well.

Raimu, Pagnol's favorite actor, gave another powerful and distinctive performance. With his remarkable screen presence it is easy to see how he was recognized as one of the world's greatest character actors. Pierre Fresnay and Orane Demazis captured their characters' great strengths and emotions while Charpin was poignant as the dying Panisse.

Although Pagnol tried to make *César* the most cinematic work of the trilogy by writing many exterior scenes and giving it a fluid camerawork, it is still the film's unforgettable characterization which makes acceptable its length and verbosity.

How paradoxical that *The Marseilles Trilogy,* one of the most regional of works and full of the flavor of the Midi in which characters speak a dialect, should go on to become an international triumph. The trilogy, combining romance, comedy, sentiment, and all the animation and color of Marseilles, obviously had a world-wide and long-lasting appeal. Unlike *Marius* and *Fanny,* which were plays first before films, *César* was eventually performed as a play, with Henri Vilbert as César and Orane Demazis as Fanny, which opened at the Théâtre Des Variétés in Paris on December 18, 1946.

Because M-G-M controlled the rights to the Pagnol material, *César* did not appear in America until 1948. The trilogy became an art house favorite. In 1954 David Merrick presented a musical version on Broadway called *Fanny,* adapted and condensed by S.N. Berman and Joshua Logan, which starred Ezio Pinza as César and Walter Slezak as Panisse. Harold Rome contributed outstanding music to the show which ran three years and totalled 888 performances. Warner Brothers acquired the film rights and released the popular *Fanny* in 1961. Replete with beautiful color, music, and photography, Leslie Caron and Horst Buchholz as the youthful, attractive lovers, and veterans Charles Boyer as César and Maurice Chevalier as Panisse, *Fanny* certainly had fine entertainment values but was rendered slick and sentimentalized. Joshua Logan directed in an obvious, unsubtle way with excessive close-ups and zoom shots. In no way does it approximate the impact and scope of the original.

The Marseilles Trilogy is one of the few successful trilogies in cinema history. Its combined length runs over seven hours but what a rewarding time spent with ebullient, lovable characters who possess a zest for living and dwell forever with us in pleasant memory.

A paen to parental love (César-Marius, Panisse-Césariot, Marius-Césariot)—and certainly the great Raimu is *the* archetypical father—*The Marseilles Trilogy* with its rich humanity and enduring traditional values has justifiably achieved classic stature.

PEPE-LE-MOKO

PARIS FILMS PRODUCTION   1937

CREDITS

Adaptation: Julien Duvivier and Henri Jeanson, based on the novel by Détective Ashelbé [Henri La Barthe] (1931); *Dialogue:* Henri Jeanson; *Director:* Julien Duvivier; *Photographers:* Jules Krüger, Marc Fossard; *Assistant Director:* Robert Vernay; *Editor:* Marguerite Beaugé; *Music:* Vincent Scotto, Mohammed Yguerbuchen; *Running Time:* 93 minutes; *Paris Premiere:* January 28, 1937; *New York Premiere:* March 3, 1941; *16 mm. Rental Source:* Audio Brandon.

CAST

Pépé-Le-Moko: Jean Gabin; *Gaby:* Mireille Balin; *Carlos:* Gabriel Gabrio; *Inspector Slimane:* Lucas Gridoux; *L'Arbi:* Marcel Dalio; *Grandfather:* Saturnin Fabre; *Régis:* Fernand Charpin; *Inès:* Line Noro; *Pierrot:* Gilbert Gil; *Jimmy:* Gaston Modot; *Max:* Roger Legris; *Tania:* Fréhel; *Maxime:* Charles Granval; *Aicha:* Olga Lord; *Meunier:* René Bergeron

BACKGROUND

Between *Poil de Carotte* and *Pépé-Le-Moko* Julien Duvivier directed ten films, notably *Maria Chapdelaine* (1934), *Le Golem* (1935), and *La Belle Equipe (They Were Five)* (1936) which reflected the spirit of the Front Populaire.

Pépé-Le-Moko was a novel written by Détective Ashelbé (a pseudonym) who had worked in Algiers. It was based on a real criminal who had eluded the French police for years by hiding out in the Casbah, the native quarter of Algiers. The man was a native of Languedoc in Provence which accounted for his nickname describing his complexion ("le moko"). A real Don Juan with the ladies, he boasted that when and if the police got him "three hundred widows would attend his funeral." This seemed a "natural" for the cinema and

Grandfather (Saturnin Fabre), right, examines the jewels from a recent heist by Pépé-Le-Moko's gang: Pierrot (Gilbert Gil), Pépé (Jean Gabin), Max (Roger Legris), Jimmy (Gaston Modot), and Carlos (Gabriel Gabrio).

the Hakim brothers decided to produce it with Duvivier directing.

Charles Boyer, then in Hollywood, was offered the role of the colorful rogue but he turned it down. (Ironically after Jean Gabin's personal triumph in the part, Boyer agreed to star in *Algiers,* the American remake.) The production company went to Algiers for exteriors (the location footage added a documentary authenticity to the film) and brought back a native composer, Mohammed Yguerbuchen, to score the work in Paris. The Casbah was reconstructed with such meticulous care at the Pathé Nathan Studios that contemporary reviewers reported that the film was shot in Algiers.

Jean Gabin, who had appeared earlier in Duvivier's *Maria Chapdelaine,* was now cast as the doomed Pépé-Le-Moko, a part he played to perfection. This role was to be his best screen performance thus far and propelled him into the orbit of international stardom. *Pépe-Le-Moko* became Duvivier's best-known film.

SYNOPSIS

Both the French and native police are hamstrung in catching Pépé-Le-Moko (Jean Gabin), a notorious thief who has been hiding in safety in the Casbah protected by his gang and many friends.

Tipped off by the informer Régis (Fernand Charpin), the police venture a raid on the Casbah to trap Pépé at the home of Grandfather (Saturnin Fabre), who acts as a fence for the gang. However, an intricate system of warning signals and the direct intervention of Pépé's mistress Inès (Line Noro) put him on guard. Although he is wounded slightly in the ensuing gunfight he manages to escape and meets the lovely, bejewelled Gaby (Mireille Balin), a French tourist being escorted in the Casbah by Slimane (Lucas Gridoux), the native police inspector. Slimane observes that the pair are immediately drawn to each other.

Pépé is bored with his life with Inès and longs to return to Paris. The police get Régis to lure Pierrot (Gilbert Gil), a young member of Pépé's gang, out of the Casbah to see his "sick" mother. When the youth returns, dying from police gunshot wounds, Régis is killed in retaliation.

The love between Pépé and Gaby blossoms while a jealous Inès watches. Slimane plans to capitalize on their affair. Accordingly, to lure Pépé out of the Casbah, he tells Maxime (Charles Granval), the rich, older man who is keeping Gaby, about Pépé and Gaby. Maxime forbids Gaby to visit the Casbah but she storms out to go to her lover. Slimane lies and tells her that Pépé has been killed. She makes plans to leave the port city.

An anxious Pépé waits for a response from Gaby. Informed that she is sailing that day, he decides to join her. Inès fails to prevent Pépé from leaving—his last, desperate chance at love and freedom. Jealous, she informs Slimane about Pépé's plans. While searching for Gaby on the ship, Pépé is arrested and handcuffed by Slimane and taken ashore.

Inspector Slimane (Lucas Gridoux) vows to a wounded Pépé (Jean Gabin) that he will capture him some day.

In the Casbah, Gaby (Mireille Balin) and Pépé (Jean Gabin) find themselves strongly attracted to each other.

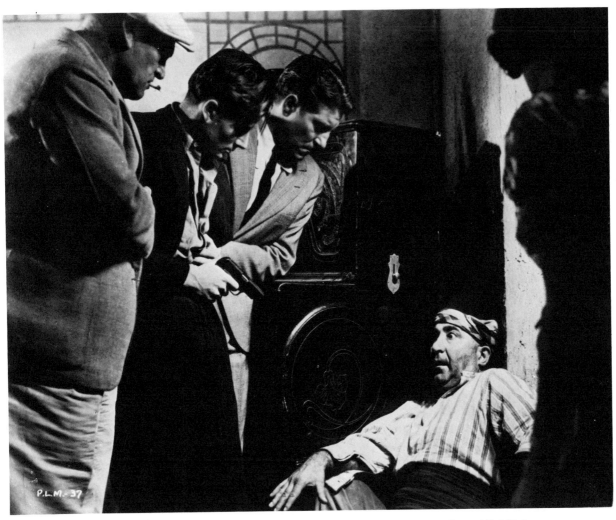

Carlos (Gabriel Gabrio) and Pépé (Jean Gabin) help their dying buddy Pierrot (Gilbert Gil) kill the terrified squealer Régis (Fernand Charpin), while Pierrot's girl friend Aicha (Olga Lord) watches.

Pépé requests a final favor from his friendly adversary—to be allowed to watch the ship leave. His wish granted, he comes up to the symbolic iron gates alone, notices Gaby onboard staring at the Casbah, and shouts her name, but the ship's whistles drown out his cry. Helplessly trapped, the unhappy Pépé stabs himself while the *Ville D'Oran* sails away.

COMMENTARY

Pépé-Le-Moko was a huge success. Duvivier was able to imbue his film with a strong sense of atmosphere. As is typical of much of the director's work, there is fluid camerawork, particularly in the scenes when Pépé is fleeing the terraced steps of the Casbah.

By downplaying Pépé's criminal career and emphasizing his loneliness and ability to be regenerated through love, the character of Pépé-Le-Moko is made most sympathetic and attractive. Jean Gabin brought to the role a powerful masculine presence and much charm. Mireille Balin was beautiful and properly alluring for Pépé to risk all for a chance to love her.

Pépé-Le-Moko was influenced by the American gangster film *Scarface* (director Howard Hawks, 1932). Yet there are elements in the film which raise it above its genre. These elements relate to the character Jean Gabin played which, combined, created a new and powerful myth for the cinema—the "myth of Jean Gabin," which continued for over a decade. The hero would be a fugitive from justice, in private revolt against a corrupt world. The loner chances upon a beautiful woman who offers an ideal, redeeming love and hope for a better life. Before the hero can escape, he is thwarted by the various agencies of fate or destiny which conspire to trap and destroy him. All his dreams would prove unattainable. *Pépé-Le-Moko* provided a framework for this myth which Jean Gabin was soon to bring to its richest development in the films of Marcel Carné.

Pépé-Le-Moko is also significant for expressing an ardent theme of escape and a brooding sense of fatalistic despondency which became more prevalent in films as the troubled decade headed toward a devastating war.

On the strength of the film's enormous success, M-G-M acquired the American remake rights. However, fearing that the story would be too offensive for the Hays Office censors to pass, M-G-M sold the rights to Walter Wanger, who called his version *Algiers* (1938) and cast Charles Boyer and Hedy Lamarr, making her American dèbut in it.

Algiers was shown in America first. Pépé-Le-Moko followed three years later. Although many scenes were copied directly from the French version, *Algiers* turned out to lack conviction and was a pallid imitation of a brilliant original.

It is interesting to compare the two treatments because one can see the greater freedom which the French filmmakers enjoyed at that time. In *Algiers*, love scenes were toned down. Maxime, the rich, old fat man who in the French film was keeping Gaby, becomes in the American version her fiancé! And since the depiction of suicide was discouraged, Charles Boyer had to be shot to death instead, under the ploy of having an aide think he was escaping. *Algiers,* directed by John Cromwell, retains interest for Boyer and the ravishing presence of Hedy Lamarr. (Another American version, *Casbah,* 1948, is distinguished solely for its Harold Arlen songs.)

After spending the war years in America, Julien Duvivier tried in France without success to regain the place of international eminence he held in the 1930's. Possibly the diversity of genres he worked in—comedy, thrillers, historical dramas, musicals, biblical epics, adaptations of classics, etc.,—and his prolific output (one should mention his lyrical *Marianne of My Youth (Marianne de Ma Jeunesse,* 1954))—made him appear more of a craftsman than an artist and his fame suffered accordingly.

If Duvivier outlived his once brilliant reputation, nonetheless we should not neglect his splendid achievement in his most fruitful period, the 1930's, and cherish such works of poetic realism as *Poil de Carotte, Pépé-Le-Moko, Le Fin du Jour* (1939), among others.

Julien Duvivier died in Paris on October 29, 1967. Jean Renoir paid homage to him by stating: "This great technician, this precisionist, was a poet."

Pépé-Le-Moko (Jean Gabin), caught at last, asks Inspector Slimane (Lucas Gridoux) to be allowed to watch the ship with Gaby onboard depart.

GRAND ILLUSION

(La Grande Illusion)

R.A.C. (RÉALISATION D'ART CINÉMATOGRAPHIQUE)   1937

CREDITS

Screenplay: Charles Spaak and Jean Renoir; *Director:* Jean Renoir; *Photographer:* Christian Matras; *Assistant Director:* Jacques Becker; *Editor:* Marguerite Renoir; *Music:* Joseph Kosma; *Song:* "Si Tu Veux Marguerite" ("If You Wish Marguerite") by Vincent Telly and Albert Valsien; *Running Time:* 117 minutes: *Paris Premiere:* June 4, 1937; *New York Premiere:* September 12, 1938; *16 mm. Rental Source:* Janus.

CAST

Commandant von Rauffenstein: Erich von Stroheim; *Lt. Maréchal:* Jean Gabin; *Capt. de Boëldieu:* Pierre Fresnay; *Rosenthal:* Marcel Dalio; *Elsa:* Dita Parlo; *The Actor:* Julien Carette; *The Engineer:* Gaston Modot; *The Teacher:* Jean Dasté; *Demolder:* Sylvain Itkine; *Cartier:* Georges Péclet; *The English Officer:* Jacques Becker; *Arthur Krantz:* Werner Florian.

BACKGROUND

As WWII seemed unavoidable, Jean Renoir felt compelled to make a final, rational appeal to the German people to ignore their jingoistic leaders. The origins of the resulting *Grand Illusion* lay in Renoir's friendship with a colorful, daring aviator named Pinsard. In 1915 Renoir was a pilot with the French squadron carrying photographers on re-

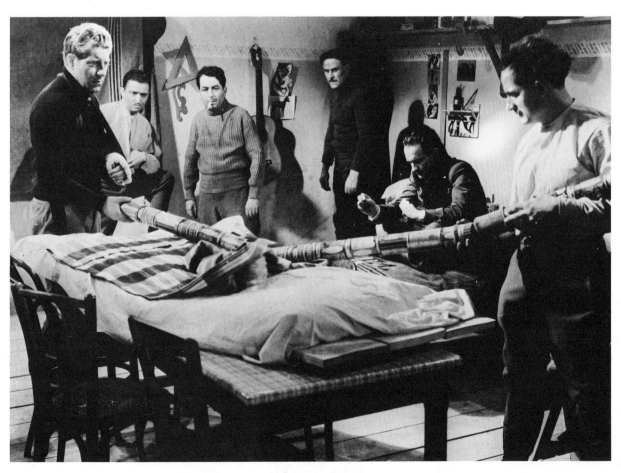

At the P.O.W. camp at Hallbach, Maréchal (Jean Gabin), Rosenthal (Marcel Dalio), the actor (Julien Carette), the engineer (Gaston Modot), Boëldieu (Pierre Fresnay), and the teacher (Jean Dasté) prepare for their nightly work making a tunnel to escape.

connaisance flights. On several occasions German planes endangered their lives, but Pinsard appeared and chased the assailants away. Years later, while filming *Toni*, Renoir met Pinsard, now a general, who related to him an account of how he was shot down seven times by the Germans, taken prisoner, but managed to escape his captors on each occasion. Thinking this would make an exciting adventure story, Renoir with the assistance of Charles Spaak prepared a sketch for a film with the tentative title, *Les Evasions du Capitaine Maréchal.*

The project transcended a story of escape to eventually become, in Renoir's words, "a statement of man's brotherhood beyond political borders." Then for three years Renoir tried to interest producers in his unusual project. When Jean Gabin agreed to appear in it several producers finally decided to take the risk. Louis Jouvet was offered the role of Boëldieu but he did not wish to leave

Paris for location shooting. Pierre-Richard Willm also turned it down and the part went to Pierre Fresnay.

The role of the German commandant was initially small. When the production manager recommended Erich von Stroheim, who had come to France in the hope of salvaging his acting career, Renoir was eager to hire the man whose work had been a life-long inspiration to him. The part was enlarged and Stroheim suggested the iron corset and chinstrap to heighten the severity of the character and his sense of defeat. He contributed dialogue as well as advice on military matters. The role became for Stroheim the most notable performance of his career.

Shooting took place in the 1936/37 winter. Interiors were the Billancourt and Eclair studios; exteriors were shot in Alsace: the Colmar barracks, the environs of Neuf-Brisach, and, for the fortress

With great dignity Maréchal (Jean Gabin) and Boëldieu (Pierre Fresnay) shake hands in parting before the escape plan from Wintersborn is set in motion.

Wintersborn, the chateau of Haut-Koenigsbourg.

Ignoring simplistic categorizing—noble French, villanious Germans ("I found it impossible to take sides with any of the characters," Renoir said)—avoiding even actual scenes of conflict (the cost of aerial combat was prohibitive), Renoir opted for a film in which rich characterization and a significant theme dominate. With *Grand Illusion* Renoir achieved his greatest international success and created his most popular film.

SYNOPSIS

On a reconnaissance flight during WWI Lt. Maréchal (Jean Gabin) and Capt. de Boëldieu (Pierre Fresnay) are shot down by the German Commander von Rauffenstein (Erich von Stroheim), who then invites them to lunch. Sent to the P.O.W. camp at Hallbach, they share their barracks with, among others, a wealthy and generous Jew, Rosenthal (Marcel Dalio). At night the two newcomers join in the difficult digging of a tunnel under the barracks' floor.

The French prisoners join several interned British soldiers in presenting a musicale to which they invite the German officers. During the show Lt. Maréchal interrupts and announces that the

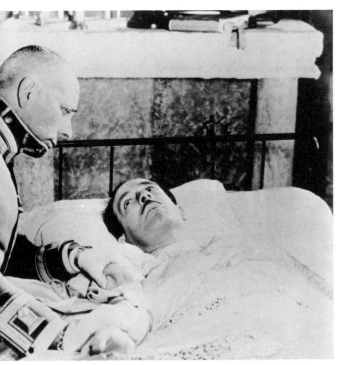

A solicitous Rauffenstein (Erich von Stroheim) comforts the dying Boëldieu (Pierre Fresnay).

French forces have just then retaken Douaumont. The British soldiers remove their wigs and join in the singing of "La Marseillaise." For his pains, Maréchal is sent to solitary confinement. When at last he's released the tunnel is nearly completed. However, on the day when escape is planned the officers learn that they are changing camps. Not knowing English, Maréchal is unable to tell an incoming English officer about the tunnel.

Wearing a brace for his fractured spine, a severely handicapped Commandant von Rauffenstein welcomes once more Boëldieu and Maréchal, this time to the impregnable fortress Wintersborn which holds prisoners who have attempted escape elsewhere (including Rosenthal). He defers to Boëldieu as a fellow career officer who shares a similar code of values and fears that the war's end will be the knell of his class.

When Russian soldiers create a ruckus over the Czarina's gift of books, not food, Boëldieu conceives a plan to create a distraction so as to afford Maréchal and Rosenthal a chance to escape. Although he will sacrifice himself for these men, he cannot break down his formal reserve before an embarrassed Maréchal.

A noisy outburst forces the commander to hold a roll-call. When Boëldieu's absence is noted, flute music is heard from the ramparts. In the ensuing confusion Maréchal and Rosenthal lower a rope and flee without detection. Rauffenstein pleads in English with the heroic flute player (Boëldieu) to surrender, then fires a shot aimed at his leg but which proves fatal. On his deathbed in Rauffenstein's room, Boëldieu declares that this was "a good solution" to the problem of maintaining a useless existence.

Maréchal and Rosenthal suffer from hunger and exhaustion in their two-hundred-mile trek to freedom. In addition, Rosenthal's ankle is painfully swollen. They are discovered by a German widow, Elsa (Dita Parlo), who cares for Rosenthal's injury. Elsa and Maréchal fall in love. Vowing to return and marry her when the war ends, Maréchal leaves with his friend. Together they make a successful flight across the snow-capped Swiss frontier.

COMMENTARY

Renoir's humanitarian and fraternal appeal to the Germans went unheeded. Dr. Goebbels (who referred to it as "cinematographic enemy No. 1") had *Grand Illusion* banned in the Reich and pressured Mussolini to undercut its chances at the 1937 Ven-

The German widow Elsa (Dita Parlo) with her child Lotte sadly watches Maréchal and Rosenthal leave her farm.

"Oscar" nomination in the "Best Picture" category for that year, the first time a French film was so honored.

During the Occupation all available prints were confiscated. Later the negative was destroyed during air raids on Paris. After the war, a second negative was discovered by the Americans in Munich. Miraculously, the Nazis had preserved it. Renoir supervised the restoration of the film, bought the commercial rights to it, and successfully reissued it in 1958. Jean Gabin as Maréchal, this time outside the myth as doomed hero, gives a great performance. Pierre Fresnay is perfect as the aristocrat Boëldieu, and Erich von Stroheim brings memorable nuance to a powerful role as Commandant von Rauffenstein.

Grand Illusion is a beautifully written and structured film. The parallel opening, showing first a

ice International Exposition. As a sop to their conscience, the critics there created a prize for it, "Best Artistic Ensemble." Nevertheless, the film was banned in Italy. When the Nazis entered Vienna, police officers halted the screening of the film at a theatre. (Renoir wrote, "I do not consider this a military decoration, but a moral one.")

Grand Illusion received the New York Film Critics Award in 1938 for "Best Foreign Film" and won an

French mess and then a German mess, suggests visually that both sides are similarly human, that nationality is a false divider of men. In addition, its splendid characterization, its brilliant technique (Renoir employs striking long takes in deep focus with fluid camerawork), its realism (there's the innovation of each character speaking his own language), its thematic richness help make *Grand Illusion* an unforgettable and rewarding experience.

More than a lament for the decline of the aristocracy, the film delves into the difficult, complex problems of human brotherhood. "The world is more divided by social conceptions than by the color of flags," Renoir wrote, and in *Grand Illusion* we find there's a stronger rapport between the two enemy officers, Boëldieu and Rauffenstein, than between the two Frenchmen of different classes, the aristocrat Boëldieu and the mechanic Maréchal.

At the time of *Grand Illusion*'s release, when asked what the title referred to, Renoir said: "The war! With its hopes never realized, its promises never kept." Later the director commented: "When I wrote it, I had in mind a phrase we used to repeat during the war, in the trenches. It was '*la der des ders*,' 'the last of the last'." Although this clear reference to the "war to end all wars" is one satisfactory explanation, Renoir conceded that the title could be open to other interpretations.

Among the many memorable scenes in *Grand Illusion* are Maréchal's agony in solitary confinement, the dignified passing of Boëldieu with Rauffenstein clipping his lone geranium afterwards symbolizing his personal despair, and the poignant departure of Maréchal from Elsa in which each speaks words of love in a language foreign to the other.

"The day will come," Renoir wrote in 1938, "when men of good faith will find a common meeting ground. Cynics will say that my words at this point in time are naive. But why not?" Let us hope that this will not be the ultimate illusion concerning the monumental classic, *Grand Illusion*.

Near the Swiss border Maréchal (Jean Gabin) and Rosenthal (Marcel Dalio) prepare to make a run for freedom.

79

Jean (Jean Gabin) and Nelly (Michèle Morgan) have just met at Panama's and together watch the sun rise.

PORT OF SHADOWS

(Le Quai des Brumes)

CINÉ-ALLIANCE   1938

CREDITS

Screenplay: Jacques Prévert, based on the novel by Pierre Mac Orlan [Pierre Dumarchais] (1927); *Director:* Marcel Carné; *Photographer:* Eugène Schuftan; *Assistant Directors:* Claude Walter and Guy Lefranc; *Editor:* René Le Hénaff; *Music:* Maurice Jaubert; *Running Time:* 91 minutes; *Paris Premiere:* May 18, 1938; *New York Premiere:* October 27, 1939; *16 mm. Rental Source:* Budget.

CAST

Jean: Jean Gabin; *Nelly:* Michéle Morgan: *Zabel:* Michel Simon; *Lucien Laugardier:* Pierre Brasseur; *Michel Krauss:* Robert Le Vigan; *Lucien's Friend:* Jenny Burnay; *Chauffeur:* Marcel Pérès; *Doctor:* René Génin; *Panama:* Edouard Delmont; *Quart-Vittel:* Raymond Aimos.

BACKGROUND

Marcel Carné was born in Paris on August 18, 1909. He rejected apprenticeship in cabinet making, his father's trade, and became an assistant director to Jacques Feyder (1928-35) and René Clair and produced his first film, the short *Nogent, Eldorado du Dimanche,* in 1929. Both Feyder and Clair, with their studio-built sets presenting, as Carné wrote, "an interpretation of life more real than life itself," impressed the emerging filmmaker. Carné has also acknowledged as influences Joseph von Sternberg, F. W. Murnau, Lupu Pick, and Fritz Lang.

Carné was a film critic and journalist as well. In a significant essay entitled "When Will the Cinema Descend into the Street?" (1933), he attacked the tendency in current cinema "to flee from life in order to find its pleasure in scenery and artifice" and called for filmmakers "to depict the simple life of the little people, render the atmosphere of working class humanity which is theirs."

Jenny (1936), Carné's first feature (with Jacques Prévert as one of the screenwriters), anticipates his later work with its theme of unrequited love and its doomed hero (Albert Préjean) unable to escape fate.

After the failure of the outrageous comedy, *Bizarre, Bizarre (Drôle de Drame)* (1937), Carné was approached by Raoul Ploquin, then director of French production at U.F.A. in Berlin, to make a film there from the Pierre Mac Orlan novel, *Le Quai des Brumes,* starring Jean Gabin. At first Carné conceived of it as a sketch film. Goebbels, however, thought the story of an army deserter decadent and sold the rights to a French producer.

The film was eventually made in France after the Minister of War demanded that the word "deserter" never be uttered and that when Gabin rids himself of his uniform he would fold the clothing carefully on a chair and not throw it pell-mell in a corner. Carné requested Michèle Morgan, the promising actress Marc Allégret launched in *Gribouille* (1937), and Michel Simon and Pierre Brasseur for supporting roles.

Jacques Prévert updated the novel, whose action

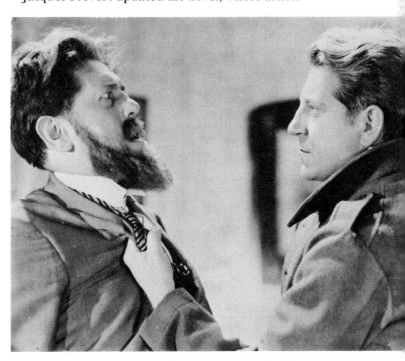

Jean (Jean Gabin) tells Zabel (Michel Simon) that he reminds him of a disgusting beast after Zabel offered a passport and money in exchange for Lucien's murder.

begins in 1909, and changed the locale from Montmartre to Le Havre. He merged two characters into Gabin's part and drastically transformed the character of Nelly who in the novel has her pimp killed and winds up a rich prostitute when the story ends in 1919! Prévert infused the melodramatic action with his brooding, philosophical concerns. In spite of all the alterations, Mac Orlan commended Carné for "recovering entirely the spirit of the book."

Carné had to fight constantly with his producer who wanted a lighter, happier film. Shooting lasted from January through February 1938. Interiors were shot at the Pathé-Nathan Studios; exteriors in Le Havre.

Appearing at a time when the screen was filled with sunny comedies and musicals, *Port of Shadows* was revolutionary for its murky photography and pessimistic tone. A success in France, it went on to achieve an international reputation and was frequently copied.

SYNOPSIS

Jean (Jean Gabin), a deserter from the French colonial army, arrives in fog-bound Le Havre seek-

"The ideal couple of French cinema": Jean (Jean Gabin) and Nelly (Michèle Morgan) share an intimate moment at the fair.

After confessing to Nelly (Michèle Morgan) that he killed Maurice out of jealousy, Zabel (Michel Simon) reveals his passion for her.

ing passage to some distant country. He is led by the derelict Quart-Vittel (Raymond Aimos) to a dive run by Panama (Edouard Delmont) where he befriends the young and beautiful Nelly (Michèle Morgan), who is waiting in vain for her boyfriend Maurice to show up.

Lucien (Pierre Brasseur), from Le Havre's underworld, appears looking for Maurice. After he's refused admittance, gunshots are heard from outside, then the sinister Zabel (Michel Simon), Nelly's guardian, enters the bar with blood on his hands. He departs without spotting his ward.

Nelly and Jean are attracted to each other and wander along the docks at daybreak. Michel Krauss (Robert Le Vigan), a despairing painter, leaves behind his passport, valise, and clothing for Jean to use in his escape, then walks out to drown himself.

Lucien visits Zabel in his boutique, actually a front for illicit goods. They're involved in some shady deal. Zabel knows that Lucien fired at him the night before and warns him that the police will receive incriminating evidence should he be harmed. Later Jean enters the shop intent on buying a gift for Nelly before he leaves Le Havre. Zabel recognizes the soldier from Lucien's description and invites him in. When Nelly comes upon Maurice's cuff links in the cellar she faints. A crafty Zabel tries to interest Jean in killing Lucien in return for a passport and money. Jean is disgusted with Zabel's despicable character and leaves.

At Panama's, Jean finds the clothes and his new identity, then makes arrangements to sail to Venezuela the following day. He meets Nelly at the fair that night and slaps a bothersome Lucien, humiliating him in front of his girl friend (Jenny Burnay). The new lovers spend a romantic night together at a hotel. Then a horrified Nelly learns from the morning paper that Maurice's body has been found in the bay. She fears being separated from Jean but he promises to send for her from South America.

Later that day Jean quits his cabin to see Nelly again. He returns to the boutique to find her grappling with her guardian. Zabel had confessed to killing Maurice in a fit of jealousy over his ward, whom he lusts after. Jean fights Zabel and bashes his face in with a brick. As Jean is attempting to return to the ship, Lucien guns him down from his car and the fated man dies in Nelly's embrace. The ship departs. . . .

COMMENTARY

"This will be one of the great French films of the year . . ." predicted critic Roger Régent when *Port of Shadows* opened. "Behold the work of a great director." The film shared the Prix Méliès with Renoir's *La Bête Humaine* (1938). It shared a Special Mention Medal for direction at the Venice International Exposition (1938) and was awarded the Prix Louis Delluc (1939). The young Carné was now regarded as an important director.

Because the film conveyed so accurately the general mood of doom and despair in pre-war France, a Vichy spokesman exaggerated later: "If we have lost the war, it is through the fault of *Port of Shadows*." Carné responded by stating that one cannot accuse the barometer for the storm it predicts; the mission of the filmmaker is to be a barometer of his time. The film was banned during the Occupation.

Port of Shadows indeed captures the dominant mood of defeat, the sense of pessimism and corruption in the bleak period prior to World War II. The all-encompassing fog of the port becomes metaphysical. Even the anguished visionary artist Krauss paints "in spite of himself" what lies behind the surface of things: "A swimmer for me is already a drowned man." Both he and Quart-Vittel serve as agents of destiny for Prévert.

Port of Shadows is the first classic of poetic realism. "Carné's realism tends toward the poetic transposition of a setting, while remaining meticulously true to life," writes critic André Bazin. Alexandre Trauner's remarkable sets for Carné were thoroughly documented, authentic in appearance, and carefully stylized to emphasize a certain atmosphere ("releasing its inherent poetry"—Bazin). Carné exerted a powerful international influence with his celebrated poetic realism.

So successful were Jean Gabin and Michèle Morgan together that they were quickly dubbed "the ideal couple of French cinema" and went on to make four more pictures together. Miss Morgan with her beautiful eyes and exquisite femininity was now firmly established as a star. The film solidified the "myth of Jean Gabin" previously established in *Pépé Le Moko* (1936). Again, there is the outcast at odds with society, wishing for peace and freedom, longing to escape with the woman he loves to some illusory "elsewhere" but trapped by various agents of an implacable and merciless fate. Jean Gabin incarnates the "myth" to perfection. Michel Simon contributes another brilliant characterization in his long and distinguished career.

In its classical structure and use of the unities of time, place, and action, *Port of Shadows* limns a dark world where evil triumphs via the operation of some malevolent destiny. Much in the plot is left unspecified (as in the relationship between Zabel and Lucien), with the result that the melodramatic aspects give way to a philosophical emphasis of a general, all-encompassing evil menacing the world. In its brooding atmosphere it anticipates the postwar movement of existentialism. Maurice Jaubert's score heightens the mood memorably.

Although imitated frequently, *Port of Shadows* remains a powerful and significant film.

As he is finally heading to the ship and freedom, Jean (Jean Gabin) is gunned down by Lucien (Pierre Brasseur) from his car. Alexandre Trauner's striking set effectively evokes Le Havre.

THE BAKER'S WIFE

(La Femme du Boulanger)

LA SOCIÉTÉ DES FILMS MARCEL
PAGNOL   1938

CREDITS

Screenplay: Marcel Pagnol, based on an episode
from Jean Giono's novel *Jean Le Bleu* (1932), published in New York as *Blue Boy* (1946); *Director:*
Marcel Pagnol; *Photographer:* Georges Benoit; *Editor:* Suzanne de Troeye; *Music:* Vincent Scotto;
Running Time: 130 minutes; *Paris Premiere:* September 7, 1938; *New York Premiere:* February 26, 1940;
16 mm. Rental Source: Images.

CAST

Aimable Castanier: Raimu; *Aurélie:* Ginette Leclerc;
Le Marquis Castan de Venelles: Fernand Charpin;
Dominique the Shepherd: Charles Moulin; *The Priest:*
Robert Vattier; *The Schoolteacher:* Robert Bassac;
Céleste: Alida Rouffe; *Maillefer:* Edouard Delmont;
Antonin: Clarles Blavette; *Casimir:* Paul Dullac;
Pétugue: Julien Maffre; *Barnabé:* Maupi.

BACKGROUND

Marcel Pagnol had a long and successful collaboration which lasted for a decade with the French
novelist Jean Giono (1895-1970) who celebrated
the pastoral life of his native Provence. His first
Giono-based film was *Jofroi* (1934) which came
from a short story "Jofroi de la Maussan" published
in *La Solitude de la Pitié* (1932). *Angéle* (1934) was
baed on Giono's novel *Un de Baumugnes* (1929)
(*Lovers Are Never Losers,* 1931). Then, after *César,*
Pagnol made *Regain (Harvest)* (1937) with Orane
Demazis and Fernandel which was derived from

the 1930 Giono novel. The best known Pagnol film
derived from Giono is, however, *The Baker's Wife.* It
originated as a short chapter entitled "Le
Boulanger, le Berger, Aurélie" in his novel, *Jean le
Bleu,* published in 1932.

Unfortunately, a complicated series of misun-
derstandings between Pagnol and Giono led to a
rift, followed by a lawsuit, and the termination of
their long and fruitful collaboration, one of the
greatest in cinema history.

Pagnol did a marvellous job in *The Baker's Wife* of
enriching the characterization and expanding the
short and simple story into a full-length movie.
With the availability of Raimu for the role of the
middle-aged baker, Pagnol had a great opportunity to develop a rich and multifaceted part for
him. Raimu himself contributed ideas to the film,
notably the wonderful bit about scolding Pomponnette the cat.

Fernand Charpin, Robert Vattier, Alida Rouffe
and other Pagnol "regulars" were recruited to lend
their talents to help make the small village of the
story authentic, colorful, and alive. The film was

made in the spring of 1938. Interiors were shot at the Studios Pagnol in Marseilles; exteriors in the village of Castelet, west of Toulon. *The Baker's Wife* proved to be a highly successful and memorable film.

SYNOPSIS

In a little, unnamed village in Provence, townspeople gather around the bakery where the new baker, Aimable Castanier (Raimu), is readying his first batch of bread. The Marquis (Fernand Charpin) arrives and introduces his shepherd, Dominique (Charles Moulin), who will be picking up his bread for him.

The shepherd is attracted to Aurélie (Ginette Leclerc), the baker's young and attractive wife, and returns that evening to serenade her. Aimable, thinking this is the young man's way to thank him for making good bread, sends his wife downstairs to give him a little present.

Aurélie, much younger than her husband and unhappy in her passionless marriage, is drawn to the muscular shepherd and agrees to run away with him in the early morning. She meets Dominique on horseback near the church and they ride off together. Consequently Aimable oversleeps and the Sunday bread is burnt. When he doesn't find Aurélie at home he convinces himself she's gone to visit her mother in a neighboring town.

In spite of an eyewitness report Aimable refuses to believe his wife has abandoned him. The Marquis, upset at the theft of his horse, visits the baker with another witness but the stubborn man will not believe the mounting evidence of his wife's infidelity. He looks for Aurélie at mass and hears the priggish priest (Robert Vattier) deliver an indelicate sermon with obvious references to his marital problem. Then he heads to a café and consumes a bottle of Pernod. When the villagers ask him about their bread, Aimable says he will resume baking only when his wife returns. Neighbors bring him back to the bakery, where he falls asleep.

The loss of bread is serious and the Marquis assembles the villagers to confront the crisis. They agree to form a searching party to find Aurélie.

Waiting for the new baker's first bread: The shepherd Dominique (Charles Moulin), Aimable the baker (Raimu), Antonin (Charles Blavette), partially hidden, the Marquis (Fernand Charpin).

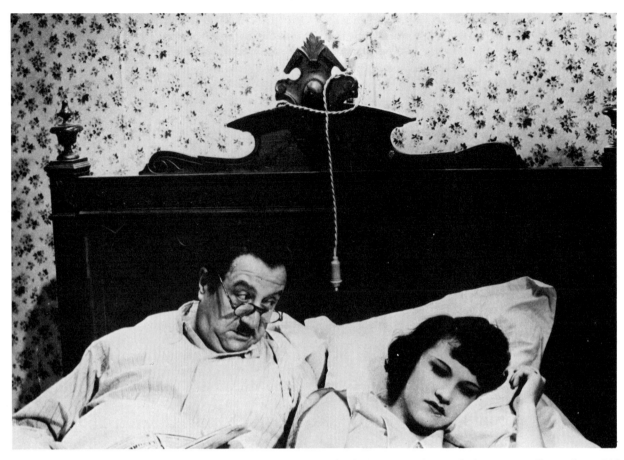

A tired Aimable (Raimu) reads his paper later that evening next to his bored wife Aurélie (Ginette Leclerc).

Aimable (Raimu) learns from the Marquis (Fernand Charpin) that Aurélie has run off with his shepherd.

The baker promises to bake extraordinary bread if they are successful.

The Marquis organizes the group like a military campaign. Some of the party get drunk and for a jest present Aimable with a pair of stag's antlers and "honor" the cuckold with a song. Thoroughly dispirited, the baker tries to hang himself in the cellar but his companions save him in time.

After Aurélie has been spotted living on an island with Dominique, a small expedition sets out to bring her back. Although they are constantly bickering over religion, the priest rides piggyback on the freethinking schoolteacher (Robert Bassac) through the marshes to get to the retreat. At the sight of the priest, the guilt-ridden shepherd deserts Aurélie and swims away. She is shocked at his cowardly behavior and leaves with the men. Ashamed, she waits until it is dark before she returns to her husband. At home the repentant Aurélie is forgiven by Aimable and the happily reconciled couple resume their life.

COMMENTARY

Besides being a success in France, *The Baker's Wife* was an enormous hit in America, setting the record at that time for the run of a French film by playing seventy-five weeks in New York alone before entering into wide national distribution and outgrossing such popular French films as *Mayerling* and *Grand Illusion*. It received the New York Film Critics Award for "Best Foreign Film" (1940) and became the best known work of both Pagnol and Raimu in America, prompting Albert Einstein to exclaim: "It is the finest, the most human film which I have ever seen."

Using a simple setting and a basic situation, Pagnol was able to create real, recognizable characters with all their strengths, weaknesses, and even—with their capacity to forgive—nobility, and to invest the narrative with pathos, comedy, and rare wisdom.

Raimu triumphs in the role of the betrayed husband who wins his wife back because of his moral superiority to his rival. In the memorable scene when his wife returns and wishes to be punished, the baker reveals the great character of his gentle and forgiving nature and only expresses his anger obliquely at the cat Pomponnette who had abandoned her mate for a spree and finally came back. Will you leave in the future? he addresses the cat in a low voice. If so, it would be less cruel to go immediately than wait a while and ... Aurélie says that the cat will never leave again. Together they quietly start the fire for the new bread.

It is a beautifully moving and controlled scene and Raimu is nothing less than magnificent in what is considered to be his best film. Ginette Leclerc is sensual and noteworthy in her finest role.

What could have been a bawdy farce about a cuckold turns out instead to be a serious comedy with tragic dimensions. Raimu invests such dignity and tenderness in the role of Aimable that we are moved to awe when he shows mercy to his wife in spite of his terrible agony.

Although its critics have claimed that *The Baker's Wife* is more theatre than cinema with its heavy reliance on dialogue, Pagnol nonetheless scored again with vigorous, human characterization and succeeded in creating a village life with such authenticity that we can almost smell that good, honest bread baked for us by a lovable and unforgettable character.

After *The Baker's Wife* Pagnol directed *The Well-Digger's Daughter (La Fille du Puisatier)* (1941), with Raimu and Fernandel, and several other films.

Critic Pierre Leprohon said of Pagnol: "He makes talky films that are often full of other faults, but they all have the authentic flavor, the look and

smell, of the soil of southern France."

Pagnol was officially received into the Académie Française on March 27, 1947, the first representative of the cinema arts to become an "immortal." In 1954 he completed his last film, *Letters From My Windmill (Les Lettres de Mon Moulin)* and retired from movies in order to write plays, novels, and a series of memoirs.

On April 18, 1974, Marcel Pagnol died in Paris. A musical version of *The Baker's Wife* produced by David Merrick starring Chaim Topol and Patti Lu Pone closed on the road in 1976 before its scheduled New York opening.

The Baker's Wife is vintage Pagnol and has endured as a film classic.

Casimir (Paul Dullac), the Marquis (Fernand Charpin), the priest (Robert Vattier), Antonin (Charles Blavette), and Maillefer (Edouard Delmont) attempt to console Aimable (Raimu), center, who has tried to drown his sorrow in Pernod.

The moving reconciliation scene: Aurélie (Ginette Leclerc) holds the heart-shaped bread baked by her adoring and forgiving husband (Raimu).

pher: Curt Courant; *Assistant Directors:* Pierre Blondy, Jean Fazy; *Editor:* René Le Hénaff; *Music:* Maurice Jaubert; *Running Time:* 93 minutes; *Paris Premiere:* June 17, 1939; *New York Premiere:* July 29, 1940; *16 mm. Rental Source:* Budget.

CAST

François: Jean Gabin; *M. Valentin:* Jules Berry; *Françoise:* Jacqueline Laurent; *Clara:* Arletty; *Concierge:* René Génin; *Concierge's Wife:* Mady Berry; *Gaston:* Bernard Blier; *Paulo:* Marcel Pérès; *The Inspector:* Jacques Baumer; *Café Proprietor:* René Bergeron; *Old Woman on the Stairs:* Gabrielle Fontan; *M. Gerbois:* Arthur Devère; *Blind Man:* Georges Douking; *Singer:* Germaine Lix.

BACKGROUND

After *Port of Shadows,* Marcel Carné directed *Hotel du Nord* (1938) which had in its distinguished cast Annabella, Arletty, Louis Jouvet, and Jean-Pierre

LE JOUR SE LEVE

PRODUCTIONS SIGMA   1939

CREDITS

Story: Jacques Viot; *Adaptation and Dialogue:* Jacques Prévert; *Director:* Marcel Carné; *Photogra-

On a delivery, Françoise (Jacqueline Laurent) wanders into François' factory by mistake.

Aumont. A story by Jacques Viot was next suggested as a vehicle for Jean Gabin, and Jacques Prévert set to work adapting it and bringing to *Le Jour se Lève* his extraordinary gifts for screenwriting. Director and critic Roger Leenhardt said of Prévert: "The brilliance of his film dialogue is composed of a thousand pearls of the human language: its words are commonplaces."

What would be melodrama in the hands of a less gifted artist became for Prévert another variant of his tragic vision of an ordinary mortal struggling against a cruel destiny bent on destroying him, finding the solace of a genuine love after much loneliness, then being deceived and deprived of all his dreams with such finality that he is driven to murder and then suicide. Jean Gabin would brilliantly personify this man, "a hero of the sprawling metropolis," critic André Bazin wrote, "a suburban, working-class Thebes where the gods take the form of the blind but equally transcendent imperatives of society."

We discover in the film such typical Prévert touches as the symbol of Fate (this time in the person of the blind man) and the longing to escape to a better world (François reads off ship movements from a newspaper in his barricaded room).

The metaphysical implication of an all-powerful evil dominating the world has special relevance to a doomed France fearfully awaiting the dreaded war in 1939. *Le Jour se Lève* perfectly conveyed the sense of hopelessness and paralysis in that fatal period.

War was thought unavoidable, Carné later said, desperation was general, and he acknowledged that this was his blackest film. The mood of despondency is much more intense here than it was in *Port of Shadows*.

In depicting the story of a trapped killer who takes his life, the film resembles Joseph von Sternberg's classic *Underworld* (1927). Carné wrote: "I wanted a set completely enclosed in order to give the impression of a man shut in, in some way walled in this room where he was passing his last night as the image of a man condemned to death in his cell." To achieve certain stark photographic effects Carné engaged the services of the German cinematographer Curt Courant who worked on Renoir's *La Bête Humaine* (1938). The film was shot at the Paris Studios Cinema at Billancourt from March to June 1939. *Le Jour se Lève* (known in America for a time as *Daybreak)* is Carné's prewar film.

SYNOPSIS

In the late afternoon in a working-class suburb of an unspecified industrial city in Normandy* shots are heard coming from an apartment. A dying Valentin (Jules Berry) stumbles down the stairs. The police arrive but François (Jean Gabin), the murderer, won't admit them and they exchange

*Some critics, however, refer to the locale as a suburb of Amiens.

(Opposite Page)Alexandre Trauner's distinguished recreation of a suburban square for *Le Jour se Lève*. "We see how the set plays as great a part as the acting in justifying situations, explaining characters, and giving credibility to the action," André Bazin wrote of this set designer's brilliant achievement of poetic realism.

At La Fauvette an embittered Clara (Arletty) strikes up a conversation with François (Jean Gabin) and discusses the corrupted Valentin whom she has just walked out on.

In his room, François (Jean Gabin) threatens Valentin (Jules Berry) after hearing nasty innuendos about Françoise.

90

gunfire. Alone in his room, François recalls the recent past.

First flashback sequence: The lovely Françoise (Jacqueline Laurent) wanders into the factory where François works as a sandblaster. Each discovers the other is an orphan and François is drawn to her.

One evening he visits her and reveals that he wants to marry her. Françoise tells him she has to see someone even though it is late at night. François is curious and follows her to La Fauvette, a café music-hall where Valentin performs a dog speciality number. His assistant Clara (Arletty) walks out during his act and befriends François who is watching from the rear bar. Soon Valentin leaves with Françoise but returns alone to pester Clara. François orders him to leave her alone.

The present: Crowds of onlookers swarm in the streets. The police attempt to storm the room but François blocks their gunfire by moving a large wardrobe in front of the door.

Second flashback sequence: François and Clara have become lovers even though he is still courting Françoise. He encounters Valentin and in a bar the odious man tries to sever François' attachment to Françoise by claiming that he's her concerned father. François is disgusted with him and orders him out of the place. Françoise denies that Valentin is her father. François finds her relationship with the aging man puzzling and disturbing. She gives him a brooch and tells him she loves him. Later François tries to break with Clara, who pretends not to be hurt by this man whom she really loves. She strikes back by showing him a brooch the lecherous Valentin gave her, a souvenir she says which the man presents to all his mistresses. A dejected François sees that it is identical with Françoise's.

The present: It's early morning and the sympathetic spectators unsuccessfully urge a despairing François to give himself up. Françoise is brought to the scene to aid François but she is hurt in the crowd and Clara brings her to her hotel to care for her. The riot squad arrives.

Third flashback sequence: The previous afternoon, upset that Françoise will no longer see him, Valentin storms into François' room. An angry François nearly throws him out of the window. When calm is restored, momentarily, Valentin announces that he had come there to kill him but couldn't bring it off. The masochist puts his pistol deliberately on a table near François and starts talking about Françoise provocatively. When François at last hears the dreaded truth that this perverted man and his beloved were lovers, the goaded man seizes the gun and instinctively fires at Valentin.

The present: Later that morning the riot police climb to the roof in order to employ tear gas. Meanwhile a thoroughly beaten and disconsolate François aims the pistol at his heart and fires. The tear gas grenade explodes in the room as the alarm clock dutifully goes off.

COMMENTARY

In *Le Jour se Lève,* released less than three months before Hitler invaded Poland, Carné and his group once more proved that they were "barometers" in capturing the dominant atmosphere. Although it was banned as "demoralizing" by the French military censor in September 1939, the film went on to be widely distributed and gained an international reputation.

The three flashback sequences signalled by long dissolves are most effectively employed with the result that the events of the past and the present are kept in equal tension. The audience at first found these flashbacks confusing and Carné had to add an explanatory title card. The film's pacing is deliberately slow, appropriate to a long night of brooding introspection.

Jean Gabin is outstanding as the doomed hero, a performance considered by many to be the peak of his artistry, underscoring memorably François' sense of feeling trapped. It is subtle acting and absolutely convincing. *Le Jour se Lève* represents as well the apogee of the myth of Jean Gabin which was fashioned before in *Pépé-le-Moko* and *Port of Shadows.* Here the mythic character is compelling and most articulate concerning his existential plight.

Jules Berry is unforgettable as the slimy, albeit charming villain who delights in destroying the happiness of others. Valentin, the personification of corruption, remains Berry's best remembered screen performance. The beautiful Arletty is wonderful as the kind-hearted, worldly Clara and Jacqueline Laurent is as delicate as her flowers, the ideal mate for the lonely François. Revelations of her affair with Valentin produce an understandable shock.

The studio-constructed sets by Alexandre Trauner are remarkable. "Trauner designed this small suburban square the way a painter composes his canvas," wrote André Bazin. "While remaining faithful to the exigencies of reality, he succeeded in giving it a delicately poetic interpretation."

Maurice Jaubert's musical accompaniment to the film is notable. The haunting drum-roll for François brilliantly underlines the man's sense of feeling trapped.

In Hollywood, Anatole Litvak directed a mediocre remake entitled *The Long Night* (1947), totally lacking in conviction and significance. Not only was it out of synchronization with the optimistic postwar years but it vitiated the original by dishonestly tacking on a happy ending.

"Out of the darkness of the approaching war, Carné emerged with his masterpiece." . . . wrote critic Georges Sadoul. "Offspring of crisis, turmoil and soul-searching, *Le Jour se Lève* was a perfect example of artistic achievement." The finest representation of Carné's poetic realism ("a poetic intensification of authentic human experience"—critic Roger Manvell), the atmospheric and psychological *Le Jour se Lève* has a deserved and secure status as a classic.

In the early morning the doomed hero François (Jean Gabin) takes his life.

THE RULES OF THE GAME

(La Règle du Jeu)

N.E.F (LA NOUVELLE EDITION FRANÇAISE)   1939

CREDITS

Screenplay: Jean Renoir in collaboration with Karl Koch; *Direction:* Jean Renoir; *Photographer:* Jean Bachelet; *Assistant Directors:* André Zwobada, Henri Cartier-Bresson, and Karl Koch; *Editor:* Marguerite Renoir: *Music:* Selections from Mozart ("Danse Allemand"), Chopin ("Waltz"), Saint-Saëns ("Danse Macabre"), Johann Strauss ("Die Fledermaus"), and Monsigny ("Le Deserteur") arranged by Roger Désormières and Joseph Kosma; *Songs:* Selections from G. Claret and Camille François, Désormes and Delonnel-Garnier, E. Rosi, Salabert, Vincent Scotto, etc.; *Running Time:* initially 113 minutes;

At La Colinière Christine (Nora Grégor) welcomes Jurieu (Roland Toutain) while his friend Octave (Jean Renoir) looks on.

Paris Premiere: July 7, 1939; *New York Premiere:* April 8, 1950; *16 mm Rental Source:* Janus.

CAST

Le Marquis, Robert de la Chesnaye: Marcel Dalio; *Christine, his Wife:* Nora Grégor; *André Jurieu:* Roland Toutain; *Octave:* Jean Renoir: *Geneviève de Marrast:* Mila Parély; *Lisette:* Paulette Dubost; *Marceau:* Julien Carette; *Schumacher:* Gaston Modot; *Jackie:* Anne Mayen; *Saint-Aubin:* Pierre Nay; *The Général:* Pierre Magnier; *Charlotte de la Plante:* Odette Talazac; *Corneille, the Majordomo:* Eddy Debray; *South American:* Nicolas Amato; *Berthelin:* Tony Corteggiani.

BACKGROUND

After *La Bête Humaine* Jean Renoir formed his own production company, La Nouvelle Edition Française. *The Rules of the Game,* its initial effort, was accorded a substantial budget and was announced as the most prestigious French film of 1939. (Earlier provisional titles of the film were *Les Caprices de Marianne, Fair Play,* and *La Chasse en Sologne.*) Renoir thought the elegant form of eighteenth-century French comedy might serve as a suitable vehicle in which to express his personal feelings about a society on the verge of collapse on the eve of WWII.

In a 1938 interview, Renoir stated that the film would be "a precise description of the bourgeois of

In his Paris home the Marquis (Marcel Dalio) displays a mechanical bird from his collection for Octave (Jean Renoir).

our age. I want to show that for every game, there are rules. If you don't play according to them, you lose." Later he commented: "My ambition . . . was to illustrate this remark: we are dancing on a volcano."

For inspiration, Renoir turned to French classical comedy. He based his dramatic situation on Musset's *Les Caprices de Marianne* (written in 1833) and drew details of characterization and elements of plot from such comedies of manners as Marivaux's *The Game of Love and Chance (Le Jeu de l'Amour et du Hasard)* (1730) and Beaumarchais' *Le Mariage de Figaro* (1784). The fact that Beaumarchais criticized a decadent society on the eve of the French Revolution made critics draw parallels of it to Renoir's film which he dubbed a "divertissement" in its preface.

For the pivotal role of Christine, Renoir wanted Simone Simon but couldn't afford the high fee she demanded. Instead he chose Nora Grégor, a stage and acreen actress who fled her native Austria at the time of the Anschluss. Renoir himself assumed the role of Octave after his brother Pierre declined it; Gaston Modot replaced Fernand Ledoux as Schumacher. The casting triumph, however,

turned out to be the role of the Marquis. Instead of perpetuating another cinematic cliché of the "refined" French aristocrat, Renoir picked the short and swarthy Marcel Dalio—"the only actor," the director later said, "who could express the feeling of insecurity which is the basis of the character."

Renoir wanted to make the film in Technicolor but this did not prove feasible. Shooting ran from late February through late May 1939. Exteriors were shot in the Sologne (south of Orléans): Brinon-sur-Sauldre, Château de la Ferté Saint-Aubin, Lamotte-Beuvron, and Aubigny. Interiors were done at the Pathé studios in Joinville where Eugène Lourié and Max Douy had created lavish and beautiful sets. Heavy rains caused delays and the film ran well over the budget.

"When I made *The Rules of the Game*. . .", Renoir later related, "I knew the malady which was afflicting my contemporaries . . . . My awareness of the danger we were in enabled me to find the right situations, gave me the right words. . . . I think the film is good. But it is not very difficult to work well when your anxiety acts as a compass pointing you in the right direction." The director reported in his autobiography, *My Life and My Films (Ma Vie et Mes*

The Celebration at La Colinière. Taking part in the show: Jurieu (Roland Toutain) "threatening" a cowering bear (Jean Renoir), Saint-Aubin (Pierre Nay), a Tyrolean Christine (Nora Grégor), South American (Nicolas Amato), Berthelin (Tony Corteggiani), gypsy Geneviève (Mila Parély), and Robert (Marcel Dalio).

Films) (1974), that during the shooting of this greatly improvised film "I was torn between my desire to make a comedy of it and the wish to tell a tragic story. The result of this ambivalence was the film as it is."

After a hostile reception and subsequent obstacle-strewn history, *The Rules of the Game* would eventually triumph.

SYNOPSIS

André Jurieu (Roland Toutain) is an heroic aviator who lands at Le Bourget after a record transatlantic flight. He's disappointed that Christine (Nora Grégor), whom he wanted to impress with his feat, is not there to greet him. His buddy Octave (Jean Renoir), a failed musician and Christine's long-time friend, tries to console his unhappy pal by getting him invited to La Colinière, the château of the Marquis, Robert de la Chesnaye (Marcel Dalio), Christine's aristocratic husband. The Marquis is aware of the aviator's interest in his wife, but is nonetheless willing to take the risk. Among the many guests who will be converging at the country estate is Robert's mistress Geneviève (Mila Parély). The Marquis finds it difficult to end this affair.

At La Colinière the testy gamekeeper Schumacher (Gaston Modot) is glad to see again Lisette (Paulette Dubost), his perky and flirtatious wife who prefers to stay in Paris as Christine's maid. While examining the grounds Schumacher and the Marquis discover the rabbit poacher Marceau (Julien Carette). Robert is amused with this crafty fellow and humors him by offering him a position as servant.

Jurieu is welcomed; Marceau is introduced to the staff and immediately notices Lisette. In the course of a rabbit shooting party, Christine, through her field glasses, inadvertently spots Robert embracing Geneviève and is terribly shattered. Angry at the poacher's attention to his wife, Schumacher threatens Marceau.

A celebration with formal dress is held in the aviator's honor. Decorum disappears quickly. Geneviève wants Robert to go away with her. André discovers Saint-Aubin (Pierre Nay) embracing Christine and starts fighting with him. Then the aviator and Christine proclaim their love and decide to run off together. When the gamekeeper spots Marceau sneaking away from Lisette in the kitchen, he starts chasing him through the house. Robert accidently comes upon André in the arms

of his wife and the two men are quickly at each other's throats.

Order is restored—momentarily. The Marquis bids his guests good evening and dismisses both Schumacher and Marceau. Then he and Jurieu calmly discuss Christine. Meanwhile the Marquise and Octave take a walk on the chilly grounds. Lisette lends Christine her warm cape, a recent present from Schumacher. The gamekeeper spots Christine and Octave entering the greenhouse and believes the caped woman is his wife. He leaves to fetch his gun. Inside the greenhouse the couple discover their love and agree to leave together. Octave returns to the house to fetch Christine's coat. However, talking with Lisette he realizes how ineffectual he is and decides that André would be the better man, so he sends him to Christine. As the aviator runs toward the greenhouse Schumacher, thinking he's Octave, fires and kills him instantly. A dejected Octave and Marceau leave. The Marquis covers everything up by announcing that the gamekeeper thought he was shooting a poacher. This announcement is received ironically by the guests.

COMMENTARY

Before the release of *The Rules of the Game* the distributors demanded about thirteen minutes be

94

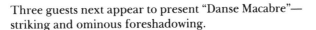

Three guests next appear to present "Danse Macabre"—
striking and ominous foreshadowing.

Interloper and ex-poacher Marceau (Julien Carette)
conveys his profound gratitude to Charlotte (Odette
Talazac), since he successfully hid behind her from the
vengeful Schumacher.

cut from its initial lentgh of 113 minutes. Although
it received some good notices, at its premiere the
audience booed and nearly rioted. Renoir observed
someone setting fire to his newspaper and trying to
burn the back of his chair, stating that any theatre
screening such a film ought to be destroyed.

In desperation Renoir cut the film to ninety
minutes but it was still a total fiasco. In October
1939 it was banned by the censors as "demoralizing." The N.E.F. went bankrupt. "I depicted pleasant, sympathetic characters," Renoir wrote, "but
showed them in a society in process of disintegra-
tion, so that they were defeated at the outset. . . .
The audience recognized this. The truth is that
they recognized themselves. People who commit
suicide do not care to do it in front of witnesses."

Allied bombings destroyed the laboratories
where the film's master negative had been stored.
After the war only a few cut versions in poor
condition were circulated. However, in 1946 a
brand new print was discovered in northern
France and an eighty-minute negative was made.
Renoir's great film, albeit truncated, was kept alive
in ciné clubs. In this abbreviated and confusing
state it opened in New York in 1950 and was
dismissed by the *Times* critic as "one for the buz-
zards." Then in 1956 three cinéphiles, Jean Ga-
borit, Jacques Maréchal, and Jacques Durand, at-

tempted to restore the film. They obtained world
rights to it and after discovering two hundred
boxes of film material recovered from the bombing, set about their long, painstaking labor. Finally,
with about a minute missing (three brief exchanges
during the hunting sequence), the reconstructed
film—now 112 minutes—was screened at the 1959
Venice Film Festival and reopened in Paris on
April 23, 1965. Since its triumphant restoration,
The Rules of the Game has appeared on many of the
"Ten Best Films of all Time" lists.

Renoir's masterly organization of camera movements, especially his striking use of depth-of-field
photography to develop dramatic contrasts between foreground and background action (thus
reducing the necessity of breaking up a scene into
many separate shots) has received much critical
praise.

The beautifully edited hunting sequence is justly
famous. The shocking cruelty and callous brutality
of the shooting party foreshadow Jurieu's hasty
dispatch. "He rolled over like an animal," Marceau
reports. The fête is also highly regarded, whose
highlight is the figure of death and three ghosts

95

performing a foreboding "danse macabre."

Although many critics complain that Nora Grégor is rather cold and fails to project the charisma which would motivate all the film's havoc, the director himself is wonderful as Octave, a sort of ursine court jester, and "Carette, once more, is perfect," said Renoir. Marcel Dalio is outstanding as the Marquis.

From a traditional point of attack, described by the director as "what would happen to the stranger who wants to belong to a milieu which is not his," Renoir composed his richly textured screenplay developed in parallel structure. Both the aviator ("a foreign substance entering the organism"—Renoir) and the poacher attempt to penetrate an alien world with confusing and tragic consequences.

"Beneath its seemingly innocuous appearance," Renoir wrote, "the story attacks the very structure of our society." When Christine tells Octave that she's suddenly realized that her life has been based on a lie, her confidant replies "We're in a period when everyone tells lies: pharmacists' handbills, Governments, the radio, the cinema, the newspapers. . . . So how could you expect us poor individuals not to lie as well?" The film's most quoted line is Octave's disturbing observation expressing his confusion in distinguishing good from evil: "On this earth, there is one thing which is frightful, and that is that everyone has his reasons."

In America during WWII Renoir directed five films, the finest being *The Southerner* (1945). *The River* (1951), shot in India, marks the start of the final phase of his career in which he directed seven more features.

In 1975 Renoir received an honorary Academy Award and was described as "a genius who, with grace, responsibility and enviable devotion through silent film, sound film, feature, documentary, and television, has won the world's admiration." He died in Los Angeles on February 12, 1979. *The Rules of the Game* is generally regarded as the master's greatest achievement.

A depth-of-field shot capturing irony: in the foreground Robert (Marcel Dalio), right, confides to Jurieu (Roland Toutain), left, that he's going to begin believing in friendship, while in the background Octave (Jean Renoir) tells Lisette (Paulette Dubost) his plans to run off with the Marquis' wife.

THE ETERNAL RETURN

(L'Eternel Retour)

AN ANDRÉ PAULVÉ PRODUCTION FOR
DISCINA INTERNATIONAL FILMS
CORPORATION   1943

CREDITS

Screenplay: Jean Cocteau; *Director:* Jean Delannoy;
Photographer: Roger Hubert; *Editor:* Suzanne
Fauvel; *Music:* Georges Auric; *Running Time:* 100
minutes; *Paris Premiere:* October 13, 1943; *New York
Premiere:* January 3, 1948; *16 mm. Rental Source:*
Janus.

CAST

Patrice: Jean Marais; *Nathalie:* Madeleine Sologne;
Marc: Jean Murat; *Gertrude:* Yvonne de Bray; *A-
chille:* Pierre Piéral; *Amédée:* Jean d'Yd; *Nathalie II:*
Junie Astor; *Lionel:* Roland Toutain; *Anne:* Jane
Marken; *Morolt:* Alexandre Rignault.

BACKGROUND

Prolific film director Jean Delannoy was born on
January 12, 1908, in Noisy-Le-Sec, a suburb of
Paris. He studied philosophy at the Sorbonne before entering film, first as an actor then as a director of shorts in the early 1930's, followed by a
period as film editor. He made his first feature,
Paris-Deauville, in 1935.

During the Occupation he directed an historical
film, *Pontcarral, Colonel d'Empire* (1942), which
amused and heartened audiences with its clever
parallels to the Vichy government. (A leader of the
Resistance was to adopt "Pontcarral" as his code-
name.) Delannoy next intended a version of the

Portrait of Madeleine Sologne as Nathalie, a modern-
day Iseult.

Tristan legend as an historical film, but it proved to
be too costly so it was decided to film it in modern
dress instead.

Poet Jean Cocteau, attracted to the theme of
thwarted love, prepared the adaptation and dialogue for the film, intended as a vehicle for Jean
Marais. It was to be called *The Eternal Return.* Its
title, Cocteau wrote, "is borrowed from Nietzsche
and suggests that the old myths may be reborn
without their heroes knowing it." ("All things eter-
nally return and ourselves with them," Nietzsche
wrote in *Thus Spake Zarathustra.)*

Cocteau's version is faithful to the original legend. He wanted Michèle Morgan for the lead but
she had left for America. Madeleine Sologne was
then selected to play Nathalie/Iseult. To underline
their Celtic derivation, Cocteau insisted on his
screen lovers dyeing their hair blond.

The Germans, feeling that the Tristan legend
was their exclusive possession via Wagner, at first
did not want the film to be made, then later refused
to let Delannoy film along the occupied Brittany
coast, the legendary setting of the story. Finally it
was shot during March 1943. Interiors were filmed

SYNOPSIS

Marc (Jean Murat) is a wealthy landowner who lives in a seventeenth-century castle with his young nephew Patrice (Jean Marais) and his sister-in-law's family, the Frossins: the scheming Gertrude (Yvonne de Bray), her weak husband Amédée (Jean d'Yd), and their malevolent dwarf son, Achille (Pierre Piéral), an agent of fate in the story.

Patrice feels that his unhappy widowed uncle needs a woman and brashly offers to find a bride for him. Soon after Patrice visits a nearby fishermen's island and witnesses a bully, Morolt (Alexandre Rignault), threatening a beautiful young woman, Nathalie (Madeleine Sologne). He defends her but is stabbed in the thigh.

Nathalie's guardian, Anne (Jane Marken), skilled in herbs, heals the young man. Recovering, Patrice offers marriage to his wealthy uncle to Nathalie but she is bitterly hurt, for she has fallen in love with the youth. Nonetheless, to avoid a destructive mar-

Patrice (Jean Marais) interferes with the brutal treatment of Nathalie (Madeleine Sologne) by Morolt (Alexandre Rignault).

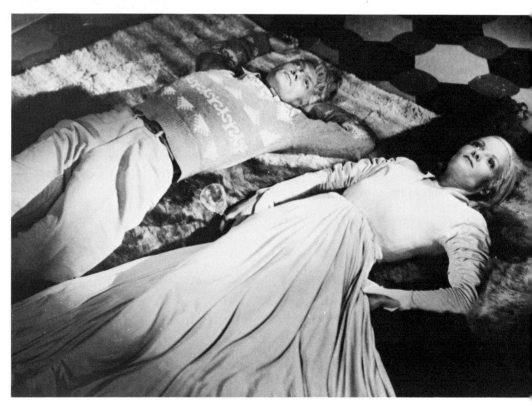

Patrice (Jean Marais) and Nathalie (Madeleine Sologne) after they have imbibed Anne's potion.

at the Studios de la Victorine in Nice, exteriors by Lake Geneva. The locale in the film is unspecified, with the implication that this myth could occur anytime, anyplace.

The Eternal Return was an enormous success, served as an important apprenticeship for Cocteau, and solidified Jean Delannoy's reputation.

riage to the drunken Morolt, she decides to flee with Patrice that evening.

Anne prepares a herbal philter for Nathalie and her husband. It has the magical power of binding the pair to eternal love. Cautiously, she labels it "Poison." Marc marries Nathalie and the Frossins, fearing eviction, plan to spy on the bride.

Marc (Jean Murat), Nathalie (Madeleine Sologne), and Lionel (Roland Toutain) rush to the dying Patrice. (The "flag" is Cocteau's homage to dancer Isadora Duncan, who was strangled to death by her long scarf.)

During a storm the vicious Achille pours Anne's "poison" into a drink Patrice prepares for Nathalie. Later, Marc's suspicions are aroused and he agrees to a ploy with the Frossins of pretending to depart. Patrice is caught talking with Nathalie in her bedroom. He is banished while she will be returned to her island. Patrice abducts Nathalie and they share an idyllic scene in a mountain hut until Marc tracks them down and brings her back.

Patrice goes to work in a garage run by his friend Lionel (Roland Toutain). His sister, also called Nathalie (Junie Astor), falls in love with Patrice, but he is obsessed with Marc's wife. Amédée comes snooping by and creates an erroneous impression that Nathalie no longer cares for him. Feeling rejected, Patrice proposes to Nathalie II and she accepts.

The engaged couple and Lionel return to the fisherman's island. Nathalie II learns from Anne the reason for Patrice's disturbing aloofness and fears she'll never marry him. Patrice confesses the truth to Lionel and begs him to accompany him to Marc's castle for one final test: if Nathalie indeed has forgotten him, why then he'll be a devoted husband to his friend's sister.

Patrice is distraught when his signals go unheeded beneath Nathalie's bedroom—actually the frail and fading woman had earlier asked Marc to change rooms, for Patrice's spirit haunted the place. Achille spots Patrice and shoots him in the leg. Fleeing through the marshes, Patrice gets his wound infected.

Back on the island he's put in a boathouse and the dying man begs Lionel to ask Marc for permission to see Nathalie once more. If she comes, please fly a white scarf from the mast so that he'll spot it. Nathalie II spends a vigil near Patrice and in a fit of jealousy lies about the oncoming boat with the designated scarf. Patrice dies.

The party arrives. A weak Nathalie rushes to Patrice's body then expires alongside her beloved.

COMMENTARY

The Eternal Return was a huge popular and critical success in France. The appeal of a tragic love story with two alluring stars was magnetic to an oppressed audience seeking escapist fare. It made Jean Marais a film star who was idolized by French girls, and set fashion trends with Marais' heraldic pullover sweater and Mlle. Sologne's hair style. The reception was altogether different when it appeared in England as *Love Eternal* in 1946. With its blond Aryan heroes it was mistaken for a Nazi film: "a nightmare of Teutonic mysticism" (critic Richard Winnington), "mysticism of the cult of death. . . . There is nothing French here" *(Daily Express)*, etc. Jean Marais was signaled out as a "Nazi type, something between Lohengrin . . . and Horst Wessel. . . ." *(Daily Telegraph)*.

Cocteau wisely observed, "Epochs dominated by politics (partisan epochs) are inappropriate to criticism." The story of Tristan and Iseult, originally a Welsh legend, was a permanent part of France's cultural heritage since the twelfth century. Ignoring the other vicious allegations, no one could accuse the man who made *Pontcarral* of collaboration with Vichy!

Jean Delannoy directed with firm control and precision. With his striking good looks and strong physique, Jean Marais was the perfect incarnation of a mythical hero superbly paired with the languorous and ethereal beauty of Madeleine Sologne. They made attractive and thoroughly con-

vincing romantic lovers. Piéral was unforgettable as the destructive dwarf and both Jean Murat and Yvonne de Bray contributed distinguished performances. The winsome dog Moulouk was the beloved pet of Jean Marais.

Besides the fine screenplay in which Cocteau weds, as he wrote, "the real and the unreal," credit should be given also to the vast and luxuriant sets of Georges Wakhévitch and to the delicate, misty photographic effects of Roger Hubert. Georges Auric managed to escape the dominance of Wagner and to create a haunting and atmospheric score. As a result of the film's success, which Cocteau attributed to the "irresistible, never-fading charm of the legend," the poet-scenarist was greatly stimulated and encouraged to continue work in film.

As a poet Cocteau sought in all his various forms of expression to instill a sense of the "marvellous" into our everyday lives. The "marvellous" he defined as that which "removes us from the confines within which we have to live." The public, he felt, was accustomed to perceiving poetry in the traditional places, as in the lovers' castle in the film. However, Cocteau felt that in the realistic garage scenes "poetry functions best." One can question the effectiveness of this observation. Are we not more impressed, for example, with the haunting potion-drinking scene in the castle than with the garage scenes which critic Roger Régent dismissed as "an interlude among the monkey wrenches and carburetor breakdowns"?

The death scene (Patrice: "I cannot hold onto my life any longer") with an immediate apotheosis of the couple is particularly remarkable and moving. A brilliant fantasy, a film of rare plastic beauty, a great love story, the poetic classic *The Eternal Return* is one of Delannoy's most memorable films.

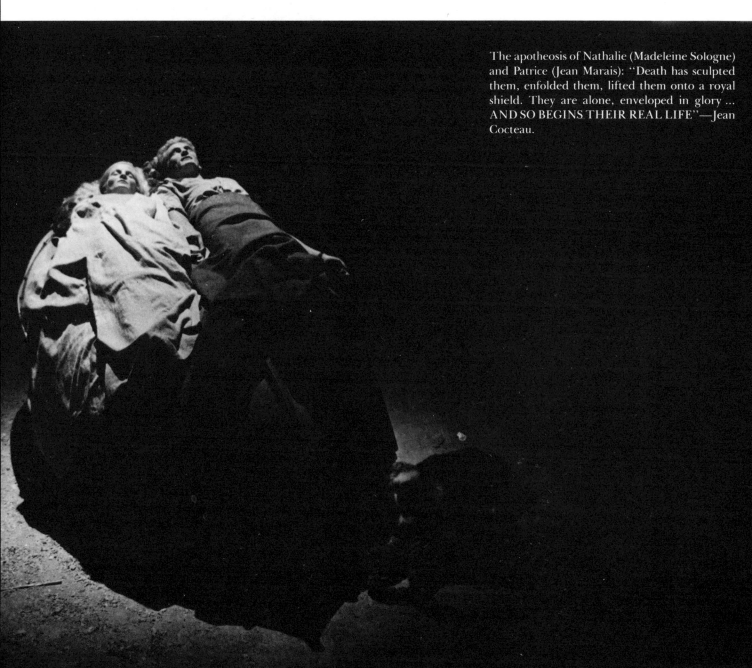

The apotheosis of Nathalie (Madeleine Sologne) and Patrice (Jean Marais): "Death has sculpted them, enfolded them, lifted them onto a royal shield. They are alone, enveloped in glory ... AND SO BEGINS THEIR REAL LIFE"—Jean Cocteau.

CHILDREN OF PARADISE

(Les Enfants du Paradis)

SOCIÉTÉ NOUVELLE PATHÉ CINÉMA   1945

CREDITS

Screenplay: Jacques Prévert; *Director:* Marcel Carné; *Photographer:* Roger Hubert; *Assistant Directors:* Pierre Blondy and Bruno Tireux; *Editors:* Henri Rust and Madeleine Bonin; *Music:* Maurice Thiriet in collaboration with Joseph Kosma; *Pantomime Music:* Georges Mouqué; *Running Time:* 195 minutes; *Paris Premiere:* Gala at Palais de Chaillot, March 9, 1945; Public release March 22, 1945; *New York Premiere:* February 19, 1947; *16 mm. Rental Source:* Films Incorporated.

CAST

Garance: Arletty; *Baptiste Debureau:* Jean-Louis Barrault; *Frédérick Lemaître:* Pierre Brasseur; *Pierre-François Lacenaire:* Marcel Herrand; *Jericho, the Old Clothes Man:* Pierre Renoir; *Nathalie;* Maria Casarès; *Count Edouard De Montray:* Louis Salou; *Anselme Debureau:* Etienne Decroux; *Avril, Lacenaire's Accomplice:* Fabien Loris; *Stage Doorman, 'Funambules':* Léon Larive; *Stage Manager, 'Funambules':* Pierre Palau; *Director, 'Funambules':* Marcel Pérès; *Scarpia Barrigni:* Albert Rémy; *Madame Hermine:* Jane Marken; *Fil de Soie, the 'Blind' Beggar:* Gaston Modot; *Little Baptiste:* Jean-Pierre Delmon; *Police Inspector:* Paul Frankeur.

BACKGROUND

During the Occupation Carné made *Les Visiteurs du Soir* (1942). Afterwards, Carné and Prévert were searching for a new project and met Jean-Louis

(*Opposite page*) Outside the Théâtre des Funambules the mime Baptiste (Jean-Louis Barrault) enacts the theft of a watch which he has witnessed.

Barrault in Nice in January in 1943. He suggested they make a film based on the life of Jean-Gaspard Debureau (1796-1846), France's greatest mime of the nineteenth century. Barrault related a dramatic event in the man's life which would be powerful in a film: Debureau and his wife and family were taking a walk and bumped into a hostile young man who started to insult him viciously. The angry artist hit him on the head with his cane and the man died a short time later. The trial was sensational, for a curious Paris descended on the courthouse to hear the celebrated mime speak for the first time in public. He was acquitted of the charge of manslaughter.

This incident and the challenge to evoke the atmosphere of the so-called "Boulevard of Crime" in Paris (in actuality the Boulevard du Temple but given the notorious soubriquet due to the many theatres there which specialized in gory melodramas to please their thrill-seeking clientele) aroused much enthusiasm in Carné and Prévert and they began their extensive research on Debureau's epoch. (A stamp from the period inspired the famous concluding carnival scene.) Ironically the Debureau killing was later found unsuitable and abandonded. The scenario's working title was *Les Funambules* and was based on such actual characters besides Debureau as Frédérick Lemaître, the celebrated actor, and Pierre-François Lacenaire, a well-known dandy of the period. However, the events in the film are imaginary.

The film was to be initially a French-Italian co-production and large sums of money were put at Carné's disposal. Considering its incredible production history—it was shot during the height of World War II—it is in the nature of the miraculous that *Children of Paradise* was ever finished.

First of all there was the problem of length. The Nazis insisted that no film could exceed ninety minutes in order to maintain strict curfew control. However, the film would need at least two and a half hours to do justice to the action which takes almost a decade (approximately 1828-36) to unfold. André Paulvé, the producer, suggested that the film be made in two parts. Carné agreed ostensibly but privately hoped the Germans would be gone from Paris before they finished it, for he wished the entire work to be shown at one time to preserve the spirit of the film.

Two artists in Carné's group, the composer Joseph Kosma and the set designer Alexandre Trauner, had to work clandestinely since Jews were forbidden employment in the film industry. Ini-

103

tially, the film was to be shot completely at the Studios de la Victorine in Nice. In spite of severe wartime shortages, enormous quantities of plaster, nails, glass, scaffolding, etc., were needed to recreate the thriving "Boulevard of Crime" of the late 1820's, one of the largest (the height reached 500 feet), expensive, and complex sets ever constructed for a French film.

Shooting began August 16, 1943, at the time when the German forces were being routed in Sicily. In the midst of the filming Allied ships were sighted sailing past the Riviera! Early in September when the Italian Armistice was signed, Carné received orders from Paris that the production be shut down and the entire group return to the capital immediately. Carné begged for a postponement. He needed only two more weeks to complete the exterior shots but his request was refused. Two months were wasted waiting for equipment to arrive from Nice before shooting could resume at the Pathé Studios in Joinville.

Meanwhile the Italian funding was withdrawn and the project nearly abandoned until the Société Pathé decided to take the risk and picked up the film's costs. During this time the collaborationist press demanded that the film be stopped. Shooting resumed on November 9. The interior theatre scenes were filmed but not without further difficulty. There was constant interference by the Germans, a lack of gasoline and transportation, scarcity of fabrics, bombings, disrupting air-raid alarms, etc.

Carné managed to complete the interior sequences and, since the Allied advance in Italy was proceeding very slowly, received permission to resume shooting in Nice. Robert Le Vigan, who had played the role of Jerico, refused to leave Paris. He had made compromising radio broadcasts for the Propagandastaffel and received threats of death if he were to go to Nice. All of his work in the film had to be reshot with his replacement, Pierre Renoir. Then the crew discovered that the sets had deteriorated in Nice and work was halted while they were restored at great expense. Further, additional shooting of night scenes was required at Pathé at the time when the electricity supply was unreliable. Amazingly, the film was finally completed on March 15, 1944.

After the Allied invasion of Normandy, Carné deliberately slowed down the editing so that the film would be ready when Paris was liberated. Great secrecy had to be maintained to prevent a possible seizure of the film by the Germans. The negatives were deposited in various hiding places without arousing the suspicion of the enemy.

After nearly two years of work, Carné managed to complete his masterpiece. The total cost ran to over sixty million francs (the equivalent at the time of $1,250,000.00), making *Children of Paradise* one of the most ambitious films ever shot in France. In the midst of all the obstacles and hardships resulting from the Occupation and the devasting war, the determination and dedication of the perfectionist Carné and his fellow artists managed somehow, astonishingly, to produce the most beloved and esteemed film in the history of French cinema.

SYNOPSIS

PART ONE: THE BOULEVARD OF CRIME

The action begins near the end of the reign of Charles X (1824-30). A theatre curtain rises. We are in Paris and it is nearly Spring. In the bustling "Boulevard of Crime" filled with theatres and cafés, Garance (Arletty), a spirited and beautiful young woman, is falsely accused of stealing a fat man's watch. Baptiste (Jean-Louis Barrault), the dreamy and spurned son of Anselme Debureau (Etienne Decroux) of the Théâtre des Funambules, has wit-

"The Gods! . . . the cheapest seats in the theatre [des Funambules], the worst, the furthest away from the stage, for the 'people,' that is why it was called Paradise, in those days. . . ."—Jacques Prévert.

nessed everything and mimes an account of the real thief at work. Freed, the grateful young woman throws a rose to the smitten youth.

When a family of actors, the Barrignis, quits the Funambules after a quarrel, an opportunity to appear onstage arises for Baptiste and Frédérick Lemaître (Pierre Brasseur), who aspires to be a great Shakespearean actor.

Nathalie (Marie Casarès), the Stage Manager's daughter, loves Baptiste, but he daydreams over Garance. In Ménilmontant a "blind" begger, Fil de Soie (Gaston Modot), befriends Baptiste and takes him to the notorious Le Rouge-Gorge for a drink. There he sees Garance in the company of Lacenaire (Marcel Herrand), an intelligent yet cruel figure from the underworld. Baptiste dares to dance with her but the criminal's henchman Avril (Fabien Loris) throws him out of the place. The brave Baptiste returns and punches the bully, to Garance's delightful surprise.

Garance and Baptiste take a walk and she tells him of her poverty-stricken background. They kiss, and when a thunderstorm comes up he finds a room for her at his place, the Grand Relais, where he expresses his devotion to her then shyly retires to his quarters.

Frédérick is staying there and he and Garance

At Le Rouge-Gorge Avril (Fabien Loris), left, interrupts the dancing couple and threatens Baptiste (Jean-Louis Barrault), while an angry Garance (Arletty) watches.

Baptiste (Jean-Louis Barrault) proclaims his love for Garance (Arletty) later that evening at the Grand Relais.

become lovers for a while. Baptiste, who worships her, creates a mime drama of his unhappy situation, *The Palace of Visions* or *The Lovers of the Moon*. A suitor, Count Edouard de Montray (Louis Salou), tries to impress Garance with his wealth, but she isn't moved in the least. Baptiste tells Garance he despairs of ever being loved by her. However, she finds herself drawn to the sensitive man. Nathalie interrupts the scene by claiming that Baptiste belongs to her alone. Lacenaire rents a room at the Grand Relais to perpetrate a robbery. Garance is implicated in this affair because of her friendship with the scoundrel and to escape a threatening imprisonment produces a card the Count left her should she ever need his protection.

PART TWO: THE MAN IN WHITE

Several years have passed. We are now in the early period of the reign of Louis Philippe (1830-48). Garance has become the Count's mistress but secretly holds the image of Baptiste in her heart. Baptiste and Nathalie had been married six years and have a son named after him (Jean-Pierre Delmon). The mime has become famous as Pierrot with his loose, white costume. Frédérick Lemaître, too, has achieved success in the theatre and leads a carefree, flamboyant existence.

The second part opens with Frédérick coping with his creditors and mocking the three hack authors of the melodrama he's currently appearing in. When he burlesques his role during a performance they challenge him to a duel.

Frédérick, wounded slightly, attends the new mime drama at the Funambules and encounters a veiled Garance who has been seeing every performance of her adored Baptiste. She tells him of her life with the Count and their travels. She would love to see Baptiste again. Frédérick leaves to inform the mime of her presence.

A nervous Nathalie learns from Jericho (Pierre Renoir), the ubiquitous, sinister rag dealer, that Garance is in the house and sends her son to inform her that she and Baptiste are living very happily together. Feeling she's not wanted, Garance leaves. When Baptiste learns that Garance awaits him, he rushes offstage to her box and is crushed to find it empty.

Lacenaire visits Garance and gives an account of his criminal career. When he leaves he runs into the Count who treats him haughtily. Lacenaire insults him and outrages him further when he refuses to duel with him.

The Count is embittered that Garance cannot love him and that he has an unknown rival. Frédérick scores a triumph with *Othello* at the Grand Théâtre. The Count and Garance watch the play. He thinks the actor is the one she loves and plans to challenge him to a duel. Baptiste discovers Garance in the theatre and leads her to a balcony where they proclaim their undying love for each other. Meanwhile the Count attempts to bait Frédérick. Lacenaire appears and taunts the Count. He maliciously draws back a curtain revealing the lovers on the balcony, then leaves. The Count forces Frédérick to duel with him on the following day.

Garance and Baptiste spend the night in their moonlit room. In the morning it is carnival time. Lacenaire, wishing to take personal vengeance on the Count, visits him at the Turkish Baths and stabs him.

Garance wants to leave Baptiste to persuade the Count not to fight Frédérick. She will go away with him to spare the actor's life. Nathalie appears and, in her second confrontation with these two, fights for her marriage.

Garance leaves quickly and takes a carriage. Baptiste runs after her shouting her name but is prevented from catching up with her by the enormous crowds of revelers, among them many mocking figures costumed as Pierrot. The curtain falls.

COMMENTARY

Carné had his wish: *Children of Paradise* was the first French film shown in his country when it was liberated. Also the two parts were shown together. The film was a triumph. On a reserved-seat basis it ran for over a year in Paris alone. Critic Jacques Natanson wrote: "Behold the monument of the French cinema."

Children of Paradise was cited for "Special Mention" along with seven other films at the 1946 Venice Film Festival, and went on to become a resounding world-wide success. Almost an hour was cut from it when it was first shown in America in 1947. Since then, in a restored version, *Children of Paradise* has become a staple in revival houses and on television. For this film Jacques Prévert was nominated for an "Oscar" for "Writing (Original Screenplay)" (1946).

The pivotal role of Garance is played to perfection by the lovely Arletty. Were she not convincing, a true woman, without haunting beauty or a sense of mystery, the film would seem unreal.

Equally perilous is the character of Baptiste, the ethereal dreamer, the exile from the moon. Were

Jean-Louis Barrault unable to project his underlying strong masculinity, his enduring passion for Garance would ring false. Having rigorously trained in mime with Etienne Decroux (who plays his father in the film), Barrault had the rare talent to project a most powerful and eloquent use of mime. In his white Pierrot costume he has been identified forever with the role of Baptiste.* "In so far as one's astral complexion harmonizes more or less completely with certain characters that one

interprets," Barrault writes in his autobiography *Memories for Tomorrow,* published in New York in 1974 (*Souvenirs pour Demain,* Paris, 1972), "I think the closest to me was Baptiste."

For Pierre Brasseur, bursting with energy as the egotistic yet dedicated actor, Frédérick Lemaître, along with Marcel Herrand as the cold and ruthless

*He performed the mime drama *Baptiste* (1946), based on the film, throughout the world.

The Funambules' mime drama, *The Palace of Visions* or *Lovers of the Moon:* while Pierrot (Jean-Louis Barrault), right, sleeps, the bold Harlequin (Pierre Brasseur) woos the statue of the moon goddess Phoebe (Arletty).

107

In the wings of the Funambules Jericho (Pierre Renoir) informs Nathalie (Maria Casarès) that her rival Garance is watching the performance.

Lacenaire and Louis Salou as the jealous Count, as well as for Arletty and Barrault, *Children of Paradise* remains the most noted film of their careers.

Marcel Carné is justified in referring to the screenplay as "the most beautiful script Prévert ever wrote.* The impassioned period is recreated with the gusto of a Dumas or a Balzac. Prévert projects his vision into the work and we recognize the traditional Figure of Destiny (Jericho—Lacenaire also) as well as the theme of fate separating the lovers.

Children of Paradise is a film of superb characterizations. There is the multi-faceted Garance. We first meet her in a sideshow as a vision of "Truth"; accordingly each of the four men will see in her a different aspect of the Eternal Woman: A vision of spiritualized love for Baptiste, a worldly and gay companion for Frédérick, an elegant courtesan for the Count, and an uncorrupted challenge for the cynical Lacenaire.

The delicate, sensitive Baptiste, constantly associated with the moon ("One night . . . when the moon was full . . . he fell down," his father says; Baptiste declares later "the moon is my country!"), must learn to function on the earth.

*In 1973 poet Jacques Prévert received the Grand Prix de la Société des Auteurs for the total body of his work; in 1975 he received the Grand Prix National du Cinéma.

108

The characters grow. At the end of the film Baptiste's influence has kept Garance unspoiled and has made her become more serious and sensitive. Baptiste, for his part, has become more earthly. When the two lovers finally meet again there is at last a harmonious consummation before fate intervenes once more.

The film has an incredibly complex structure incorporating much parallel action and utilizing the device of a play-within-a-play for a total of six times (there are four mime dramas and two plays) to comment on the action and to reinforce thematic associations.

Children of Paradise is capable of varied interpretation. The relation between the "Gods" in "Paradise" (the boisterous poor who take the cheapest seats in the top gallery of the Funambules) and the "Children of Paradise" ("the actors, the beloved heros of the public"—Carné) suggests affinities between the nature of life and art, reinforced by events in the narrative which are recreated in pantomime dramas.

The film can also be seen as a meditation on the nature of love: there is the idealistic and romantic

love of Baptiste; the carefree, profane love of Frédérick; the possessive and jealous love of the Count; the carnal and selfish love of Lacenaire, etc.

The movie can be viewed as well as a debate on the relative merits of mime and theatre and their analogies of silent cinema and films of the sound period.

And, above all, the film's a commentary on the human condition in which love is elusive in men's illusion-filled, fate-dominated lives.

Marcel Carné reached his peak as a director in this towering work. There is the consistent, eloquent style, the skill in handling thousands of extras and in making the whole epoch come alive for a contemporary audience. *Children of Paradise* remains his undisputed masterpiece. In 1979 the French Academy of Cinema Arts and Techniques placed it first among the ten best French films made since 1929. *Children of Paradise* ("this magnificent and sumptuous film, this gigantic, philosophical ballet"—critic Georges Sadoul) is generally and understandably regarded as the most stunning achievement in the history of French cinema.

In the Green Room at the Grand Théâtre Frédérick (Pierre Brasseur) as Othello is insulted by the Count (Louis Salou), right, while Lacenaire (Marcel Herrand) bides his time before humiliating the Count by exposing to view the lovers, Garance and Baptiste, on the balcony.

On the balcony of the Grand Théâtre the lovers meet again after years of separation: Baptiste (Jean-Louis Barrault) and Garance (Arletty).

109

SYMPHONIE PASTORALE

(La Symphonie Pastorale)

LES FILMS GIBÉ   1946

CREDITS

Adaptation: Jean Aurenche and Jean Delannoy, from the novel by André Gide (1919), published in New York in *Two Symphonies* (1931); *Dialogue:* Pierre Bost and Jean Aurenche; *Director:* Jean Delannoy; *Photographer:* Armand Thirard; *Assistant Directors:* Jack Sanger and Roger Calon; *Editor:* Suzanne Fauvel; *Music:* Georges Auric; *Running Time:* 105 minutes; *Paris Premiere:* September 26, 1946; *New York Premiere:* September 13, 1948; *16 mm. Rental Source:* Facsea.

CAST

Gertrude: Michèle Morgan; *Pastor Martin:* Pierre Blanchar; *Amélie:* Line Noro; *Jacques:* Jean Desailly; *Piette:* Andrée Clement; *Casteran:* Louvigny; *Charlotte:* Rosine Luguet.

BACKGROUND

After *The Eternal Return,* Jean Delannoy's next project was *La Symphonie Pastorale* (the article was dropped for its American release), a well-known short novel which André Gide wrote in 1918. Relating the story of a self-deluded Swiss minister,

The Pastor (Pierre Blanchar) brings the gift of a rabbit to his blind ward Gertrude (Michèle Morgan).

Amélie (Line Noro), the sadly neglected wife, seeks attention in vain from her husband (Pierre Blanchar).

this novel was properly classified by Gide as a *récit*, a serious, ironical, and critical brief narrative. The work's original title was *L'Aveugle* (the French word for a "blind person" can apply to either sex), which could represent the central character's spiritual blindness as well as the physical blindness of Gertrude, the young girl he brings into his home and later falls in love with.

The subsequent title refers to Beethoven's Sixth symphony the pastor takes Gertrude to hear. The exquisite evocation of a serene Nature in the second movement symbolizes an ideal image of the world he is misrepresenting to her as reality. "These ineffable harmonies," Gide wrote, "painted the world as it might have been, as it would be without evil and without sin, rather than the world as it really was."

"With what scruples Jean Aurenche, Pierre Bost and I approached the adaptation of this story," Jean Delannoy commented. "We had to translate into images a work almost exclusively introspective without castrating the spirit of it. The minister's uneasy and passionate character, the continuous flowing of the conscious to the unconscious had to be as perceptible on the screen as it was in the words—and what words—from which we derived our inspiration."

In the book Gide subordinated the plot to stress the moral problem: Disaster follows when the pastor disguises to himself—as Christ's commandment

to love—his true feelings for the blind girl while he ignores the moral strictures of St. Paul. Raised by the pastor to believe the world is totally beautiful and to be unaware of sin, Gertrude is devastated when she gains her sight and bears witness to the words of St. Paul: "For I was alive without the law once; but when the commandment came, sin revived, and I died" (*Romans* 7:9). In the film these theological issues are less emphasized than the plot, the complex interrelationships, and the actual physicality of the setting. The adapters changed the first-person narrative (the pastor's notebooks) and introduced Piette as a plot complication, a character who expands the theme of jealousy and unrequited love. They dropped the pastor's seduction of Gertrude before her operation and Jacques' decision to enter the Catholic priesthood. Whereas Gide was criticized for hurrying to a climax, the film allows for a slower and more richly textured development.

The role of Gertrude was offered to Michèle Morgan, who was in Hollywood where she had spent the war years pursuing a disappointing career with five mediocre films. She quickly accepted the challenging role and returned to France to revive her career. She prepared for the role painstakingly by visiting l'Institut des Jeunes Aveugles and familiarizing herself with the gestures and reactions of the blind.

Symphonie Pastorale was filmed during the 1945/

At his homecoming party Jacques (Jean Desailly) teaches Gertrude (Michèle Morgan) the waltz.

At the clinic a cured Gertrude (Michèle Morgan) realizes her visitor is Jacques (Jean Desailly), not the Pastor.

46 winter. Locations were the Swiss villages of Château d'Oex and Rossinière with interiors being shot at the Neuilly studios in Paris.

At the Paris premiere Delannoy asked Gide to autograph a copy of the novel and the famous writer inscribed: "To Jean Delannoy, for whom this little volume has served as a pretext to create a beautiful film."

SYNOPSIS

In an unspecified mountainous region in Switzerland, Pastor Martin (Pierre Blanchar) is summoned to a remote area to attend to a dying woman. Shocked at the animalistic state the woman's blind and filthy daughter is in, he decides to raise her himself so that he can lead her to God.

The pastor supervises the education of the child, now called Gertrude, who blossoms into a beautiful young lady (Michèle Morgan). A jealous Amélie (Line Noro), the pastor's long-suffering wife, realizes that he is not aware of the extent of his love for Gertrude, all the while neglecting his wife and his family.

The son Jacques (Jean Desailly) returns from his studies in England. He teaches Gertrude to dance at a homecoming party. The pastor observes them and burns with jealousy.

Piette (Andrée Clement), a young neighbor, loves Jacques but soon discovers she has a rival in Gertrude whom he spends time with, teaching her to play the organ. Jacques wishes to marry Gertrude, but the pastor attempts to persuade him that one doesn't marry a blind girl. The son, however, senses the real reason: his father cannot let her go.

Piette has a doctor examine Gertrude's eyes—in ten years the pastor has never had her eyes checked!—for she realizes Jacques is drawn to the blind girl because of her fragility. Were Gertrude cured she feels he could freely choose between two normal women. It turns out Gertrude has cataracts.

When the operation on Gertrude's eyes is successful, Jacques visits her in the clinic. Her sight now restored, she mistakes him for the pastor. They kiss but she recognizes him when she touches his hand and withdraws. Jacques feels hurt that she prefers his father. Gertrude returns and, unprepared for pain and evil, sees for the first time the toll of the pastor's obsessive love: an unhappy Amélie, Jacques estranged from his father, the pastor blind to all the misery he's caused. . . .

Before departing, Jacques tells his father he wants to marry Gertrude, but the pastor claims she loves him more than she does his son. Gertrude decides to leave. The pastor begs her to stay. A tortured Gertrude tells him that she has discovered it is Jacques whom she really loves but that the pastor prevented their marriage. . . .

Next morning the pastor notices her missing and runs out after her. He sees her body being dragged from a stream. The tormented woman had internalized all the guilt and committed suicide. He takes her in his arms.

COMMENTARY

Symphonie Pastorale was a great success. At the first Cannes Film Festival in 1946 the film shared the Grand Prize with six other films. Michèle Morgan received the prize for "Best Actress" and, in addition, won a "Victoire" as the most popular French actress of the year. Georges Auric won the "Best Musical Score" award.

The film made Miss Morgan a star all over again in France. With her high cheek bones and large, magnificent blue eyes, she was breathtakingly beautiful as the doomed Gertrude. Projecting a spiritual as well as a physical beauty, Miss Morgan was radiant in this, her best-remembered role. Raimu said: "She is magnificent . . . in *Symphonie Pastorale* she surpasses herself."

In the difficult part as a modern Pygmalion, which could easily veer into caricature, Pierre Blanchar makes the pastor understandable, convincing,

and even sympathetic. *Le Figaro* commented: "You can see in him a soul measured out to his part." Jean Desailly as the unhappy son and Line Noro as the shunted wife are excellent.

A tightly structured and skillful adaptation, Georges Auric's atmospheric score, and Armand Thirard's impressive photography which captures the isolation of the snowy Alpine region contribute to the film's striking impact.

Jean Delannoy's direction is at all times sure, restrained, and precise. Many powerful scenes linger in one's memory:

Gertrude leaves the clinic as snow falls. "Is that snow?" she inquires, her face luminous.

Vision restored, Gertrude enters the church during the service and walks among the congregation while the organ is playing. The pastor, arms outstretched, thanks the Lord for her sight while fighting back tears.

In the final scene the pastor chases away the men who've retrieved Gertrude's body from the stream. "She's mine," he blurts out, then closes her eyes and carries her away in his arms.

Symphonie Pastorale set a standard for a long time in America for what had come to be expected from the best of French cinema: sensitivity, psychological acuity, and rich poetry. Since that film, Delannoy's output has been prolific: historical films, police thrillers, melodramas—all marked by craftsmanship and technical proficiency. In the 1950's he was attacked by the New Wave critics who found his work cold and unemotional. In recent years M. Delannoy has worked in French television. His international reputation as a filmmaker, however, rests chiefly on his work in the 1940's and *Symphonie Pastorale* remains his best-loved film.

The confrontation scene: The Pastor (Pierre Blanchar) begs Gertrude (Michèle Morgan) to stay; she reveals that it is his son Jacques whom she really loves.

BEAUTY AND THE BEAST

(La Belle et la Bête)

AN ANDRÉ PAULVÉ PRODUCTION FOR
DISCINA INTERNATIONAL FILMS
CORPORATION   1946

CREDITS

Screenplay: Jean Cocteau, based on the classical tale by Mme. Leprince de Beaumont written in 1757; *Director:* Jean Cocteau; *Photographer:* Henri Alékan; *Editor:* Claude Ibéria; *Music:* Georges Auric; *Running Time:* 96 minutes; *Paris Premiere:* October 29, 1946; *New York Premiere:* December 23, 1947; *16 mm. Rental Source:* Janus.

Avenant (Jean Marais) offers marriage to the exploited Beauty (Josette Day).

BACKGROUND

Born July 5, 1889, in the Parisian suburb of Maisons-Laffitte, Jean Cocteau, an internationally known figure in France's cultural life for many years as poet, novelist, dramatist, essayist, etc., turned to the cinema in 1930 when the Vicomte de Noailles gave him a million francs to make a film with total freedom. The result was *The Blood of a Poet (Le Sang d'un Poète)* (1932), which Cocteau described as "documentary scenes from another realm." Although this unusual, experimental film became very influential, the poet was not drawn to the cinema until almost a decade later. Then he began his formal apprenticeship, writing dialogue for and acting in Serge de Poligny's *Le Baron Fantôme* (1942), preparing the screenplay for *The Eternal Return,* and contributing dialogue to Robert Bresson's *Les Dames du Bois de Boulogne* (1945). The concept, as Cocteau put it, of "a poet telling a story through the medium of the camera" fascinated him and he then plunged into what he called "the lustral bath of childhood" to create his version of Mme. de Beaumont's "Beauty and the Beast." This would be the first film since *Blood of a Poet* for which he assumed total responsibility.

Although Cocteau made some minor changes (he dropped the fairies, added the character of Avenant, etc.) he nonetheless remained completely faithful to the spirit of the original tale. The indeterminate time and locale of the story became in Cocteau's treatment seventeenth century Holland. He introduced such elements of the fantastic as the enchanted castle with arms supporting candelabra jutting from walls, Diana's pavilion, Magnifique the horse, etc. The film was to be another attempt at a "realistic documentary of unreal happenings."

Jean Marais was to meet his greatest challenge in film as the Beast. He had to project many emotions underneath a lion's head. Marais did not wear a mask; the daily ordeal of applying hairs to his face lasted from three to five hours. The glue interfered with his circulation and the nightly removal process was an agony. Josette Day, who had trained as a dancer and acted in Pagnol's *The Well-Digger's*

The entrance of Beauty (Josette Day) in the Beast's enchanted castle.

The Beast (Jean Marais), not finding her in her room, desperately questions his magic mirror, "Where is Beauty? Where is Beauty?"

Daughter (La Fille du Puisatier) (1941), was chosen to play Beauty.

A gifted group of assistants contributed their talents, among them: Artistic Director Christian Bérard who created the wondrous sets, costumes, and the extraordinary mask design which made the Beast far from frightening, but sympathetic, even seductive; Make-Up Artist Hagop Arakélian; and Technical Advisor René Clément.

The décor of the castle was influenced by Gustave Doré's illustrations for Charles Perrault's fairy tales; the bourgeois household shows traces of the paintings of Jan Vermeer among others. Shooting began on August 26, 1945, and was completed on January 11, 1946. Exteriors were the manor house Rochecorbon in Ille-et-Vilaine (Touraine) and the Château de Raray with its bizarre terrace of animal statuary near Senlis. Interiors were shot at the studios of Epinay and Saint-Maurice in Joinville. Cocteau regretted that color was unavailable to use at that time.

Cocteau kept a detailed account of the making of the film (*La Belle et la Bête: Journal d'un film,* Paris, 1947) published in New York in 1950 as *Beauty and the Beast: Diary of a Film.* The travails of working in postwar France with stringent economy, limited technical equipment, power failures and the almost insurmountable bouts with accidents and illness— the film was shut down at one point to permit Cocteau's hospitalization—etc. provide fascinating insights into the creative process of filmmaking and reveal the determined efforts of all involved to make a beautiful picture. Their labor of love was justified in the film's critical and commercial success.

SYNOPSIS

A merchant (Marcel André), reduced to straitened circumstances, resides in the country with his children: the vain and selfish Félicie (Mila Parély) and Adélaïde (Nane Germon), a ne'er-do-well son, Ludovic (Michel Auclair), and his virtuous and unselfish youngest daughter, Beauty (Josette Day).

Beauty is courted by Avenant (Jean Marais) but she feels she must put aside thoughts of marriage to care for her beloved father.

News comes of the arrival of a ship and the merchant revives hopes of prosperity. As he leaves, the older daughters request extravagant presents but all Beauty asks for is a rose. However, the merchant discovers that his creditors arrived before he did. Returning home without money that evening he loses his way in the forest and comes upon a mysterious castle where he spends the night.

Before departing he plucks a rose for Beauty. An angry Beast (Jean Marais) appears and sentences him to death for the offence. He grants a concession, however. Either the man or one of his daugh-

ters must return in three days to pay the penalty. The merchant agrees and the Beast lends him his white horse, Magnifique, to take him home.

Beauty decides to save her father and is taken by the horse to the enchanted castle. When she meets the ferocious-looking beast, she faints. Later, he informs her he will visit each evening at seven while she dines and ask her to be his wife. Repulsed by his appearance, Beauty nonetheless senses his underlying kindness. Anxious to see her ailing father again, she asks permission to return home. When she promises to return in a week, the Beast, worshipping her and fearing to lose her to Avenant, agrees and gives her as proof of his trust the golden key to his pavilion, which houses his riches, along with his glove which magically transports her home.

The sick father revives at the sight of Beauty. The jealous sisters plot to seize the Beast's wealth. They feign love for Beauty to detain her at home and steal her key. After the week's up, the Beast sends Magnifique to remind Beauty of her promise. Avenant and Ludovic, however, mount the horse in their plan to slay the Beast and capture his treasure.

When Beauty looks into the magical mirror carried by the white horse she is horrified to see an image of a tortured Beast. Immediately she uses her glove to return to the castle. She comes upon a dying Beast besides a pool. Her efforts to save him fail.

Meanwhile Avenant and Ludovic break into the pavilion. A statue of Diana comes to life and shoots an arrow into Avenant. He transforms into the Beast. Beauty is startled to see a handsome young Prince (Jean Marais) resembling Avenant appear in lieu of the Beast. He tells her he was under a spell and could only be saved by a look of love. Together the ecstatic couple fly away to his kingdom for a life of happiness.

COMMENTARY

Beauty and the Beast won the Prix Louis Delluc (1946). Cocteau aimed for an "anti-pompous" style and deliberately curtailed camera movement. His masterly direction shows rigor, restraint, precision, and an eschewing of sentimentality and clichés.

Jean Marais, in his best remembered screen role, projects a suffering soul which makes the Beast seem human, noble, and profoundly stirring. One might quibble that after his haunting presence as the Beast with his unpenetrable depths of pain and

Beauty (Josette Day) describes life at the castle to Ludovic (Michel Auclair) and Avenant (Jean Marais).

feelings, Márais' sudden metamosphosis into a "wedding cake" prince comes as something of an anticlimax and one can well sympathize with Greta Garbo who's reputed to have cried out after viewing this transformation: "Give me back my Beast!" Josette Day conveys the right grace and simplicity to make her Beauty convincing.

The daily life on the farm as well as the enchanted castle with such phenomena as eyes-moving, smoke-exhaling busts in the mantelpiece is infiltrated with that sense of the "marvellous" associated with Cocteau.

George Auric composed one of his most haunting and atmospheric scores for the film. Henri Alékan achieved that photographic tone that Cocteau sought: "the soft gleam of hand-polished old silver."

Interpretation of the film is varied and interesting. Critic Clément Borgal defines the Beast's precious treasure in his pavilion, "the source of his power," as "the treasure of childhood. If jealously preserved, it can enrich our interior worlds and thus become an inexhaustible source of poetry." Dr. Joseph L. Henderson interprets the myth in a Jungian analysis: Beauty undergoes an "initiation" and must learn "to come to terms with the erotic animal side of her nature [the Beast]. . . ." in order to achieve "a true relationship with a man."

In such a realistic medium as the cinema Jean Cocteau accomplished the miraculous. The sumptuous and dream-like *Beauty and the Beast* remains one of the great screen fantasies of all time.

(Opposite page) In his garden the Beast (Jean Marais) questions Beauty (Josette Day): Has a young man asked to marry her and was he handsome?

DEVIL IN
THE FLESH

(Le Diable au Corps)

TRANSCONTINENTAL FILMS   1947

CREDITS

Screenplay: Jean Aurenche and Pierre Bost, based on the novel by Raymond Radiguet (1923), published in New York, (1932); *Director:* Claude Autant-Lara; *Photographer:* Michel Kelber; *Assistant Director:* Ghislaine Autant-Lara; *Editor:* Madeleine Gug; *Music:* René Cloërec; *Running Time:* 110 minutes; *Paris Premiere:* September 12, 1947; *New York Premiere:* May 9, 1949.

CAST

Marthe Grangier: Micheline Presle; *François Jaubert:* Gérard Philipe; *M. Jaubert:* Jean Debucourt; *Mme. Grangier:* Denise Grey; *M. Marin:* Pierre Palau; *Jacques Lacombe:* Jean Varas; *Mme. Marin:* Jeanne Pérez; *Anselme:* Charles Vissières; *Mme. Jaubert:* Germaine Ledoyen; *Doctor:* Maurice Lagrenee; *Headwaiter:* Richard Francoeur; *Soldier in Bar:* Jacques Tati.

BACKGROUND

Claude Autant-Lara was born on August 5, 1903, in Luzarches (Seine-et-Oise) to an architect father and an actress mother. He studied art and at the age of sixteen was painting sets for Marcel L'Herbier's films. He designed costumes and sets for L'Herbier and Renoir; directed an avant-garde short, *Fait-Divers* (1923); and was an assistant director for René Clair.

In 1930 he went to Hollywood for a few years to direct French versions of American films and, on

Portrait of a confused and anguished adolescent: Gérard Philipe incarnating the Radiguet hero, François Jaubert, a role which made him an international star.

returning to France, created a number of shorts and documentaries. Opportunity came with the exodus of established directors during the Occupation. *Douce* (1943) signalled a new director of significance.

Always a critic of conventional morality, after the war Autant-Lara proposed to film *Devil in the Flesh*, the brilliant and precocious first novel of Raymond Radiguet (1903-23)* ("The work of a boy who has lived through many of the experiences of manhood"—Aldous Huxley) completed when the youth was eighteen. In attacking accepted values of the army and patriotism, Radiguet's novel provoked a scandal and was a huge success. The novel was mistakenly considered autobiographical.

Although there were some necessary changes to tighten the leisurely-paced narrative and stress the dramatic incident at the expense of the analytic digression, adapters Jean Aurenche and Pierre Bost—who prepared many screenplays for Autant-Lara—succeeded in not violating the spirit of the novel. Rendered faithfully was the hurt and confu-

*Contrary to certain published accounts of his "suicide" in this country, Radiguet died of typhoid fever on December 12, 1923.

sion of a "boy-man" suffering from the throes of an intense first love who could declare in the novel: "I exhausted my nervous energy swinging between cowardice and boldness, suffering the innumerable contradictions inherent in the situation of a boy of my age attempting to come to grips with a man's adventure."

The use of flashbacks which correspond to the first person narration adds momentum to the chronologically structured and slowly paced novel. The characters in the film are made more sympathetic than in the novel. François is now less offensively egotistic and arrogant than immature and vulnerable; Marthe appears less selfish by her volunteer hospital work (which was not in the novel).

The director wanted Gérard Philipe to play François. The scrupulous actor hesitated at first, thinking that, at twenty-four, he was too old for the part. Established screen actress Micheline Presle made a perfect co-star. The film was shot from August 26 through December 21, 1946 at the Neuilly and Boulogne studios. A small provincial town was authentically recreated down to its cob-

bled streets for the film. Exteriors were the banks of the Marne, the Charenton bridge, and the railway station at La Varenne-Chennevrières.

"It was not an easy film to make," Autant-Lara commented, "but we claim the merit of handling this story without flinching." Aurenche and Bost observed "it is this fragrance of temporariness, this 'sand castle which the tide will carry away,' which gives this love story its poignant character." *Devil in the Flesh* would prove to be a sensational triumph.

SYNOPSIS

At the end of WWI François (Gérard Philipe), a morose adolescent, enters the deserted apartment of his dead mistress in a Parisian suburb and retraces their meeting:

Marthe (Micheline Presle) comes to the hospital next to François' school to do volunteer work. Not yet seventeen, he's attracted to the older woman immediately and soon cuts class to spend the day with her in Paris. He learns she's engaged to marry a soldier, Jacques (Jean Varas), but she's not in love

François (Gérard Philipe) cuts classes and sells his stamp collection so he can spend the day in Paris with Marthe (Micheline Presle).

Marthe (Micheline Presle) tends a rain-soaked François (Gérard Philipe) during their first night together.

with him. A jealous François follows Marthe and the soldier, who is on an overnight pass, to their new apartment where the couple spend the night.

François' understanding father (Jean Debucourt) consoles his suicide-contemplating son; he had intercepted Marthe's note arranging a rendezvous for that night. They decide to head to the boat landing and spot Marthe waiting for him but the confused youth, feeling betrayed and hurt, begs his father to send him away for a while.

During the requiem mass for Marthe, François recalls their affair:

After a six-month interval they meet again. Now married, Marthe still finds François attractive and invites him to visit her the next evening. . . . Soon she shows him Jacques' letters complaining of her indifference to him and tells François that had he kept their rendezvous she wouldn't have married. Marthe is aware that their relationship is intense, but transient.

She becomes pregnant. When Jacques requests Marthe visit him at his camp, François, full of bravado, offers to accompany her and tell him everything, but the next day he loses courage and pleads the excuse of school. A dejected Marthe leaves alone.

As the service concludes, François relives their separation:

The youth discovers that a frail Marthe is being sent by her stern mother (Denise Grey) to spend her confinement in the country where no one

knows about the scandal. He finds her in a train compartment.

Later, on the verge of collapse, Marthe reveals her profound love for the irresponsible and callow but still desirable youth. Her mother is summoned but blocks François from accompanying them to the hospital. At home, a dying Marthe shouts "François!" but the mother tells Jacques, who has returned, that that's the name of his child.

Outside the church François' sense of loss is drowned in the joyful celebration of the armistice.

COMMENTARY

Devil in the Flesh was selected by the government to represent French cinema at Brussels' first World Film Festival in 1947. It won the International Critics prize and Gérard Philipe was voted best actor. However, during the screening the French Ambassador to Belgium walked out—a gesture perceived as an insult by the director and the movie people present. After twenty-four years the literary scandal would be repeated as a cinematic scandal.

A member of the Bordeaux City Council unsuccessfully petitioned the government to revoke the film's license "in the name of French veterans of this war and the last. . . ." The idea that a soldier fighting at the front should be deceived in a more or less sympathetic manner, rather than the sexual

Oblivious to the air raid siren, François (Gérard Philipe) shares an intimate dance with Marthe (Micheline Presle).

candor of the film, was what was deeply offensive to many people.

Although boycotted by "moral action" groups, the film was shown simultaneously in three first-run houses in Paris to record business and became an international hit: Sweden, Hungary, Poland, Argentina, Mexico, etc.

Banned in Canada and by the New York State Censors, it was finally approved for America after an appeal and a slight cut. The Legion of Decency condemned it, naturally ("a sordid and suggestive atmosphere pervades the film"), but it went on to a successful career here.

The critics extolled Gérard Philipe's performance: "He has the intuitive genius which makes great actors by the simplest means, the gift of being able to identify one's self with the screen character by a sort of natural adhesion. His acting is as pure as a tear." Strikingly handsome with a haunting, tragic face, Gérard Philipe caught the turmoil of adolescence with great emotional urgency and sincerity. This role launched the gifted actor into

In the midst of rumors of an armistice, François (Gérard Philipe) tries to comfort an exhausted Marthe (Micheline Presle) at the onset of her labor pains.

international stardom; until his early death in 1959 he was *the* great romantic star of his generation. *Devil in the Flesh* remains his most memorable screen appearance and Micheline Presle's as well. Thin-boned, with delicate features, hers was an exquisite, feminine beauty. Denise Grey's severe Mme. Grangier and Jean Debucourt's kindly M. Jaubert lent strong support.

Marthe's death is revealed at the outset, under-cutting needless suspense, and establishes an elegiac tone which is sustained throughout, aided by Michel Kelber's somber lighting effects and Max Douy's atmospheric sets.

Autant-Lara's direction is precise and authoritative. One remembers that wonderful dissolve at the start of the first flashback with Marthe appearing slowly in her bedroom mirror while church bells come to a dissonant halt. François is constantly seen behind fences and grills which underline his sense of imprisonment and his position as outsider. There are also many skillful parallel shots and scenes and a frequent use of close-ups which create a sense of intimacy.

For all its controversy, the film does not operate in a moral vacuum. The lovers, who are not without guilt feelings—after all, Jacques is presented as a decent husband—have sufficient failings to create some distance in the audience to reflect on their behavior, yet have abundant appeal and humanity to involve us powerfully in their plight. Done without sentimentality, with exquisite taste and delicacy, *Devil in the Flesh* holds up after many years as a lyrical, spellbinding film.

Autant-Lara went on to be a prolific filmmaker producing films of varying quality, none of which has brought him the international acclaim or the controversy of *Devil in the Flesh,* which remains his masterpiece.

LES ENFANTS TERRIBLES

MELVILLE PRODUCTIONS   1950

CREDITS

Adaptation: Jean-Pierre Melville and Jean Cocteau based on the latter's novel (1929), published in New York as *The Holy Terrors* (1957); *Dialogue:* Jean Cocteau; *Director:* Jean-Pierre Melville; *Photographer:* Henri Decaë; *Assistant Directors:* Claude Pinoteau, Jacques Guymont, Michel Drach, and Serge Bourguignon; *Editor:* Monique Bonnot; *Music:* Bach's Arrangement in A Minor for Four Pianos of Vivaldi's Concerto in B Minor for Four Violins, Opus 3; and Vivaldi's Concerto Grosso in A Minor; *Song:* "Were You Smiling at Me?"—words and music by Melvyn Martin; *Running Time:* 107 minutes; *Paris Premiere:* March 29, 1950; *New York Premiere:* July 28, 1952; *16 mm. Rental Source:* Cinema 5.

CAST

Elisabeth: Nicole Stéphane; *Paul:* Edouard Dermit; *Gérard:* Jacques Bernard; *Dargélos/Agathe:* Renée Cosima; *Gérard's Uncle:* Roger Gaillard; *Michael:* Melvyn Martin; *The Doctor:* Maurice Revel; *Mariette:* Adeline Aucoc; *The Mother:* Maria Cyliakus; *Head-Master:* Jean-Marie Robain; *Vice-Principal:* Emile Mathis; *Narrator:* Voice of Jean Cocteau.

BACKGROUND

Jean-Pierre Melville was born in Paris on October 20, 1917. (His family name was Grumbach but he changed it out of deep admiration for his favorite American novelist, Herman Melville.) Film was a lifelong obsession with him. He made amateur films in childhood and was heavily influenced by

the American cinema of the 1930's. During WWII he served with the British army, then with the Free French forces. Demobilized, unable to gain entry into French film companies, Melville boldly decided to set up his own production company and made a short with raw stock bought on the black market, *Vingt Quatre Heures de la Vie d'un Clown (Twenty-Four Hours in the Life of a Clown)* (1946).

In 1947, on a shoestring budget, without permission of the author, and with no arrangement for distribution, Melville made his first feature, *Le Silence de la Mer (The Silence of the Sea)*, based on the celebrated novel of Vercours which had circulated clandestinely during the Resistance. Impressed, as he said, with Melville's "free-lance style" and "improvised '16 mm' air," Jean Cocteau decided to let the director film his most important and popular novel, *Les Enfants Terribles*. This influential and disturbing book, written by Cocteau in a clinic after a cure for opium addiction, had a profound impact

Gérard (Jacques Bernard), left, brings news of Dargelos's expulsion from school to Paul (Edouard Dermit), right, and his sister Elisabeth (Nicole Stéphane).

upon the youth of the 1930's, including Jean-Pierre Melville, with its brilliant and compelling depiction of the intense, private world of arrested adolescence cut off from encroaching adult values.

The action of the novel, which occurs over a period of five years, is much condensed. Melville at first wanted to place the film in the 1925 period; Cocteau preferred to give it a contemporary setting. Nicole Stéphane, the gifted young actress who had appeared in Melville's first feature, was chosen to play the demanding role of Elisabeth. Cocteau insisted that his artist protégé Edouard Dermit play Paul, a role which the poet hoped would launch him as another Jean Marais.

Les Enfants Terribles was filmed between November 1949 and January 1950. With no budget for the vast sets, the film had to be shot in actual settings. Melville rented a dingy apartment where most of the early domestic scenes were filmed. Interiors were also shot at the Théâtre Pigalle with its re-

In a quiet moment, Elisabeth (Nichole Stéphane) tries to lead Paul (Edouard Dermit) into playing the Game.

markable movable stages as well as the director's own Studios Jenner in Paris; exteriors were Paris, Montmorency, and Ermenonville. While Melville was ill, Cocteau shot the shoplifting sequence—supposedly a summer beach scene—in wintertime Montmorency. The two directors can be spotted walking in the dining car scene while the camera tracks to the vacationers' table. A critic was to declare: "There isn't a single gaiter-button missing" and Cocteau said of the film: "Of all my writings which have been filmed, I feel it is the most faithfully presented."

Individual and uncompromising, *Les Enfants Terribles* is an unusual, off-beat film. Melville confessed he made it "essentially to please myself, without much thought about the public." Over the years the film has developed a cult status.

SYNOPSIS

During a snow ball fight near his Lycée, Paul (Edouard Dermit) is hit severely in the mouth and chest by missiles thrown by the school tough, Dargélos (Renée Cosima), whom he idolizes. A loyal friend Gérard (Jacques Bernard) brings the wounded youth home to Paul's sister Elisabeth (Nicole Stéphane), who has her hands full caring for their invalid mother (Maria Cyliakus).

Brother and sister—in their late adolescence—unselfconsciously share the same bedroom full of magical objects and adorned with many photo-

123

A jealous Paul (Edouard Dermit) rages at his sister Elisabeth (Nicole Stéphane) and Agathe (Renée Cosima) for alleged sexual misconduct, while Gérard (Jacques Bernard) defends them. ("Suicide is a mortal sin" is inscribed on the mirror).

graphs. They live as if they were, as Cocteau relates, "twin halves of a single body." Frequently they "go away"—play the Game wherein they lose themselves in fantastic reveries.

The kindly doctor (Maurice Revel) orders a long rest for Paul; Gérard later reports on the expulsion of Dargélos from school. The spoiled and selfish Paul and Elisabeth bicker constantly but, underneath, the sister worships her brother to a degree bordering on incest.

Gérard comes to adore Elisabeth secretly but her brusque manner intimidates him. The mother dies and the children continue their intense, hermetic existence which is briefly interrupted by a seaside vacation sponsored by Gérard's uncle (Roger Gaillard).

Gérard is attached to the curious ménage. A bored Elisabeth gets a job as a model and meets Agathe (Renée Cosima). Paul finds himself strangely drawn to the shy, docile girl who bears an uncanny resemblance to Dargélos. Agathe joins the "gypsy camp" and falls in love with Paul.

Elisabeth quietly dates Michael (Melvyn Martin), a fabulously wealthy American. At first Paul is jealous and makes nasty accusations before he's reconciled to their marriage. Michael dies alone in a car accident before his honeymoon and the now rich widow is installed in a huge town house in which the original quartet reassemble.

It is a hothouse of repressed emotions: Paul and Agathe for each other; Elisabeth for Paul and Gérard for Elisabeth. Finally Agathe declares her hopeless love for Paul—she fears he hates her—to Elisabeth who must act quickly to thwart it. When she learns that Paul is dying of love for Agathe and has sent a letter to her, she offers to act as go-between—and promptly destroys the letter. Elisabeth lies to Paul that Agathe and Gérard love each other, then deviously pushes the unwitting couple toward marriage.

The honeymooning pair return later and Gérard unknowingly gives Paul a poisonous plant, a gift from Dargélos whom he had met. A weakened and miserable Paul at last takes Dargélos's poison. Agathe and Paul confront each other and discover the sister's treachery. A frantic Elisabeth confesses that she was jealous and couldn't bear to let Agathe take him away from her.

Elisabeth turns Paul on to a final "Game" and then, as he succumbs, she positions a revolver next to her temple and fires.

COMMENTARY

Cocteau reported to his English translator that *Les Enfants Terribles* was "torn to pieces by completely ignorant critics" and added "but the trees are in flower, and the world still turns accompanied by

124

flying saucers. . . ." The film was called *The Strange Ones* in its initial release in the United States.

If Renée Cosima is too soft to convey the rugged masculinity of Dargélos and Edouard Dermit is too athletic to convince us of the delicate nature of Paul, there can be no quarrel with the choice of Nicole Stéphane as Elisabeth, a triumph of casting. Imperious, despotic, with a presence which dominates the film, she gives what amounts to a legendary performance. "The slightest gesture of Nicole Stéphane took on a terrifying power of those of Electra," Cocteau said. When she sets about breaking up the budding romance between Paul and Agathe she is a hypnotic, captivating, avenging fury.

Cocteau's lifelong obsessions with fate, death, love and narcissism are successfully conveyed. The Room, resplendent with the strange trophies of the adolescents, admirably evokes that sense of the marvellous so prominent in Cocteau's aesthetics.

Jean Cocteau narrates the film in his inimitable, spellbinding manner. Melville said he used his voice "because I thought it was marvellous. Such a beautiful voice deserves to be preserved." The narration acts like a Greek chorus commenting on the events and bestowing a mythic dimension to the film.

It was a stroke of genius on Melville's part to hit upon the Bach-Vivaldi score for background music which stunningly suggests, in Cocteau's words, "the step of destiny which goes now slowly now swiftly up the stairs." The use of classical music was haunting and innovative. What an interesting contrast between Michael's ordinary ballad and the fiery baroque music which describes the fated brother and sister.

Melville's skillful and fluid direction permits us to eavesdrop on a rarefied, bizarre world. When Elisabeth shoots herself and falls back knocking over the screens as the camera mounts for a long shot, we come to the powerful ending of a riveting and unique film. Cocteau's special poetry is captured and faithfully rendered by an enormously talented director who proceeded to go his independent way making very interesting and very personal films.

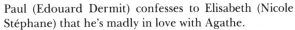

Paul (Edouard Dermit) confesses to Elisabeth (Nicole Stéphane) that he's madly in love with Agathe.

In a strange foreboding dream sequence, Elisabeth (Nicole Stéphane) comes across the dead body of Paul (Edouard Dermit) on a billiard table atop a hill.

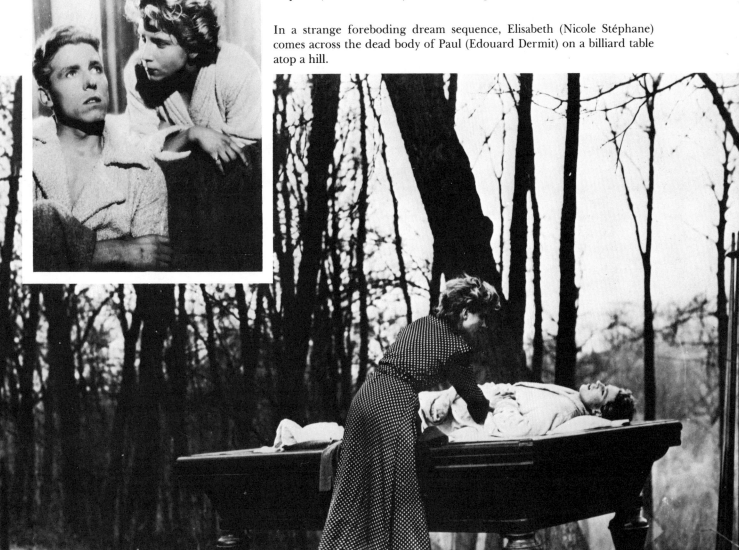

126   Orpheus (Jean Marais), on the right, follows the mysterious Princess
(Maria Casarès) and her motorcyclist aides bearing the body of Cégeste
(Edouard Dermit) into the chalet.

ORPHEUS

(Orphée)

PRODUCTIONS ANDRÉ PAULVÉ/LES
FILMS DU PALAIS-ROYAL   1950

CREDITS

Screenplay: Jean Cocteau (a major reworking of his 1926 play); *Director:* Jean Cocteau; *Photographer:* Nicholas Hayer; *Assistant Directors:* Claude Pinoteau, Claude Clément; *Editor:* Jacqueline Sadoul; *Music:* Georges Auric, also themes from Gluck's opera *Orfeo ed Euridice* (1762); *Running Time:* 112 minutes; *Paris Premiere:* October 3, 1950; *New York Premiere:* November 29, 1950; *16 mm. Rental Source:* Janus.

CAST

Orpheus: Jean Marais; *The Princess:* Maria Casarès; *Eurydice:* Marie Déa; *Heurtebise:* François Périer; *Aglaonice:* Juliette Gréco; *Cégeste:* Edouard Dermit; *Friend in Café:* Henri Crémieux; *Police Commissioner:* Pierre Bertin; *Writer:* Roger Blin; *Judge:* Jacques Varennes; *Judge:* André Carnège; *Judge:* René Worms; *A Bacchante:* Renée Cosima; *Hotel Manager:* Jean-Pierre Melville; *Narrator:* Voice of Jean Cocteau.

BACKGROUND

After *Beauty and the Beast,* Jean Cocteau directed two films drawn from his plays: *The Eagle With Two Heads (L'Aigle à Deux Têtes),* (1947, play 1946), both versions starring Edwige Feuillère and Jean Marais, and *Les Parents Terribles* (1948, play 1938), both versions starring Jean Marais, before embarking on his extraordinary treatment of the Orpheus legend.

Orpheus, for Cocteau, was *the* archetypal poet

Orpheus (Jean Marais) "in pursuit of the unknown" is obsessed with the broadcasts over the car radio and ignores his wife Eurydice (Marie Déa) and the advice of Heurtebise (François Périer), left: "Your voice is the best one. Be happy with your voice."

and his own mythic prototype. His *Orphée,* a one-act play which premiered at the Théâtre des Arts in Paris on June 15, 1926, was an imaginative dramatization of the creative process of a poet. Later Cocteau realized the cinematic potential of this myth: "I wanted to express something that could not be expressed through any other medium but the cinema."

Through his identification with Orpheus Cocteau would do more than retell the legend, he would depict in the film his personal vision of the poet's role in society as well as his preoccupations with death and eternity.

Cocteau "opened up" his play to take advantage of the screen's possibilities for spectacle, as in the stunning depiction of the Zone ("the No Man's Land between life and death," as Cocteau wrote.) The locale for the Zone was the ruins of the Saint-Cyr barracks (near Versailles) which were bombed during the war.

The mythic characters in the play are reduced to a more human and accessible scale: Death is now the Princess, a functionary of Death; Orpheus is no longer a high priest but a celebrated poet; Heurtebise is an angel no more but a newly dead young man assigned to be a chauffeur. Characterization is enriched: the abstract figure of Death in the play

127

"Mirrors are the doors through which Death comes and goes": Orpheus (Jean Marais) follows Heurtebise (François Périer) through the bedroom mirrors into "The Zone."

becomes the highly individualized Princess. Orpheus's stature is increased and made more heroic.

The oracular horse is replaced by a very physical, luxurious Rolls Royce with its alluring radio transmitting cryptic messages. (Cocteau claims he was inspired by the British broadcasts to France during the Occupation.) Said the poet: "The closer one approaches to mystery, the more important it becomes to remain a realist."

The film project was turned down by producers as "incomprehensible" and definitely uncommercial. A determined Cocteau had to organize a small company, experience difficulty in raising capital, and engage a cast willing to work for delayed payment. His energy and enthusiasm overcame every obstacle. At one time Jean-Pierre Aumont and Maria Montez were considered for the parts of Orpheus and the Princess—Cocteau even envisioned Garbo and Marlene Dietrich for this role—and Gérard Philipe for Heurtebise before the roles went respectively to Jean Marais, Maria Casarès, and François Périer.

*In André Fraigneau's interview with the director, published in New York in 1954 as *Cocteau on the Film* (*Jean Cocteau: Entretiens autour du Cinématographe recueillis par André Fraigneau*, Paris, 1951), Cocteau explains how he achieved his special effects.

After his death, Orpheus (Jean Marais) and Heurtebise (François Périer) struggle in their difficult passage through the Zone. (Jean Cocteau is the old "woman" huddled in the window.)

Orpheus was shot between September 12 and November 16, 1949. Other exteriors, besides Saint-Cyr, were Paris and the Vallée de Chevreuse. Interiors were done at the Studio Francoeur. The trick shots (the famous scene of Orpheus walking into his bedroom mirror for instance) are not disconcertingly ostentatious but organic and vital to the film.*

In the hands of a lesser artist *Orpheus* could be arty, pretentious, and self-indulgent. It is to Cocteau's credit that *Orpheus*, which he described as "a detective film, bathed on one side in myth, and on the other in the supernatural," avoids these pitfalls and succeeds in being one of the most original and striking films ever made.

SYNOPSIS

Orpheus (Jean Marais) is a famous poet married to Eurydice (Marie Déa). At the Café des Poètes he witnesses a young, inebriated poet, Cégeste (Edouard Dermit), get run over by sinister motorcyclists after a disturbance. Cégeste's patroness, the elegant Princess (Maria Casarès), orders Orpheus to come along as witness. To Orpheus's surprise they do not drive to a hospital but to a strange chalet.

Inside, Cégeste is "resurrected" and pressed into service for the Princess. Orpheus is astounded to see the group exit by passing through a mirror. When he comes to, he finds the chauffeur Heurtebise (François Périer) and the Princess's Rolls Royce at his disposal. Back home, he ignores his wife and spends his time studying the mysterious car radio messages (actually fragments broadcast by Cégeste to draw him to the Princess). Heurtebise falls in love with Eurydice and warns Orpheus to listen only to his own voice. The Princess appears nightly to watch Orpheus in his sleep.

Deeply hurt by her husband's indifferent behavior, especially since she's pregnant, Eurydice leaves to seek advice from Aglaonice (Juliette Gréco), leader of a group of women known as the Bacchantes, only to be killed by the motorcyclists. The Princess appears to prepare Eurydice for the next world and Heurtebise accuses her of acting without orders to have Orpheus to herself.

Orpheus agrees to journey with Heurtebise, both to rejoin Eurydice and to encounter the Princess with whom he's obsessed. By means of the Princess's gloves which she left behind, Orpheus passes though the mirrors into the Zone. At the chalet, he hears the Princess confess her love for him during an interrogation. A tribunal grants the

"The Death of the Poet must sacrifice herself to make him immortal": The Princess (Maria Casarès) orders Cégeste (Edouard Dermit) and Heurtebise (François Périer) to "kill" Orpheus (Jean Marais) to enable him to return to life and his poetry.

Princess provisional freedom and returns Eurydice to life on condition that Orpheus never looks at her again. Tensions mount in his household until he loses her by accidently peering into the car's rear-view mirror.

Accusing Orpheus of killing Cégeste to steal his poems, Aglaonice rouses a frenzied mob who attack and kill him. Heurtebise escorts him through the Zone. The Princess makes a heroic act of sacrifice by ordering Orpheus to be symbolically "strangled" and thus returned to life and immortality through pursuing his destiny as a Poet. She and Heurtebise are arrested for their unauthorized actions while, back in life, in their "muddy waters" to cite Cocteau's phrase, Orpheus and Eurydice are joyfully reconciled.

COMMENTARY

Orpheus was a success and won an International Criticis Award at the 1950 Venice Film Festival. Cocteau's direction is controlled and brilliant. Jean Marais is convincing and ideally cast as the poet. Maria Casarés is splendid in her best screen role as the icily efficient Princess, "full of contained fire" (critic René Gilson). Marie Déa as the devoted Eurydice and François Périer as the sensitive Heurtebise are both excellent. Credit should be given to Nicolas Hayer's superb photography, Georges Auric's evocative score, and Marcel Escoffier's elegant costumes.

"I have had a thousand exegeses," Cocteau wrote, "from all the universities of the world" concerning the interpretation of *Orpheus,* including critic Jean-Jacques Kihm's which finds parallels between the film and the *Tibetan Book of the Dead.* It is safer to see the film as a meditation upon poetry rather than death.* Two major themes emerge from the film: the poet must undergo many types of "death" in order to achieve immortality through his art and he must listen to his own voice which comes from his "nocturnal factory." "Everything starts to go wrong when Orpheus ignores his own messages and agrees to accept messages coming from outside," Cocteau wrote.

One could also see the film as autobiography (the Bacchantes representing Cocteau's career-long conflict with the Surrealists etc.) "Even those who see it [*Orpheus*] without understanding it," Cocteau wrote, "keep pictures from it in their minds and think about it. This is what matters."

Orpheus is a film of daring, a visually stunning and hypnotic film, full of the sense of the marvelous, which attains a tragic splendor. It is, for me, Cocteau's cinema masterpiece.

François Truffaut donated earnings from *The Four Hundred Blows* to help the director realize what was to be his final film, *The Testament of Orpheus (Le Testament d'Orphée)* 1960. Jean Cocteau, best known outside of France for his films, died at his country house at Milly-la-Forêt, near Fontainebleau, on October 11, 1963.*

When Cocteau was formally admitted to the Académie Française on October 20, 1955, André Maurois said: "The art of the screen tempted you. You have succeeded in it, and it is one of the domains to which your contribution has been incomparable. You were one of the first writers to comprehend that cinematography, in addition to fiction and the theatre, can engender works of art ... *The Blood of a Poet, Beauty and the Beast, The Eternal Return, Orpheus* are, and will remain, classics in every country of the world. . . ."

---

*For a useful analysis see *Jean Cocteau and His Films of Orphic Identity* by Arthur B. Evans (1977).

Cocteau, Francis Steegmuller's admirable biography, was published in 1970.

DIARY OF A COUNTRY PRIEST

(Le Journal d'un Curé de Campagne)

U.G.C. (UNION GÉNÉRALE
CINÉMATOGRAPHIQUE)   1951

CREDITS

Screenplay: Robert Bresson, based on the novel by Georges Bernanos (1936), published in New York, 1937; *Director:* Robert Bresson; *Photographer:* Léonce-Henry Burel; *Assistant Director:* Guy Lefranc; *Editor:* Paulette Robert; *Music:* Jean-Jacques Grünenwald; *Running Time:* 120 minutes; *Paris Premiere:* February 7, 1951; *New York Premiere:* April 5, 1954; *16 mm. Rental Source:* Audio Brandon.

CAST

The Priest of Ambricourt: Claude Laydu; *The Count:* Jean Riveyre; *The Priest of Torcy:* André Guibert; *Louise:* Nicole Maurey; *Chantal:* Nicole Ladmiral; *The Countess:* Marie-Monique Arkell; *Séraphita:* Martine Lemaire; *Dr. Delbende:* Antoine Balpêtré; *Oliver:* Jean Danet; *The Canon:* Gaston Séverin; *Housekeeper:* Yvette Etiévant; *Louis Dufréty:* Bernard Hubrenne.

BACKGROUND

Robert Bresson was born on September 25, 1907, in Bromont-Lamothe (Puy-de-Dôme). At the Lycée Lakanal in Paris he studied classical languages and philosophy before interesting himself first in painting, then later in cinema. In 1939 he made a comedy of medium length, *Les Affaires Publiques,* of which no copy survives.

The priest (Claude Laydu) learns about his illness from the troubled Dr. Delbende (Antoine Balpêtré) soon to take his life. The downcast eyes are a Bresson trademark.

In 1943 Bresson made an impressive début with his first feature, *Les Anges du Péché.* In 1945 appeared his remarkable *Les Dames du Bois de Boulogne* with Maria Casarès. In spite of his growing critical recognition, the director had to wait five years—a projected life of St. Ignatius de Loyola went unrealized—before he could make his next film, an adaptation of the celebrated novel by Georges Bernanos, *The Diary of a Country Priest,* which was awarded the Grand Prix du Roman by the French Academy and was regarded as the author's masterpiece.

Although Bernanos was eager to have his acclaimed novel filmed he rejected two prior treatments, one prepared by Jean Aurenche and Pierre Bost and another by Fr. Raymond Brückberger, feeling the liberties taken tended to falsify the work. It was Bresson's faithful yet orthodox treatment which won the approval of the author's literary executor—Bernanos died in 1948.

Bresson maintained the spirit of the work and its journal structure. Nothing was added; most of the dialogue in the film comes from the book. Cut were the long theological debates with the priest from Torcy and the latter's excessive fulminations against existing conditions. "I'm eliminating any-

The powerful confrontation scene: The priest (Claude Laydu) attempts to reconcile the embittered Countess (Marie-Monique Arkell) to God.

Chantal (Nicole Ladmiral) pours out her bitterness to the priest (Claude Laydu) after her mother's death.

thing which may distract from the interior drama," Bresson said.

The director chose to work with unknowns—Balpêtré and Mme. Arkell were the only professional actors used—and interviewed a great many actors for the lead (non-believers were disqualified) before selecting young Belgian-born Swiss Claude Laydu (born 1927), who seemed to the director "to incarnate with simplicity and truth the 'saint' of Bernanos." Bresson coached him for over a year and even had him live in a monastery for a period so that his gestures and mannerisms would appear authentic. Laydu identified with the role completely and even dieted to accentuate the priest's ascetic look. His clothing was genuine—cassock and boots lent by priests.

After many delays in obtaining the necessary financing, the film was shot between March and May of 1950 along the north coast of Pas de Calais and in the village of Hesdin. A perfectionist, Bresson subjected his cast to interminable rehearsals and shot a scene many times to achieve the correct one.

The producers demanded that the original version of 160 minutes be shortened and the director cut one-fourth of it. Bresson's film proved to be a critical triumph and earned him an international reputation.

SYNOPSIS

An unnamed, introverted young priest (Claude Laydu), dedicated but in frail health, comes to his first parish, the small village of Ambricourt (Pas de Calais) whose inhabitants are suspicious and chiefly indifferent to religion. The priest is drawn into the anguished world of the neighboring chateau inhabited by a withdrawn Countess (Marie-Monique Arkell) embittered over the loss of her son, the cold and reserved Count (Jean Riveyre), and his mistress Louise (Nicole Maurey), who is the governess of the sullen and unhappy daughter Chantal (Nicole Ladmiral).

Throughout the film the priest confides his discouragement and feelings of failure to his journal. Forced to subsist on dry bread and wine—the only fare his sick stomach can tolerate—the priest is mocked as an alcoholic by the villagers. His only friend is the older and far more practical priest of Torcy (André Guibert), who comes to see the youth as a "prisoner of the Holy Agony."

In a powerful confrontation scene, the priest manages to break down the Countess's wall of

The solicitious priest from Torcy (André Guibert) expresses concern about the health and suffering of the young priest from Ambricourt (Claude Laydu).

hatred toward God and unloosen her pent-up emotions. He is able to bring her that peace which he himself does not possess. She dies during the night and Chantal spitefully causes trouble by blaming her mother's death on him.

The weakened priest collapses on his rounds and must quit his parish to seek medical care. In Lille he learns that he's dying of stomach cancer and expires at the shabby apartment of his ex-priest friend Louis Dufréty (Bernard Hubrenne).

Louis writes an account of the priest's passing for the Torcy priest. The dying priest had asked Louis for absolution and the scrupulous ex-priest hesitated. "What does that matter?" the priest said and then uttered his magnificent last words from St. Thérèse of Lisieux, "All is grace."

COMMENTARY

Diary of a Country Priest was received with much critical acclaim. "This new Bresson film . . . ," novelist Julien Green observed, "proves . . . that a work entirely of the interior life can pass to the screen without the slightest concession. It took courage to give us a film of a purity so uncompromising." The film won the Prix Louis Delluc as the most distinguished French film of 1950; it was awarded the Grand Prix du Cinéma Français (1951); and at the Venice Film Festival (1951) it received an International Prize and shared with Kurosawa's *Rashomon* the Italian Critics Prize, while Léonce-Henry Burel's camerawork was voted "Best Photography."

Since it is so highly unconventional, Bresson's film style should be discussed. The director carefully differentiates between "cinema," the traditional approach which he defines as "photographed theater" restricted to the display of the external aspects of men and women, and "cinematography," which attempts to reveal the character's hidden, inner spirit. To that end, actors whose gestures and speech patterns are too theater-oriented for him ("acting is for the theatre") are replaced with "models," non-actors ("precious raw material") carefully trained not to display emotion or thought, "mechanized externally" so that involuntarily they may reveal "the enigma peculiar to each living creature."

Bresson wrote, "For me, the cinema is an exploration within" and to reach his goals he must "express things with a minimum of means, showing

133

The priest (Claude Laydu) records in his journal the devastating news concerning his terminal illness.

By the use of many close-ups without either establishing shots or reaction shots vis-à-vis the other characters, we are locked intimately in the priest's world and are forced to accompany him without interruption through his painful inward journey. The scenes are brief with fade-outs for transition.

Bresson makes frequent use of "ellipsis," reducing a scene to its absolutely essential minimum. The priest visits a specialist in Lille to have his illness diagnosed. What could have been a standard, high-powered revelation scene in the doctor's office is replaced with one terse, disturbing shot of the doctor's door opening and the priest leaving with a look of doom on his face. It is as shattering as it is economical.

Claude Laydu was perfect as the tragic priest and dominates the film in a quiet, subtle, and understated way. Typical of Bresson's manner, the actors frequently address each other with downcast eyes and neutral voices. "What we are asked to look for on their faces," observed critic André Bazin, "is not for some fleeting reflection of the words but for an uninterrupted condition of soul, the outward revelation of an interior destiny."

Avoiding a traditional dramatic development leading to a climax, Bresson relies on the journal—the pages on the screen, the off-screen narration of portions of it, and the recreation of episodes from it as remembered incidents in the film—to both convey the priest's internal conflicts and self-awareness and act as a unifying device for the film.

Both Burel's harsh, autumn-evoking photography and Grünenwald's restrained and sensitive music contribute much to the mood of the film.

Those who see the central character as simply a doomed, passive victim or perhaps as a scapegoat figure atoning for the sins of his parish miss the main point that, throughout the "dark night of the soul," beset with doubts and despair, the priest has somehow triumphantly managed to surrender his will to God's. What we have here is actually the process toward sainthood; the saint is at all times believable, convincing, and very much human. *Diary of a Country Priest* is a challenging, uncompromising masterpiece, as intense as it is profound. With this film Bresson became the most successful cinematic explorer of the inner spiritual state since Carl Dreyer.

nothing that is not absolutely essential." Thus, he suppresses plot; avoids presenting motivation according to the accepted psychological theories; curtails camera movement; eschews excessive, ornate dialogue; ignores distracting photographic effects, décor, and an overreliance on music.

LE PLAISIR

STERA FILMS/C.C.F.C. COMPAGNIE
COMMERCIALE FRANÇAISE
CINÉMATOGRAPHIQUE   1952

CREDITS

Adaptation: Jacques Natanson and Max Ophüls from three stories by Guy de Maupassant, "The Mask" ("Le Masque" 1889), "The Model"* ("Le Modèle" 1883), and "The House of Madame Tellier" ("La Maison Tellier" 1881); *Dialogue:* Jacques Natanson; *Director:* Max Ophüls; *Photographers:* Christian Matras ("The Mask" and "The House of Madame Tellier") and Philippe Agostini ("The Model"); *Assistant Directors:* Tony Aboyantz and Jean Valère; *Editor:* Léonide Azar; *Music:* Joe Hajos and Maurice Yvain, based on themes of Offenbach;

*A.k.a. "The Artist's Wife"

Running Time: 95 minutes; *Paris Premiere:* February 29, 1952; *New York Premiere:* May 19, 1954; *16 mm. Rental Source:* Images.

CAST

"THE MASK": *The Doctor:* Claude Dauphin; *Ambroise, "The Mask":* Jean Galland; *Denise, his Wife:* Gaby Morlay; *Frimousse, The Mask's Partner:* Gaby Bruyère. "THE MODEL": *Jean:* Daniel Gélin; *Joséphine:* Simone Simon; *The Friend:* Jean Servais; *The Journalist:* Michel Vadet. "THE HOUSE OF MADAME TELLIER": *Madame Tellier:* Madeleine Renaud; *Joseph Rivet:* Jean Gabin; *Rosa:* Danielle Darrieux; *Julien Ledentu, The Travelling Salesman:* Pierre Brasseur; *Flora:* Ginette Leclerc; *Fernande:* Paulette Dubost; *Raphaële:* Mira Parély; *Louise:* Mathilde Casadesus; *Marie, Joseph's Wife:* Héléna Manson; *Constance, their Daughter:* Joëlle Jany; *Mr. Tourneveau:* Louis Seigner; *Mayor:* René Blanchard; *Voice of de Maupassant, The Narrator:* Peter Ustinov (English Version), Jean Servais (French Version), and Anton Walbrook (German Version).

BACKGROUND

Max Ophüls was born Max Oppenheimer on May 6, 1902, in Saarbrücken, Germany. To prevent "disgrace" to his family who operated a department store in the city, he changed his name to "Ophüls" when he decided to embark upon a theatrical career.

In the merry Palais de la Danse, Ambroise, "The Mask" (Jean Galland), executes a lively quadrille with his partner (Gaby Bruyère) before his startling collapse.

Joséphine (Simone Simon), the model, finally meets up with Jean (Daniel Gélin), her artist lover who abandoned her.

Unsuccessful as a stage actor, he became for a decade a prodigious theatrical producer, which included a post at the Burg Theater in Vienna when he was only twenty-three. After being an assistant director to Anatole Litvak he directed his first film in 1930, the featurette *Dann Schon Lieber Lebertran*. His adaptation of the Arthur Schnitzler play *Liebelei* (1933) earned for him a brilliant reputation as a film director. In Nazi Germany, neither the playwright nor the director, both Jews, was cited in the credits.

Ophüls left for France where he made several films before eventually coming to America. There he directed five films, most notably *Letter From An Unknown Woman* (1948), before returning to France to adapt Balzac's *The Duchess of Langeais*, an unrealized project which was to have starred Greta Garbo and James Mason.

With *La Ronde* (1950), based on Schnitzler's ground-breaking play, this truly international director who had made films in Germany, France, Italy, Holland, and the United States began his last and finest period of achievement. *La Ronde* set the standard for his next three films: elegant direction, use of a glittering cast, collaboration with distinguished artists in an expensive production aimed at a worldwide audience.

After *La Ronde's* commercial success, Ophüls decided to make a triptych of tales by Guy de Maupassant. "Paul's Wife" ("La Femme de Paul") was initially considered, then dropped—partly due to

financial reasons—and replaced with "The Model." Shooting took place in the summer and fall of 1951. Interiors were shot in several studios in Saint-Maurice, Boulogne, and Joinville; exteriors were shot at Clécy and neighboring region (the "Tellier" sequence) and at Trouville and Parisian locales ("The Model").

With the sketch film *Le Plaisir* Ophüls had another chance to display his dazzling personal style.

SYNOPSIS*

"THE MASK": At a lively ball in Paris, a doctor (Claude Dauphin) is summoned to attend to a masked man (Jean Galland) who collapsed while dancing. He removes the mask and discovers underneath an old, white-haired man. The doctor returns him to his shabby quarters and learns from the man's long-suffering wife (Gaby Morlay) that Ambroise, her husband, was once a handsome man who always had great success with the ladies. Unable to bear the passing of time he uses a mask to continue playing Don Juan. The wife encourages him nonetheless, since this keeps his spirit alive. She requests the doctor's address should he be needed again. The doctor then returns to the ball.

"THE MODEL": At a seaside resort a middleaged man (Jean Servais) relates to a journalist (Michel Vadet) the story of his friend Jean, the famous painter (Daniel Gélin), who is seen approaching them pushing his wife Joséphine (Simone Simon) in an invalid's chair. He recounts Jean's frantic pursuit of the young woman over thirty years ago, her posing for him, their early idyllic romance, then, months later, the start of a violent series of quarrels. Jean sells a painting, leaves the money for her in their atelier as a parting gift, then moves in with his friend.

Joséphine tracks him down and throws the money at his feet. To placate her, the friend tells her that Jean's family is forcing him to marry someone else and she then threatens to kill herself. Jean, bored with her histrionics, dares her and Joséphine, on impulse, hurls herself out the window and breaks both legs. The guilt-ridden painter, vowing eternal love, marries her. . . .

The morose couple pass the narrator and snub him. The friend mentions that he has never been forgiven for interfering in Jean's life. Also, the only happiness the painter found was in his work.

*In the French version, the "Tellier" sketch is in the middle, followed by "The Model."

"THE HOUSE OF MADAME TELLIER": On a Saturday night in Fécamp, Normandy, the clients of Mme. Tellier's brothel are astonished to learn the place is shut. M. Tourneveau, the fish curer (Louis Seigner), discovers a notice which states that the house is closed on account "of the first communion."

The respectable proprietress (Madeleine Renaud) has a brother, Joseph Rivet (Jean Gabin), a carpenter in a small village some distance away, who had invited his sister to attend the first communion of his daughter Constance (Joëlle Jany). Mme. Tellier decided to take along her five ladies rather than let the house be unsupervised for the night. On the train a salesman (Pierre Brasseur) boards and has some fun with the ladies until Mme. Tellier throws him off for unspecified liberties.

The villagers consider the women elegant town ladies. In church Rosa (Danielle Darrieux), one of the group, starts crying over her lost innocence and soon the entire congregation joins in the contagious bawling. Mme. Tellier must depart because business is business. Attracted to Rosa, Joseph says he'll come and see her.

That evening the brothel comes alive again. Tourneveau orders champagne and even propositions Mme. Tellier, who's in an agreeable mood. The narrator remarks that what started as a party, grew to be a ball, then rose to be a festival!

COMMENTARY

Le Plaisir met with an unjustly hostile reception—it was dismissed by a critic as "useless games with the camera"—and it took a while to gain popular favor and a well-deserved reputation. In America, where it was known for a time as *House of Pleasure, Le Plaisir* met with a kinder critical reaction.*

The brief, opening scenes of "The Mask" with Ophüls' almost vertiginous tracking shots at the ball evoke with cinematic brilliance the frenzied and heady pursuit of pleasure which is the film's theme. In style it represents a perfect Ophüls miniature. And in "The Model" the camera races up stairs to capture the whirlwind pursuit of kittenish Joséphine by the young artist Daniel Gélin, then later feverishly follows the angry painter as he chases his unhappy mistress throughout his studio. Such camerawork, almost in constant flux, has received much critical attention. Words such as "decorative" and "baroque" are employed in an attempt to define Ophüls' idiosyncratic style, which has come to be called "Ophülsian."

Critic Andrew Sarris reminds us that the director's fluid style has an unltimate meaning: "time has no stop." As the tracking camera underlines "inexo-

*Robert Christidès, Jean d'Eaubonne, and Jacques Guth were nominated for an "Oscar" for "Art Direction—Set Decoration (Black-and-White)" (1954).

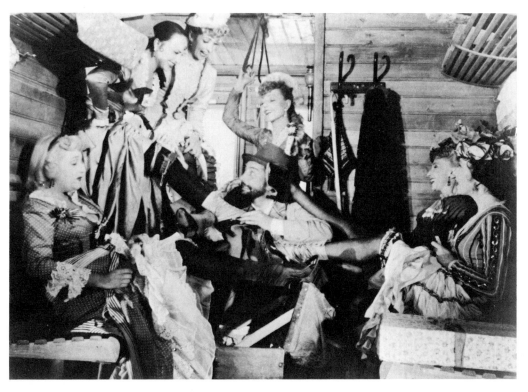

In the train, travelling salesman Ledentu (Pierre Brasseur) begins to distribute garters to a bevy of "ladies" making a trip to the country: Louise (Mathilde Casadesus), Flora (Ginette Leclerc), Rosa (Danielle Darrieux), Fernande (Paulette Dubost), Mme. Tellier (Madeleine Renaud), and Raphaële (Mila Parély).

137

During the First Communion Service, Joseph (Jean Gabin) tries to get the attention of Rosa (Danielle Darrieux). The Mayor (René Blancard) looks on. Others in the pew: Flora (Ginette Leclerc) and Raphaële (Mila Parély). In the front pew: Fernande (Paulette Dubost), Louise (Mathilde Casadesus), Mme. Tellier (Madeleine Renaud), and Marie (Héléna Manson), Joseph's wife.

Open for business once more, Mme. Tellier (Madeleine Renaud) entertains Tourneveau (Louis Seigner), the fish curer.

rably the passage of time" we sense that the characters are trapped in time but that "they will never lose their pose and grace. . . ."

"The lesson is clear," writes critic Claude Beylie, "throughout the ages pleasure is an easy thing but nearly always thwarts true happiness. 'Happiness is not gay,' concludes the narrator. Happiness is a long perseverance, not a swirling folly."

The last episode, whose lyrical, impressionistic country scenes pleasingly recall Renoir's *A Day in the Country*, stays longest in the viewer's mind, especially the wonderful epilogue, the brothel's re-opening, in which the screen seems to burst with zest and brio as the camera darts all over the exterior of Mme. Tellier's establishment eavesdropping on the merriment within.

It's neither a quiet, subdued Jean Gabin as a Norman peasant nor a wistful, lovely Danielle Darrieux who dominates this episode, but the formidable Madeleine Renaud who triumphs in one of her infrequent screen appearances. Tough, shrewd, winsome—a "no-nonsense" businesswoman—she steals the show and creates an archetypal madam for posterity.

We can easily concur with critic Bosley Crowther who wrote in his review: "*Le Plaisir* affords such pleasures as are few and unrestrained in this hard world." After more than thirty years, this charming film continues to delight and entrance.

CASQUE D'OR

SPÉVA FILM/PARIS FILMS PRODUCTION   1956

At an outdoor suburban cabaret Marie (Simone Signoret), the "Casque d'Or," meets Manda (Serge Reggiani), right, while his old buddy Raymond (Raymond Bussières), center, looks on.

CREDITS

Story and Adaptation: Jacques Becker and Jacques Companeez; *Dialogue and Direction:* Jacques Becker; *Photographer:* Robert Le Febvre; *Assistant Directors:* Marcel Camus and Michel Clément; *Editor:* Marguerite Renoir; *Music:* Georges Van Parys; *Song:* "Le Temps des Cerises" ("The Time of the Cherries"); *Running Time:* 96 minutes; *Paris Premiere:* April 16, 1952; *New York Premiere:* August 18, 1952; *16 mm. Rental Source:* Janus.

CAST

Marie ("Casque d'Or"): Simone Signoret; *Manda:* Serge Reggiani; *Félix Leca:* Claude Dauphin; *Raymond:* Raymond Bussières; *Roland:* William Sabatier; *Danard:* Gaston Modot; *Léonie Danard:* Loleh Bellon; *Fredo:* Claude Castaing; *Ponsard:* Paul Azaïs; *Billy:* Emile Gènevois; *Paul:* Jean Clarieux; *Anatole:* Roland Lesaffre; *Inspector Juliani:* Paul Barge; *Superintendent:* Tony Corteggiani; *Julie:* Dominique Davray; *La Mère Eugénie:* Odette Barencey.

BACKGROUND

Jacques Becker was born in Paris on September 15, 1906. His mother was a Scot; his father was a French industrialist who wanted his son to be an engineer. However, Jacques became an assistant director to his friend Jean Renoir from 1932 through *La Marseillaise* (1938) and even took small roles, notably in *La Grande Illusion* (1937). In 1934 he co-directed with Pierre Prévert *Le Commissaire Est Bon Enfant;* the following year he directed *Tête de Turc,* which he was to later disavow. In 1939 he began work on *L'Or du Cristobal* but financial difficulties shut the production down and he was eventually replaced. His real cinematic career began after his release from a P.O.W. camp.

Becker established a reputation as a promising director during the Occupation with an American style gangster film, *Dernier Atout* (1942), and a comic melodrama set in a rural village, *It Happened at the Inn (Goupi Mains Rouges)* (1943). After the war Becker made several films capturing the "feel" of contemporary youth such as *Antoine et Antoinette* (1947) before making his classic *Casque d'Or.*

"I have constructed my film upon an historical fact", Becker said of *Casque d'Or.* Newspapers at the turn of the century capitalized on the lurid Leca-Manda affair and sensationalized the underworld of the "apache" (a newly coined word for the Parisian gangster) with his savage code of honor. In addition there was a reigning courtesan among the cutthroats whose lovers met violent deaths.

All this seemed a "natural" for the movies. Before the war intervened, Duvivier considered directing Jean Gabin in a film version of it. After the war Becker was involved in the project and prepared a screenplay. This didn't materialize, however, and such directors as Yves Allégret and

Henri-Georges Clouzot were interested before Becker was finally given another chance to make it.

He rewrote the entire screenplay eliminating Manda's formation of a rival gang. In keeping with his stated views: "Only the characters of my story (and who become *my* characters) obsess me truly to the point of thinking about them without stop," the director de-emphasized the melodrama, demythologized the picturesque apache underworld, and, instead, concentrated on characterization. "I'm not interested in recounting clinical cases, but in human beings" he said. An apache melodrama became an atmospheric love story. Becker had a great fondness for the period of his childhood and it gave him much pleasure to recreate it cinematically.

For the legendary Casque d'Or (literally "helmet of gold," the nickname describing both the style of Marie's coiffure which resembles that of an old Spanish helmet and the color of her hair) he chose Simone Signoret and selected Serge Reggiani to be her co-star. Claude Dauphin was the gang leader Leca.

Shooting lasted from late September through mid-November 1951. The lovely, Renoir-inspired country scenes were shot at Annet-sur-Marne; interiors were done at the Paris Studios Cinema (Billancourt). Becker was a precise and exacting filmmaker. He had said: "I believe that the effectiveness of a film is dependent on the application of a rigorous logic to the development of a narrative. . . . In a true film everything should be convincing: the least suspect detail destroys the value of the whole." Reggiani's costume, for example, was carefully reproduced from the pages of an old magazine.

Becher's painstaking labor and vigorous realism gave a sense of authenticity to *Casque d'Or* which would eventually join the ranks of the great screen masterpieces after a troubled start.

SYNOPSIS

Around 1900, members of the Belleville (a Parisian suburb) Leca gang and their mistresses go on an outing to an outdoor cabaret in Joinville. Gang member Raymond (Raymond Bussières) runs into Manda (Serge Reggiani), a childhood friend now doing carpentry there. Marie (Simone Signoret), bored with gang member Roland (William Sabatier), is attracted to Manda and they dance. Roland picks a quarrel with the carpenter but Manda knocks him out.

Gang leader Félix Leca (Claude Dauphin) desires Marie and is willing to buy her off Roland. However, she's interested in Manda. When Manda visits Marie at the gang's hideout, L'Ange Gabriel, he's summoned to an alleyway and, following the apache code, is forced to fight Roland to the death to gain his woman. The men wrestle and Manda knifes Roland.

Manda receives Raymond's note which sends him to Mère Eugénie (Odette Barencey) in the country. Marie joins Manda there and the two share a brief, romantic idyll. A jealous Leca plots to destroy Manda by first pinning the blame for Roland's death on Raymond, then visiting the happy couple to inform them of the arrest of his childhood buddy. The loyal Manda cannot betray Raymond and so turns himself in.

Marie visits Leca to get him to help her lover. Here is his chance to seduce her. Afterward, typically, he refuses to aid Manda. Enroute to prison Raymond tells Manda that he has learned Leca used him as a pawn. The two men, with Manda's help, make a break for it, but Raymond is fatally shot.

Out for vengeance, Manda searches Leca's house, finds one of Marie's slippers, and guesses her sacrifice for him. He spots Leca in the street and pursues him furiously into a police station where he shoots him repeatedly in front of the startled gendarmes. Later Marie keeps vigil in a hotel overlooking a prison courtyard and in the morning watches her beloved Manda get guillotined.

COMMENTARY

Casque d'Or had a disastrous premiere in Brussels and proceeded to flop as well in Paris. However, the British Film Academy voted Simone Signoret "Best Foreign Actress" (1952) and eventually the French rediscovered Becker's neglected masterpiece.

Under Becker's supple and authoritative direction, using minimal dialogue, the period and the vivid characters come strikingly alive. Critic Jean Couturier wrote: "Becker employs a language amazing in its simplicity; not an unusual angle, a clever shot, or the self-styled 'aesthetic' pursuit. The camera position and the chosen angle seem to impose themselves . . . which is the height of great art."

Casque d'Or "is perhaps the finest film I ever made," Simone Signoret wrote. Director Lindsay

Gang leader Félix Leca (Claude Dauphin) expresses his interest in Marie (Simone Signoret) after he's learned she has quarreled with Roland.

At L'Ange Gabriel with her friend Julie (Dominique Davray), right, nearby, Marie (Simone Signoret) taunts Roland as he waltzes with a society lady.

"It clicks well, you two, huh?" is how Mère Eugénie greets the lovers, Manda (Serge Reggiani) and Marie (Simone Signoret), in the morning after they spent a happy night together in the country.

Anderson commented that her Marie was "a creation entrancingly feminine, with a range of intuition that compasses the arrogant (and irresistible) willfulness of the earlier sequences as persuasively as the later warmth of a woman passionately and constantly in love." Reggiani, Signoret wrote, had a "surface fragility, which concealed a staggering, inner strength." Together they were able to evoke genuine and powerful love and passion. Immaculately attired, Claude Dauphin gives a richly individualized performance of a civilized scoundrel. For Signoret, Reggiani, and Dauphin *Casque d'Or* remains their best remembered screen performances. Veteran character actor Raymond Bussières was most impressive also.

Critic Claude Beylie wrote that *Casque d'Or* "is . . . a poem of friendship and shared love, rendered illustrious with a sobriety and . . . a rare dignity." Robert Le Febvre's fine photography and Georges Van Parys' lovely score help create the film's memorable atmosphere.

The climax is painful and devastating as Becker avoids a slow pace to build suspense with the execution scene and, instead, rushes headlong to the shocking, tragic ending. At the moment of Manda's guillotining. Marie forcibly drops her head. There's a rapid dissolve to a poignant memory of the lovers waltzing al fresco on a deserted dance floor at Joinville.

Becker went on to make six more films, notably *The Night Watch (Le Trou)* (1960) before his death from haemochromatosis in Paris on February 21, 1960. Becker's credo was: "I believe in the possibility of entertaining friendship and in the difficulty of maintaining love. I believe in the value of effort. And I believe above all in Paris. In my work I do not want to prove anything except that life is stronger than everything else."

Of his thirteen eclectic films, *Casque d'Or* remains Becker's masterpiece ("the crown of a great cinéaste"—Jacques Doniol-Valcroze), a work of great plastic beauty.

142

Marie (Simone Signoret) and Manda (Serge Reggiani) watch a wedding in progress. Marriage will be denied to them in their doomed relationship.

FORBIDDEN GAMES

(Jeux Interdits)

SILVER FILMS   1952

CREDITS

Adaptation: Jean Aurenche, Pierre Bost, and René Clément, based on the novel, *Les Jeux Inconnus* (1947) by François Boyer, published as *The Secret Game* in New York, 1950; *Dialogue:* Jean Aurenche, Pierre Bost; *Director:* René Clément; *Photographer:* Robert Juillard; *Assistant Directors:* Claude Clément, Léonard Keigel; *Editor:* Roger Dwyre; *Music:* Traditional "Romance" for guitar arranged and performed by Narciso Yepes; *Running Time:* 102 minutes*; *Paris Premiere:* May 9, 1952; *New York Premiere:* December 8, 1952; *16 mm. Rental Source:* Janus.

CAST

Paulette: Brigitte Fossey; *Michel Dollé:* Georges Poujouly; *Dollé (the Father):* Lucien Hubert; *Mme. Dollé:* Suzanne Courtal; *Georges Dollé:* Jacques Marin; *Berthe Dollé:* Laurence Badie; *Gouard (The Father):* André Wasley; *Francis Gouard:* Amédée; *Jeanne Gouard:* Denise Pérronne; *Priest:* Louis Saintève.

BACKGROUND

René Clément was born on March 18, 1913, in Bordeaux and studied architecture at the Ecole des Beaux-Arts. He directed ten shorts (including *Soigne Ton Gauche,* 1937, Jacques Tati's screen début) before making his first feature, *Battle of the*

*The film's short prologue and epilogue were cut from the foreign prints. Length of the version shown in America is 90 minutes.

Rails (La Bataille du Rail) (1946), a powerful, reconstructed documentary of the French railway workers activities in the Resistance. This film, shot in a neo-realistic style, shared a Grand Prize at the Cannes Film Festival (1946) and Clément was cited "Best Director." *The Damned (Les Maudits)* (1947) dealt with a submarine carrying Nazis and collaborators fleeing Europe at the end of the war. And after two other features Clément turned once more to the subject of WWII.

He originally intended to make a three-part sketch film to be entitled, *Cross of Wood, Cross of Iron,* which concerned the problems of childhood. While working on the first sketch, based on a novel by François Boyer, *Les Jeux Inconnus,* Clément realized that it had the potential to be a self-contained work

A bewildered Paulette (Brigitte Fossey) clutches her dead dog after the Nazi air strike on the refugees.

The chic little Parisienne (Brigitte Fossey) is cared for by Berthe (Laurence Badie), the farmer's daughter.

Michel (Georges Poujouly), her protector and friend, and Paulette (Brigitte Fossey) at the initiation of the "forbidden games."

and so the remaining sketches were abandoned. The resultant film was *Forbidden Games*.

The adapters changed the novel's ending. In the book Michel climbs to the church belfry to loosen an admired stone cross atop the edifice. He falls along with the cross and is crushed to death. The more subdued film ending of adult betrayal and Paulette's departure makes a much greater impact without recourse to melodrama.

Clément used no known actors. "I wanted emotions to move across faces that were new," he said. The casting of Paulette, the little girl who dominates the film, was a stroke of luck. Clément tested hundreds of children in Nice for the part until he found five-year-old Brigitte Fossey (born in 1947) who was vacationing with an aunt in Cannes. He originally wanted a girl of eight who could pass for six in order to comprehend the role and felt Brigitte was too small and too young. However, he was struck by her intelligence and delicate emotional quality and decided to try her in the part. (Her actual parents play Paulette's parents in the film.) He found his Michel in Georges Poujouly who was in a vacation colony for underprivileged Parisian boys.

Besides evincing great care for realistic detail (flies crawl over the congregation in the country church), Clément was concerned with the visual aspect of his film and drew inspiration from such seventeenth century Dutch painters as Pieter de Hooch and Jan Vermeer in creating lighting effects for his interior scenes with the assistance of his cameraman Robert Juillard.

The film was made in the autumn of 1951. Exteriors were shot in La Foux (Basses-Alpes) and Puget-Théniers (Alpes-Maritimes). This beautifully crafted film was destined for international acclaim and success.

SYNOPSIS

It is June 1940 and hordes of Frenchmen, including five-year-old Paulette (Brigitte Fossey) and her parents, are making a desperate exodus to the South of France, Nazi planes fly over and strafe the bridge, killing the girl's parents and dog. When someone hurls the dead animal into the river Paulette follows it and meets Michel (Georges Poujouly), an eleven-year-old son of local farmers. He brings her back to his home and the frightened child is made welcome by the Dollé family. An older brother, Georges (Jacques Marin), was hurt that day, having been kicked in the groin by a runaway horse. The Dollés are constantly quarelling with their neighbors, the Gouards.

When Paulette learns that those killed by the planes are to be buried in a common grave, she asks if this is done so that they won't get wet, and then worries about her dog. The next day Paulette and Michel bury the animal in a deserted mill, and when she fears that her dog will be lonely, Michel hits upon the idea of making a secret cemetery there replete with crosses, flowers, and burial prayers. Her interest is immediately aroused and Michel starts making crucifixes for the "forbidden games."

Georges dies of his wound and the family prepares for his funeral. Michel swipes the crucifixes from atop the hearse and when his father (Lucien Hubert) notices the missing crosses during the service the boy lies and blames the "spiteful" Gouards for it. Michel even attempts to steal the altar cross but the priest (Louis Saintève) catches him at it.

The "cemetery" expands to include dead moles, chicks, mice, insects, and at Paulette's instigation the pair get a wheelbarrow and steal the crosses from the graveyard by the church during an air raid. The next day Dollé and Gouard (André Wasley) fight in the churchyard owing to the confusion arising from the missing crosses, and the priest restores order by blaming Michel for the theft.

Michel hides from his outraged father, but Dollé catches him, demands the crosses, and beats him. Police drive up to the farm; they've come for Paulette. Michel, upset, tells his father he'll reveal where the crosses are if he promises to keep Paulette. Dollé agrees, then betrays his word by turning the girl over to the authorities. The furious boy rushes over to the mill and destroys the crosses. In a crowded railway station, a disconsolate Paulette waits to be sent to an orphanage.

COMMENTARY

Presented out of competition at the Cannes Film Festival in 1952, *Forbidden Games* won the Grand Prix Independant. Later at the Venice Film Festival it earned the Grand Prize (1952) with the following citation: "for having known how to raise up, with a singular lyric purity and an exceptional force of expression, the innocence of childhood over the tragedy and desolation of war." Receiving the New York Film Critics Award for "Best Foreign Film" (1952), *Forbidden Games* went on to obtain an Honorary "Oscar" for "Best Foreign Language Film" (1952).* In Tokyo it was awarded the Japanese

*François Boyer later received an "Oscar" nomination for *Forbidden Games* in the "Writing (Motion Picture Story)" category (1954).

Dollé (Lucien Hubert), Michel (Georges Poujouly) and Paulette (Brigitte Fossey) watch Georges Dollé die.

Critics Prize (1953) and the British Film Academy cited it as "Best Film" (1953).

Forbidden Games is an extraordinary, powerful, and poetic film. Clément was able to let the children act in a completely natural, spontaneous, and unsentimentalized fashion. The lovely, delicate Brigitte Fossey, who immediately arouses our protective instincts and sympathy, turns in a performance which is poignant and unforgettable. (Mlle. Fossey resumed her movie career with Jean-Gabriel Albicocco's *The Wanderer* (1967), the film of the classic *Le Grand Meaulnes* by Henri Alain-Fournier.)

Are we to understand that these "forbidden games" are a traumatized child's way of indirectly dealing with war and the death of her parents? Are the dead animals and insects the recipients of the love which she is unable to bestow upon her mother and father? Are these "forbidden games" somehow a contagious ritual which shows the power that death holds over children? The scenarists wisely refrain from presenting a glib, facile explanation. Instead, with great skill and understanding the unique world of childhood is recreated and we, as adults, are invited to eavesdrop but ultimately refrain from judging the children's irreverent, even sacriligeous "games," since Clément himself warns: "For me foremost of the forbidden games is war."

Forbidden Games is a rich, provocative film indicting man's cruelty, stupidity, and horror in a subtle, never bombastic, way and contrasting the deceptive values of the adults with the forthright honesty of the children.

Critics praised the brilliant and shocking opening sequence, done in an authentic documentary manner, of the air attack on the civilians followed by a close-up of little Paulette trying to rouse her dead mother. And nothing can surpass the devastating conclusion in the railway station in which a terrified Paulette cannot be comforted by a nun. She hears someone call out "Michel" and rushes off calling his name expecting to meet her friend. When she sees that "Michel" is an older man embracing a woman, she cries "Mama," then "Michel!" over and over as the camera moves to a high angle shot revealing the tragic child being swept up in the mass of displaced persons. It is one of the most harrowing scenes in cinema and inflicts an immortal wound on the spectator.

The haunting guitar music played by Narciso Yepes—the only music in the film—heightens the mood. Painfully sensitive, delivering an unforgettable impact, *Forbidden Games* is Clément's most memorable film and is undoubtedly his masterpiece.

146

Betraying his promise to his son, Dollé (Lucien Hubert) turns Paulette (Brigitte Fossey) over to the authorities while Raymond and his brother Michel (Georges Poujouly) and Mme. Dollé (Suzanne Courtal) look on.

MR. HULOT'S HOLIDAY

(Les Vacances de Monsieur Hulot)

CADY FILMS/DISCINA INTERNATIONAL
FILMS CORPORATION/ECLAIR JOURNAL   1953

CREDITS

Screenplay: Jacques Tati and Henri Marquet, with the collaboration of Pierre Aubert and Jacques Lagrange; *Director:* Jacques Tati; *Photographer:* *Jacques Mercanton and Jean Mousselle; Assistant Directors:* Bernard Maurice and Pierre Aubert; *Editors:* Suzanne Baron, Charles Bretoneiche, and Jacques Grassi; *Music:* Alain Romans; *Running Time:* 96 minutes; *Paris Premiere:* February 27, 1953; *New York Premiere:* June 16, 1954; *16 mm. Rental Source:* Images.

CAST

M. Hulot: Jacques Tati; *Martine:* Nathalie Pascaud; *Fred:* Louis Perrault; *The Aunt:* Michèle Rolla; *Commandant:* André Dubois; *Commandant's Wife:* Suzy Willy; *Englishwoman:* Valentine Camax; *Hotel Proprietor:* Lucien Frégis; *Strolling Woman:* Marguerite Gérard; *Strolling Man:* René Lacourt; *Boy:* Raymond Carl; *Businessman:* Jean-Pierre Zola.

BACKGROUND

Jacques Tati (family name was Tatischeff) was born on October 9, 1908, at Pecq (Seine-et-Oise). He discovered rugby when he was sent to England to learn the family picture-framing business and his deft interpretations of both that sport and tennis so amused his friends that they urged him to try the music halls.

M. Hulot (Jacques Tati) arrives for his vacation in his 1924 Amilcar, an extension of himself: old-fashioned, unconventional, but persistent.

Back in France he started in cafés and performed in music halls and circuses with increasing success. Between 1931-38 he made five shorts, his apprenticeship in film, where the character of Hulot—his screen persona—took gradual shape.

After the war he played the ghost in Claude Autant-Lara's film *Sylvie and the Phantom (Sylvie et le Fantôme)* (1945) and had a bit part in *Devil in the Flesh (Le Diable au Corps)* (1947). In 1946 Tati directed and appeared in a short, *L'Ecole des Facteurs* ("School for Postmen"), which was so well-received he was encouraged to expand his account of a gangling rural postman into a feature film. Subsequently, *The Big Day (Jour de Fête)* (1949) was made and won the Grand Prix du Cinéma Français (1950). Critics marked the début of a fresh and original talent.

Tati then decided to make a film based on his funny creation, the singular Monsieur Hulot. From the observation of an architect with an odd walk and a fellow soldier who was likeable and good-natured, Tati derived his unique character: "I invented him because I wanted to find a man who would be simple and honest and also a little bit out of control." Unlike other comic characters Hulot doesn't set out to win the girl or achieve fame and fortune. He is, rather, a timid, early middle-aged man—the eternal outsider—who nonetheless attempts to cope. Tati said of Hulot: "He is different. When people say 'Go right,' he nods nicely and

M. Hulot (Jacques Tati) displays his personal tennis form.

goes left, because it happens his mind is on the moon at the time."

Hulot has a funny, bouncy walk landing only on the forepart of his foot. He wears baggy trousers which are too short for his spindly legs, an old raincoat, felt hat, has an umbrella and a perennial pipe. With his deferential politeness and old-world manners he is out of synchronization with modern life. Bumbling, unprepossessing, Hulot does amusing things without realizing they are in any way unusual.

Tati's clown character and use of sight gags have been influenced by Max Linder and other early French comedians and by such great performers in American silent comedy as Charlie Chaplin, Buster Keaton (especially in his deadpan manner and expressive body movements), Harold Lloyd, and Harry Langdon. Keaton acknowledged that Tati was continuing the great comic tradition in film.

As in his first feature, Tati preferred to work chiefly with non-professional actors ("I do not want a performer who everyone will know is playing a part. . . . My films are concerned with real people coming up against the absurdities of life") in natural locations.

Tati started shooting *Mr. Hulot's Holiday* in St. Marc-sur-Mer in Brittany in July 1951. Aside from a few actors, most of the cast was drawn from

148

Searching for his Ping-Pong ball, M. Hulot (Jacques Tati) is unaware that he is disrupting a tranquil scene. Martine (Nathalie Pascaud) observes his chaos-strewn movements.

Mr Hulot (Jacques Tati) demonstrates his equestrian skill.

visitors and residents there. Interiors were done at the Studios de Billancourt. A meticulous and painstaking filmmaker—every gag was carefully prepared prior to shooting and not improvised on location—Tati completed the film in October 1952—financial difficulties contributed to the delay as well. He regretted he was unable to shoot it in color.

In giving us a finely observed slice of life, Tati tried to make us feel the lazy unrollment of each sun-drenched day which includes the inevitable presence of monotony and boredom. Much of the humor derives from the frantic way vacationers "relax." "People's seriousness when they are having fun is funny," Tati said. "Why do they approach the holidays so seriously? They make it seem like a new job to be undertaken every year."

At first producers were unsure of this off-beat film's marketability, but *Mr. Hulot's Holiday* proved a hilarious and engaging hit.

SYNOPSIS

Bachelor M. Hulot (Jacques Tati) arrives at a middle-class seaside resort in Brittany. Among the guests staying at the Hôtel de la Plage are Martine (Nathalie Pascaud), a pretty young woman whom he shyly courts from a distance, and various, recog-

At the hotel's masked ball, the "pirate" (Jacques Tati) dances with the "harlequin" (Nathalie Pascaud).

149

nizable "types": The businessman who toils unceasingly while "vacationing," etc.

Hulot is involved in a series of misshaps: His kayak breaks in half and is mistaken for a shark floating in the water. He intrudes accidentally upon a funeral at a cemetery and attempts amusingly to fit in. While retrieving a runaway Ping Pong ball, he inadvertently moves a cardplayer's chair and causes the man to lay his card on the neighboring table where a second game's in progress, and squabbling follows. A dog chases Hulot late at night. He retreats to a shed, which holds fireworks, and lights a match to see where he is. The ensuing display wakes up the household and alienates almost all of the guests from Hulot.

At departure time he is snubbed by all save two adults and the children. Undaunted, Hulot drives away.

COMMENTARY

Mr. Hulot's Holiday was a worldwide critical and commercial success. Among the prizes which it won were the International Critics Award at the Cannes Film Festival (1953). and the Prix Louis Delluc (1953).* Tati realized that non-Frenchmen could identify with his hero: "Hulot is a bit of everybody magnified."

Tati prefers to mine the ordinary, not the dramatic, for his comedy. The result is a low-keyed style, an avoidance of such "spectaculars" as the chase. To prevent excess he is not adverse to breaking off a gag, cutting for example the card playing scene before the mixup results in further violence than a face slap. "I loved slapstick," Tati said, "but I wanted to find another sort of visual comedy. Not the ancient formula."

Tati frequently allows the other characters to be as funny or funnier than Hulot himself. The surly waiter and the henpecked husband and bossy wife, forever strolling but always first for dinner, are priceless. The story line is thin and the dialogue minimal in this episodically structured film.

Director Tati dislikes the obtrusive close-up ("I have no right to bang anyone's nose against the screen") and prefers wide-angle long shots, approximating stage action, "because they allow the audience to participate and choose what to look at."

This restraint both in style and in camera movement creates an impression of naturalness, not contrivance. And Tati's timing is marvellous.

When a dog refuses to budge from the center of a street to give way to Hulot in his bizarre car we have clever, visual exposition near the film's beginning as to the man's commanding presence in the world. Although Hulot is an easily embarrassed loner, an "innocent," Tati wisely refrains from arousing pathos for him or letting his hero indulge in self-pity. When rejected, he intrepidly moves on to something new.

There is no character growth or recognition in Hulot; it is we the audience who gain the perceptions which are revealed in the film. The tone is one of gentle caricature.

There is a clever employment of natural sound which characterizes inanimate objects: the swinging door in the hotel dining room, Hulot's spluttering car, etc. "I believe," Tati said, "in using sound in a funny way but not in exaggeration." Alain Romans' music captures the mood of a languorous summer vacation; the effective photography of Jacques Mercanton and Jean Mousselle contribute to the authentic "feel" of the film.

One of the hilarious and memorable scenes is the opening sequence at the railroad station in which the haggard travellers are constantly being dispatched to various platforms for the arriving train by a muddled and garbled voice over a loudspeaker. This recalls the confusion attendant on the meeting of Hynkel and Napaloni in Chaplin's *The Great Dictator* (1940).

Tati went on to make: *My Uncle (Mon Oncle)* (1958), the neglected *Playtime* (1967) which created great financial difficulties for the director, *Trafic* (1971), and *Parade* (1973), a feature made for Swedish television. Tati said in 1976: "My aim is to get the spectators to see all the funny things which surround them." In a film career spanning over twenty-five years, the independent, uncompromising comedian has only been able to make six films. In 1979 he was awarded the Grand Prix National du Cinéma. Jacques Tati died in Paris on November 5, 1982.

André Bazin commented that M. Hulot "is all gracefulness, he is a scatterbrained angel and the disorder he produces is that of tenderness and of liberty." *Mr. Hulot's Holiday* remains Tati's most popular film. It doesn't seem to date and continues to delight and entertain each succeeding generation.

---

*In addition Jacques Tati and Henri Marquet received an "Oscar" nomination for *Mr. Hulot's Holiday* for "Writing (Story and Screenplay)" (1955).

Terreur des Batignolles, then went to Berlin in 1932 where he became an assistant-director to Anatole Litvak and E. A. Dupont and an adapter-director of French versions of several German films.

Bad health interrupted his career in 1934 and he spent the next four years recuperating in various sanatoria. He returned to his screenwriting career in 1938 and directed his first feature, *The Murderer Lives at No. 21 (L'Assassin Habite au 21)* (1942). His

THE WAGES OF FEAR

(Le Salaire de la Peur)

COMMERCIALE CINÉMATOGRAPHIQUE/
FILMSONOR PRODUCTION/VÉRA FILMS
(PARIS)/FONO ROMA (ROME)   1953

CREDITS

Screenplay: .Henri-Georges Clouzot and Jérome Géronimi, based on the novel by Georges Arnaud [Henri Georges Charles Achille Girard] (1950), published in New York in 1952; *Director:* Henri-Georges Clouzot; *Photographer:* Armand Thirard; *Assistant Directors:* Michel Romanoff, Roberto Savarese; *Editors:* Henri Rust, Madeleine Gug, and Etiennette Muse; *Music:* Georges Auric; *Running Time:* 156 minutes; *Paris Premiere:* April 22, 1953; *New York Premiere:* February 16, 1955; *16 mm. Rental Source:* Images.

CAST

Mario: Yves Montand; *Jo:* Charles Vanel; *Linda:* Véra Clouzot; *Luigi:* Folco Lulli; *Bimba:* Peter van Eyck; *Bill O'Brien:* William Tubbs; *Hernandez:* Dario Moreno; *Smerloff:* Jo Dest; *Camp Chief:* Centa; *Bernardo:* Luis de Lima; *Dick:* Jeronimo Mitchell.

BACKGROUND

Henri-Georges Clouzot was born in Niort (Deux-Sèvres) on November 20, 1907. He studied law at Brest and political science in Paris before switching to journalism. He began his apprenticeship in film by working on the adaptation and storyboard for several movies. In 1931 he directed a short, *La*

Portrait of Yves Montand as the desperate Mario willing to risk his life for a chance at escape.

A rare light moment: Mario (Yves Montand) playfully dabs the nose of Luigi (Folco Lulli), his roommate, as he prepares for a meeting with Jo.

next film, *Le Corbeau* ("The Raven")*(1943), a thriller about an epidemic of poison pen letters in a provincial town, proved to be very controversial. After the Liberation Clouzot was accused of serving the enemy propaganda by his bleak depiction of corruption in rural France and was prevented from working in film for a period. (It is not true that *Le Corbeau* was screened in Nazi Germany under the title *A Little French Village;* the film was never released there during the war.) He resumed his career with *Jenny Lamour (Quai des Orfèvres)* (1947) and *Manon* (1948), among others. In 1950 Clouzot went to Brazil on a honeymoon with his wife Véra. Although his documentary project on that country failed to materialize, his experiences there helped him recreate an authentic atmosphere in his next film.

Georges Arnaud's best-selling thriller *The Wages of Fear* became Clouzot's sixth feature. The director added a long prologue which sets the mood and delineates characterization before the exciting central action starts. The locale of Guatemala becomes unspecified in the film. The port city of Las Piedras

*Remade in Hollywood as *The Thirteenth Letter* (1951) directed by Otto Preminger and starring Charles Boyer and Linda Darnell.

152

is more of a cul-de-sac as a landlocked village in the movie.

Clouzot changed the Mario-pimp-Linda-whore relationship and dropped the novel's harsh anti-clerical tone. He introduced the character of Jo, contributed a philosophical dimension to the suspenseful narrative, and added the thrilling episodes of the perilous turn on the wooden platform and the demolition of the obtruding boulder in the road.

Clouzot wanted popular music hall singer Yves Montand for the role of Mario. At first, recalling his miscasting in Carné's *Gates of the Night,* Montand refused but let himself be persuaded. Reluctant to play a coward, Jean Gabin turned down the role of Jo. Charles Vanel accepted the part which became a significant comeback vehicle for him.

Clouzot said: "An important setting, complex human material, and this terrifying prop which is a truck loaded with explosives have allowed me . . . to aim at the epic. . . . Yes, an epic whose major accent should bear upon courage. And upon its opposite, because contrast is for me the basis of my cinematographic conception."

Forced to execute a dangerous turn during a mountainous climb, Mario (Yves Montand) backs his nitroglycerin-laden truck to the edge of the rotted wooden platform, then searches for the missing Jo.

The village of Las Piedras was painstakingly constructed in Saint-Gilles near Nîmes in the Camargue; the truck journey was shot in the Gardon valley. Other exteriors were the Nîmes Airdrome and Galician refineries; interiors were done in studios in Nice. Shooting began September 1951. Conditions were dreadful: torrential rain which ravaged the sets, the fatiguing mistral, illness, and financial difficulty. The film was suspended in November and production begun again only in June and lasting through September 1952.

The Wages of Fear proved an international critical and commercial success and is generally regarded as perfectionist Clouzot's greatest achievement.

SYNOPSIS

Among the uprooted Europeans stranded in Las Piedras, a poverty-stricken Latin American village with lepers, are the Corsican Mario (Yves Montand), his Italian roommate Luigi (Folco Lulli), and the embittered Germans, Bimba (Peter van Eyck) and Smerloff (Jo Dest). Linda (Véra Clouzot), a native woman, adores Mario but he treats her

An angry Mario (Yves Montand) beats up Jo (Charles Vanel) after his frightened co-driver deserted the truck a second time.

callously. Southern Oil Company, an American firm managed by O'Brien (William Tubbs), dominates the economy. Jo (Charles Vanel), an aging French gangster on the run, arrives and befriends Mario who's impressed by his courage. There is an undertone of homosexual tension among Mario, Luigi, and Jo.

An accident and potentially unmanageable fire in a distant oil field force O'Brien to take an emergency step. He must hastily dispatch two unsafe trucks loaded with nitroglycerin to the area. Although the risks seem overwhelming, the offer of two thousand dollars to drive signals escape to the trapped men. Mario, Luigi, Bimba, and Smerloff are selected.

At 3 A.M. departure time Jo—rejected for his age—appears in lieu of Smerloff whom he apparently did some dirty work to.* He and Mario lead the perilous three-hundred-mile trek. The least jolt and the deadly explosives . . . Mario executes a nerve-racking turn on a shaky wooden platform which collapses as he pulls away. Jo loses his courage and quits Mario temporarily. Bimba,

*Some commentators report that Jo killed Smerloff. However, near the film's end we spot him dancing in the café. No explanation is provided for Jo's replacing him for the trip.

153

Mario (Yves Montand) hastily tends to a wounded Jo (Charles Vanel) before returning to his truck bogged down in a pool of oil.

who has passed Mario's truck, confronts the obstacle of a huge boulder in the path by skillfully and harrowingly blowing it up with some nitroglycerin. Later, Mario and Jo see a cloud of smoke—Bimba and Luigi's truck has blown up. Mario has to beat up a frightened Jo to prevent him from deserting him. The truck's explosion created a crater which is rapidly filling up with oil from the broken pipelines. Mario drives into it and crushes Jo's leg which was caught underneath and later turns gangrenous. Mario manages to extricate the truck from the crater. Comradeship is rekindled between Mario and the dying Jo. An exhausted Mario successfully arrives at the oil field.

Returning home the next day Mario, heady with his triumph and $4,000 reward, drives recklessly and crashes to his death over a precipice while clutching a Métro ticket in his hand.

COMMENTARY

The Wages of Fear received the Grand Prize and Charles Vanel was voted "Best Actor" at the Cannes Film Festival (1953). The British Film Academy voted it "Best Film" (1954). It won an Audience Award at the Berlin Film Festival (1953). Unfortunately, when it opened in New York, the film was bowdlerized. Almost an hour had been cut and the result was a confusing film. (The deletions were subsequently restored.)

The Wages of Fear presented a new and virile image of Yves Montand and firmly established him in his career as an important screen actor with international fame. The film gained recognition for Clouzot outside of France as a brilliant master of suspense. "In *The Wages of Fear*," the director said, "I have sought an editing based on constant shocks."

A very visual film—"The dialogue occupies here, above all, the role of a resonant background," Clouzot said—*The Wages of Fear* evinces a powerful and meticulous sense of atmosphere which heightens the film's realism. "To move the viewer," Clouzot commented, "I am always concerned with emphasizing chiaroscuro, opposing light with shadow."

The Wages of Fear presents a pessimistic existential commentary on the human condition. For Bimba, to relocate is merely "a change of mosquitoes." The dying Jo asks Mario what was behind a fence in a familiar Parisian neighborhood and is told, significantly, "There's nothing . . . a bit of waste ground." There is as well strong social criticism of Latin America's exploitation by U.S. business interests. Armand Thirard's photography evokes a hot, bright hellhole aptly with some striking chiaroscuro effects.

Clouzot followed his success with *Diabolique (Les Diaboliques)* (1955). Ill-health restricted his productivity. He directed Brigitte Bardot in *The Truth (La Verité)* (1960); *La Prisonnière* (1968) was his last film. Clouzot died in Niort on January 12, 1977.

William Friedkin's expensive, boring, and totally pointless remake of *The Wages of Fear*, called *Sorcerer* (1977), did nothing to diminish the memory of the original, a masterpiece of excruciating suspense and unrelenting tension. As critic Bosley Crowther succinctly put it, "You sit there waiting for the theatre to explode."

don (1952); *Dialogue:* Marcel Achard; *Director:* Max Ophüls; *Photographer:* Christian Matras; *Assistant Directors:* Willy Picard and Marc Maurette; *Editor:* Boris Lewyn; *Music:* Georges Van Parys (theme of Oscar Straus) and excerpts from Gluck's *Orfeo ed Euridice; Running Time:* 105 minutes; *Paris Premiere:* September 16, 1953; *New York Premiere:* July 19, 1954; *16 mm. Rental Source:* Images.

THE EARRINGS OF MADAME DE . . .

(Madame De . . .)

FRANCO-LONDON FILMS
(PARIS)/INDUSFILMS/RIZZOLI (ROME)   1953

CREDITS

Adaptation: Marcel Achard, Annette Wademant, and Max Ophüls from the novel by Louise de Vilmorin (1951), translated and published in Lon-

CAST

Countess Louise de . . .: Danielle Darrieux; *Général André de . . .:* Charles Boyer; *Baron Fabrizio Donati:* Vittorio de Sica; *Mme. de . . .'s Nurse:* Mireille Perrey; *M. Rémy, the Jeweler:* Jean Debucourt; *Jérôme, his Son:* Serge Lecointe; *Lola, the Général's Mistress:* Lia di Léo; *M. de Bernac:* Jean Galland; *Henri de Maleville:* Hubert Noël; *Theatre Manager:* Léon Walther; *Mme. De . . .'s Friend:* Madeleine Barbulée; *Julien, the Général's Valet:* Guy Favières.

BACKGROUND

After *Le Plaisir,* Max Ophüls' next film was *The Earrings of Madame De . . . .* Louise de Vilmorin's terse analysis of a "grand amour" which changes a

At the opera, Mme de. . .(Danielle Darrieux), right, feigns the loss of her earrings to her husband, the Général (Charles Boyer).

The Général (Charles Boyer) meets his friend, Baron Donati (Vittorio de Sica), at an official function and humorously cautions him that his wife Louise (Danielle Darrieux) is fickle.

frivolous society lady of an unspecified period and place to a serious woman who dies of love became in Ophüls' masterful hands another stunning achievement.

Ophüls wisely set the story in Paris at the time of the Belle Epoque which concretizes the novel's ambiguous period and allows his elegant, almost "operatic" style to be more acceptable than would a contemporary staging. The screenwriters tightened the book's narrative flow and by providing a duel as a resolution to the dilemma of the husband-wife-lover triangle added a tragic dimension to the film. (In the novel the Countess expires clutching an earring in each hand with the two men who loved her standing by. The husband then gives an earring to the lover.)

Ophüls assembled a very powerful cast, reuniting the celebrated lovers of *Mayerling* (1936): Danielle Darrieux and Charles Boyer and presenting the distinguished Italian actor-director Vittorio de Sica as the Baron, a role ideally suited to the former matinee idol. Interiors were shot at the Boulogne studios; exteriors in the forest of Rambouillet within the d'Uzès domain.

What could have been a dated, even trite, melodrama turned out to be one of the most ravishingly beautiful and richly cinematic films of all time. More than one critic was to cite Ophüls' *The Ear-

rings of Madame De . . . as his personal favorite film.

SYNOPSIS

To pay some debts, Countess Louise de . . . (Danielle Darrieux)—no last name is provided—casually sells her diamond earrings, a present on her wedding night from her husband, Général André de . . . (Charles Boyer), to her jeweler, M. Rémy (Jean Debucourt), then feigns losing them when she attends the opera with her spouse.

When an item about the "theft" appears in the newspapers, M. Rémy, feeling compromised, takes the jewels to the Général who purchases them back, then presents them as a parting gift to his mistress Lola (Lia di Léo) who is leaving for Constantinople. There she loses them gambling at the casino. Months later they are bought by diplomat Baron Donati (Vittorio de Sica).

While traveling, the Baron and the Countess meet, but their relationship takes a serious turn during the Parisian social season. He sends her the earrings; she receives his token of love ecstatically. The Général, usually amused by his fickle wife's innocent flirtations, gives way to jealousy and sends Louise to Italy. "I don't love you" she unconvincingly dissembles before the Baron at departure. The lovers have a rendezvous after several torturous months of separation. Her earrings were her only consolation she tells him.

Back in Paris, anxious to wear them at a ball, the Countess pretends to "find" the earrings in a glove. Provoked beyond endurance, the Général demands the jewels and tells the Baron that his honor forbids him to allow his wife to accept them. Understandably hurt when he learns his gift's origin, the Baron confronts the Countess who finally admits the truth after first lying. Devastated by her apparent shallowness, he disposes of them at M. Rémy's.

Hoping to renew his marriage, the Général purchases the earrings again and presents them to his ailing wife. Noticing her weep at the sight of them and realizing the depth of her love for the Baron, he humiliates the Countess by forcing her to present the pair to his niece who has just had a baby.

Once more M. Rémy offers the earrings for sale—the niece was in need of money—but the Général refuses angrily. The Countess, however, in desperation sells her jewels to buy back the precious stones. The Général, feeling rejected, his renewed love turning to hate, seeks a husband's

In the course of a beautiful waltz montage, the love between Louise (Danielle Darrieux) and Baron Donati (Vittorio de Sica) grows steadily.

revenge by challenging the Baron to a duel. The Countess begs the Baron to flee and confesses her frivolity, but he has no wish to live without her.

She rushes to the site of the duel in time to hear one shot—the Général apparently killed the Baron instantly—then collapses and dies. On an altar we see candles and the enshrined earrings with the inscription "In memory of Madame De. . . ."

COMMENTARY

Unlike the reception accorded *Le Plaisir,* the critics were much impressed with Ophüls' dazzling personal style in *The Earrings of Madame De. . . .* The camerawork is breathtaking, in particular the director's endless tracking shots sweeping along with his characters and conveying their restless, frenetic existence as they dress, dance, love, duel, and finally die. A justly celebrated sequence is the depiction of the growing ardor between the Countess and the Baron over a period of time through the device of a waltz montage: It begins with the couple dancing in a crowded ballroom; then proceeds through a series of graceful tracking shots—which cut or dissolve to the next scene—of the pair dancing in different costumes; and concludes with the lovers alone on an empty floor. This delicate and economical device—there's a total of six brief

The lovers have a tryst in the Baron's carriage. The Baron (Vittorio de Sica) teases Louise (Danielle Darrieux) to utter his favorite phrase: "I don't love you."

At the ball, the angry Général (Charles Boyer) demands without any explanation that his wife (Danielle Darrieux) give him the diamond earrings which she is flaunting.

scenes—recalls Welles' "breakfast montage" detailing the souring of Kane's first marriage in *Citizen Kane* (1941).

Ophüls manages to avoid both indulgence and sentimentality and an icy detachment which would have produced a dull and sterile film and to maintain a careful balance of restraint, emotion, and even reflection: this "grand amour"—albeit sexually innocent—can enrich and ennoble these characters' lives and yet at the same time destroy them. There is criticism implicit in the narrow range of their world, with its rigid, stifling mores, and compassion as well in his treatment of Madame de . . . as we see her character develop from frivolity to depth of feeling. How different from the early scene when the Countess enters a church to pray to a hopefully indulgent God that her husband will understand and forgive her selling the diamond earrings is the scene near the end when a grave and dying woman begs the Lord to spare the Baron's life in the pending duel and places those precious jewels on an altar in a painful sacrifice.

With her expressive face, slendor body, and her natural delicate grace and beauty, the ravishing Danielle Darrieux is the quintessential Ophülsian heroine who convinces us that she could indeed die for love. In one of his strongest film roles in a long career, Charles Boyer conveys the arrogance, bearing, and troubled feelings of a proud Général who prefers honor to love. And Vittorio de Sica is suave and impeccable in his subtle and underplayed role of the gallant yet hapless Baron who seeks death as a way out of his unhappy plight.

Georges Annenkov and Rosine Delamare received an "Oscar" nomination (1954) for "Costume Design (Black-and-White)" for *The Earrings of Madame De. . .* Tribute should be paid to Oscar Straus's haunting theme (orchestrated by Georges Van Parys) which comments perfectly on the film's action, a lilting waltz when the Countess and the Baron begin their courtship and a sombre requiem with tolling bells at her death.

The Earrings of Madame De . . . is a great film, in my opinion Ophül's masterpiece, a work which will continue to enrich those viewers' lives who would agree with the lines written by Mme. de Vilmorin in *Madame De . . .* that "whenever love touches history, events of the past belong to the present."

Ophül's next and last film was the sumptuous *Lola Montès* (1955), which flopped and then was drastically cut and reedited. A reconstructed version was reissued in 1969 to critical acclaim. The great director died in Hamburg on March 26, 1957. His son, Marcel Ophüls, is the well-known and controversial documentary filmmaker.

"I believe in a certain current. . . ." Max Ophüls wrote. "It is the current of the imagination. It runs across all the arts and if, from time to time, it sprinkles the cinema a little, we should feel joy and contentment. . . . To keep this current from drying up is our duty. . . ." He concludes: "As long as we do that, in spite of crisis, our *métier,* I believe, will continue to exist. To be able, one day, to say to onself that one was lucky enough to help keep it alive should be the most beautiful and essential experience one could have."

158

GERVAISE

C.I.C.C. (COMPAGNIE INDUSTRIELLE
COMMERCIALE
CINÉMATOGRAPHIQUE)/DISCINA
INTERNATIONAL FILMS
CORPORATION/SILVER FILMS/AGNÈS
DELAHAIE PRODUCTION
CINÉMATOGRAPHIQUE   1959

CREDITS

Adaptation and Dialogue: Jean Aurenche and Pierre Bost, based on the Emile Zola novel, *L'Assommoir* (1877); *Director:* René Clément; *Photographer:* Robert Juillard; *Assistant Directors:* Claude Clément and Léonard Keigel; *Editor:* Henri Rust; *Music:* Georges Auric; *Lyrics:* Raymond Queneau; *Running Time:* 116 minutes; *Paris Premiere:* September 5, 1956; *New York Premiere:* November 11, 1957; *16 mm. Rental Source:* Budget.

CAST

Gervaise: Maria Schell; *Henri Coupeau:* François Périer; *Virginie:* Suzy Delair; *Lantier:* Armand Mestral; *Goujet:* Jacques Harden; *Mme. Boche:* Mathilde Casadesus; *M. Boche:* Jacques Hilling; *Père Colombe:* André Wasley; *M. Lorilleux:* Hubert de Lapparent; *Mme. Lorilleux:* Jany Holt; *M. Poisson:* Lucien Hubert; *Nana:* Chantal Gozzi.

BACKGROUND

After completing a comedy with Gérard Philipe, *Lovers, Happy Lovers* (Monsieur Ripois)* (1954), René

*Now better known here under its British title, *Knave of Hearts.*

The celebrated fight scene in the public wash-house between Gervaise (Maria Schell) and Virginie (Suzy Delair).

Clément made *Gervaise*, based on the Emile Zola novel, *L'Assommoir*. Zola's powerful study of the effects of alcohol on the struggling working class was a popular subject in the early French cinema. Starting with Ferdinand Zecca's *Les Victims de l'Alcoolisme* (1902), there were several more treatments before and after WWI as well as a version directed by Gaston Roudès in 1933.

L'Assommoir is the seventh in the ambitious twenty volume "Rougon-Macquart" novels in which Zola, expressing deterministic views of human nature of the so-called school of "Naturalism," combined the observation of a scientist with the compassion and skill of an artist to demonstrate the destructive influences of heredity and environment on the Rougon-Macquart family (1850-70).

Zola wrote in his preface to *L'Assommoir:* "I wanted to depict the inevitable downfall of a working class family in the polluted atmosphere of the urban areas. The logical sequel to drunkenness and indolence is the loosening of family ties, the filth of promiscuity, the progressive loss of decent feelings, and, as the climax, shame and death. It is morality in action, just that."

Gervaise (Maria Schell) reveals her dream of owning her own laundry shop to her husband, Coupeau (François Périer).

After the birthday dinner, Gervaise (Maria Schell) is comforted by the blacksmith Goujet (Jacques Harden), who loves her.

Jean Aurenche and Pierre Bost remained faithful to the spirit of this great novel but made several changes for cinematic purposes. While Zola created a collective drama about a doomed milieu, the adapters decided to let the individual tragedy of Gervaise dominate the film. The audience is quickly drawn into her struggles for a better life and her devastating defeat.

The time span, almost twenty years in the novel, was reduced to about half that length for the sake of pacing in the film. Nana is still a child at the film's end and not a young woman as in the book. The use of Gervaise as a narrator occasionally and of flashbacks helps to tighten the plot and thrust the action forward. Goujet's political activism and eventual departure and Coupeau's destruction of the laundry shop are some of the additions, while many of the novel's anticlerical touches were passed over for the film.

Already noted for his striking realism, Clément took great pains in *Gervaise* to capture the atmosphere of the period even to the extent of buying and dismantling a genuine public wash-house from the time of Zola and rebuilding it in the studio. Assembling a great cast headed by Maria Schell and François Périer, Clément created his best known film since *Forbidden Games*.

SYNOPSIS

The film is set in the 1850's; the locale is the working-class district of Barbes-Rochechouart in Montmartre, Paris. Gervaise (Maria Schell) has been living for the past eight years with her drifter-lover Lantier (Armand Mestral) and their two boys. When she goes to the public wash-house she learns that Lantier has run off with the sister of a neighbor, Virginie (Suzy Delair). Hurt and humiliated by the news, she indulges in a bitter fight with the taunting woman. Although a cripple, she overpowers Virginie and spanks her fiercely.

Later Gervaise marries Coupeau (François Périer), a kindly repairer of roofs. A daughter is born. Gervaise dreams of owning her own laundry shop and saves for it diligently. Just as she is nearing her goal, Coupeau falls off a roof and hurts himself. She overprotects him by nursing him at home for half a year and goes through her savings. Coupeau becomes more and more dependent on his wife and loses his pride and desire for work. Coupeau's strong blacksmith friend Goujet (Jacques Harden), secretly in love with Gervaise, generously offers her five hundred francs to open her laundry.

Gervaise, at last a hard working shopkeeper, runs into Virginie, now respectably married, who feigns friendship in order to eventually wreck her vengeance for the earlier humiliation. A recovered Coupeau takes up drinking and starts stealing from the shop.

Gervaise celebrates her birthday by giving a mammoth dinner in the store. Virginie, secretly in league with Lantier, informs the assembly that Lantier is across the street. Coupeau leaves and returns, perversely, with him. A fearful Gervaise is aware that Lantier still exerts power over her and finds solace in the arms of Goujet, who openly declares his love for her. Coupeau and Lantier become buddies and Coupeau invites him to stay with them in an extra room.

Goujet is sent to prison for being involved in a strike and when he returns he is unhappy to see Lantier installed in Gervaise's home. In a flashback we learn how Lantier became Gervaise's lover again: The couple returned one night to find Coupeau asleep in his vomit and Lantier forced Gervaise into his room, her daughter Nana (Chantal Gozzi) observing the while. Goujet, disillusioned with her weakness, leaves Paris, taking her son into apprenticeship with him. Her one chance at love has gone.

Coupeau, distintegrating rapidly, drinks constantly. Gervaise learns that the parasitic Lantier is deceiving her with Virginie. Business falls off and debts pile up. Still, Gervaise has enough pride to angrily refuse Virginie's "helpful offer" to buy the store. In a fit of the D.T.'s, Coupeau demolishes the

Gervaise (Maria Schell) lashes out at the treacherous Virginie (Suzy Delair) and Lantier (Armand Mestral) for trying to take her shop away from her.

His sister (Jany Holt), left, daughter Nana (Chantal Gozzi), and wife (Maria Schell) are horrified at the delirium tremens of Coupeau (François Périer).

shop which Gervaise slaved so long for and is taken away to a hospital. Defeated and thoroughly demoralized, she turns to drink.

The laundry shop is now a candy shop supervised by Virginie, her husband (Lucien Hubert), and a cozy Lantier to complete the latest ménage à trois. The final scene shows Nana leaving her drunken mother in a tavern and running wild in the streets.

COMMENTARY

At the 1956 Venice Film Festival *Gervaise* shared the International Critics Award with Juan Antonio Bardem's *Calle Mayor* (1956). Maria Schell was voted "Best Actress." The British Film Academy cited *Gervaise* "The Best Film from any Source" (1956) and François Périer received the "Best Performance by a Foreign Actor" award. *Gervaise* was

nominated by the Academy of Motion Picture Arts and Sciences for best "Foreign Language Film" (1956) and won the New York Film Critics Award for "Best Foreign Film" (1957).

As in all the best work of Clément, *Gervaise* captures the climate of the period and possesses a unity of atmosphere. The remarkable art direction of Paul Bertrand which effectively reconstructs the Second Empire period; the striking photography of Robert Juillard which presents arresting images of a bleak and overcast Paris; the simple but moving music of Georges Auric which subtly evokes the moods of longing and nostalgia; and of course the firm hand of Clément's direction, never flashy or resorting to sensationalism, all contribute to a memorable film faithful to the intentions of Zola which retains the author's tone of compassion and pity.

The cast is superlative. Maria Schell captures all the strengths and weaknesses of the victimized heroine. Gervaise's essential vulnerability, her wistful sadness, her pathetic aspirations are delicately conveyed in a performance which is Miss Schell's best on screen so far. Outstanding as well are François Périer's weak and ultimately self-destructive Coupeau; Suzy Delair's bitchy, vengeful Virginie; Armand Mestral's self-serving, opportunistic Lantier; and Jacques Harden's warm and sympathetic Goujet.

Certain scenes stay with us: The realistic fight scene in the laundry. The amusing outing to the Louvre to kill time on Gervaise's wedding day. The birthday dinner splurge. The disgusting sight of Coupeau sleeping on his vomit-soaked bed which activates Gervaise's degrading liaison with Lantier. Coupeau's frightening bout of delirium tremens with Nana staring at his feet shaking in convulsive movements, culminating in his shocking destruction of the laundry shop and a now-defeated Gervaise turning to drink for solace. And lastly the final long shot of a neglected Nana, her mother now an alcoholic, showing off her ribbon flirtatiously to the neighborhood boys—her fate, that of the future notorious courtesan, being sealed.

It is interesting to note that Gervaise was also the mother of Jacques Lantier who had been left in Provence when his parents came to Paris and who is the doomed central character of Zola's *The Human Beast (La Bête Humaine)* (1890).

A superb adaptation, beautifully directed and acted, *Gervaise* retains its power and is among Clément's best work.

Lt. Fontaine: François Leterrier; *François Jost:* Charles Le Clainche; *de Leiris, the Pastor:* Roland Monod; *Blanchet:* Maurice Beerblock; *Orsini:* Jack Ertaud; *Terry:* Roger Tréherne; *Hébrard:* Jean-Paul Delhumeau; *Prisoner #110:* Jean-Philippe Delamare; *Chief Warder:* Jacques Oerlemans; *German Intelligence Officer:* Klaus Detlef Grevenhorst.

A MAN ESCAPED

(Un Condamné à Mort s'Est Echappé or Le Vent Souffle Où Il Veut)

S.N.E. GAUMONT (SOCIÉTE NOUVELLE
DES ESTABLISSEMENTS
GAUMONT)/N.E.F. (NOUVELLES
EDITIONS DE FILMS)   1956

CREDITS

Screenplay: Robert Bresson, based on André Devigny's account published in *Le Figaro Littéraire* (November 20, 1954); *Director:* Robert Bresson; *Photographer:* Léonce-Henry Burel; *Assistant Directors:* Michel Clément and Jacques Ballanche; *Editor:* Raymond Lamy; *Music:* The "Kyrie" from Mozart's Mass in C Minor; *Running Time:* 102 minutes; *Paris Premiere:* November 9, 1956; *New York Premiere:* August 26, 1957; *16 mm. Rental Source:* New Yorker Films.

BACKGROUND

Despite the enormous critical acclaim which *Diary of a Country Priest* earned, Robert Bresson had to wait over five years before he could make another film.

In 1954 André Devigny, a Resistance hero, published an account of his daring escape, just hours before he was to be executed by the Nazis, from a heavily guarded prison in Lyons in 1943 during the time of the Occupation. Bresson read it and felt that he must bring it to the screen: "I remember that it affected me as something of great beauty."

Concerning his escape, Devigny had written: "There were two parts in it, mine and God's. Where was the limit? I did not know but I felt that heaven would cast its glance upon this deaf and resolute struggle only to the extent that I would put the most hidden of my physical and moral resources into the balance."

Here was an opportunity for this gifted, instinctive director to make another deeply personal, even autobiographical film—Bresson himself was a P.O.W. at the beginning of WWII—a vehicle to

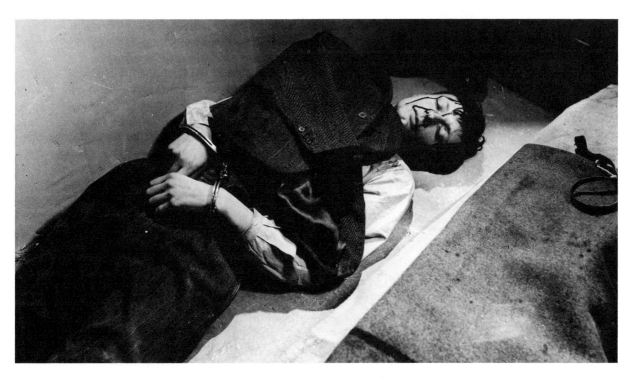

After being beaten for trying to escape enroute to prison, Lt. Fontaine (François Leterrier) is left on his cell floor at Fort Montluc.

After weeks of painstaking effort Lt. Fontaine (François Leterrier) manages to loosen the wooden panels of his cell door with only his sharpened spoon.

demonstrate the workings of God's mercy or grace on our lives. Significantly the two working titles for the project were *Help Yourself* (*Aide-toi*—with the idea that "heaven will help you") and *The Wind Bloweth Where It Listeth* (John: 2:8) which eventually became the film's alternate title.

Bresson said: "I would like to show this miracle: an invisible hand over the prison, directing what happens and causing such and such a thing to succeed for one and not for another. . . . The film is a mystery. . . . The Spirit breathes where it will." Bresson wrote the screenplay, omitting Devigny's explanation for his intitial capture and subsequent story after his escape, thereby concentrating on the escape exclusively. He announces, in the film's preface, "This story is true. I present it as it is, without embellishment."

As in his prior film, Bresson chose to work with non-professionals, this time totally. "My interpreters must have a moral resemblance to the characters in my film," Bresson said. Accordingly,

The prisoners are lined up and ordered to surrender their clandestine pencils. Front row left: the Pastor (Roland Monod, partially hidden), and next to him Lt. Fontaine (François Leterrier).

he rejected a young parachutist who strongly resembled Devigny physically and chose instead François Leterrier, a graduate of philosophy who had finished his military service and was both the same age (27) and rank (Lt.) as Devigny in 1943. (Leterrier went on to have a career as a film director.) Roland Monod, who had studied theology, was selected to play the Pastor who had encouraged Devigny to pray while they were imprisoned together.

For the sake of authenticity much of the film was shot at the actual Lyons prison, even in Devigny's original cell, and at a replica carefully designed by Pierre Charbonnier at the Saint-Maurice studio. Devigny himself acted as a technical adviser. Bresson strove for perfection with his incessant rehearsals and shooting more than twenty times the number of feet eventually used in the film. Monod recalls: "During the shooting, and as the rushes were projected in the evenings, one realized that this literal faithfulness was only a marvellous pretext for Bresson; that out of the 'exceptional' adventure, he was creating an 'eternal' work, devoted to the glory of the Divine Grace and Will." More than a precise documentary and a breathtaking suspenseful prison break, *A Man Escaped* is a magnificent drama of the triumphal human spirit.

SYNOPSIS

The young Lt. Fontaine (François Leterrier) attempts to flee from his German captors taking him by car through Lyons to prison, but is caught. He is badly beaten and thrown into a cell in Fort Montluc where he recovers slowly. Contact through his bars with Terry (Roger Tréherne) and other inmates in a courtyard renews a sense of hope in the despairing man. He is able to send off a message to his Resistance group and begins communicating with his fellow prisoners.

He starts a meticulous plan of escape. Changed to a cell of the top floor, Fontaine files down a spoon and spends seven weeks painstakingly loosening the panels of his wooden cell door. He meets the Pastor, de Leiris (Roland Monod), a continuous source of spiritual encouragement to him. Fontaine in turn tries to bolster the morale of his neighboring cellmate Blanchet (Maurice Beerblock), a suicidal old man sunk in despair.

Fontaine furtively pries apart his bed springs yielding forty yards of strong wire which, combined with cloth from bedding and clothing, forms a sturdy rope. Orsini (Jack Ertaud), a fellow prisoner, makes an unsuccessful escape attempt. How-

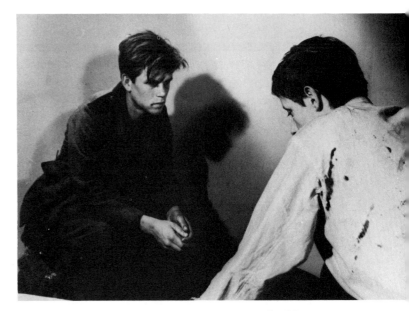

Lt. Fontaine (François Leterrier) is in a state of crisis: Should he enlist the new cellmate Jost (Charles Le Clainche), a deserter, in his escape plans or kill him?

ever, before his execution, he manages to tell Fontaine to break up his window frame to make stronger hooks; the ones he made couldn't support his weight.

Interrogated by the Nazis, Fontaine learns he's been found guilty of espionage and sentenced to die before the firing squad soon. François Jost (Charles Le Clainche), a sixteen-year-old French boy who deserted from the German army, is thrown into his cell. Fontaine ponders: Is he a spy? Can he be trusted? He has to decide quickly whether to kill him or take him along with him. He opts for the latter and pressures the boy to join him.

On a dark evening they leave the cell and reach the roof through the skylight which is raised at night. After a wait, Fontaine lowers a rope and descends to the courtyard where he's forced to kill a guard. They climb to another roof and toss their rope across a passage to the outside wall. The hooks are secured and after a nervous wait with a sentry bicycling past below they crawl across to the wall and leap to freedom. Fontaine is grateful for the providential Jost, for he realizes that he may not have made it alone. Elated with their triumph, they hurry off into the night.

COMMENTARY

For his achievement with *A Man Escaped*, Robert Bresson was unanimously voted "Best Director" at

Waiting for the right moment to crawl across the rope to the outer wall and the leap to freedom: Lt. Fontaine (François Leterrier) and Jost (Charles Le Clainche). (The "rope" has been made from wire, clothing, and bedding.)

the 1957 Cannes Film Festival. The French Film Academy named it the best picture of the year.

With this film once more the director was on the track of the ineffable: "To translate the invisible wind by the water it sculpts in passing." "All of the drama is interior," Bresson said of *A Man Escaped*, and to have us concentrate on Fontaine's inner state the director deliberately avoids establishing and reaction shots and presents everything from the point of view of the protagonist. Frequent close-ups of Fontaine contribute to the effect of intimacy.

Bresson understates sensational aspects through ellipsis: while Fontaine makes a dash for freedom in the German car at the film's start, the camera remains focused on the empty seat while selected sounds record the man's capture and return. His subsequent beating and later killing of a guard are not shown but conveyed through ellipsis as well. Fontaine's off-screen commentary helps infuse spiritual insight into the perilous action.

Bresson uses great economy of means and a rigorous exactitude. The short scenes and rapid cutting create a powerful tension. François Truffaut observed that *A Man Escaped* "once set on its perfectly staright path, rushes into the night with the same rhythm as a windshield wiper. . . . It's one of those films which can be said not to contain a single useless shot or a scene that could be cut or shortened."

From the "raw material" of his "models" Bresson through his disciplined direction strove to achieve, as he wrote, "the constant, the eternal beneath the accidental." François Letterier was an ideal choice for Devigny; his remarkable face shows intelligence, gentleness, sensitivity, and an inner strength.

There is a striking use of sound: the noise from a distant trolley car and train evokes the world beyond the prison; the sound of the guard's key as it hits the bannister summons up the menacing presence of the enemy. . . . There is also a sparse but powerful use of music which underlines the spiritual dimension of the work. A Mozart "Kyrie" is played while the inmates empty their wastes in the courtyard. "This music lifted this scene to another level," Bresson said. "It is not possible now to think of those men without remembering their dignity, and they were dirty, ragged, and dishevelled." After the pair make their arduous break for freedom, the "Kyrie" returns in a glorious outburst of exultation. Burel's somber photography captures the dreary atmosphere of the prison.

A Man Escaped remains Bresson's masterpiece. If one were required to list ten of the greatest French films of all time, this transcendental work would certainly be included. It is one of a handful of films from the entirety of world cinema which can honestly and precisely be called "sublime."

166

THE FOUR HUNDRED BLOWS

(Les Quatre Cents Coups)

LES FILMS DU CARROSSE/S.E.D.I.F.
(SOCIÉTÉ D'EXPLOITATION ET DE
DISTRIBUTION DE FILMS)   1959

CREDITS

Story: François Truffaut; *Adaptation and Dialogue:* François Truffaut and Marcel Moussy; *Director:* François Truffaut; *Photographer:* Henri Decaë (Dyaliscope); *Assistant Directors:* Philippe de Broca, Alain Jeannel, Francis Cognany, Robert Bobert; *Editor:* Marie-Josèphe Yoyotte; *Music:* Jean Constantin; *Running Time:* 101 minutes*; *Paris Premiere:* June 3, 1959; *New York Premiere:* November 16, 1959; *16 mm. Rental Source:* Janus.

CAST

Antoine Doinel: Jean-Pierre Léaud; *Gilberte Doinel:* Claire Maurier; *Julien Doinel:* Albert Rémy; *"Little Sheet," the Teacher:* Guy Decomble; *René Bigey:* Patrick Auffay; *M. Bigey:* Georges Flamant; *Mme. Bigey:* Yvonne Claudie; *Director of the School:* Robert Beauvais; *Examining Magistrate:* Claude Mansard; *Commissioner:* Jacques Monod; *Nightwatchman:* Henri Virlojeux; *Woman with dog:* Jeanne Moreau; *Man in Street:* Jean-Claude Brialy; *Policeman:* Jacques Demy.

BACKGROUND

François Truffaut was born on February 6, 1932, in Paris. Many aspects of his troubled childhood and

*Original release was 94 minutes; 7 more minutes were added in the 1967 reissue.

Portrait of Jean-Pierre Léaud as the incarcerated, troubled adolescent, Antoine Doinel. One of several shots underlining the youth's isolation and sense of confinement.

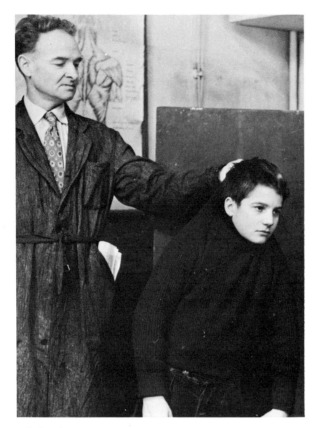

"Little Sheet", the teacher (Guy Decomble), discovers that his pupil, Antoine Doinel (Jean-Pierre Léaud), has written some verse on the classroom wall while being punished for having a pin-up photo.

adolescence, which include detention at the reformatory at Villejuif at age sixteen, appear in his first feature.

At the age of twelve Truffant decided to become a film director and at fifteen made an unsuccessful attempt at running a film club. Through this, however, the youth was fortunate in befriending film critic André Bazin. Bazin not only managed to have him subsequently released from the reformatory in his custody but also came to his rescue later when Truffaut was in a military prison for desertion. Bazin served as a mentor to the young cinéaste and started his career as a film critic in 1953 by having him write for the influential *Cahiers du Cinéma* which Bazin helped launch in April 1951. Over the next five years Truffaut became a very formidable and outspoken critic.

In 1955 Truffaut made his first film, the short *Une Visite*, shot in 16 mm. His next short was the well-received *The Mischief Makers (Les Mistons)* (1958). *The Four Hundred Blows* was initially conceived as an autobiographical, twenty-minute sketch entitled *Antoine Runs Away (La Fugue d'Antoine)* for a compilation film dealing with childhood which was to include *The Mischief Makers* and three other sketches which were never filmed. Truffaut decided to expand the Antoine segment into a chronicle of adolescence.

Though the film is autobiographical ("The ad-

After school, Antoine (Jean-Pierre Léaud) discusses his problems with "Little Sheet" with his friend René Bigey (Patrick Auffay).

168

ventures which Antoine Doinel experiences in *The Four Hundred Blows* are mine," Truffaut said), the director set the story in contemporary Paris, for he didn't feel sufficiently competent at that time to recreate the Occupation. He collaborated with writer Marcel Moussy: "Our main purpose," Truffaut wrote, "was not to depict adolescence from the usual viewpoint of sentimental nostalgia but . . . to show it as the painful experience it is. . . . The affective weaning, the coming of puberty, the wish for independence and the inferiority complex are characteristic symptoms. . . . During this stage, a simple disturbance, or upset, can spark off a revolt and this crisis is precisely described as adolescent rebellion: the world is unjust . . . and one way to cope is to raise hell. In France this is known as *'faire les quatre cents coups.'* " Of all those tested for the leading role, Truffaut was most impressed with young Jean-Pierre Léaud (born in Paris on May 5, 1944).

Through borrowing, hiring actors on a deferred payment basis, and economizing Truffaut was able to shoot his film for approximately one-fourth the cost of an average feature at that time. Shooting began on November 10, 1958, and was completed on January 5, 1959. No studios were used, just apartments, schools, and streets of Paris as well as the natural setting of Honfleur.

The Four Hundred Blows, dedicated "to the memory of André Bazin" who died on the second day of shooting, was an immediate success and confirmed Truffaut's belief that "a child's truth is something I think I feel absolutely."

SYNOPSIS

The neglected, thirteen-year-old Antoine Doinel (Jean–Pierre Léaud) lives in Paris with his indifferent mother (Claire Maurier) and ineffectual father (Albert Rémy) who raises the illegitimate boy as his son. Antoine does poorly in school and dislikes his unsympathetic teacher, "Little Sheet" (Guy Decomble). He plays hooky with his friend René (Patrick Auffay) and goes to an amusement center.* Later he sees his mother embracing a lover on the street.

At school, pressed to explain his absence, Antoine blurts out to his teacher that his mother died. His parents' appearance at the school traps him in his lie and, terrified, he spends the night away from

---

*François Truffaut is one of the adults in "The Rotor" sequence.

home. A worried mother affects a brief, friendly reconciliation.

When "Little Sheet" accuses Antoine of plagiarizing a passage from Balzac, the boy decides to quit school and run away from home. René hides him in his house. Needing money, Antoine decides to steal a typewriter from his father's office with René's help. Unable to pawn it, Antoine returns it and is caught by the nightwatchman (Henri Virlojeux). His exasperated father takes him to the police station and confesses to the chief (Jacques Monod) that he and his wife can't handle this impossible child. Antoine is questioned and, shockingly, locked up with criminal types and prostitutes.

He is sent to the Observation Center for Delinquent Minors. He reveals aspects of his unhappy family life to a lady psychologist. Antoine's mother visits and tells him his father is no longer interested in him. An opportunity to escape arises during a soccer game. Antoine flees to a Normandy beach and the sea he always longed for, which symbolizes freedom for him. He stops at the water's edge and turns to the camera—his fate uncertain in a famous concluding freeze frame.

COMMENTARY

François Truffaut was voted "Best Director" at the 1959 Cannes Film Festival. Ironically, he had been barred from attending the previous year for his attacks on the commercial exploitation of the festival. *The Four Hundred Blows* shared the Prix Méliès (1959) with *Hiroshima Mon Amour.* Among many other awards it received the New York Film Critics Award for "Best Foreign Film" (1959). François Truffaut and Marcel Moussy were nominated for an "Oscar" for "Story and Screenplay—Written Directly For The Screen" (1959).

Critics commented on the stimulating and appealing freshness of the direction. The "open" narration as opposed to the typical tightly structured plot was trend-setting. Truffaut employed brief shots, simple editing, and a documentary style. "I made that film in a very instinctive way," Truffaut said.

Truffaut and Moussy avoided the temptation to establish a black and white demarcation: innocent children and corrupt adults. Instead, all his characters are richly complex, recognizably human, and vulnerable. They were able to keep the central character of Antoine in focus and not use him as a symbol with which to attack society or make the work a filmed thesis. Truffaut managed to main-

After finding out that Antoine (Jean-Pierre Léaud) caused a fire in their apartment with his candle-lit "homage to Balzac," M. Doinel (Albert Rémy) threatens him, while his wife (Claire Maurier) protests.

tain a non-judgmental, objective tone and to eschew any self-pity or sentimentality.

Critics praised the scene of the psychologist's interview in which the camera remains trained on Antoine as he responds to an off-screen voice without traditional reaction shots of the interviewer and with dissolves used to bridge topics.

The closing freeze frame was ambiguous, celebrated, and widely imitated. "A totally happy ending would be completely false," Truffaut said. "So I was obliged to have a conclusion that was sort of hanging in mid-air." He told Léaud to turn and stare into the camera. "But," Truffaut continued, "his look wandered. So, in the lab, I stopped the image on that moment when he was looking into the camera. And I enlarged the face. For me, it was as if the face came down into the audience. It was also to instill in the audience a form of guilt; a tacit accusation."

Typical in Truffaut's films was the act of homage to a favorite director. Here he pays tribute to Jean Vigo: the group of boys jogging after the gym teacher who start disappearing down side streets recalls *Zero for Conduct;* Antoine's rush to the sea evokes Jean Dasté's similar race in *L'Atalante.* Jean-Pierre Léaud brought the character of Antoine Doinel to life unforgettably. "He was a 'natural,' " Truffaut said, "and I encouraged him to play it 'by

170

ear.' He performed freely, reacting in his own manner and responding in his own words." The subdued lighting of Henri Decaë pinpoints Antoine's grey and bleak world.

Truffaut started a twenty-year Antoine Doinel cycle continuing with the sketch *Antoine et Colette* for the compilation film, *Love at Twenty (L'Amour à Vingt Ans)* (1962), *Stolen Kisses (Baisers Voles)* (1968), *Bed and Board (Domicile Conjugal)* (1970), and concluding with *Love on the Run (L'Amour en Fuite)* (1979).

The Four Hundred Blows helped launch the New Wave and establish Truffaut internationally as a major director. It remains one of those rare films which captures childhood in an authentic and compelling manner.

Antoine (Jean-Pierre Léaud) runs away from the Observation Center for Delinquent Minors and confronts the sea for the first time.

HIROSHIMA MON AMOUR

ARGOS FILMS / COMO FILMS (PARIS) /
DAÏEÏ MOTION PICTURE CO. LTD.
(TOKYO) / PATHÉ OVERSEAS
PRODUCTION   1959

CREDITS

Screenplay: Marguerite Duras, published in Paris (1960) and in New York (1961); *Director:* Alain Resnais; *Photographers:* Sacha Vierny (in France) and Takahashi Michio (in Japan); *Assistant Directors:* Tanneguy Andréfouet, Jean-Pierre Léon, René Guyonnet, I. Shiraï, Iroi, and Hara; *Editors:* Henri Colpi, Jasmine Chasney, and Anne Sarraute; *Music:* Giovanni Fusco and Georges Delerue, with additional Japanese music for the parade and jukebox; *Running Time:* 91 minutes; *Paris Premiere:* June 10, 1959; *New York Premiere:* May 16, 1960; *16 mm. Rental Source:* Images.

CAST

She: Emmanuèle Riva; *He:* Eiji Okada; *The German Soldier:* Bernard Fresson; *Her Mother:* Stella Dassas; *Her Father:* Pierre Barbaud.

BACKGROUND

Alain Resnais was born on June 3, 1922, in Vannes (Morbihan). His father was a pharmacist. In 1940 he left Brittany to study education in Paris but switched to acting then later enrolled at

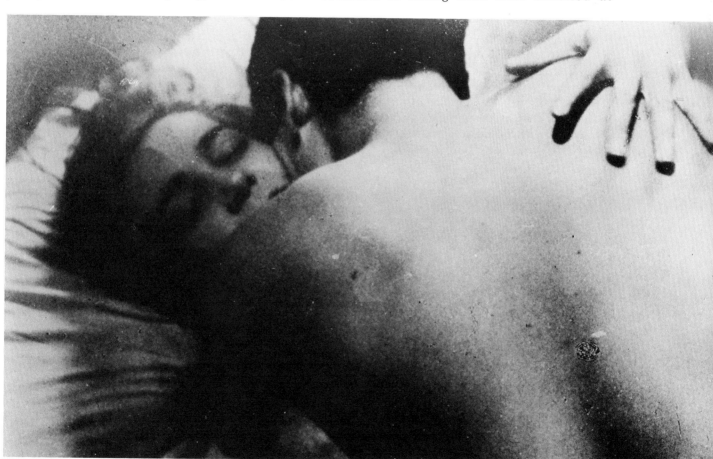

In the early morning in her hotel room, the newly met lovers (Emmanuèle Riva and Eiji Okada) embrace.

171

I.D.H.E.C.* to learn editing. His short, *Van Gogh* (1948), initially shot in 16 mm., established him as a documentary filmmaker of note and won an "Oscar" for "Short Subject" (2-reel category) (1949). For the next decade he produced seven remarkable shorts (in 35 mm.), the most extraordinary being the prize-winning *Night and Fog (Nuit et Brouillard)* (1955), a compelling study of our memory of Nazi concentration camps.

On the strength of his reputation, Resnais was approached by a group of Japanese and French producers wishing to sponsor a documentary film on the way Hiroshima appeared twelve years after its destruction on August 16, 1945, by an atom bomb. The director was guaranteed complete freedom with the stipulations that the film would be an hour long, feature one Japanese and one French actor, and contain episodes based in Japan and France.

Resnais, reluctant to repeat himself after *Night and Fog*, decided after several fruitless months to approach novelist Marguerite Duras (Françoise Sagan earlier turned down an invitation to write the script) and discuss the feasibility—since it was impossible to deal with the overwhelming subject of Hiroshima directly—of doing it as a love story, a fictional but stylized narrative, "but one in which," Resnais explained, "the atomic agony would not be absent." A sparse, lyrical script was completed by the summer of 1958 and served as basis for Resnais' first feature film, *Hiroshima Mon Amour*. Resnais said "I intended to compose a sort of poem in which the images would act as counterpoint to the text."

Preferring stage actors to film actors, Resnais cast Emmanuèle Riva, who had a successful career in French theatre, in the lead. He admired the quality of her voice as well as her beauty and emotional range. Eiji Okada, prominent on the stage and in films in Japan, was her co-star. Exteriors were shot in Hiroshima, interiors at Tokyo during August and September 1958, then, in France, exteriors at Nevers and Autun that December and interiors at Paris.

Unconventional and difficult, *Hiroshima Mon Amour* scared off potential distributors who saw it only as an uncommercial avant-garde film and had to wait until the Cannes Film Festival where its premiere was an event. The career of a director of genius was brilliantly launched.

*Initials of Institut des Hautes Etudes Cinématographiques, the prestigious Paris film school co-founded by Marcel L'Herbier in 1943.

SYNOPSIS

The action occurs in little more than twenty-four hours. There's a startling, dream-like prologue composed of brief shots of two naked torsos in an embrace intercut with shots of a hospital and museum, newsreels of Hiroshima's atomic devastation, footage from the 1953 semi-documentary Japanese film *Hiroshima* (directed by Hideo Sekigawa) which was a reenactment of the holocaust, and views of the rebuilt city accompanied by a duologue consisting of the French woman's incantatory report and the Japanese man's repeated denial of what she "saw."

A short realistic scene follows of the unnamed lovers talking at 4 A.M. She (Emmanuèle Riva) is a French actress making a film on peace in Hiroshima. He (Eiji Okada) is a Japanese architect she met the day before and brought back to the Hotel New Hiroshima. Later that morning she notices his hand tremble a little in his sleep and has an involuntary memory of the dead German soldier (Bernard Fresson) she loved during the war. . . . The couple separate.

He finds her on location in the afternoon during the film's shooting. The architect brings her to his home. We learn each is happily married. After they have made love, he probes into her past and she tells of her blissful first love with the soldier in Nevers, France. He senses that Nevers is a way to come to understand her. She must leave soon to return to Paris.

Later, the couple are in a riverside café and she recalls (but in nonchronological order) the traumatic events at Nevers: her lover killed on the day of the Liberation, her head shaved for consorting with the enemy, her going temporarily insane and

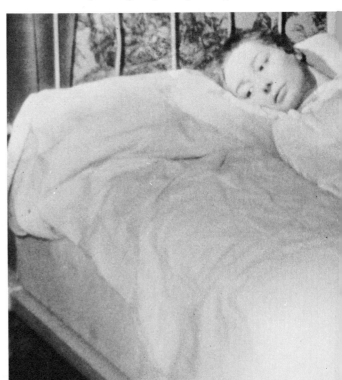

being hidden in the cellar by her shamed parents. . . . At one point so absorbed is she in her remembered pain that the architect slaps the hysterical woman to restore her to herself. She resumes: Slowly she forgot this first love, then left for Paris and arrived at the time of the bombing of Hiroshima. . . . Realizing that this present intense love is doomed to oblivion, she parts from him.

She cannot stand being alone in her hotel room and leaves. He meets her and asks her to stay in Hiroshima. She is tortured by love and indecision and wanders restlessly, he following. Returning, eventually, to her hotel she moans to her lover who enters, "I'll forget you! I'm forgetting you already!" He holds her wrists while each intuitively calls the

Later, the architect (Eiji Okada) finds the troubled actress (Emmanuèle Riva) on location for a film and tells her, "You give me a great longing for love. . ."

He (Eiji Okada) brings her (Emmanuèle Riva) back to his home in Hiroshima.

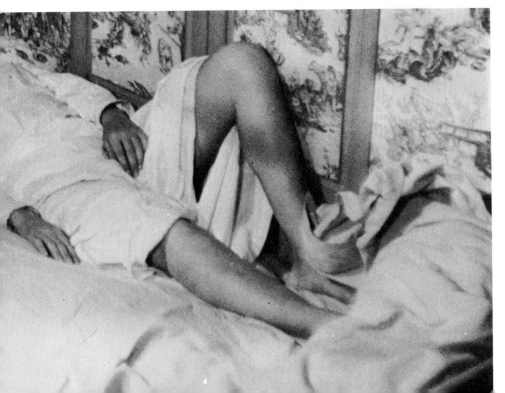

She (Emmanuèle Riva) painfully remembers her room at Nevers and how she was tortured with desire for her dead German soldier.

173

other the emblematic names: "Hiroshima" and "Nevers."

COMMENTARY

Shown out of competition "for diplomatic reasons" (presumably so as not to offend the United States) at the 1959 Cannes Film Festival, *Hiroshima Mon Amour* nonetheless shared with the Venezuelan film *Araya* (1958) the International Critics Award and received the Film Writers Award, presented for the first time. It also shared a Prix Méliès with Truffaut's *The Four Hundred Blows* (1959). Resnais's film was successful and universally praised. It received the New York Film Critics Award for "Best Foreign Film" (1960) and Marguerite Duras was nominated for an "Oscar" for "Story and Screenplay—Written Directly for the Screen" (1960).

The director made radical departures in directing his first full-length film which critics claimed were as revolutionary as those made by Orson Welles in *Citizen Kane* (1941). Chief among these was the introduction of the subliminal flash cut. In the morning the actress sees her Japanese lover's hand quivering slightly in his sleep. Suddenly there is a quick cut to a four second shot of a dying soldier, lying elsewhere, hand extended and jerking in a similar gesture. There is a cut to her distressed face, then to the lover who wakes up. Here is a cinematic use of the Proustian device of recapturing the past fragmentarily through the operation of involuntary memory by which an object or bodily attitude in the present can accidentally trigger off a recall of past feelings or incidents associated with it. No explanation is provided at the time, no traditional dissolve to cue us that this is a flashback; the audience must pay undivided attention to the flow of imagery. Such a device indicates the interaction between the past and the present. This direct cut to past experience has a shock value and has often been imitated.

In the heroine's flashback sequence at Nevers, Resnais daringly uses a subjective order— prompted by her emotional state—rather than a chronological order of events. Thus we see her in the cellar before the scene of her head being shaved after the soldier's death.

Resnais' beautiful tracking shots have been praised, especially those employed in the sequence when the heroine wanders the streets of Hiroshima while recalling Nevers. There is a marvellous use of parallel montage (shot at identical speed by the separate Japanese and French photographers who didn't know the other's work) in which views of the Japanese city are gracefully intercut with those of the French city to create the visual impression of the unity of past and present in her mind. There is as well a striking use of the soundtrack to achieve a similar effect of simultaneity: Japanese music and sounds underscore shots of Nevers; musical motifs for Nevers are heard in the Hiroshima scenes.

The jolting opening shots of the enlaced couple have been described by Resnais as "a sort of dream, a voice coming from the unconscious, which is at one and the same time that of the authors and that of the spectators, which will only later become that of the principal characters. It is a kind of great advancing tracking shot into the clouds of the unconscious to reach the two characters, a way of painting a sensory atmosphere which perhaps allows us, afterwards, to give this love story a new resonance."

The Japanese man's repeated denial of what the woman "saw" in Hiroshima indicates that the full meaning of the atomic catastrophe lies beyond the ability of the visitor's intellect to grasp by merely frequenting a museum and implies, by extension, that the whole phenomenon of Hiroshima cannot be captured by filmmakers attempting a documentary. "All one can do is talk about the impossibility of talking about Hiroshima," Duras commented.

The dropping of the atom bomb and the personal tragedy at Nevers are not meant to be considered equal in significance. Resnais maintains: "We contrast the immense, monstrous, incredible aspect of Hiroshima with the tiny, little story of Nevers which to us is reflected through Hiroshima as the glimmer of a candle is magnified and reversed by a lens." Hiroshima and Nevers can only be evaluated on the level of the macrocosmic with the microcosmic, a tragedy for mankind in general linked tentatively to an individual's agony in wartime.

The film's central theme is that of memory and forgetfulness which first appears as a leitmotif announced and repeated in the hypnotic prologue. (At no point does the film explore the ethical problems inherent in the extramarital relationship.) All experiences in time are subject to oblivion, even those which seem "unforgettable" as Hiroshima's destruction. Forgetting is inevitable (the French girl inflicts pain on herself in the cellar in Nevers in order to keep alive the wound of love but ultimately says, "I tremble at the thought of having forgotten so much love. . . .") and necessary ("If one does not forget," Resnais said, "one can neither live nor act.")

The actress and the architect will in time forget

each other, but Nevers and Hiroshima will remain as symbols of love. (There is obviously concern for the future in that the lesson of Hiroshima's destruction must never be lost to the world.)

The characters in this superbly written screenplay are complex, real, and undergo change. Emmanuèle Riva gives an astonishing performance in her screen début; Eiji Okada is convincing and effective as her lover. Giovanni Fusco provided a remarkably original and atmospheric score; Georges Delerue contributed a haunting waltz in the café scene.

As much a poignant love story as a visual meditation between past and present and a strong anti-war movie, this seminal film, this formally dense and musically structured work, exerted a profound influence by suggesting new approaches for the narrative film, creating a new film vocabulary, and pointing out ways to treat the manifestation of time cinematically. Intense, lyrical, provocative and mature, *Hiroshima Mon Amour* retains its power after more than twenty years and justly deserves its reputation as a screen classic.

After leaving the café, realizing that their affair is doomed as was her first love, she (Emmanuèle Riva) tells her lover (Eiji Okada) to please go away, that they will probably die without seeing each other again. The shot effectively expresses their pending separation.

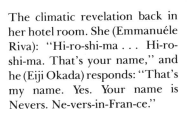

The climatic revelation back in her hotel room. She (Emmanuéle Riva): "Hi-ro-shi-ma . . . Hi-ro-shi-ma. That's your name," and he (Eiji Okada) responds: "That's my name. Yes. Your name is Nevers. Ne-vers-in-Fran-ce."

BREATHLESS

(A Bout de Souffle)

S.N.C. (SOCIÉTÉ NOUVELLE DE
CINÉMA)   1960

CREDITS

Screenplay and Direction: Jean-Luc Godard, based on a story by François Truffaut; *Photographer:* Raoul Coutard; *Assistant Director:* Pierre Rissient; *Editor:* Cécile Decugis; *Music:* Martial Solal and Mozart's Clarinet Concerto (K. 622); *Running Time:* 89 minutes; *Paris Premiere:* March 16, 1960; *New York Premiere:* February 7, 1961; *16 mm. Rental Source:* Corinth.

CAST

Michel Poiccard, alias Laszlo Kovacs: Jean-Paul Belmondo; *Patricia Franchini:* Jean Seberg; *Inspector Vital:* Daniel Boulanger; *Antonio Berrutti:* Henri-Jacques Huet; *Parvulesco:* Jean-Pierre Melville; *Journalist Van Doude:* Van Doude; *Minouche:* Liliane Robin; *Carl Zombach:* Roger Hanin; *Claudius, the Used Car Dealer:* Claude Mansard; *Informer:* Jean-Luc Godard.

BACKGROUND

Jean-Luc Godard was born in Paris on December 3, 1930. His mother was French; his father was a Swiss physician who operated a clinic in Nyon (Canton of Vaud). In 1949, Godard was a student

Returning to Paris, Michel (Jean-Paul Belmondo) meets Patricia (Jean Seberg) sellling the *Herald Tribune* along the Champs-Elysées and invites her to go with him to Rome.

(Opposite page) Portrait of the disconnected young lovers: Michel (Jean-Paul Belmondo) and Patricia (Jean Seberg) in her hotel room.

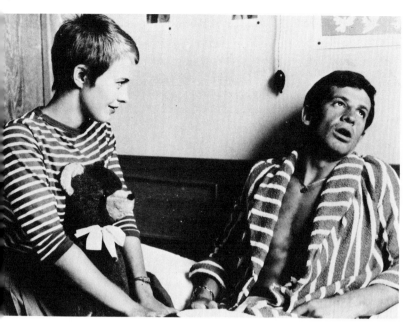

In her hotel room, Michel (Jean-Paul Belmondo) is exasperated when Patricia (Jean Seberg) expresses reluctance to make a commitment to a man she's quite unsure of.

Patricia (Jean Seberg), wearing Michel's shirt, in a pensive moment standing near her portrait in her hotel bathroom.

at the Sorbonne—eventually taking a degree in Ethnology—but spent most of his time devouring films at the Cinémathèque and cinéclubs along with such cinéastes as Eric Rohmer, Jacques Rivette, and François Truffaut. Godard co-founded the short-lived *La Gazette du Cinéma* (1950), contributing articles under the name Hans Lucas, then wrote

intermittently for *Cahiers du Cinéma* and *Arts*. In 1954 he directed the first of his five shorts, *Opération Béton,* in Switzerland (released in 1958) before he was finally able to make his first feature.

In 1959 he offered producer Georges de Beauregard four projects, including a fifteen-page outline about a young alienated gangster written by François Truffaut and conceived as a potential sequel to *The Four Hundred Blows* as he imagined a future Antoine Doinel after reform schools and the army. Unable to realize his project—based on a news item—Truffaut let Godard have it. Since the early New Wave films were successful at international festivals, Beauregard decided to take a chance on letting Godard do the gangster story, especially since there were the supposed safeguards of Truffaut as scriptwriter and Claude Chabrol as production supervisor. Actually these two directors merely lent their names to help Godard get financing and that was the extent of their participation.

By not supplying a completed script to his producer, technicians or his actors, Godard was able to maintain total control of the film. On a small budget of $90,000, *Breathless* was shot between August 17 and September 15, 1959, in Paris and Marseilles. "I wanted to end the old tradition in a spectacular way," Godard admitted, "so I made a gangster film, using all the effects that were supposed to be impossible. It's a film where anything goes." This remarkable film broke all the established rules for filmmaking: Instead of stars with big box-office draw, Godard cast in the leads a former boxer and bit player, Jean-Paul Belmondo, and an Iowa-born actress, Jean Seberg, trying to recover from the disaster of her screen début in Otto Preminger's *Saint Joan* (1957). Instead of following a completed script, Godard each morning wrote the scenes to be shot that day. Instead of working with elaborate studio-built sets and carefully controlled lighting, he shot his film on the city streets—even in a friend's bedroom—utilizing available natural light. Instead of employing traditional technical equipment, he placed his photographer in such makeshift conveyances as a wheelchair, twin-sized baby carriage—even a postman's mail cart with peepholes drilled in the sides—and then pushed him along to shoot the action with his hand-held camera. It was even shot as a silent film with the sound post-synchronized in the editing stage. "What I wanted," Godard wrote, "was to take a conventional story and remake, but differently, everything the cinema had done. I also wanted to give the feeling that the techniques of filmmaking had just been discovered or experienced for the first time."

Dedicated to Monogram Pictures, the former Hollywood studio of low-budget, quickly-made "B" movies that Godard admired, *Breathless* was a startling film which, critic Jean Clay wrote, "burst like a thunderbolt in the troubled sky of the French cinema." This liberating, personal work became a landmark film and one of the greatest achievements of the New Wave.

SYNOPSIS

Enroute from Marseilles in a stolen car, Michel Poiccard (Jean-Paul Belmondo) kills a cop attempting to arrest him for speeding. In Paris he tries to persuade a reluctant Patricia (Jean Seberg), an American student who hawks newspapers, to go to Italy with him.

Michel's crime has made the papers. He obtains a check for some unspecified deal but it needs the signature of his hard-to-find friend, Antonio Berrutti (Henri-Jacques Huet). Patricia and Michel have a long scene in her hotel room. She's pregnant by him. Although he proclaims his love for her, she finds him indecipherable. They banter, then make love.

The next day a passerby (Jean-Luc Godard) recognizes Michel and informs the police. Inspector Vital (Daniel Boulanger) visits Patricia at the *Herald Tribune* and shows her a news story about her criminal boyfriend. If she won't cooperate with the law, she'll encounter difficulty with her passport.

A dragnet is spread for the cop killer. Patricia helps Michel find Antonio. The couple spend the night at a friend's apartment. Next morning, she calls Vital and tells him where Michel is, then announces her betrayal to her lover. In the street he meets Antonio who gives him the money. Vital spots Michel and shoots him. He staggers along, then collapses. As Patricia coolly watches, Michel utters his last words, "It's truly disgusting."

COMMENTARY

Breathless won the Prix Jean Vigo (1960) and at the Berlin Film Festival (1960) Godard was cited for "Best Direction." Raoul Coutard received the German Critics' Prize for Photography. A financial success, *Breathless* remains Godard's most popular film to date.

Here was an accurate portrait of two nihilistic young people living on impulse in an aimless and irresponsible manner which seemed to reflect the disorder and existential weariness of its period. The anarchistic Michel is unforgettably portrayed by Jean-Paul Belmondo. Commanding and virile, the young actor was soon to become the biggest French male star since Jean Gabin and Gérard Philipe. Godard conceived the character of Patricia as an extension of the spoiled and inconsiderate girl played by Jean Seberg in Otto Preminger's *Bonjour Tristesse* (1957). Callow and vacillating, Patricia is one of the many bitches who will destroy their men in Godard's films. Although Miss Seberg acted until her tragic death in 1980 she is best remembered as the shallow American girl with close-cropped hair and photogenic features in *Breathless*.

After spending the night together at a friend's studio, Patricia (Jean Seberg) prepares to leave Michel (Jean-Paul Belmondo) to inform the police where he can be found.

Godard's direction was innovative and iconoclastic. He disregarded the formal conventions of film narration: he minimized exposition, leaving the characters' motivations to the viewer to analyze; presented a fragmented narrative; shifted the tone to alternate comedy with tragedy, realism with melodrama; and paid no attention to consistency in shot duration. Most striking of all was his use of "jump cuts," Godard's clever solution to the problem of editing a film which initially ran over three hours. Jean-Pierre Melville commented, "Instead of cutting whole scenes as was the practice then, he had the brilliant idea of cutting more or less at random within scenes. The result was excellent." Instead of a seamless continuity Godard unsettles the viewer by excising smooth transitions and aggressively linking unmatching adjoining shots to propel the action forward, to indicate passing of time, and to suggest structurally the central characters' disjointed life style. The use of jump cuts, the hand-held camera, unusual camera angles, and elliptical editing forces us to regard what is familiar in a new and fresh manner. These techniques produce a directness and immediacy and create, as photographer Raoul Coutard said, "its sense of living in the moment."

Godard employs frequent cultural references, whether to other films (there are significant allusions to the films of Humphrey Bogart, whom Michel idolizes and imitates), directors (Godard pays homage to Jean-Pierre Melville by casting him as the novelist Parvulesco whom Patricia interviews at the Orly airport), writers (William Faulkner), etc. The references can be a private joke (a girl tries to sell Michel a copy of *Cahiers du Cinéma*) or a useful "distancing" device to reinforce the film's theme.

Liberating film from its inherited conventions and employing a collage of innovative film techniques which were quickly absorbed, *Breathless* had a powerful and profound impact. Critic Raymond Sokolov observed that "its careening, anarchic style rewrote the textbooks and opened the way to a freer, more personal kind of cinema." The film demonstrated that the manner in which a story is told can be more important than the story itself. With *Breathless** the career of the most influential and controversial film director of the 1960's, Jean-Luc Godard, was brilliantly launched.

*In August 1982 an American remake of *Breathless* starring Richard Gere and Valerie Kaprisky, directed by Jim Mc Bride, went into production.

LAST YEAR AT MARIENBAD

(L'Année Dernière à Marienbad)

TERRA FILM / SOCIÉTÉ NOUVELLE DES
FILMS CORMORAN / PRÉCITEL / COMO
FILMS / ARGOS FILMS / LES FILMS
TAMARA / CINÉTEL / SILVER FILMS
(PARIS) / CINÉRIZ (ROME)   1961

CREDITS

Screenplay: Alain Robbe-Grillet, screenplay *(ciné-roman)* published in Paris (1961) and New York (1962); *Director:* Alain Resnais; *Photographer:* Sacha Vierny (Dyaliscope); *Assistant Directors:* Jean-Pierre Léon and Volker Schlöndorff; *Editors:* Henri Colpi and Jasmine Chasney; *Music:* Francis Seyrig, performed by organist Marie-Louise Girod; *Running Time:* 94 minutes; *Paris Premiere:* September 29, 1961; *New York Premiere:* March 7, 1962; *16 mm. Rental Source:* Images.

CAST

The Woman (A): Delphine Seyrig; *The Stranger (X):* Giorgio Albertazzi; *The Escort/Husband (M):* Sacha Pitoëff; *with* Françoise Bertin, Luce Garcia-Ville, Héléna Kornel, Françoise Spira, Karin Toeche-Mittler, Pierre Barbaud, Wilhelm von Deek, Jean Lanier, and Gérard Lorin.

The stranger, X(Giorgio Albertazzi), "recalls" the explanation he had given of this emblematic statue at Frederiksbad to the woman, A(Delphine Seyrig).

BACKGROUND

After the successful launching of *Hiroshima Mon Amour* producers Pierre Courau and Raymond Froment arranged in 1960 for Alain Resnais to meet with Alain Robbe-Grillet, prominent in *"le nouveau roman"* ("the new novel") movement which attracted attention in France since the early 1950's and which questioned man's ability to grasp "reality" in the traditional sense and favored ambiguous plots. Robbe-Grillet gave Resnais four brief script projects. They agreed on one and the writer set to work on what was to become famous as *Last Year at Marienbad.*

Resnais felt "the time has come to address [the] public in a new language." He wished, he said, "to train a camera on the inner minds of the characters rather than on their external behavior." The images we see would not be those of objective reality but a subjective vision of what the characters are thinking. The film would represent, Resnais said, "an attempt, still crude and primitive, to approach the complexity of thought and of its mechanisms."

As before, the director chose actors with a theatrical background: Giorgio Albertazzi worked on the Italian stage; Delphine Seyrig and Sacha Pitoëff came from the Paris stage. The film was shot between September and November 1960, exteriors in Munich (the Nymphenburg, Schleissheim, and Amalienburg castles) with interiors at the Photosonor Studios in Paris.

During the editing, Resnais revealed, "we had the feeling we were dealing with something very mysterious. . . . that we were stepping on the toes of unconsciousness. . . ."

However, its producers got nervous and distributors backed away from a movie they thought would confuse and frustrate the public. Since his signature on the "Free Algeria Manifesto" prevented the film from being shown in competition at Cannes, Resnais resorted to entering it at the Venice Film Festival where its triumph guaranteed it a release. Resnais declared: "We hope that the lyrical dream world that is to be found in the picture will appeal to the collective unconscious of people in all countries."

SYNOPSIS

Because of the film's paralogical and nonlinear development, its existence apparently outside of time, its nameless characters without psychological definition (referred to by letters, for convenience

182

only, in the screenplay), and its overwhelming ambiguity—shifts in present, past, future, and conditional tenses; variations and repetitions of scenes; and uncertainty of narrator ("We never really know if the scenes are occurring in the man's mind or the woman's"—Resnais), it is impossible to present an adequate plot summary but merely a rudimentary and tentative guideline.

While the camera tracks through a huge, elegant baroque hotel—an unnamed and mysterious closed world—a man's voice narrates an extended description: "Once again—I walk on. . . ." We witness the conclusion of a play, *Rosmer.* Among shots of the subdued guests speaking cryptic dialogue, a stranger, X (Giorgio Albertazzi), the film's intermittent narrator, announces to a beautiful and stylish woman, A (Delphine Seyrig), that she doesn't seem to remember him and recalls a meet-

Famous shot of the gardens at Frederiksbad which play an important part in the hero's "recollections." In other scenes the statuary and sculpted schrubbery cast shadows, but illogically and mysteriously not here; we see only those of the guests.

ing a year ago at the Frederiksbad gardens where they discussed a statue. When the puzzled woman denies ever visiting the place, he says perhaps it was Marienbad or even here. . . .

There is an older, sinister-looking man, M (Sacha Pitoëff), who accompanies A and who may or may not be her husband. M is triumphant in playing a variant of the Nim game—with cards, matchsticks, dominoes—with X and others.

X pursues A, evoking sundry "memories," and states that she had asked him to wait a year before returning and claiming her. A, at first amused, is gradually drawn to her persistent suitor but fears the distruption of her sedate world. When she's close to the point of surrender there follows a series of hypothetical scenes, each one depicting a possible aftermath which include a fantasy of a jealous M shooting A and a "rape" scene.

M. tells her he knows she's leaving; A begs him not to let her go. During a performance of the play which we saw at the beginning, X and A depart at midnight. In a long shot with the hotel in the distance, X's voice reveals that "you were now already getting lost, forever, in the calm night, alone with me."

COMMENTARY

Last Year at Marienbad won the Grand Prize at the 1961 Venice Film Festival, later the Prix Méliès (1961). This film, possibly the most enigmatic in motion picture history, proved surprisingly successful. Alain Robbe-Grillet was nominated for an "Oscar for "Story and Screenplay—Written Directly for the Screen" (1962).

What might seem terribly literary is a remarkably visual film. Mental processes are rendered in appropriate cinematic forms: Resnais' celebrated exploratory tracking shots—anticipated in his 1956 short on the Bibliothèque Nationale, *Toute la Mémoire du Monde*—suggest the relentless and obsessive pattern of a recurring dream; overexposed shots, as those in the "rape" sequence, denote emphasis; the flow of imagery represents the stream of consciousness, etc. Resnais' direction is totally assured and brilliant.

The plot can be seen as structured in a circular pattern. The film then ends at the point where it starts. Resnais said, "Perhaps at the last image . . . all begins again." Are the hotel and the gardens equal labyrinths, one feeding into the other, with no escape? If the action is "circular" and hence recurring, all distinctions of past, present, and future are hopelessly blurred.

When you have a difference between the screenwriter ("One must remember that the man is not telling the truth. The couple did not meet the year before") and the director ("I could never have shot this film if I had not been convinced that their meeting had actually taken place"), the viewer is free to decide for himself what, if anything, did occur.

While critic John Ward believes that M killed A and X projects fantasies of wish fulfillment, many other diverse interpretations abound, among them: X is a psychiatrist trying to get A to acknowledge what she had repressed; the hotel is a huge necropolis—X, A, and M are all dead; the film depicts parallel universes ("It is quite possible that all the characters are speaking the truth"—Resnais); it retells the old Breton legend of Death (X)

Through the baroque hotel's labyrinthine corridors, the stranger, X(Giorgio Albertazzi), aggressively pursues the woman, A(Delphine Seyrig), attempting to convince her of their "affair" the year before.

The stranger, X(Giorgio Albertazzi), tries to persuade the woman, A(Delphine Seyrig), to leave with him.

coming to fetch his victim (A) after allowing her a year's respite; within an individual three forces vie for dominance: the id (X), ego (A), and superego (M); A sees a play and imagines herself in the heroine's situations; the hotel is a clinic and A is a patient there (M: "You should get some rest. Don't forget, that's why we're here"); M is a vampire. . . . One can discern the legends of Orpheus and Eurydice in the underworld, Don Juan, Sleeping Beauty or even that of the Grail. However, the director warns that if you look for parallels to these themes or myths in the film "you will arrive at a correct interpretation of sixty or eighty percent of the film. But your interpretations will never hold good for the film as a whole." Resnais declared: *"Marienbad* is an 'open' film which proposes to everyone an involvement, a choice."

Among the important "keys" to consider in trying to understand it one could mention:

Rosmer, the play-within-the-film, is being performed at the start and close of the film. Is this a variant on Ibsen's *Rosmersholm* (1887) which concludes with the pastor persuading the heroine to join him in a suicide pact? *Rosmer*'s indicative dialogue and familiar backdrop representing a garden, statuary, balustrade, etc., suggest that the play is a mirror image to the main story.

The nameless guests can be seen as a Greek chorus whose fragmented conversation ("murder," "lying," "there's no way of escaping," etc.) foreshadow and comment on the central plot, especially their mention of "Frank's story"—an attempted seduction in a former year—which bears a parallel to X's behavior.

The statue (built specially for the film and modelled after figures in a Poussin painting) serves as a focal point in X's persuasion. "It could just as well be you and I" X tells A. Is the pair "frozen" in time, like the statue?

There's the recurrent game in which X (and others) continually lose to the invincible M. Does this symbolize an unchangeable fate? X keeps trying "to win" (both the game and A) but invariably "loses."

The stylized acting of the three leads makes the film remarkably effective as well as the eerie organ music of Francis Seyrig (the brother of the actress) which helps, in Resnais' words, "to bring out the oneiric atmosphere." Credit also Jacques Saulnier's marvellous sets, Sacha Vierny's striking photography, and the Colpis' extraordinary editing.

While some dismiss the entrancing *Last Year at Marienbad* as a hollow, sterile exercise in style, this viewer considers it the most brilliant, daring, and provocative experiment in film history.

The stranger, X(Giorgio Albertazzi), is about to begin the game—this time with dominoes—with his invincible opponent, M(Sacha Pitoëff). More seems to be at stake here than the game.

186   In Paris the two Bohemians, Jim (Henri Serre), left, and Jules (Oskar Werner), right, form a close friendship and share many things, including boxing at the gymnasium.

Robert Bobert; *Editor:* Claudine Bouché; *Music:* Georges Delerue; *Song:* "Le Tourbillon," words and music by Boris Bassiak; *Running Time:* 110 minutes; *Paris Premiere:* January 24, 1962; *New York Premiere:* April 23, 1962; *16 mm. Rental Source:* Janus.

CAST

Catherine: Jeanne Moreau; *Jules:* Oskar Werner; *Jim:* Henri Serre; *Thérèse:* Marie Dubois; *Gilberte:* Vanna Urbino; *Albert:* Boris Bassiak; *Sabine:* Sabine Haudepin; *1st Customer in Café:* Jean-Louis Richard; *2nd Customer in Café:* Michael Varesano; *Drunkard in Café:* Pierre Fabre; *Albert's Friend:* Danielle Bassiak; *Merlin:* Bernard Largemains; *Mathilde:* Elen Bober; *Narrator:* Voice of Michel Subor.

JULES AND JIM

(Jules et Jim)

LES FILMS DU CARROSSE / S.E.D.I.F.
(SOCIÉTÉ D'EXPLOITATION ET DE
DISTRIBUTION DE FILMS)   1962

CREDITS

Screenplay: François Truffaut and Jean Gruault, based on the novel by Henri-Pierre Roché (1953), published in New York, 1967; *Director:* François Truffaut; *Photographer:* Raoul Coutard (Franscope); *Assistant Directors:* Georges Pellegrin and

BACKGROUND

Shoot the Piano Player (Tirez sur le Pianiste) (1960), his homage to the American gangster film, was François Truffaut's second feature. His next film was a project which had been incubating for several years. Back in 1956 he had discovered *Jules and Jim*

"The statue comes alive"—the fateful meeting of Jim (Henri Serre) and Jules (Oskar Werner) with the mysterious Catherine (Jeanne Moreau) in Jules' garden.

A triumphant Catherine (Jeanne Moreau) disguised as "Thomas" beats Jim (Henri Serre), center, and Jules (Oskar Werner), right, in a race across the footbridge by starting ahead of them.

in a secondhand bookstall. The author, Henri-Pierre Roché (b. 1879), a Parisian dandy who became an art-dealer, had published this, his first novel, in 1953 when he was in his seventies. This partly autobiographical novel—the character Jim is reputed to be the author's persona—described events which occurred over fifty years before.

Truffaut started to correspond with Roché, who became convinced that the young director would be ideal for bringing his novel to the screen and approved of his choice of Jeanne Moreau for the feminine lead, even noting that she bore a striking resemblance to his heroine. Roché, however, died in 1959 before meeting her or seeing the eventual film.

"I believe *Jules and Jim* is a perfect hymn to love," Truffaut declared, "and perhaps even a hymn to life." The novel "was so little known," the director said, "and I wanted to increase its popularity by calling it to the attention of a large audience." He said he was intrigued by "a project which inspires ideas at once formal and moral, visual and intellectual." Truffaut and his co-adapter, Jean Gruault, did an extraordinary job of condensing and tightening a very diffusive and episodic novel set in a twenty-year period (1907–27). The scenarists rear-

The future "Queen of the Hive": Catherine (Jeanne Moreau) is carried by Jim (Henri Serre) and Jules (Oskar Werner).

While a complacent Jules (Oskar Werner) and Jim (Henri Serre) stroll along, Catherine (Jeanne Moreau) prepares to jump into the Seine—an ominous foreshadowing of her later suicidal plunge.

ranged incidents, merged several women into the formidable Catherine, and simplified a very complicated plot. They decided, for thematic reasons, to update the time span (now 1912–33), concluding with bookburning by the Nazis which, Truffaut said, "marks the end of an epoch—an epoch of artists and dilettantes."

The characters' backgrounds—Kate, as Catherine is called in the novel, is German along with Albert, and Jules is a German Jew—were changed. The adapters toned down their weaknesses—Jules's streak of masochism, Kate's viciousness, and Jim's vacillation—to create finer, more sympathetic subjects.

Jules and Jim was shot between April 10 and June 3, 1961, in and around Paris, Alsace, and near St. Paul de Vence on the French Riviera. The film was an enormous critical and popular success and became the director's best-loved film to date.

SYNOPSIS

In pre-World War I Paris Jules (Oskar Werner), a German, and Jim (Henri Serre), a Frenchman—

both young writers—meet and become inseparable friends. In their Bohemian world is Albert (Boris Bassiak) who shows them slides he took of a fascinating statue he found of a woman with an arresting smile. The two set out to visit the Adriatic island where the statue had been excavated. Shortly after, they meet Catherine (Jeanne Moreau) who is French and possesses the statue's smile. Jules is captivated by her and asks Jim not to interfere in his courtship. The three spend an idyllic vacation together in the South of France, where Jules proposes marriage.

Later, in Paris, they attend a Swedish play about a modern woman which interests Catherine. When Jules criticizes the work and starts a glib dismissal of women in general, Catherine asserts herself by suddenly jumping into the Seine, an act which shocks Jules, inflames Jim with devotion, and foreshadows her ultimate act of destruction.

Catherine agrees to marry Jules. War breaks out and the two men fight in opposing armies. After the Armistice Jules invites Jim to his chalet in the Rhineland. He now has a daughter, Sabine (Sabine Haudepin). Jim arrives and senses the tensions in the household. He learns that Catherine is almost ready to flee for a liaison with Albert. Jules is resigned by now to her adulteries but cannot bear to have her desert him. Seeing the growing attraction between Jim and his wife, he exhorts his friend to marry Catherine and not feel that he is in the way. He would agree to a divorce and be content simply to see her.

Jim and Catherine begin an intense love affair. He is forced to return to Paris for his work and resumes seeing Gilberte (Vanna Urbino), his long-time lover who is satisfied with their non-marital arrangement. He cannot bring himself to break with her.

Catherine, feeling insecure, runs off to have a fling with Albert. When Jim returns, she tells him that "Albert equals Gilberte." They reconcile and Catherine tries desperately to conceive a child, a sign for her that she and Jim are meant to be a couple. Apparently failing in this, they agree to a trial separation.

Back in Paris Jim learns from Jules' letter that Catherine had miscarried her child by Jim and wishes no further communication from him. After some time passes, the two estranged friends meet. Catherine beckons Jim to their home and greets him amorously. Jim, however, starts to analyze their failed romance, points out each's major character faults, and then announces his intentions of marrying Gilberte and having children. Feeling rejected, Catherine tries to shoot Jim.

Later, all three meet again by accident and go off in Catherine's car to a café. Leaving with Jim accompanying her, Catherine instructs Jules to watch carefully. Behind the wheel she flashes her perverse, triumphant smile at Jim and then deliberately drives off a broken bridge to their deaths. A devastated yet relieved Jules witnesses their cremation and interment at the film's end.

COMMENTARY

Jules and Jim received the Prix de l'Académie du Cinéma for "Best French Film" and Jeanne Moreau was awarded the Grand Prix for "Best Actress." The film went on to garner awards in Denmark and Italy and at festivals in Mexico, Venezuela, and Columbia. Truffaut displayed a technical mastery of his medium with his amazingly varied and always functional camera movements. In the famous opening montage with its rapid, breathtaking cutting (and grainy print to simulate period photography), the director has found a style to match the exuberance and frantic excitement of his young Bohemians. The frenetic pacing at the beginning gives way to slow, longer-held shots later on as the characters' early high spirits wear off and deep troubles set in.

Though some critics have objected to Truffaut's use of an omniscient narrator, this is justified—Bresson and Cocteau have employed narrators in a similar way—as a "distancing" device to downplay excessive emotion and to stimulate reflection in the viewer, as a means of providing insights which lie beyond the grasp of the principals, and as a way to help unify the film. There is an effective use of natural settings, especially evident in the trio's vacation in the South of France where they are blissfully united with nature.

Among the many cinematic allusions we come to expect in Truffaut's work we might mention Renoir (a rowing scene at the beginning recalls *A Day in the Country*) and Laurel and Hardy (Catherine and Jules imitate the team's routine of putting on each other's hat).

"I wanted people to be aware of the possibility of seeking other ethics, other ways of life," Truffaut wrote, "even knowing that all such arrangements would be doomed to failure." Accordingly, Jules, Jim, and Catherine set out to find a new code since they reject traditional conventions. Truffaut merely presents their life and refrains from judgment. "There are two themes," Truffaut said, "that of the friendship between the two men, which tries to remain alive, and that of the impossibility of living *à trois*. The idea of the film is that the couple is not really satisfactory but there is no alternative." It is a tribute to Truffaut's genius that we are convinced of their love, of their innocence, and are deeply involved with all of them.

Although the two men lend their names to the title, the film is dominated by the willful, complex, and elusive Catherine. As desirable as she is "demonic," Jim perceives that "she is an apparition for all to appreciate, perhaps, but not a woman for any one man." Catherine is a richly developed character, totally engrossing and unpredictable. She is fascinated with Napoléon and critics have pointed out her links with the opposing elements of fire (the burning of her letters, her vitriol—"liquid fire"—which she carries with her) and water (her jump into the Seine, her death by drowning) which characterize her nature.

Catherine's suicide has drawn varied critical reaction from "psychologically inevitable" (Andrew Sarris) to the "pettish caprice" of a "psychopath"

(Stanley Kauffmann). Truffaut commented, "I can't say why she killed him because the book doesn't say. It isn't a psychological novel." Catherine has a certain androgynous side, best expressed in the early scene when she dresses up like Jackie Coogan in Chaplin's *The Kid* (1921) and, as "Thomas," successfully impersonates a man. She challenges Jules and Jim to a race across the foot bridge and wins by starting before the official count is over. Not only does she desire the freedom of a man, but she demonstrates she will break any rule to achieve her own ends. Jules comes to see her as a "force of nature" who "expresses herself in cataclysms."

Jules is the passive, gentle, sadly disenchanted husband. His earlier lack of success with the free-spirited Thérèse (Marie Dubois) presages his later failure in controlling his wife. "The gamble for me," Truffaut said, "was to see if I would be able to make the woman sympathetic rather than whore-like (without making the film itself melodramatic), and if I could keep the husband from seeming ridiculous."

In the chalet, after arguing with Jim, Catherine (Jeanne Moreau) finds solace with her husband Jules (Oskar Werner) who avows his love for her.

Their attempted relationship at an impasse, Catherine (Jeanne Moreau) and Jim (Henri Serre) prepare to spend their last night together as lovers in a hotel room.

Jim is reserved, self-assured, loyal and, unlike Jules, a success with women. We never learn of Gilberte's reaction to Jim's death. Was it relief for her as well as it was for Jules?

It is inconceivable that anyone but Jeanne Moreau could be cast as Catherine. If she did not incarnate all the allure and mystery of this fascinating character, we would be forced to take everyone's word that she was extraordinary without seeing any evidence of it. Fortunately, Miss Moreau realizes Catherine totally. She has a great presence and displays enormous range and versatility in a role which solidified her international reputation and which remains her best screen appearance to date. Both Oskar Werner, who later appeared in Truffaut's *Fahrenheit 451* (1966), and Henri Serre are ideally cast and give outstanding performances. Marie Dubois is delightful in her sparkling cameo role.

"I wanted the film to look like an album of old photographs," Truffaut said and Raoul Coutard succeeded admirably with his striking photography. Georges Delerue composed one of the most memorable scores in film history ranging from the exhilarating, riotous music which launches the film to the haunting theme for the statue which becomes an ominous motif for Catherine as it accompanies both her leap into the Seine and her fatal car ride. The Bassiak song, "Le Tourbillon" ("The Whirlwind"), telling of lovers who meet, love, part, then repeat the cycle, charmingly sung by Jeanne Moreau, prepares us for Catherine's pattern of lovemaking in her coming affair with Jim.

Among the many striking scenes in *Jules and Jim* one could cite:

The amusing reunion in a café of Jim with the zany Thérèse who proceeds to render a long, non-stop account of her crazy adventures while Jim ignores her and greets old friends.

Bizarre and disturbing is the scene near the end in which Jim is awakened by the loud honkings of a car. He looks out of his window and catches sight of Catherine's vehicle swerving dangerously among the lamp-posts and trees like "a phantom ship" on the deserted square. It is her way of summoning him and creates a chilling sense of foreboding.

Then there is the shocking suicide scene: Catherine beaming her signatory smile at Jim and next we see—in a long shot photographed in slow motion—the car driving off the damaged bridge.

This eerie effect is heightened by the subsequent close-up after their cremation when the camera startlingly reveals charred fragments of bones. Was this all that was left of their energy and spirit?

Roché's second and even more autobiographical novel, *Les Deux Anglaises et la Continent* (1956) was later filmed by Truffaut (released 1971.) (American title: *Two English Girls*.)

Jules and Jim is a poem of youth and miraculously captures the essence of what it is like to be young. It happens to be this writer's personal favorite French film of all time.

The *Time* critic wrote that Truffaut's genuine feeling "bubbles up like the spring of life itself. A spectator who sits down to this picture feeling old and dry will rise up feeling young and green." This rich, celebrational film—frequently imitated but never surpassed—has achieved the status of a classic. Critic Pauline Kael predicted: "I think it will rank among the great lyric achievements of the screen, right up there with the work of Griffith and Renoir."

THE FIRE WITHIN

(Le Feu Follet)

N.E.F. (NOUVELLES EDITIONS DE FILMS)   1963

CREDITS

Screenplay and Direction: Louis Malle, based on Pierre Drieu La Rochelle's novel (1931), published in New York (1965); *Photographer:* Ghislain Cloquet; *Assistant Director:* Volker Schlöndorff; *Editor:* Suzanne Baron; *Music:* Satie's "Gymnopédies" and "Gnossiennes," performed by Claude Helffer; *Running Time:* 110 minutes; *Paris Premiere:* October 15, 1963; *New York Premiere:* February 17, 1964; *16 mm. Rental Source:* New Yorker Films.

CAST

Alain Leroy: Maurice Ronet; *Lydia:* Léna Skerla; *Mlle. Farnoux:* Yvonne Clech; *d'Averseau:* Hubert Deschamps; *Dr. La Barbinais:* Jean-Paul Moulinot; *Mme. La Barbinais:* Mona Dol; *Dubourg:* Bernard Noël; *Fanny:* Ursula Kobler; *Jeanne:* Jeanne Moreau; *Urcel:* Alain Mottet; *Cyrille Lavaud:* Jacques Sereys; *Solange:* Alexandra Stewart; *Brancion:* Tony Taffin; *Frédéric:* Henri Serre.

BACKGROUND

Louis Malle was born October 30, 1932, in Thumeries (Nord), France. After majoring in political science at the Sorbonne, he studied filmmaking at I.D.H.E.C., then made his first short, *Fontaine de Vaucluse* (1953). He became an assistant director on Jacques-Yves Cousteau's award-winning underwater documentary, *The Silent World (Le Monde du Silence)* (1956), then directed his first feature, the thriller *Ascenseur pour L'Echafaud* (1958) (called *Frantic* here in 1961, later *Elevator to the Gallows*)

starring Maurice Ronet and Jeanne Moreau which won him the Prix Louis Delluc. His next film was the daring *The Lovers (Les Amants)* (1958) which brought him international fame.

The versatile young director decided to adapt as his fifth feature film *The Fire Within*, a powerful novel about a dissolute suicide-to-be by Pierre Drieu La Rochelle published in 1931. The author based the central character of Alain on a friend, the surrealist writer Jacques Rigaut, who committed suicide in 1929. The novelist himself took his life in 1945; he had been a collaborationist and directed the important publication *Nouvelle Revue Française* during the Occupation.

Lydia (Léna Skerla) and Alain (Maurice Ronet) dress quietly in the early morning after spending the night together at a hotel.

193

Alone in his room at the clinic, Alain (Maurice Ronet) contemplates suicide: "Life does not move fast enough for me. So I quicken it, I put it right."

Although the novel, Drieu's most famous work, depicted the moral malaise of the inter-war years Malle decided, partly to avoid the expense, not to make his film a period piece and, instead, updated the story to the present. He changed Alain's drug addiction in the book to alcoholism, which he felt far more comfortable in dealing with. Feeling, as Malle said, that "such as he is, I believe that the character arouses great tenderness for his aggravated humanity—one is moved and concerned," he permitted his chief character to be depicted sympathetically. Maurice Ronet memorably essayed the doomed Alain in this haunting and poignant film.

Shooting began in mid-April 1963; Paris and Versailles were used for exteriors. "It wasn't the subject of suicide that drew me . . . ," Louis Malle said, "it was the night."

SYNOPSIS

The Fire Within records the last two days in the life of Alain Leroy (Maurice Ronet), a doomed thirty-year-old Parisian playboy with a "handsome, eroded face" who spent his youth living off women. Although he completed a cure for alcoholism, Alain remains at his Versailles clinic because he's terrified of resuming his destructive drinking habits.

The film opens in a hotel, where he is unsuccessful at making love to Lydia (Léna Skerla), a friend of his American wife Dorothy from whom he's been long estranged. His impotency symbolizes his

A wearied Jeanne (Jeanne Moreau) resting in the home of her addict friend Urcel after bringing Alain there.

194

devastating inability to love or connect with anyone, a major factor propelling him to suicide. Alain accepts Lydia's gift of money but rejects her offer of marriage since he feels "it's too late."

Back at the clinic in his room Alain tells the director, Dr. La Barbinais (Jean-Paul Moulinot) that he's in a state of perpetual anxiety but all the doctor can do is urge Alain to cable his wife and state, without much conviction, that "life is good." He wants him to leave, since he's cured; Alain promises to be gone by the weekend. The mirror in the room of this death-obsessed young man is covered with newspaper clippings of suicides including prominent photos of Marilyn Monroe and a date scrawled on the glass, July 23, his approaching rendezvous with death.

The next day he decides to return to Paris to bid adieu to his friends but also to reach out to them, a sort of final cry for help. He visits his old companion Dubourg (Bernard Noël) and glimpses underneath the friend's scholarly preoccupations, emptiness and a complaisant marriage. Then his artist friend Jeanne (Jeanne Moreau) leads him to the home of an opium user, Urcel (Alain Mottet), where Alain recognizes the traps of addiction. There is nothing to sustain him, and he takes his first drink at a café, gets ill, then rests at the home

At the Lavaud dinner party, realizing that all his life he has reached out but touched nothing, a desperate Alain (Maurice Ronet) extends his hands to Solange (Alexandra Stewart) for help.

of his socially prominent friend Lavaud (Jacques Sereys). He dines there later, drinks much, and unsuccessfully attempts to seek comfort from his host's wife, Solange (Alexandra Stewart).

His room at the clinic in disorder, an intoxicated Alain (Maurice Ronet) sleeps restlessly on the morning of his suicide. Newspaper clippings of Marilyn Monroe are posted on the walls.

195

The following day is July 23. He rouses himself from sleep in his disarrayed room, completes reading a book, then calmly takes a revolver, points it at his heart, and fi..es.

COMMENTARY

A critical success, considered by many to be Malle's best film to date, *The Fire Within* won a Special Jury Prize at the 1963 Venice Film Festival along with the Italian Critics Award for "Best Foreign Film." Unfortunately but understandably it was a commercial failure. "It is such a harsh subject," Malle said, "and it's such a depressing movie."

The director was able to get at the interior life of his character and explore the vast territory of a troubled soul. Alain Leroy is presented to us without any self-pity, mawkish pleading, judgment or melodrama. "The only possible angle in which to see this film," Malle wrote, "is with the knowledge from the very beginning that it is the story of a man who is going to kill himself. The film must be seen in the past tense, as if it were nothing but a long flashback."

The director avoids the trap of a glib psychological or sociological analysis of Alain's "condition." A sense of mystery about the man's character is maintained and enables us to ponder his suicide from many points of view.

Among the many factors besides the realism of its natural settings which make *The Fire Within* a remarkable film is the restrained, sympathetic, and unsensational treatment of a very delicate subject matter. The pacing is deliberately slow to encourage a meditative response. This subtlety, this Bresson-like quality of precision and discretion, makes viewing the film a quietly overwhelming experience. The suicide scene is all the more jolting for being terse and played down.

Maurice Ronet brilliantly registers every nuance of the tortured, complex Alain in an outstanding performance. He makes the character come alive, commanding our interest and solicitude. Ronet acknowledged that the role of Alain was the greatest opportunity in his career.

It was a wise choice to use Satie's melancholic music to add a mood of ineffable sadness to the film and to shoot it in expressive black and white so as to control the movie's atmosphere. Ghislain Cloquet's remarkable photography is most effective.

In a way, *The Fire Within* bears a resemblance to Fellini's celebrated *La Dolce Vita* (1960). Each detailed the odyssey of a weak, disintegrating character who is vainly searching for some meaning in his life. Whereas the Roman version was of epic length and had the full orchestration of a symphony, the Parisian counterpart was brief, and had the intimacy and poignancy of chamber music.

Malle pays homage to F. Scott Fitzgerald. On a shelf in his room Alain keeps a copy of *Babylon Revisited*, a collection of the master's short stories. The title story adds resonance to the film since its central character returns to Paris and the haunts of his former dissipation. Whereas hope is held out to Charlie Wales, Fitzgerald's hero, in the possible reunion with his daughter and the assumption of responsibilities, by contrast there is nothing in Alain's life to which he can cling. The brief episode of Alain's return to his old hotel, not in the novel, was inspired by Fitzgerald's story.

Some thirty years after its release, *The Fire Within* still remains a neglected film which has failed to find an audience. By no means dated, this sombre, elegiac film forces us not only to examine the spiritual and social isolation of its hero but also the delusions and "props" which somehow sustain the survivors. It is a profound and challenging experience. Alain's disturbing meditation appears onscreen after his suicide: "I kill myself because you have not loved me, because I haven't loved you. I kill myself because the bonds between us were loose, and to tighten those bonds. I will leave an indelible stain on you."

Malle continued to make original and provocative documentaries and features, including *Lacombe Lucien* (1974), before beginning his distinguished career in the United States with the stunning and controversial *Pretty Baby* (1978).

THE UMBRELLAS OF CHERBOURG

(Les Parapluies de Cherbourg)

PARC FILMS / MADELEINE FILMS
(PARIS) / BETA FILM (MUNICH)   1964

Mme. Emery (Anne Vernon) tries to discourage her young daughter Geneviéve (Catherine Deneuve) from considering marriage.

CREDITS

Screenplay and Direction: Jacques Demy; *Photographer:* Jean Rabier (Eastmancolor); *Assistant Directors:* Jean-Paul Savignac and Klaus Muller-Laue; *Editor:* Anne-Marie Cotret; *Music:* Michel Legrand; *Lyrics:* Jacques Demy; *Running Time:* 92 minutes; *Paris Premiere:* February 19, 1964; *New York Premiere:* December 16, 1964; *16 mm. Rental Source:* Audio Brandon.

CAST

Geneviève Emery: Catherine Deneuve; *Guy Foucher:* Nino Castelnuovo; *Mme. Emery:* Anne Vernon; *Roland Cassard:* Marc Michel; *Madeleine:* Ellen Farner; *Tante Elise:* Mireille Perrey; *Aubin:* Jean Champion; *M. Dubourg:* Harald Wolff; *Jenny (Woman in Nightclub):* Dorotheé Blank.

BACKGROUND

Jacques Demy was born in Pontchâteau (Loire Atlantique) on June 5, 1931, and grew up in Nantes, where his father owned a garage. He pursued art studies at the Ecole des Beaux-Arts in Nantes, then film at the Ecole Technique de Photographie et de Cinématographie in Paris. He became an assistant to animator Paul Grimault, then to documentary filmmaker Georges Rouquier. Demy made the first of his five shorts, *Le Sabotier du Val de Loire,* in 1955 and released his first feature,

Lola, dedicated to Max Ophüls, in 1961. He married the well-known director Agnès Varda in 1962.

His most popular film to date, *The Umbrellas of Cherbourg,* encountered obstacles and delays. "One day," Demy said, "I confided to Michel Legrand that it was my ambition to make a film musical, a film which would owe nothing to American musical comedy, or to French operetta. I had in mind a film entirely sung. . . . A kind of opera in a way." Legrand liked the concept and the two collaborated closely for almost a year. Demy wanted to film it in 1962 but producers thought the idea idiotic so in the interim he shot *Bay of the Angels (La Baie des Anges)* (1963) with Jeanne Moreau. Then producer Mag Bodard became interested in the project. She relates that Demy called and told her "he was tired of the kitchen sink trend, and wanted to make a film of ravishing beauty—a mixture of poetry, color, and music. . . . Cherbourg would provide the *mise-en-scène,* for harbors are nostalgic and suggest the siren's song." The money was eventually raised.

In addition to Catherine Deneuve the cast included the Italian actor Nino Castelnuovo and the

Called up for military service, Guy (Nino Castelnuovo) leads his beloved Geneviéve (Catherine Deneuve) to his room where they will spend the night.

German actress Ellen Farner. Demy offered the role of the mother first to Micheline Presle, then to Danielle Darrieux, before selecting Anne Vernon for the part. All these non-singing leads had their voices dubbed by professional singers.

After the music was recorded, the film was shot in its entirety in Cherbourg—interiors were shot in a museum—and the inhabitants willingly consented to let their town be painted in startling colors and act as extras in the film. Since the story covers the four seasons, tons of fake snow were dumped on the summer streets to simulate winter. The film is punctuated with dates, a device to make it more realistic. "I need to hold on to something down-to-earth," Demy explained.

The most ordinary of plots was rendered fresh, vibrant, and memorable. "I'm trying to create a world in my films," Demy said and referred to *The Umbrellas of Cherbourg* as a *"film en-chanté"* which, besides denoting "a film sung" also means—and how aptly—"enchanted."

SYNOPSIS

LOCALE: Cherbourg

PART ONE: DEPARTURE

November 1957. Geneviève (Catherine Deneuve) is the pretty seventeen-year-old daughter of widowed Mme. Emery (Anne Vernon) who runs a

The soon-to-be-parted lovers, Geneviéve (Catherine Deneuve) and Guy (Nino Castelnuovo), share a tender moment in a café.

198

shop, "The Umbrellas of Cherbourg." Geneviève is deeply in love with twenty-year-old Guy Foucher (Nino Castelnuovo) who works in a service station and has been raised by his invalid Aunt Elise (Mireille Perrey).

December 1957. The couple wish to marry but her mother thinks she's too young. Financial difficulties force Mme. Emery to sell her pearl necklace. Roland Cassard (Marc Michel), a wealthy diamond merchant, happens to be in the jewelry store at the time and, smitten with Geneviève's beauty, offers to purchase the jewels. The Algerian War is on and Guy is called up for two years' military service. Before their painful parting Geneviève gives herself to her beloved.

PART TWO: ABSENCE

January 1958. A pale Geneviève languishes with no word from Guy. Mme. Emery learns her daughter's pregnant. Roland comes to dinner and offers marriage.

February 1958. Guy finally writes. He says he's happy about the baby.

March 1958. At carnival time Mme. Emery pressures her daughter to accept Roland's proposal.

April 1958. Roland returns and is willing to marry her and rear the child as his own.

June 1958. Geneviève marries Roland.

PART THREE: RETURN

March 1959. Guy, who incurred a leg injury in the war, returns and is upset to learn that Geneviève has married and left for Paris. Madeleine (Ellen Farner) has been caring for Aunt Elise for a long time and secretly loves Guy.

April 1959. Guy has difficulty adjusting to civilian life. He quits his job and dissipates. The godmother dies and a lonely Guy asks Madeleine to stay.

June 1959. Guy buys a garage station with a bequest from Elise. He owes his transformation to Madeleine and asks her to marry him. She fears he's still involved with Geneviève but Guy offers his devotion.

December 1963. It is a snowy Christmas Eve. A happy Madeleine leaves the service station with their little boy François to see the toy shops. A wealthy Geneviève with her daughter Françoise drives up in her Mercedes. She had detoured and is surprised to see Guy again. In their poignant reunion, each maintains emotional control. Guy declines to see his daughter and says, "I think you'd better go." Geneviève drives off as Madeleine returns and embraces her husband.

COMMENTARY

The Umbrellas of Cherbourg was awarded the Prix Louis Delluc (1963) and opened to rave reviews.

A happy Roland (Marc Michel) marries Geneviéve (Catherine Deneuve), while her mother (Anne Vernon) watches.

Guy (Nino Castelnuovo), now contentedly married, awaits a joyful Christmas with his wife Madeleine (Ellen Farner).

Paris-Presse said that Cherbourg was even better than heaven! At the 1964 Cannes Film Festival the film won a Grand Prize and later received the Prix Méliès. It was nominated for an "Oscar" for best "Foreign-Language Film" (1964).* The film was a worldwide success.

Catherine Deneuve and Nino Castelnuovo made an attractive couple. The exquisitely beautiful Miss Deneuve was launched on her international career. Anne Vernon provided strong support as Mme. Emery.

The Umbrellas of Cherbourg is an unusual and experimental film. For the first time in a musical conceived for cinema every word is sung; there is no spoken dialogue. What could have been silly and pretentious turned out to be convincing and beautifully effective. The device helps maintain the illusion of fantasy.

Michel Legrand contributed a lovely, haunting score which is richly variegated with ballads, jazz,

*The following year it received four additional "Oscar" nominations: Jacques Demy for "Story and Screenplay—Written Directly for the Screen," and three in the Music category—Michel Legrand and Jacques Demy both for their Song "I Will Wait for You" and "Music Score—Substantially Original" and Legrand for "Scoring of Music—Adaptation or Treatment."

tangos, mambos, tinkling piano music, etc. Two songs from the film: "I Will Wait for You" (the main theme) and "Watch What Happens" (Roland's song, recalling his lost love, was used before in *Lola*) became standards in America; the soundtrack was to be a bestselling LP album.

Demy's skillful direction was regulated by the music. He said: "The camera movements, the movements of the actors themselves would be guided by the musical rhythm, while remaining always close to reality." The film is a treat for the eye as well as the ear. Silvery rain, a petunia umbrella shop, a flaming red portside bar, a light pink jewelry store—there is a dazzling palette of bright and pastel colors which reveals the characters' world. Jean Rabier's brilliant photography and Bernard Evein's striking sets contribute much to the film's decorative elegance.

Demy considers *The Umbrellas of Cherbourg* "a fairy tale . . . but the meaning of the story and the morality are always based on reality." He declared his aims in the film: "I am fighting against war, against nastiness, against stupidity, against many things that I don't like," and acknowledged: "The war destroys the love, and that is important to know."

The director feels that "human experience recurs constantly in the same terms and almost in the round." Accordingly, *The Umbrellas of Cherbourg* is at the center of a loosely connected triology. In Demy's first feature Roland Cassard was in love with Lola and in the third film, *The Model Shop* (1969), made in Hollywood, we follow Lola's subsequent adventures in Los Angeles. Among Demy's later features is the delightful fantasy, *Donkey Skin (Peau d'Ane)* (1970), a homage to Jean Cocteau.

In 1982 Jacques Demy was the recipient of the Grand Prix des Arts et Lettres, honoring his entire career.

A successful stage adaptation of *The Umbrellas of Cherbourg* directed by Andrei Serban opened off-Broadway at the Public/Cabaret Theatre in New York in February 1979 and was subsequently produced in London and San Francisco. A production starring Corinne Marchand opened at the Théâtre Montparnasse in Paris in September 1979.

The movie retains its irresistibly romantic, bittersweet charm. Critic François Nourissier observed: "Demy has presented the public with this marvellous song of a movie. The public sings its own life in *The Umbrellas of Cherbourg*."

200

PIERROT LE FOU

ROME-PARIS FILMS (PARIS)/DINO DE
LAURENTIIS CINEMATOGRAPHICA
(ROME)   1965

CREDITS

Screenplay and Direction: Jean-Luc Godard, based on
the novel *Obsession,* by Lionel White, published in
New York (1962) and in Paris as *Le Demon de Onze*
Heures (1963); *Photographer:* Raoul Coutard (East-
mancolor and Techniscope); *Assistant Directors:* Phi-
lippe Fourastié, Jean-Pierre Léaud; *Editor:* Fran-
çoise Collin; *Music:* Antoine Duhamel, Antonio
Vivaldi (Flute Concerto); *Song:* "Jamais Je Ne T'Ai
Dit Que Je T'Aimerai Toujours" ("I Never Told
You That I Would Love You All My Life") by Boris
Bassiak and "Ma Ligne de Chance" ("My Line of
Luck") by Antoine Duhamel and Boris Bassiak;
Running Time: 112 minutes; *Paris Premiere:* Novem-
ber 5, 1965; *New York Premiere:* January 8, 1969; *16
mm. Rental Source:* Corinth.

CAST

Ferdinand Griffon: Jean-Paul Belmondo; *Marianne
Renoir:* Anna Karina; *Fred:* Dirk Sanders; *Maria,
Ferdinand's Wife:* Graziella Galvani; *Midget:* Jimmy
Karoubi; *Gangsters:* Roger Dutoit, Hans Meyer;
Man on the Pier: Raymond Devos; *Samuel Fuller:*
Himself; *Political Exile:* Laszlo Szabo; *Young Man in
Cinema:* Jean-Pierre Léaud.

Ferdinand (Jean-Paul Belmondo) and Marianne (Anna Karina) evade pursuing gangsters
and flee Paris to begin their life of adventure together. This shot suggests one of the
several possible ways they could have made their escape.

Bombarding the viewer with provocative stimulii, Godard here juxtaposes verbal communication—Ferdinand (Jean-Paul Belmondo), dressed as a gangster, pauses in his flight to read from the well-known Pieds Nickelés comic to Marianne (Anna Karina), dressed as a guerilla—with a visual text—besides the comic book, there's the important sign "total" on the gas pump which comments on Ferdinand's commitment to her.

Ferdinand (Jean-Paul Belmondo) and Marianne (Anna Karina) share an intimate moment on a Riviera beach.

BACKGROUND

After *Breathless,* the controversial and prolific director Jean-Luc Godard turned out eight diversified features, including *My Life to Live (Vivre sa Vie)* (1962) and *Alphaville* (1965), and four sketches (for compilation films) in just six years before making

Pierrot le Fou. French poet Louis Aragon wrote of Godard: "The disorder of our world is his raw material—all this shantytown of our lives without which we couldn't live, but which we manage not to see. And of this, as of accidents and murder, he creates beauty."

Godard decided to film a thriller by Lionel White which had been translated and published in the popular "Série Noire." *Obsession* was an absorbing acount of a middle class American who abandons wife and family to run off with a young femme fatale he's infatuated with. She and her lover make him the fall guy in a Las Vegas robbery. Only when he kills them can he rid himself of his obsession. Godard, as before, chose a conventional story as a frame upon which he could then manipulate and impose his own personality. He said, "I don't really like telling a story. I prefer to use a kind of tapestry, a background in which I can embroider my own ideas."

At different times both Sylvie Vartan and Richard Burton were considered for the leads before Godard cast his then-wife, Anna Karina, and Jean-Paul Belmondo. "I wanted to tell the story of the last romantic couple, the last descendants of *La Nouvelle Héloïse, Werther* and *Hermann and Dorothea,*" Godard declared.

He shot the greatly improvised film between May and July of 1965 on locations in Paris, the South of France, and the isle of Porquerolles in the Hyères.

The couple's romantic idyll is threatened: while Ferdinand (Jean-Paul Belmondo) is absorbed with his diary, Marianne (Anna Karina) becomes increasingly bored and unhappy.

Disturbing and provocative, *Pierrot le Fou* would prove to be controversial and ultimately one of Godard's most satisfying achievements.

SYNOPSIS

Ferdinand Griffon (Jean-Paul Belmondo) feels bored and trapped in his marriage to Maria (Graziella Galvani). After walking out on a dull party, he is ripe for some excitement. Driving the babysitter Marianne (Anna Karina) home, he resumes their intimacy—they had been lovers over five years ago. In the morning in Marianne's apartment Ferdinand sees the body of a dead man, scissors embedded in his neck, on a bed. The two make a getaway by car from Paris and elude gangsters headed by a midget (Jimmy Karoubi).

The couple embark on a series of adventures. At one point Marianne sets their car on fire and inadvertently burns the money the gangsters were searching for. Marianne wishes to find her "brother" but Ferdinand persuades her to spend a romantic idyll with him in a remote cottage. He reads and keeps a diary while Marianne becomes increasingly bored and restless. At her insistence they quit their Rousseauistic sojourn and head to the Riviera to find the "brother."

They run into the midget and Marianne goes off to placate him. Later Marianne summons Ferdinand by telephone. When he rushes into the

apartment he finds the midget dead with scissors embedded in his neck and no sign of Marianne. Gangsters (Roger Dutoit and Hans Meyer) enter and torture Ferdinand to reveal where the loot is hidden.

In Toulon, after an aborted suicide attempt, Ferdinand meets up with Marianne again. She claims she thought he had been killed and so left. He meets her brother/lover Fred (Dirk Sanders) who traffics in munitions. The pair involve Ferdinand in a robbery and more killing, then double-cross him and flee to an island with the money. Ferdinand follows and in a shootout both Marianne and Fred are killed. Dying, she asks Ferdinand to forgive her but he replies, "It's too late."

Plunged into despair, Ferdinand paints his face blue, stands at the top of a cliff, wraps strings of dynamite around his head, and ties the fuse. He lights a match but then drops it accidentally. Having second thoughts about suicide, he tries unsuccessfully to put out the flame near the coiled fuse wire.

In a long shot we see a violent explosion on the top of the cliff.

COMMENTARY

Pierrot Le Fou shared the Young Critics Prize at the 1965 Venice Film Festival. A well-received film, it ran for more than a year at one theatre alone in Paris's Latin Quarter. Godard customarily referred to his filmmaking as an *essai*, which in French means both a "try" ("You could say that *Pierrot* is not really a film," he said. "It is an attempt at cinema") and an "essay" ("I consider myself an essayist," he maintained. "I construct essays in novel form and novels in the form of essays: except that I film them rather than write them.") Finding the traditional methods of narration unsuitable for his purposes and viewing cinema as a very "open-ended" form in which he could commingle various genres, shift the tone, mix poetry with the comic strip, etc., Godard produced a striking, experimental, and innovative film that is as much of a thriller as it is a probing of cinema and language, an autobiographical diary, an exploration of love, and an analysis of a disjointed world.

In *Pierrot le Fou* the director incorporated several "distancing" devices, showing the influence of playwright Bertolt Brecht, to make the audience not a passive spectator involved only emotionally in the action, but an active participant, reflecting critically on the film's ideas. He employs a running off-screen chorus-like commentary undercutting sus-

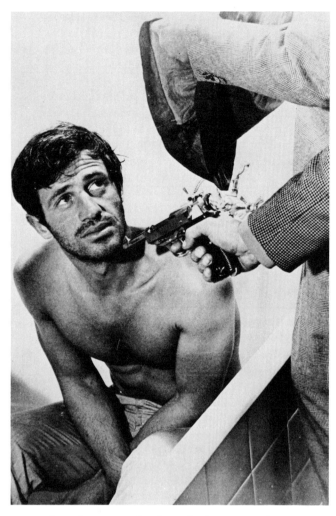

Ferdinand (Jean-Paul Belmondo) is menaced by gangsters who want to know where he's hidden the stolen money.

pense by reporting (and illuminating) the action, has the actors address the viewers directly to make us aware that we are watching a film, interrupts the narrative with songs and passages from Ferdinand's diary, etc.

The film is divided structurally into three sections. The first details the hero's sense of imprisonment in his modern, commercialized world, then his sudden departure when there's a chance at love and adventure. The second part deals with Ferdinand's unsuccessful attempt to realize an ideal romantic love in a natural setting removed from the horrors of civilization. The final segment thrusts the protagonist back into the world of violence and betrayal and concludes with his clumsy act of self-destruction.

Pierrot le Fou relies heavily on quotations and allusions—even to the American involvement in Vietnam—to develop a rich matrix of ideas. At the outset Ferdinand reads aloud a significant passage from Elie Faure's *Histoire de l'Art (L'Art Moderne I,* 1921) concerning the painter Velasquez whose world was "sad" and filled with "idiots, dwarfs, cripples, deformed clowns clothed as princes, whose only job was to laugh at themselves and amuse those lifeless outlaws who were trapped by etiquette, conspiracy, lies. . . ." This underscores Ferdinand, "the deformed clown," whom Marianne persists in calling "Pierrot" (the fool in old French pantomime). Other painters are cited (Renoir, Picasso) as well as novelists (Céline, Bernardin de Saint-Pierre), poets (Rimbaud, Lorca), directors (Sam Fuller, Jean Renoir), etc.

The exciting presence of Jean-Paul Belmondo and the mystery and beauty of Anna Karina add color and resonance to their screen characters. Godard commented: "Anna represents the active life and Belmondo the contemplative."

One of the most effective sequences is the party scene during which the guests mechanically quote commercials for cars, deodorants, and hair sprays to each other while red, yellow, blue, and green filters alternate in filling the screen. Raoul Coutard achieved many striking effects like this throughout the film.

At one point near the end Ferdinand declares, "I am only a huge question mark poised over the Mediterranean horizon." It is this sense of confusion and helplessness, of dislocation and alienation which adds power to the film. Ferdinand-Godard is very much of his time reacting against modern consumer culture, being paralyzed with intellectual malaise, feeling appalled at the violence and mechanization of life, yearning for a better world and despairing of its realization. *Pierrot le Fou* is a *cri de coeur,* an intensely personal film with genuine pain and anguish, and a work which has had lasting popularity and influence.

Godard maintained a prolific output, including the disturbing *Weekend* (1967), then with Jean-Paul Gorin, calling themselves the Dziga-Vertov group, produced a series of didactic political tracts for several years. Since then Godard has done video experimentation and features: *Every Man for Himself (Sauve Qui Peut La Vie)* (1980). The man who said in *Le Petit Soldat* (1963): "Photography is truth . . . and the cinema is the truth twenty-four times a second" continues his restless probing with his film *essais.* In 1982 Jean-Luc Godard received the Grand Prix des Arts et Lettres honoring his entire career.

BELLE DE JOUR

PARIS FILM PRODUCTION (PARIS)/FIVE
FILM (ROME)   1967

CREDITS

Screenplay: Luis Buñuel and Jean-Claude Carrière, based on Joseph Kessel's novel (1928), published in New York (1962); *Director:* Luis Buñuel; *Photographer:* Sacha Vierny (Eastmancolor); *Assistant Directors:* Pierre Lary and Jacques Fraenkel; *Editor:* Louisette Hautecoeur; *Running Time:* 100 minutes; *Paris Premiere:* May 24, 1967; *New York Premiere:* April 10, 1968; *16 mm. Rental Source:* Audio Brandon.

CAST

Séverine Sérizy: Catherine Deneuve; *Pierre Sérizy:* Jean Sorel; *Henri Husson:* Michel Piccoli; *Mme. Anaïs:* Geneviève Page; *Marcel:* Pierre Clémenti; *Hippolyte:* Francisco Rabal; *Charlotte:* Françoise Fabian; *Mathilde:* Maria Latour; *The Duke:* Georges Marchal; *Renée Févret:* Macha Méril; *Pallas:* Muni; *Asiatic Client:* Iska Khan; *Coachman:* D. de Roseville; *Footman:* Michel Charrel; *Séverine as a Child:* Brigitte Parmentier.

BACKGROUND

Luis Buñuel was born in Calanda, Spain, on February 22, 1900. The screen's foremost Surrealist received a Jesuit education then later went to the University of Madrid. In Paris he became an assistant director to Jean Epstein. With Salvador Dali's collaboration he made the classic Surrealist short, *An Andalusian Dog (Un Chien Andalou)* (1928). Buñuel's next film, *L'Age d'Or* (1930), triggered violent demonstrations and was officially banned. A fifteen

In the daydream which opens the film, Séverine (Catherine Deneuve) is dragged along the ground by a coachman (D. de Roseville) and a footman (Michel Charrel) to a tree where she'll be bound, whipped, and abused.

year hiatus in his directing career ended in 1947 when he began making a series of films in Mexico, including *The Young and the Damned (Los Olvidados)* (1950) which indicated a significant comeback. The controversial and acclaimed *Viridiana* (1961) solidifed Buñuel's international reputation and signalled a great surge of creativity which extended into his advanced years.

When a projected adaptation of the Gothic tale, *The Monk,* failed to materialize, the director was offered a novel owned by the producers Robert and Raymond Hakim, *Belle de Jour,* written by Joseph Kessel, published in 1928. The work was a realistic, psychological portrait of a frigid wife driven by her masochistic desires to become a part-time prostitute. Unimpressed with the book, Bu-

205

Later, Pierre (Jean Sorel) comforts Séverine (Catherine Deneuve), his edgy, frigid wife.

Only when Mme. Anaîs (Geneviève Page) asserts her authority does an uncooperative Séverine (Catherine Deneuve) become a submissive and compliant "Belle de Jour" at her establishment.

ñuel nonetheless recognized, as he said, its "dramatic possibilities." Accordingly, he and writer Jean-Claude Carrière used the novel as a point of departure. They set the action in the present, added the revealing flashbacks to Séverine's childhood, and changed the ending which had Séverine confess the truth to a paralyzed Pierre, then—three years have passed, we are informed, without his saying a further word to her. . . . The scenarists replaced Kessel's psychological exposition of Séverine's behavior with an invented series of erotic and mysterious daydreams and "by mixing indiscriminately and without warning in the montage the things that actually happen to the heroine, and the fantasies and morbid impulses which she imagines," Buñuel writes, changed a literal story to one open-ended and ambiguous: "As the film proceeds, I am going to increase the frequency of these interpolations, and at the end, in the final sequence, the audience will not be able to know if what is happening to her is actual or the heroine's subjective world—reality or nightmare. . . ."

Buñuel shot his film from October 10 to mid-December 1966 at the Franstudio in Saint-Maurice. Then the French censors trimmed two brothel sequences and the necrophiliac episode. After seeing the film Joseph Kessel wrote: "Buñuel's genius has exceeded by far all that I could hope for. . . . We are in another dimension: that of the subconscious, of dreams and secret instincts suddenly laid bare. And what formal beauty in the images!"

SYNOPSIS

The following represents a traditional account of the action. Séverine (Catherine Deneuve) is married to Pierre (Jean Sorel), a successful Parisian doctor patiently confronting her sexual unresponsiveness.

In her opening daydream the couple are riding in a landau. Pierre's tenderness changes to cruelty as he gives orders for Séverine to be dragged and tied to a tree where she is bound, whipped, then violated. . . .

Meeting Husson (Michel Piccoli), Pierre's libertine friend, Séverine's masochistic tendencies are aroused when he describes women "enslaved" in a brothel and mentions the address of one. A nervous Séverine hesitates before inspecting the place run by the elegant Mme. Anaïs (Geneviève Page) who is pleased with the attractive novice who can only work in the afternoon from two to five (hence her nickname "Belle de Jour"). Séverine finds her first client loathsome and is all set to flee when an annoyed Anaïs orders her back. The madam senses that the woman welcomes a firm hand. Later Séverine daydreams about being splattered with mud by Husson. Another daydream/dream involves her in a bizarre necrophiliac ritual with a Duke (Georges Marchal).*

Marcel (Pierre Clémenti), a violent young hoodlum, is drawn to an acquiescent Belle de Jour. When, inevitably, Husson shows up at Mme. Anaïs's and spots Pierre's wife, she quits the brothel, fearing that he might tell her husband. A possessive Marcel shows up at her home and threatens blackmail. Sensing that her husband is the obstacle, he shoots Pierre and is then killed by the police.

Séverine tends to her husband, now paralyzed and speechless. Husson appears to free him from feeling guilty or a burden. What follows are perhaps alternate endings: Alone, Séverine enters the drawing room. We see Pierre's tear-stained face—his reaction to Husson's disclosure. Another shot shows his hands lying motionless on his lap. . . . Then a rejuvenated Pierre rises from his chair and discusses a vacation with her. The landau arrives; as it passes we see it's empty.

COMMENTARY

Belle de Jour received the Grand Prize at the 1967 Venice Film Festival. To Buñuel's surprise the film which he thought too complex for a mass audience turned out to be a big commercial success and he a director much in demand.

Buñuel avoids a clinical approach, Freudian symbolism, sensationalism, pious moralizing, along with the conventions of cinema dream sequences (such as the use of the dissolve) to create a personal and highly original film. His masterly controlled direction is simple and straightforward and his reliance on mainly medium shots contributes to a tone of neutrality, leaving the viewer without guidelines as to how to respond to it.

A conventional interpretation would treat Séverine as a repressed woman—a child victim of molestation by a worker—who attempts to improve her marriage by entering a brothel where she can act out her masochistic tendencies. As she's awakened she's drawn closer to Pierre and when he

*At the café where the Duke meets her, we can spot a seated Buñuel. Also in the robbery sequence he can be seen walking along the Champs-Elysées.

Belle de Jour (Catherine Deneuve) finds her Asiatic client (Iska Khan) intriguing. Significantly, in his prelude to a passionate session which brings her release, he shakes a little bell. Throughout the film the sound of bells heralds her erotic fantasies.

becomes a helpless cripple she can repress her erotic nature—the carriage at the end is "empty", i.e. now lacks her active participation—to be a devoted nurse to him. Some critics regard the narrative as a variant on the legend of Beauty and the Beast in which the heroine must learn to come to terms with the erotic side of her nature.

The rather pat psychological analyses are undermined by the mysterious ending. When we have a scene of Pierre "dying" at the revelation of his wife's sordid affairs immediately followed by a scene of the husband miraculously "cured," we begin to suspect those earlier scenes we complacently divided into "fantasy" and "reality." It is even possible to consider the *entire* film as occurring in Séverine's imagination. Does the landau arrive at the conclusion to take us back to the start again—another "circular movement" à la *Marienbad*?

The fact remains that *every* apparent certainty in the film is open to question. Buñuel has succeeded in maintaining a consistent ambiguity in order to evoke a vision of Surrealism in which reality and dream are inextricably one. In his first Surrealistic Manifesto (1924) André Breton said, "I believe in the future transmutation of those two seemingly contradictory states, dream and reality, into a sort of absolute reality, 'surréalité.' " Buñuel implies that the subconscious has equal validity with the conscious mind.

Since the Surrealists place great importance on sexual drives, the return of the landau at the end can symbolize Séverine's irrepressible erotic nature. And since the Surrealists believe that reality is manifold, open to many differing interpretations, the director stresses: "ambiguity is established by the landau, which is the symbol of the irrational. When the landau comes it is a signal that you do not know whether what is seen is actual or not."

In the absence of any music in the film ("I try to keep it out of my work because it makes for a too easy effect"—Buñuel) there is a masterful use of natural sounds: the jingling bells of the landau and cowbells which connote immanent release, animal noises—hooves of wild bulls, cats' mewing—representing unfettered emotion etc.

Buñuel refrains from any moral judgment on Séverine's journey to liberation. We can notice the change in her clothing, from the earlier neutral beige dress to the later bright red one. The beautiful Catherine Deneuve is coolly elegant and enigmatic as Séverine. Buñuel said that she played her role "with great style." Geneviève Page and Pierre Clémenti lend memorable support. Sacha Vierney's photography is excellent. *Belle de Jour* brilliantly realizes an earlier dictim of Buñuel: "The cinema seems to have been invented for the expression of the subconscious, so profoundly is it rooted in poetry."

Angered at her disappearance from Mme. Anaîs's, the young gangster Marcel (Pierre Clémenti) raises his belt to strike Belle de Jour (Catherine Deneuve), who attempts to shield her face. Notice she seems to be wearing the same jacket as in the initial daydream.

208

LA FEMME
INFIDELE

FILMS LA BOËTIE (PARIS)/CINEGAY
(ROME)   1969

CREDITS

Screenplay and Direction: Claude Chabrol; *Photographer:* Jean Rabier (Eastmancolor); *Assistant Directors:* Jacques Fansten and Jean-François Detré; *Editor:* Jacques Gaillard; *Music:* Pierre Jansen; *Running Time:* 98 minutes; *Paris Premiere:* January 22, 1969; *New York Premiere:* November 9, 1969; *16 mm. Rental Source:* Hurlock Cine-World, Inc.

CAST

Hélène Desvallées: Stéphane Audran; *Charles Desvallées:* Michel Bouquet; *Victor Pégala:* Maurice Ronet; *Michel Desvallées:* Stéphane di Napoli; *Police Officer Duval:* Michael Duchaussoy; *Police Officer Gobet:* Guy Marly; *Private Detective Bignon:* Serge Bento; *Maid:* Louise Chevalier; *Charles's Mother:* Louise Rioton; *Paul:* Henri Marteau; *Frédéric:* François Moro-Giafferi; *Truckdriver:* Dominique Zardi.

BACKGROUND

Claude Chabrol was born in Paris on June 24, 1930. After earning a *licencié ès lettres* (equivalent to a masters of arts degree) and studying law for a year, he took up pharmacy for a while—he comes from a family of pharmacists—to please his parents who wouldn't let him go to I.D.H.E.C. Soon he began to write detective fiction, befriend such young film enthusiasts as François Truffaut and Jean-Luc Godard and contribute criticism to *Cahiers du Cinéma.* In 1957 he published *Hitchcock,* an analytical study of the director written in collaboration with Eric Rohmer.

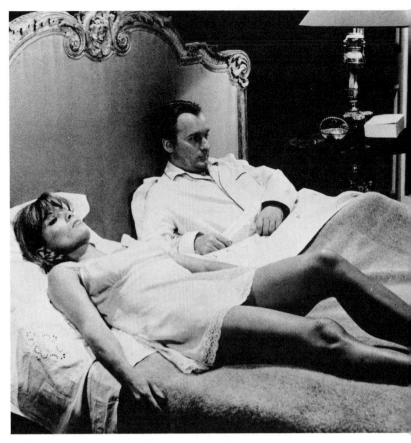

An image of a troubled marriage: The sensuous Hélène (Stéphane Audran) is neglected by her husband Charles (Michel Bouquet), who prefers to listen to Mozart.

With money inherited by his first wife, Chabrol formed a production company and made his first film, *Le Beau Serge* (1958). A very personal film, shot on location with a low-budget, using unknown actors, the film validated the filmmaking theories of the young cinéastes by being the first critically successful—it won the Prix Jean Vigo (1959)—and popular film of the New Wave. After the acclaimed *Les Cousins* (1959), Chabrol went through a temporary eclipse with a string of flops and some insignificant potboilers before entering a fertile period which re-established his career as a serious filmmaker, commencing with *Les Biches* (1968). Critics praised a stylistic advancement and a more detached attitude toward his subjects.

The director, while acknowledging that he learned very much from Hitchock, said: "Others have influenced me more. My three greatest influences were Murnau . . . Ernst Lubitsch, and Fritz Lang." Chabrol in general chooses to work within

209

the thriller genre: "I've always tried to hold on to the cinema of genre, because I think it's the only way to make films." In Chabrol's next film, *La Femme Infidèle* as well as in most of his best work, the thriller serves as only a framework for his major concerns—characterization and *mise en scène*. "The plot is just a means to get at the behavior of the characters," he said.

"I'm not at all interested in who-done-its," Chabrol remarked. "I want the audience to know who the murderer is, so that we can consider his personality." Chabrol's critical theories are amply justified in *La Femme Infidèle,* his sixteenth feature. Stéphane Audran, his leading lady in many of his films and wife since 1964, was cast in the title role. Michel Bouquet and Maurice Ronet were to play, respectively, the husband and the lover. Each had appeared in a number of the director's films.

The film was shot in Paris and in Jouy-en Josas, near Versailles, during July and August of 1968. *La Femme Infidèle* was to be Chabrol's best received movie since *Les Cousins* and prove one of his most satisfying films.

SYNOPSIS

Charles Desvallées (Michel Bouquet) manages a successful insurance firm and lives in comfortable complacency with his beautiful but unfulfilled wife Hélène (Stéphane Audran) and ten-year-old son

Charles (Michel Bouquet), left, pays a visit to his wife's lover, Victor Pégala (Maurice Ronet), right. What starts off as a relaxed, civilized interview. . .

erupts into sudden violence when Charles (Michel Bouquet) unleashes his fury by bashing Victor (Maurice Ronet) over the head with a heavy statue.

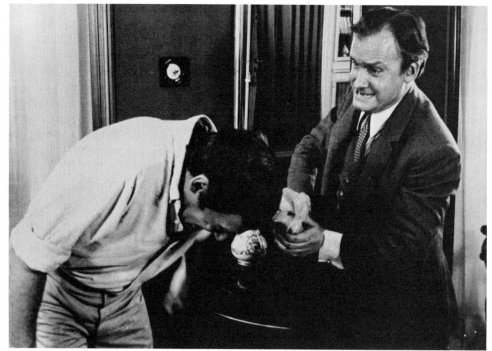

210

Michel (Stéphane di Napoli) in affluent Versailles. When he suspects his wife of infidelity, he hires a private detective, Bignon (Serge Bento), who soon produces proof.

In Neuilly Charles visits the lover, Victor Pégala (Maurice Ronet), a wealthy, dilettantish writer. Charles gets him to talk about Hélène by pretending that he and his wife have a liberal arrangement concerning extramarital affairs. However, a brooding Charles, no longer able to contain his overwhelming passion, suddenly picks up a statue and hits Victor over the head with it. Then, calmly, he goes about cleaning up the blood-strewn apartment and dropping the blanket-wrapped corpse into a pond.

Two policemen—Officers Duval (Michel Duchaussoy) and Gobet (Guy Marly)—visit the unhappy Hélène and question her about Pégala's disappearance, since her name was listed in the man's address book.

Later Hélène discovers Victor's photo in her husband's jacket. Realizing how profound is Charles's love for her, she burns the evidence in a symbolic act of renewed commitment to him.

The police return, this time to take Charles away. "I love you madly," he tells his wife after she proclaims her newly revitalized love for him.

COMMENTARY

La Femme Infidèle was a critical and popular success and displayed what a master craftsman Chabrol had become. Through a careful control of camera movement, the director is able to convey much about his central character. The opening tracking shots reveal Charles's immaculately kept suburban home and grounds. Chabrol explained that: "The principle of *La Femme Infidèle* is that the movement always ends up by returning to its starting point, as if it never moved." This pinpoints the desire of Charles to desperately maintain a status quo. When his mother tells him to exercise or else he'll wind up with *"un gros derrière,"* Charles responds by saying that he's pleased with things as they are and that "the least change in my life is able to disturb this harmony."

However, with the discovery of Hélène's infidelity, Charles's world "becomes unbalanced," Chabrol notes, "and he pushes like crazy on the unbalanced side to re-establish balance." This includes murdering the lover. In the famous concluding shot, Charles is being taken away by the police. As the camera tracks back and away slowly to denote

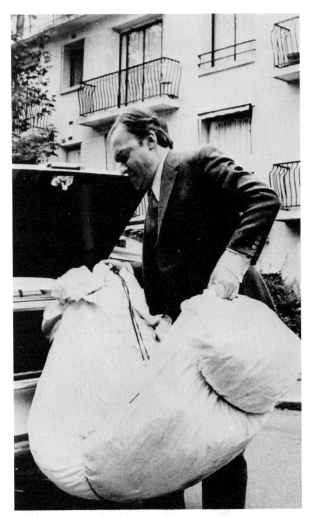

Calmly, methodically, Charles (Michel Bouquet) deposits Victor's carefully wrapped corpse into his car trunk.

separation, there is an accompanying zoom forward to the wife and child to indicate Charles's intense union with them. The image poignantly expresses his synchronous gain and loss. *La Femme Infidèle* is a very visual film and employs a minimum of dialogue.

Through the course of their marriage Charles's deep passion somehow got buried along with Hélène's responses of tenderness and sweetness—accessible to Victor, he learns, but kept from him. It is ironic that the ensuing murder results in the bringing together of husband and wife.

Michel Bouquet is outstanding as the cuckolded husband, a part which was written for him. The elegant Stéphane Audran is excellent as the wife. "I have always thought that Bouquet's wife . . . had probably been his secretary," Chabrol said. "She must have been slightly his inferior socially."

"I ask audiences to contemplate a character, not

Hélène (Stéphane Audran) discovers Victor's photo (supplied by the private detective) in Charles's jacket and realizes the depth of her husband's love for her.

identify with him," Chabrol said. To that end, he strives for a "distancing" effect. Here as in much of his other work, there is criticism of the upper middle class world: "I make films about the bourgeoisie, because I am one myself—I know them and I hate them," Chabrol said. The director dislikes what he calls the "extraordinary egoism" in that class. The least threat to its secure privileges

and it readies its attack. Charles will commit murder to hold on to what he feels is his possession. As beautiful as the Desvallées' lifestyle is we can sense the void at the heart of it. "My films don't offer solutions," Chabrol said. "One cannot solve or explain anything for other people. I dislike explanations and judgments."

Victor's murder is a great scene all the more shocking since it seems so unpremeditated and spontaneous. As Victor gives Charles a tour of his apartment the husband sees the bed, then a large Zippo lighter which he had presented to Hélène as a third wedding anniversary present and which she later gave to Victor. He feels dizzy. "When the husband notices that his wife has given it away," Chabrol observes of the lighter, "he can't bear it. It's warmth and home." All of a sudden the well-mannered Charles explodes into a violent outburst and kills Victor. The lighter served as a catalyst and made Charles realize that his prize possession was being taken away from him. There is a striking shot of Victor's body and two separate streams of blood trickling from it onto the linoleum.

Chabrol followed *La Femme Infidèle* with two impressive films: *This Man Must Die (Que la Bête Meure)* (1969) and *Le Boucher* (1970), then went into a critical decline, occasionally emerging with a success such as *Violette (Violette Nozière)* (1978). Since 1957 the prolific director has produced over thirty features, three sketches, and six television films. So far, his achievement peaked in the period from 1967-70 in which *La Femme Infidèle* remains an outstanding example of Chabrol at his most accomplished: subtle, delicate, low-keyed, and powerful. Critic George Melly observed: "Chabrol's strength is his ability to find stories which, for all their melodrama, stand as metaphors for a society which, despite faithful observation of the old forms of honesty and morality, is in fact rotting away under the surface."

Z

REGGANE FILMS (PARIS) / O.N.C.I.C.
(OFFICE NATIONAL POUR LE
COMMERCE ET L'INDUSTRIE
CINEMATOGRAPHIQUE) (ALGIERS)   1969

CREDITS

Adaptation: Jorge Semprun and Costa-Gavras, based on the novel by Vassili Vassilikos (1966), published in New York, 1968; *Dialogue:* Jorge Semprun; *Director:* Costa-Gavras; *Photographer:* Raoul Coutard (Eastmancolor); *Assistant Director:* Philippe Monnier; *Editor:* Françoise Bonnot; *Music:* Mikis Theodorakis; *Running Time:* 128 minutes; *Paris Premiere:* February 26, 1969; *New York Premiere:* December 8, 1969; *16 mm. Rental Source:* Cinema 5.

CAST

Deputy "Z": Yves Montand; *Hélène, his Wife:* Irène Papas; *Examining Magistrate:* Jean-Louis Trintignant; *Photographer-Journalist:* Jacques Perrin; *Manuel:* Charles Denner; *Public Prosecutor:* François Périer; *The General:* Pierre Dux; *The Colonel:* Julien Guiomar; *Matt:* Bernard Fresson; *Yago:* Renato Salvatori; *Vago:* Marcel Bozzufi; *Deputy Georges Pirou:* Jean Bouise; *Nick:* Georges Géret; *Nick's Sister:* Magali Noël; *Coste:* Jean Dasté; *Pierre:* Jean-Pierre Miquel.

BACKGROUND

Costa-Gavras was born in Athens on February 13, 1933. "Costa" is short for his Christian name, Konstantinos, which he added, hyphenated, to the family name Gavras, as he says, "to create confusion." Because his Russian immigrant father fought in the Greek Resistance against the Nazis he was mistakenly considered Communist and after the war found himself without work and subjected to a repeated pattern of arrest, jail, and release. This left an indelible impression upon his teenage son: "That's where I learned about oppression," he said.

Since sons of politically suspect persons were denied the right to a university education, Gavras left Greece in 1952 for Paris and studied literature at the Sorbonne before switching to film, his real interest, at I.D.H.E.C. After graduation in 1958 he was an assistant director to Yves Allégret, René Clément (whom he acknowledged influenced him the most), etc., before making his first feature, the successful suspense thriller *The Sleeping Car Murders (Compartiment Tueurs)* (1965), followed by *Shock Troops (Un Homme de Trop)* (1967).

His next film dealt with a tragedy in his native country. On the evening of May 22, 1963, at Salonika, pacifist Grégorios Lambrakis, M.D., a liberal—not a Communist—deputy in the national assembly, was fatally injured after he presided over a meeting of the Friends of Peace protesting the installation of the Polaris missile in Greece. The government was forced to appoint a judge, Christos Sartzétakis, to investigate the affair. It soon became apparent that Lambrakis was a victim of a conspiracy triggered by officials in the Establishment. (It is believed that Lambrakis might have won the coming elections and threatened the Allies' flow of money and armaments to Greece.) The actual murderers were tried and sentenced in Oc-

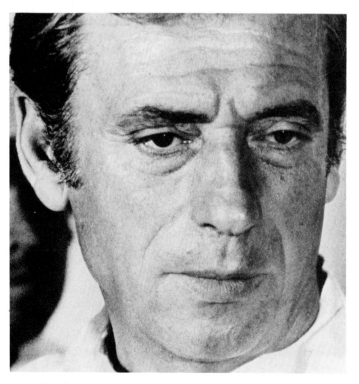

Portrait of Yves Montand as Deputy Z, the crusader for peace who will be martyred.

213

Deputy Z (Yves Montand), center, together with his lawyer friends Manuel (Charles Denner), left, and Pierre (Jean-Pierre Miquel), right, brave the counterdemonstrators as they head to the meeting. Hidden behind Manuel is Matt (Bernard Fresson), the Committee Secretary.

tober 1966. There was a military coup d'état on April 21, 1967, and a seven-year oppressive, Fascist dictatorship began. The five officials forced to resign earlier were reinstated. Judge Sartzétakis was arrested, tortured, and prevented from practicing law. Followers of the slain Lambrakis scrawled the forbidden letter "Z" (which stands for the Greek symbol *zei*, meaning "he lives") on city walls. In 1966 Greek novelist Vassili Vassilikos portrayed these events in an engrossing and suspenseful novel, Z. The action ends just before the trial in the autumn of 1966. The junta banned Z in 1967; the author went into exile.

When Costa-Gavras read the book around the time of the military takeover he was determined to film it: "For me, Z was a political action, like writing on a wall . . . I felt I had to do something against the Greek regime." He tried for almost two years to raise backing but producers turned down the project as being "too political" and therefore uncommercial. Then his friend Jacques Perrin managed to get Algeria to coproduce the film.

In the carefully constructed, highly charged Z (or *The Anatomy of a Political Assassination*) Costa-Gavras decided not to explore the intricate *motivations* of the crime, such as rumors of intervention by the CIA or the palace, but to stay with the *mechanics* of the crime: "By sticking absolutely to what was proved at the trial, we have made it all but impossible for people to say, 'How do you know? That isn't true. That's a rumor.'" Elsewhere he said:

"Expose the assassins! Police accomplices!" shout students protesting Z's death in front of his widow's hotel, as the police start to attack them brutally.

"The important thing is to point out the problems and ask the questions." The shocking events which occurred in Greece after the novel was published provide a brutal dénouement to the film.

Costa-Gavras said that Yves Montand was "the only one in France who could play Lambrakis." It was fitting that the music used was by Mikis Theodorakis, whose work had been banned by the junta. The composer was then living under house arrest. Unable to write an original score—his earlier compositions had to be adapted to the film—he nonetheless managed to smuggle out an original song sung by him and used in the film.

Z was shot mostly in Algeria during the summer of 1968 and then Paris for some interior scenes. The film was faithful to the novel—especially in spirit. Z would prove a sensational hit, a very influential film with sinister implications extending far beyond the frontiers of Greece.

SYNOPSIS

The locale is unspecified. After addressing a peace

rally, pacifist deputy Z (Yves Montand) is hit by a speeding truck driven by Yago (Renato Salvatori) and clubbed by another hired assassin, Vago (Marcel Bozzufi). Hélène, Z's wife (Irène Papas), rushes to her dying husband. Z's death is declared "accidental." Examining Magistrate (Jean-Louis Trintignant) conducts an investigation.

Varnisher Nick (Georges Géret) is cudgeled before he can testify. An inquisitive photographer-journalist (Jacques Perrin) helps uncover a secret Fascist organization, C.R.O.C. ("Royalist Fighters of the Christian West") which collaborated in the conspiracy against Z.

Public Prosecutor (François Périer) tries in vain to halt the proceedings but the uncompromising magistrate continues gathering incriminating evidence. There's an attempt on the life of Manuel (Charles Denner), a lawyer in Z's cause. Soon several officials are arrested.

In an epilogue the photographer-journalist informs us via a news report of the tragic deaths of several witnesses, the sentences of Yago and Vago, and the dropping of charges against the officers. Then comes news of the military coup prior to the elections and the vengeful actions taken against Z's supporters. A voice announces the imprisonment of the photographer-journalist. A list of prohibitions by the junta appears, including long hair, freedom of the press, Peace Movements, etc.

COMMENTARY

Z was the most popular film shown in France in 1969. At the Cannes Film Festival (1969) it was unanimously awarded the Special Jury Prize; Jean-Louis Trintignant was voted "Best Actor." In America the film was an enormous critical and popular success. The New York Film Critics Awards went to Z for "Best Motion Picture" (1969) and Costa-Gavras for "Best Direction." Z won two "Oscars" for 1969, one for best "Foreign Language Film," another to Françoise Bonnot for "Film Editing," and was nominated for an Academy Award in three other categories: "Picture," Costa-Gavras for "Direction," and Jorge Semprun and Costa-Gavras for "Writing (Screenplay—Based on Material from another Medium)."

Z was banned in Spain, India, Brazil, etc. When Greece was able to see it with the restoration of democracy in 1974, Z proved both successful and controversial. The film's "thriller" style, underlining a sense of urgency, accounts for Z's blockbuster appeal. With his use of rapid cross cutting, zoom lenses, constant tracking shots, hand-held camera

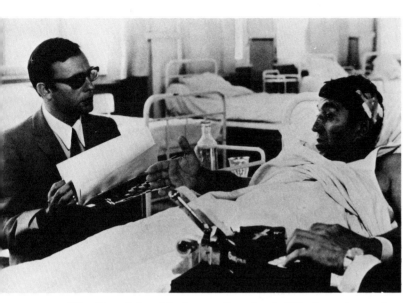

The Examining Magistrate (Jean-Louis Trintignant) questions the witness Nick (Georges Géret), who was clobbered while he was enroute to present his testimony.

Manuel (Charles Denner) zig-zags frantically through the streets to avoid being run over by the opposition's car.

shots, Costa-Gavras moves the action along at a pounding pace.

Although he's killed early in the film, Yves Montand exerts a powerful presence which dominates

Z. As the dedicated Examining Magistrate, Jean-Louis Trintignant is forceful and convincing. Raoul Coutard's grainy photography gives a documentary "feel" to *Z*. Theodorakis's music is rousing, plaintive, and quintessentially Greek.*

From the opening reversal of the usual disclaimer ("Any similarity to actual events or to people living or dead is not done by chance. It is intentional") to its closing superimposition of the phrase "He is Living" over portraits of Lambrakis and Montand, *Z* concentrates exclusively on the theme of injustice. Accused of taking a simplistic approach, Costa-Gavras said: "That's the way it is in Greece. Black and white. No nuances."

Z exposed to international scrutiny factors which led to the brutal regime of the junta in Greece. Scriptwriter Semprun warns: "Let's not try to reassure ourselves: This type of thing doesn't only happen elsewhere, it happens everywhere." "Z is Lambrakis, of course," Costa-Gavras said, "but he is also John F. Kennedy, Martin Luther King, Robert Kennedy ... Z is the just man underhandedly murdered within an oppressive climate of official hypocrisy."

Z represented a new and popular genre, the political thriller. The detective thriller in the film noir tradition has become politicized; there is the simultaneous coupling of riveting action to provocative political ideas. *Z* demonstrates that a political film could mean box office. Its popularity encouraged a flow of political thrillers, modelled on *Z*, such as Elio Petri's *Investigation of a Citizen Above Suspicion (Indagine su un Cittadino al di sopra di Ogni Sospetto)* (1970).

After *Z*, Costa-Gavras continued as a political, not a revolutionary, filmmaker ("A camera is not a gun," he said) with an account of the Slansky trials in Czechoslovakia, *The Confession (L'Aveu)* (1970); the Mitrione affair in Uruguay, *State of Siege (Etat de Siège)* (1972), and an exposé of Vichy "justice," *Section Spéciale* (1975).*

Z remains Costa-Gavras' most popular and influential film. His sense of commitment and inflammatory style continue to rouse the human spirit and appeal to man's thirst for justice.

*The composer received an award from the British Society of Film and Television Arts for his music in *Z* (1969).

*Costa-Gavras made an auspicious début in American films with the provocative *Missing* (1982), which shared a Grand Prize at the 1982 Cannes Film Festival and whose star, Jack Lemmon, was voted "Best Actor."

UNE FEMME DOUCE

PARC FILMS/MARIANNE PRODUCTIONS   1969

CREDITS

Screenplay: Robert Bresson, based on Dostoevsky's novella, *A Gentle Spirit* (1876); *Director:* Robert Bresson; *Photographer:* Ghislain Cloquet (Eastmancolor); *Assistant Director:* Jacques Kebadian; *Editor:* Raymond Lamy; *Music:* Jean Wiener, with selections from Purcell and Mozart; *Running Time:* 88 minutes; *Paris Premiere:* August 28, 1969; *New York Premiere:* May 27, 1971; *16 mm. Rental Source:* New Yorker Films.

CAST

She: Dominique Sanda; *He:* Guy Frangin; *Anna:* Jane Lobre.

BACKGROUND

"Bresson is 'apart' in this terrible profession," Cocteau wrote in 1957. "He expresses himself cinematically like a poet with his pen." Bresson was only able to make twelve films in the period 1943-1977. "The producers do not hurl themselves on my projects," he said. However, if he was not a commercially successful director he did not lack for supporters or acclaim. Jean-Luc Godard, Jacques Rivette, and Eric Rohmer among the New Wave directors and Louis Malle acknowledged him as their master; at the Cannes Film Festival in 1967 the jury paid homage to the entirety of Bresson's work.

There has been a noticeable change in Bresson's films since *Au Hasard, Balthazar* (1966) in which the central character no longer discovers spiritual redemption through grace but rather succumbs to the evil in the world or seeks release through suicide as did the young heroine of *Mouchette* (1967), his second Bernanos adaptation. His next film, *Une Femme Douce*, based on the novella by Dostoevsky, continues in this vein.

Portrait of a gentle creature. One of the many varied shots of the husband (Guy Frangin) returning to the bier of his wife (Dominique Sanda) during his agonizing re-examination of their relationship.

The wedding night. The husband (Guy Frangin) and his eager bride (Dominique Sanda). Soon he narrates: "I threw cold water on that bliss."

Husband (Guy Frangin) and wife (Dominique Sanda) on a visit to the countryside. Afraid of becoming a conventionalized wife, she will quickly throw away the bouquet.

The great Russian writer presented a disturbing account of a young wife who commits suicide without leaving an explanatory note. Her pawnbroker husband, age 41, is forced to engage in torturous, guilt-ridden introspection. The egotistical man lacks self-awareness and attempts to justify his behavior so as to acquit himself of culpability. The reader alone comes to perceive the truth behind the man's rantings and sense why the subjugated and humiliated woman took her life.

Bresson moved the locale from St. Petersburg to contemporary Paris, made the husband younger, and in general retained the original plot outline, even keeping the couple unnamed. His most radical innovation was his omission of motivation. "I never want to explain anything," Bresson said. "The trouble with most films is that they explain everything." This trait discourages our reliance on simplistic and facile psychological explanations—"No psychology (of the kind which discovers only what it can explain)," said Bresson—and forces us to explore deeper the secret of our existence.

As in Dostoevsky Bresson presented the effect (the wife's suicide) before any cause. The director commented: "I think this is a good idea because it increases the mystery; to witness events without knowing why they are occurring makes you desire to find out the reason." What results is a fascinating ambiguity.

Bresson changed the temperament of the histrionic, self-pitying husband to that of a rigid, stern, and silently subjugating character and downplayed his dominance in the novella to emphasize the alluring and enigmatic wife. The obtuseness in Dostoevsky's husband finds a cinematic equivalent in the film's husband who delivers an unconsciously ironical commentary; there is a discrepancy between the words he uses and the images we perceive. Thus he can narrate: "She never looked at me—was she shy?" while we have witnessed his continual oppressive behavior towards her.

Dominique Sanda was a sixteen-year-old model whom Bresson spotted in a fashion magazine. He was convinced she was right for the wife when he heard her voice on the telephone. *Une Femme Douce* would help launch her important film career. Guy Frangin was a painter whom the director noticed at a gallery opening. For the first time money was available for the director to use color.

While her husband pretends to sleep, the wife (Dominique Sanda) tries to shoot him but backs off.

Une Femme Douce marks another original, beautiful, and haunting Bresson film.

SYNOPSIS

A young Parisian wife (Dominique Sanda) jumps to her death from her apartment terrace at the film's start. While her body is laid out on her bed, her pawnbroker husband (Guy Frangin) recalls their relationship in front of the servant Anna (Jane Lobre): As a poor student she enters his shop to sell various items. Attracted to her, he dates her and offers marriage. She tells him she's looking for something broader than marriage but consents nonetheless to be his wife.

The husband represses her enthusiasm and soon their marriage is marked by silence. She objects to his stinginess and materialism. He is cold and withdrawn and tries to dominate her. They quarrel. When he notices a man paying attention to her in the shop his jealousy is aroused. The couple are apparently seeing each other and one evening the husband brings a gun with him and surprises her talking in a car with his "rival." That night, while pretending to be asleep, he sees her approach him with the gun and point it at his cheek, but she cannot bring herself to fire it. He installs a second bed surrounded by a screen and the wife realizes that he saw her with the gun. She falls into a long illness lasting six weeks. This elicits his pity and solicitude. The wife recovers but there is still no genuine communication between the two.

He catches her singing one afternoon and drops his cold mask to pour forth his love and devotion to her for the first time. Shocked at this unexpected outburst, she sobs uncontrollably. He makes plans for a vacation, a new life together. Can people change? she asks.

That morning she dresses and walks back and forth in a state of conflict before coming to a decision. Then she leaps to her mysterious death.

COMMENTARY

The critics were impressed with both the beauty and profundity of *Une Femme Douce*. The opening suicide sequence in four quick shots, after the film's credits, is shocking and riveting: the maid turns the handle of the glass-paned door and enters the bedroom. Next shot is that of a bentwood rocker swaying back and forth on the terrace while a table supporting a vase and plant overturns. Then a shot of a white shawl drifting to the ground. Cut to the

The wife (Dominique Sanda) sees a new, second bed in the room and realizes her husband saw her with the gun. One of several "framed" shots which convey a sense of her imprisonment.

street: a car comes to a halt. We hear brakes. A crowd gathers around the body of a young woman. This eloquent use of ellipsis is a Bresson trademark, along with brief scenes and scant dialogue.

Enhanced by Ghislain Cloquet's stunning color photography, Dominique Sanda makes a ravishingly beautiful début. There is a powerful use of sound: the harsh noises from doors slamming and footsteps underlie the couple's dreadful world of hostile silence.

By constantly returning to the present after each flashback, the director concentrates on the drama of the husband confronting his dead wife. This fragmented narration adds to the sense of a "puzzle" which the husband is trying to solve.

Much has been made of the extended closing scene from *Hamlet* which the couple view at the theatre. Does the wife relate to Hamlet's metaphysical anguish? And his desire to find escape in death? Is the play to be taken as foreshadowing her own act of revenge? Does the husband, perhaps, identify with the theme of betrayal?

The major controversy, however, centers around the wife's suicide. Are we to see it as an act of defiance against a man who would tyrannize her and destroy her spirit? Is it simply to flee the bonds of an insufferable existence? It is interesting to observe that she takes her life—we have been prepared for violence of some sort by the wife's attempted killing of her husband—soon after the husband has just revealed his vulnerability. Was it then to inflict the maximum pain? Doom him to be racked with guilt all his life? If so, the *"douce"* in the title is rather ironic. Concerning the suicide, Bresson acknowledges: "There are many motives here."

Unforgettable is the brief smile the wife flashes at a mirror before she heads to the terrace; the repetition of the suicide sequence at the end—this time the gracefully wafting shawl seems to imply "release"; and the shocking and indelible noise of the screws securing the coffin lid in close-up.

Une Femme Douce remains a superbly directed film, one of Bresson's most challenging and rewarding achievements. "My theme is the impossibility of communication," he said. Bresson adapted another Dostoevsky story, "White Nights" (1848): *Four Nights of a Dreamer (Quatre Nuits d'un Rêveur)* (1972) then did *Lancelot du Lac* (1974), and *The Devil Probably (Le Diable Probablement* (1977). In 1975 he published *Notes sur le Cinématographie* (published in New York as *Notes on Cinematography,* 1977). Robert Bresson was awarded the Grand Prix National du Cinéma in 1978.

In 1957 critic Claude Choublier commented: "A Robert Bresson film is not a collection of tricks: gray walls, low skies, immobile faces, abstract dialogue; it is, on the contrary, one of the most extraordinary of existing cinematographic languages: the perfect meeting of form and substance, of the written word and thought." This observation still holds, twenty-five years later, concerning a director who claimed: "The domain of cinematography is the domain of the ineffable."

L'ARMÉE DES OMBRES

CORONA FILMS (PARIS)/FONO FILMS
(ROME)   1969

Portrait of Simone Signoret as the Resistance fighter Mathilde making plans to invade the Gestapo HQ in Lyons to rescue Félix.

CREDITS

Screenplay: Jean-Pierre Melville, based on the novel by Joseph Kessel published in New York both in French and as *Army of Shadows* (1944); *Director:* Jean-Pierre Melville; *Photographer:* Pierre Lhomme (Eastmancolor); *Assistant Directors:* Jean-François Adam, Georges Pellegrin; *Editor:* Françoise Bonnot; *Music:* Eric de Marsan; *Running Time:* 140 minutes; *Paris Premiere:* September 12, 1969; *16mm. Rental Source:* Facsea.

CAST

Philippe Gerbier: Lino Ventura; *Luc Jardie:* Paul Meurisse; *Mathilde:* Simone Signoret; *Jean-François:* Jean-Pierre Cassel; *Le Masque:* Claude Mann; *Le Bison:* Christian Barbier; *The Barber:* Serge Reggiani; *Dounat:* Alain Libolt; *Félix:* Paul Crauchet; *Camp Commandant:* Alain Bottet.

BACKGROUND

Several years after *Les Enfants Terribles* Jean-Pierre Melville constructed his own film studio. He returned periodically to the gangster film, exploring the moral code of criminals and displaying the strong influence of American film noir. The example of his cinematic practice—making films outside of the studio system on extremely low budgets, shooting on actual locations without stars, writing his own scripts and retaining artistic control—rather than his style or themes earned him the designation as "father of the New Wave."

In 1961 Melville entered a new phase of produc-

tion, working with large budgets, using stars like Jean-Paul Belmondo and Alain Delon, and aiming for a wide audience. By 1969 he was ready to make the film he had been waiting for twenty-five years to do, his version of Joseph Kessel's powerful, fictionalized account of the early days of the French Resistance, *L'Armée des Ombres, (The Army of Shadows)*, which he had discovered in London during the war. World War II had a profound influence on the director. He was in the Resistance for two years before serving in combat in Italy with the Free French Forces. Twice before, in his first feature and in *Léon Morin, Prêtre* (1961), he had treated the subject of the Resistance.

Kessel's novel ("*The* book about the Resistance: the greatest and the most comprehensive of all the documents about this tragic period in the history of humanity"—Melville) was completed in London in 1943. Since "nothing must be recognizable," the author drew his characters out of diverse figures and deliberately rearranged and disguised events to prevent the Nazis from using the book profitably.

In bringing this exciting and fast-paced account of the dedicated "army of shadows" to the screen Melville remained absolutely faithful to the vision of nobility and sacrifice which Kessel captured. For the sake of economy some of the action had to be simplified and transposed in the film. Melville

221

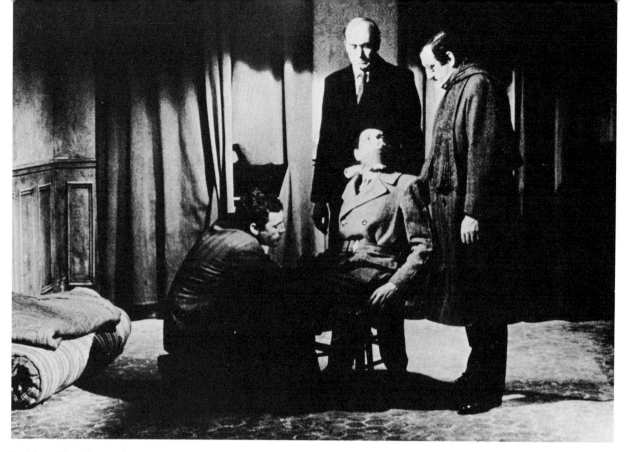

In Marseilles, the Resistance group: Le Masque (Claude Mann), Félix (Paul Crauchet), and Philippe Gerbier (Lino Ventura) is forced to kill the seated traitor Dounat (Alain Libolt).

In Paris, Jean-François (Jean-Pierre Cassel), left, newly recruited to the Resistance, meets his scholarly brother Luc Jardie (Paul Meurisse) and is unaware of Luc's position in the organization.

added such scenes as Gerbier's escape from the Gestapo Headquarters and Jean François' attempt to rescue Félix.

The characters are composites as in the novel. Philippe Gerbier represents several different people; Luc Jardie is based on, among others, the Resistance hero Jean Moulin and the philosopher Jean Cavaillès, both executed by the Nazis. For the leads Melville reunited the stars of his earlier thriller, *Le Deuxième Souffle* (1966), Lino Ventura and Paul Meurisse. Alain Delon was originally offered the role of Gerbier but he turned it down.

Melville took great pains in creating a sense of realism. The concentration camp sequence was actually shot in a camp, which Melville had to restore, originally built to hold German P.O.W.'s. Interiors were shot at the Studios de Boulogne. The film was made between January and March 1969.

L'Armée des Ombres is as personal a memoir for Melville as it was for Kessel. "Out of a sublime documentary about the Resistance," Melville said, "I have created a retrospective reverie; a nostalgic pilgrimage back to a period which profoundly marked my generation."

SYNOPSIS

The film records the terrible losses and sacrifices of the early French Resistance leaders in a period,

October 1942 through February 1943, before the full-scale military underground, the Maquis, was operating.

Philippe Gerbier (Lino Ventura), a suspected Resistance leader, is interned in a concentration camp among various political and ethnic prisoners. Before he can escape, he's taken to Gestapo Headquarters, the Hotel Majestic in Paris, for questioning. Daringly, he kills a guard and escapes. A barber (Serge Reggiani) shaves him and then quietly gives him a new overcoat to keep him from being detected.

In Marseilles, Gerbier's group seizes Dounat (Alain Libolt), a young man who was betraying them to the Nazis, and takes him to a rented room where they strangle him. Félix (Paul Crauchet) meets an army buddy, Jean-François (Jean-Pierre Cassel) and inducts him into the organization. Jean-François delivers a radio to the Resistance fighter Mathilde (Simone Signoret) in Paris then visits his aesthete brother Luc Jardie (Paul Meurisse). He returns to Provence where he helps some downed pilots escape and rows the underground's Chief to a waiting submarine, little realizing that the head of the movement is actually his scholarly brother.

In London Gerbier witnesses General De Gaulle decorating the heroic Luc. Gerbier is then parachuted over France after he learns that Félix has been arrested by the Gestapo in Lyons. Mathilde and other members of the group, including Le Masque (Claude Mann) and the "Bison" (Christian Barbier), meet to plan Félix's rescue. Gerbier warns Mathilde not to keep her daughter's photo on her. Thinking he possesses *baraka*, the Arab notion of a divine grace insuring good fortune, Jean-François has himself arrested in an effort to save Félix. He fails and takes a cyanide pill.

Gerbier is caught and later led before the firing squad in the cellar of the converted military school. The condemned are made to run—and be excellent target practice. Darting furiously, Gerbier sees smoke and a rope and climbs it quickly to freedom.

Weeks pass and Luc arrives at Gerbier's hideout to discuss a painful and dangerous development: Mathilde's been arrested in Lyons. The Gestapo learned her identity from the photo they found on her of her daughter. She is ordered to reveal all the names of the Resistance group or else the girl will be sent to a brothel in Poland for German soldiers returning from the front.

When he learns that Mathilde's temporary release coincided with two Resistance men being arrested, Gerbier orders her death over the "Bi-

In Lyons, the Resistance group: Mathilde (Simone Signoret), the "Bison" (Christian Barbier), and Philippe Gerbier (Lino Ventura) meet to plan how to save Félix, imprisoned by the Gestapo.

son's" protests. Luc hypothesizes that Mathilde desires to be killed to resolve her torturous dilemma since she can neither denounce the leaders nor commit suicide. The group drives up to a surprised Mathilde walking along the street and the "Bison" shoots her.

In a shocking dénouement, the horrible fate of each of the remaining Resistance leaders is flashed on the screen in a terse announcement as in *Z*.

COMMENTARY

L'Armée des Ombres lacked the critical and commercial success which greeted the director's next effort, *Le Cercle Rouge,* and remains a neglected work. In addition, due to the vicissitudes of film distribution, this brilliant and gripping film along with other fine Melville films was not shown commercially in America.

The episodic structure of the narrative fits the film well and suggests the varied and interrelated activities of the Resistance. Melville avoids a flamboyant, "derring-do" approach and directs in a taut, economical manner which conveys an authentic "feel" of the actual Resistance: here is the daily life of ordinary men and women, not regarding themselves as heroic, who perform out of a sense of

In Lyons, the "Bison" (Christian Barbier) has the painful duty of liquidating Mathilde. Le Masque (Claude Mann) is the driver; back seat: Luc Jardie (Paul Meurisse), partly seen, and Philippe Gerbier (Lino Ventura).

mission dangerous actions for which they were hardly prepared. The director didn't feel the need to cheapen his efforts with clichés and corny melodrama, to exploit the violence inherent in the material, or to introduce a perfectly gratuitous and distracting love affair for the sake of the box office. "The characters from *L'Armée des Ombres* are tragic characters," Melville said. "You know it from the very beginning."

The acting is superb. Lino Ventura, in particular, gives a solid performance as the leader Gerbier. He is totally convincing as an average man but one with hidden strength to overcome self-doubt. For his performance he was awarded "Etoiles de Cristal" by L'Académie du Cinéma (1970). Simone Signoret is believable and fascinating as the dedicated Mathilde. Eric de Marsan contributed an atmospheric and moving score.

The opening scene is stunning and one of the director's proudest achievements: a long shot at a low angle reveals the gradual approach of a Nazi marching band past the Arch of Triumph which ends in a freeze frame. The ugly rape of Paris is shockingly and unforgettably evoked.

Among the many suspenseful scenes is the execution of Dounat. In daytime, in a vacant apartment with paper thin walls and neighbors close by, the inexperienced and nervous Resistance men look for a way to kill the traitor since their gun has no silencer. With their bare hands, using a towel in which a knife was inserted for additional pressure, they strangle the terrified youth.

Besides being a haunting film which packs a wallop, *L'Armée des Ombres* presents a necessary and altruistic corrective to the cynical and apathetic image of Occupied France evoked by the controversial Marcel Ophuls documentary, *The Sorrow and the Pity (Le Chagrin et la Pitié)* completed in 1970. "A film-maker must be a witness of his times," Melville wrote.

He made two more films, *Le Cercle Rouge* (1970) and *Un Flic (Dirty Money)* (1972) before his death in Paris on August 2, 1973. Film historian Charles Ford referred to Melville as "one of the most original and individualistic filmmakers of contemporary French cinema."

224

faut; *Photographer:* Pierre-William Glenn (Eastmancolor); *Assistant Directors:* Suzanne Schiffman, Jean-François Stévenin; *Editors:* Yann Dedet, Martine Barraqué; *Music:* Georges Delerue; *Running Time:* 115 minutes; *Paris Premiere:* May 24, 1973; *New York Premiere:* October 7, 1973; *16mm Rental Source:* Swank.

DAY FOR NIGHT

(La Nuit Américaine)

LES FILMS DU CARROSSE/P.E.C.F. (PRODUCTIONS ET EDITIONS CINÉMATOGRAPHIQUE FRANÇAISE) (PARIS)/P.I.C. (PRODUZIONE INTERNAZIONALE CINEMATOGRAFICA) (ROME)   1973

CREDITS

Screenplay: François Truffaut, Jean-Louis Richard, and Suzanne Schiffman; *Director:* François Truf-

CAST

Julie Baker (and Pamela): Jacqueline Bisset; *Séverine:* Valentina Cortese; *Alexandre:* Jean-Pierre Aumont; *Alphonse:* Jean-Pierre Léaud; *Ferrand, the Director:* François Truffaut; *Stacey:* Alexandra Stewart; *Joëlle, the Script Girl:* Nathalie Baye; *Liliane, Apprentice Script Girl:* Dani; *Bernard, the Prop Man:* Bernard Menez; *Bertrand, the Producer:* Jean Champion; *Jean-François, 1st Assistant Director:* Jean-François Stévenin; *Odile, the Make-Up Girl:* Nike Arrighi; *Gaston Lajoie, the Production Manager:* Gaston Joly; *Mme. Lajoie:* Zénaïde Rossi; *Dr. Nelson (Julie's Husband):* David Markham; *Television Announcer:* Maurice Séveno; *Boy with Cane in Dream Sequences:* Christophe Vesque; *English Insurance Broker:* Henry Graham (British author Graham Greene in

A portrait of the *Meet Pamela* crew: Jean-François, 1st Assistant Director (Jean-François Stévenin); Liliane, Apprentice Script Girl (Dani); Ferrand, the Director (François Truffaut); and Joëlle, the Script Girl (Nathalie Baye).

225

A distraught Séverine (Valentina Cortese) is comforted by Alexandre (Jean-Pierre Aumont) after she keeps muffing her lines during the shooting of *Meet Pamela*. Odile (Nike Arrighi) watches.

Ferrand (François Truffaut), right, directs Alphonse (Jean-Pierre Léaud), left, and Julie Baker (Jacqueline Bisset) during the shooting of *Meet Pamela*.

a guest appearance); *French Insurance Broker:* Marcel Berbert (the film's Executive Producer).

BACKGROUND

François Truffaut's subsequent work after *Jules and Jim* varied between experiments with genre films, particularly the thriller as in *The Bride Wore Black (La Mariée Etait en Noir)* (1968), and more personal films, such as *The Wild Child (L'Enfant Sauvage)* (1970). *Day for Night* was his thirteenth feature.

In July of 1971 Truffaut was editing *Two English Girls* at the Victorine Studios in Nice. Constantly passing the huge outdoor set of a Parisian square built for Bryan Forbes' *The Madwoman of Chaillot* (1969), he hit upon the idea: "I would shoot a film about shooting a film—*a movie about filmmaking.*" The notion had been forming in his mind for a long time. "I would not tell *all* the truth about shooting a film," Truffant said. "That would be impossible. But I would tell *only true things:* events which had happened to me while making other films, or which had happened to other filmmakers I knew." For example, the uncooperative cat in the bungalow sequence comes from a similar situation during the shooting of *The Soft Skin (La Peau Douce)* (1964). The project would also be a means of showing how films are made, how effects of rain, fire, and snow are achieved, etc. All the characters, from star to script girl, were to be treated equally.

The plot of *Meet Pamela,* the film-in-the-making, was developed from a news item in the British press concerning the elopement of a middle-aged man with his young daughter-in-law. The story is simple and banal for a good reason: Truffaut doesn't want us to become involved with the plot per se, but only in the more interesting and rewarding matter of *how* it is filmed. Thus there is a contrast between the "serious" inner frame (the trite melodrama of *Meet Pamela*) which we treat lightly and the "light" outer frame (the comedy-drama of the making of *Meet Pamela*) which receives our serious attention. Although *Meet Pamela* is trivial, no one working on it is condescending to it; all give it their professional best. The title, *Day for Night*, refers to the use of dark filters being placed over the camera lens to create night shots during the daytime, a technique developed in making American westerns.

"I wanted to make a French film," Truffaut said, "and an exclusively French film." Yet to evoke a necessary Hollywood presence he hired British actress Jacqueline Bisset and French actor Jean-Pierre Aumont who are best known for their American films. Valentina Cortese, he said, "added still another desired element: cosmopolitanism." Truffaut decided to play the director himself because he asserted he was seeking "absolute truth" in the role, but gave him a hearing aid to distance him from his own image and "to demonstrate the voluntary isolation the director has when shooting."

Day for Night was filmed at the Victorine Studios in Nice and on locations in the French Riviera from late September through December 1972. After the credits, using a still from their first movie for Biograph—*An Unseen Enemy* (1912)—Truffaut announces his dedication of *Day for Night* "to Lillian and Dorothy Gish."

Day for Night, as personal a film about moviemaking as Fellini's *8½* (1963), was to be Truffaut's most popular film since *Jules and Jim*.

SYNOPSIS

Day for Night deals with the seven weeks shooting of *Meet Pamela*, whose plot is as follows: Alphonse (Jean-Pierre Léaud), a young Frenchman, brings his English bride Pamela (Jacqueline Bisset) to meet his father Alexandre (Jean-Pierre Aumont) and mother (Valentina Cortese). Father-in-law and bride elope and in the ensuing conflict Pamela dies in a car accident while Alphonse shoots his father in a Parisian square.

Meet Pamela serves as a pretext to explore the more complicated lives of the actors and film crew: There is concern over the unstable condition of the star, Julie Baker (Jacqueline Bisset). Séverine (Valentina Cortese) is drinking too much and fluffing her lines; later we realize she's deeply upset because her son is dying of leukemia. Alphonse (Jean-Pierre Léaud) acts possessive and jealous with Liliane (Dani), the script girl trainee who is flirting with others, etc. Coping with these temperamental

The climax of the recurring dream sequence: Boy (Christophe Vesque) steals stills from a theatre showing *Citizen Kane*. ("The film of films! Probably the one film that has stimulated more careers in moviemaking than any other"—François Truffaut.)

people and the heavy responsibility of the expensive project is the director, Ferrand (François Truffaut).

When Liliane runs off with the stunt man, Alphonse threatens to quit the film. Trying to talk some common sense into him, Julie winds up spending the night with him, a gesture more maternal than amorous. Involved with a new fantasy, Alphonse telephones Dr. Nelson (David Markham), Julie's husband, and demands a divorce! The doctor calls his wife who immediately gets hysterical and locks herself in her room. The intercession of Ferrand and the arrival of her understanding husband restore Julie's composure.

Then, catastrophe: Alexandre (Jean-Pierre Aumont) is killed while driving his car with his lover.* The film is salvaged, however, when Ferrand uses a double for Alexandre to complete the picture. *Meet Pamela* finished, the cast and crew go their separate ways.

COMMENTARY

Day for Night was an internationally acclaimed and successful film. It received the New York Film

*His death recalls that of actress Françoise Dorléac, star of *The Soft Skin,* in a car accident in Nice in 1967.

Critics Awards in three categories: "Best Motion Picture," François Truffaut for "Best Direction," and Valentina Cortese for "Best Supporting Actress" (1973). The film won an "Oscar" for best "Foreign Language Film" (1973). The following year *Day for Night* received an additional three nominations for Academy Awards: François Truffaut for "Direction," Miss Cortese for "Supporting Actress," and Truffaut, Jean-Louis Richard, and Suzanne Schiffman for "Writing (Original Screenplay)." Also, the British Society of Film and Television Arts voted *Day for Night* "Best Film," Truffaut "Best Direction," and Miss Cortese "Best Supporting Actress" (1973).

From the effective opening shot which convinces us we are at a Parisian Métro station until we hear "Cut!" and the camera tracks back to reveal a technical crew busy making a movie—the scene ends with a spectacular, high traveling crane shot of the entire set—through a series of well-executed montage sequences of rehearsals and shooting which capture the difficult but exhilarating métier of filmmaking, Truffaut directs as a virtuoso with marvellous control and imagination.

"Day for Night," Truffaut said, "revolves around one central question: 'Are films superior to life?' It gives no definite answer. For there can be none." After stating that "private life is messy for everyone," Ferrand informs Alphonse that their type is only happy in their work, making films: "Films are more harmonious than life. . . . There are no traffic jams in films, no dead waits. Films move forward like trains . . . like trains in the night." Yet to balance the argument, Alphonse rejects this and seeks fulfillment through his quest for romantic love—"Are women magical creatures?" he asks persistently.

Major among the barrage of cinema references is the prominent one in the concluding dream fragment: a well-dressed boy (Christophe Vesque), carrying a cane, approaches a theatre late at night showing Orson Welles' *Citizen Kane* (1941) and proceeds to steal all the stills—a powerful and haunting tribute to Truffaut's most revered film. Another homage is to Jean Cocteau: Alexandre's wish to make his protégé his son recalls the late director's adopting Edouard Dermit; one of Cocteau's tapestries adorns Julie's dressing room.

Unsentimental, acknowledging various hardships inherent in the undertaking—nonetheless Truffaut maintains a tone of passionate concern for his beloved medium.

Jacqueline Bisset is sensitive and lovely as the Hollywood star. Valentina Cortese, forgetting her lines, opening the cupboard door while supposedly making an exit during shooting, or presiding memorably over the farewell banquet, steals the picture. Jean-Pierre Léaud is appealing as an eternal adolescent. Truffaut's natural authority makes Ferrand convincing. The rest of the cast comes alive through fine character touches and Truffaut typically withholds any judgment on their lives. Georges Delerue's music in the baroque manner adds elegance to the film.

Since *Day for Night* Truffaut continues making films that garner acclaim, such as *The Last Métro (Le Dernier Métro)* (1980). "His films are like faces that will never show wrinkles," Henri Langlois said. *Day for Night* ("a love declaration for the cinema"—Valentina Cortese) is a beautifully crafted work which will probably remain the definitive film about moviemaking.

Julie (Jacqueline Bisset) takes leave of Alphonse (Jean-PIerre Léaud) after spending the night with him attempting to console her histrionic co-star.

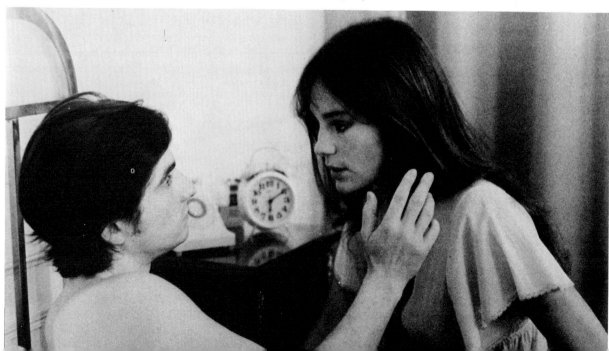

THE LACEMAKER

(La Dentellière)

CITEL FILMS (GENEVA)/ACTION
FILMS/F.R.3 (FRANCE RÉGIONS 3)
(PARIS)/FILMPRODUKTION JANUS
(FRANKFURT)   1977

CREDITS

Screenplay: Claude Goretta and Pascal Lainé, based
on Lainé's Prix Goncourt novel (1974); *Director:*
Claude Goretta; *Photographer:* Jean Boffety (East-
mancolor); *Assistant Directors:* Laurent Ferrier and
Patrick Grandperret; *Editor:* Joëlle Van Effenterre;
Music: Pierre Jansen; *Running Time:* 108 minutes;
Paris Premiere: May 25, 1977; *New York Premiere:*
October 8, 1977; *16 mm. Rental Source:* New Yorker
Films.

CAST

Béatrice ("Pomme"): Isabelle Huppert; *François:*
Yves Beneyton; *Marylène:* Florence Giorgetti;
Gérard: Christian Baltauss; *Marianne:* Renata
Schroeter; *Béatrice's Mother:* Anne Marie Düringer;
Painter: Michel de Ré; *François' Mother:* Monique
Chaumette; *François' Father:* Jean Obé; *Cashier:*
Odile Poisson.

BACKGROUND

Claude Goretta was born in Geneva on June 23,
1929. He obtained a law degree from the University of Geneva. From 1955 to 1957 Goretta was at
the British Film Institute and made a documentary
short, *Nice Time* (1957), in collaboration with Alain
Tanner. He returned to Switzerland and began
directing a series of documentaries, plays, and
films for Swiss TV. In 1968, together with Tanner,
Michel Soutter and other TV directors, Goretta

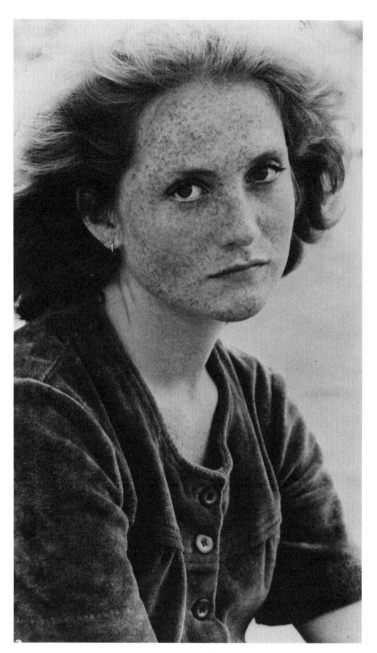

Portrait of Isabelle Huppert as "Pomme" the "Lacemaker."

founded the Group Five Production Society to
make feature films for theaters with financial backing coming from Télévision Suisse Romande. Soon
their films marked the start of the significant New
Swiss Cinema Movement.

Goretta made his first theatrical film, *Le Fou*
("The Madman"), in 1970 followed by *L'Invitation*
(1973) which received a Special Jury Prize at the
Cannes Film Festival in 1973 and an Academy
Award nomination for best "Foreign Language
Film" of 1973. Next came the comedy *The Wonder-*

229

ful Crook (Pas Si Méchant Que Ça) (1975) with Gérard Depardieu and Marlene Jobert.

As he did for his last two features, Goretta co-wrote the screenplay when he next adapted Pascal Lainé's novel, *The Lacemaker,* which was filmed in France. The story of a doomed relationship between a student, described by Goretta as one "who expresses himself through knowledge," and an uneducated young woman, "who goes straight to the realities inside," aroused the director's interest. "I'm always involved with ordinary people," Goretta said, "but my purpose is to say they're much more than they appear. The problem is, it's so hard to see exactly what they are. . . ." The director continues: "What interests me is showing what links people to others, and also what makes people unique, with their own singularities and depths. . . . In *The Lacemaker,* the audience can see things the characters don't notice in each other." Young Isabelle Huppert (born 1955) was offered the lead. Up to then she had only played bit roles since she started making movies in 1971. She incarnated the central character indelibly.

The film's title comes from a quotation from the novel used at the end of the film: "Because she was one of those souls who makes no sign but who, when the painter in times past examined with patience, would have been made the subject of a

230

In this significant scene, François (Yves Beneyton) has directed Béatrice (Isabelle Huppert) to a cliff with her eyes closed and tells her he wouldn't have let her fall.

Béatrice (Isabelle Huppert) and François (Yves Beneyton) visit the cemetery for the American soldiers killed in WWII. A visual sense of alienation and foreshadowing doom is strikingly caught.

genre painting. She would have been seamstress, water-carrier, lacemaker. . . ." Pomme's inner grace would have been recognized immediately by a Vermeer and paid homage to. Today a potential lover like François is too alienated from basic feelings of love and acceptance to perceive her special worth. Goretta succeeds beautifully in making his lacemaker a rich character portrait.

SYNOPSIS

Béatrice (Isabelle Huppert), nicknamed "Pomme" ("Apple"), is a docile, passive girl just turning nineteen who is an apprentice in a Parisian beauty salon. She lives with her mother (Anne Marie Düringer), her father having left the family a long time ago. Pomme's best friend is Marylène (Florence Giorgetti), an older and worldly co-worker who acts as a mentor of sorts to the shy and innocent girl.

When Marylène's married lover drops her after a long affair, Pomme thwarts her suicide attempt.

The two women decide to vacation at Cabourg on the Normandy Coast. Soon the extroverted, aggressive Marylène finds a man and leaves Pomme alone at the resort. François, a literature student in Paris from a middle-class background, meets her and is drawn to the attractive girl. Their obvious differences in class and education are not insurmountable barriers at this stage of their relationship. They become lovers and start living together in a Paris apartment. She doesn't fit in with his politically involved university friends; François finds Marylène shallow and boring.

François feels Béatrice should be more ambitious in life than to remain as a beautician trainee, but the self-effacing woman is simply content to be with the man she loves. When he takes her home to meet his family he is uncomfortable and realizes he needs an equal who'll be an asset to his future teaching or journalist career. Although they do not quarrel, the couple start drifting apart irremediably. He finally asks her to leave.

Béatrice returns home, becomes more and more withdrawn and ill, and finally collapses. She is apparently pregnant too. In the autumn her mother writes François and tells him that Béatrice has been in a mental hospital for the past several months.

With his friends Marianne (Renata Schroeter) and Gérard (Christian Baltauss), who had earlier taken him to task for treating Pomme more like an employee whom he fired than a lover, François visits the frail, pensive girl. He is anxious soon to get away from the solemn, defeated Pomme. However, when he rejoins his friends he breaks down and cries. Béatrice enters a recreation room and starts knitting quietly.

COMMENTARY

The Lacemaker proved to be a critical and commercial success. It received an Ecumenical Prize at the Cannes Film Festival in 1977.

Conveying a rich inner life behind a simple mask, Isabelle Huppert gives a stunning performance which helped launch her international career. The British Academy of Film and Television Arts voted her "The Most Promising Newcomer to Leading Film Roles" (1977) for this film. Her "Pomme" could very well have been the archetypal model for a Vermeer; it is significant that an artist sketches her in the film when she is with François at an outdoor inn. As an awkward youth, more callow than cruel, Yves Beneyton is excellent as François.

Goretta's direction shows remarkable restraint and control. "If you want to show what is inside people," he said, "you must not dance the camera around." The thrust is not on plot but characterization, "getting inside movement, seeing what is behind the eyes." He continues: "The eyes have a great importance in *The Lacemaker*, too. They express the tension underneath." He also points out that it is "a violent film, because it is about matters of life and death. And it is all the more violent because the people are gentle and ordinary . . . we often don't see the violence in daily life. We often destroy people without even realizing it." A measure of Goretta's artistry is that he avoids the traps of sentimentality and melodrama.

There is a subtle use of symbolism throughout. During their courtship Pomme lets herself be directed with her eyes closed to the edge of a cliff by François. This indicates to what extent she will put her life under his total control. He assures her that he wouldn't have let her fall, which becomes a glib, ironic boast. Pomme's exploitation both at her job and in her relationship with François adds a political dimension to the film.

Jean Boffety's photography is superb and Pierre Jansen's effective chamber music score adds a sense of intimacy and profundity to the work.

François (Yves Beneyton) brings Béatrice (Isabelle Huppert) to his family home and tells her he wants to spend the night with her.

The Lacemaker is, above all, an extremely delicate film. Audiences must be attentive to catch all the subtle nuances, such as Pomme's gesture of placing a shell on a cross in the G.I. cemetery or the significant revelation early in the film that Marylène, whose fate is to be disappointed and frustrated in love, had crocheted a bedspread—a hobby which Pomme subsequently adopts out of loneliness too.

The ending is devastating. In the hospital, to save face Pomme refers to a trip to Greece and encounters with men when François inquires of her recent past. Alone, she walks into a recreation room. We spot a poster of Mykonos and glimpse the shocking truth. There is a close-up of Pomme as she picks up her needlework and stares at the camera in all her vulnerability and dignity. It is a poignant, wrenching, and unforgettable moment.

Goretta comments on Pomme: "She finds a sort of refuge in madness, in silence, because society isn't the way she hoped it would be. Still, when she looks into the camera . . . there is something peaceful and strong inside her, with a sort of defiance. She is . . . struggling inside." *The Lacemaker* is a haunting, quietly overwhelming work and remains one of the most memorable of recent films.

Béatrice (Isabelle Huppert) gives herself tenderly to her lover François (Yves Beneyton).

232

MON ONCLE
D'AMERIQUE

PHILIPPE DUSSART / ANDREA FILMS /
T.F. 1 (TÉLÉVISION FRANÇAISE 1)   1980

Experiencing stress when his textile firm undergoes a corporate merger and his position is threatened by the rival Veestrate, manager RenéRagueneau (Gérard Depardieu) tries to carry on with his job.

CREDITS

Screenplay: Jean Gruault, inspired by the works of Professor Henri Laborit; *Director:* Alain Resnais; *Photographer:* Sacha Vierny (Eastmancolor); *Assistant Directors:* Florence Malraux and Jean Léon; *Editor:* Albert Jurgenson; *Music:* Arié Dzierlatka; *Running Time:* 125 minutes; *Paris Premiere;* May 21, 1980; *New York Premiere:* December 17, 1980; *16 mm. Rental Source:* Films Inc.

CAST

René Ragueneau: Gérard Depardieu; *Janine Garnier:* Nicole Garcia; *Jean Le Gall:* Roger-Pierre; *Arlette Le Gall:* Nelly Borgeaud; *Thérèse Ragueneau:* Marie Dubois; *Zambeaux:* Pierre Arditi; *Léon Veestrate:* Gérard Darrieu; *Michel Aubert:* Philippe Laudenbach; *with the participation of:* Professor Henri Laborit; *Jean's Grandfather:* Alexandre Rignault; *Jean as a Child:* Guillaume Boisseau; *M. Louis:* Jean Dasté; *Mme. Veestrate:* Laurence Badie; *Mme. Crozet:* Héléna Manson; *Narrator:* Voice of Dorothée.

BACKGROUND

In spite of his worldwide fame after his first two features, Alain Resnais' output was sporadic. *Muriel* (1963), *La Guerre Est Finie* (1966), *Je T'Aime, Je T'Aime* (1968). He was awarded the Grand Prix National du Cinéma in 1976 for his notable

achievement. Some time after *Stavisky* (1974), a phamaceutical company brought him and Dr. Henri Laborit, the well-known behavioral scientist, together to make a short devoted to a new drug which would improve memory. Although the project never materialized, Resnais studied the scientist's writings and came to see that they contained, as he said, "strong dramatic elements." Later scenarist Jean Gruault worked in close consultation with him and the initially proposed documentary became a narrative film, *Mon Oncle d'Amérique,* with a difference: "Instead of putting the thesis, the discourse, in the mouth of one of the characters," Resnais remarked, "we will put them precisely beside. A sort of documentary laid on the fiction (and vice versa)." Professor Laborit presents his theories incrementally via a voice-over narration or personal appearance.

Just two of Laborit's ideas were to be explored in relation to the characters: "One is that we all have a basic impulse to domination, either as possession or as control," Resnais stated. "The other is that when

233

Having left his wife, broadcasting executive Jean Le Gall (Roger-Pierre) moves in with actress Janine Garnier (Nicole Garcia) to share a relationship which seems promising and

Meeting her lover accidently again on an isle in the Gulf of Morbihan after two years's separation, Janine (Nicole Garcia) reaches out to Jean (Roger-Pierre), but he is cold and unresponsive.

this impulse is frustrated we can react in three ways: by violence, by flight or by a violence turned inward, which can range up from stomach pains, to serious illness, to suicide." Resnais stressed: "We sympathize profoundly with Laborit. . . . He acts on our film like a catalyzer." The scientist freely discusses his ideas but does not comment on the characters. "Without locking the characters . . . in a demonstration," the director said, ". . . . we have allowed them their autonomy." The intrusion of Laborit is a distancing device to stimulate the viewer, Resnais pointed out, so "he can think about his own actions and contemplate his own life."

For the leads, Resnais cast the popular actor Gérard Depardieu in a part written for him, stage and screen actress Nicole Garcia, and versatile comedian Roger-Pierre. The film was shot from late September through early December 1979. Exteriors were Paris and environs, Brittany—including the Isle of Logoden in the Gulf of Morbihan—and Cholet.

Resnais edited selections from the researcher's six-hour filmed conversation into the rough cut. The director admitted, "We didn't know . . . whether it would work; we were in anguish until the end." The experiment worked indeed and *Mon Oncle d'Amérique* proved to be civilized entertainment of the highest order. "We made it a kind of comedy," Resnais said, "because we were conscious that we weren't going to explain the human condition in two hours."

SYNOPSIS

First there's a capsule summary provided for the three central characters: executive Jean Le Gall (Roger-Pierre), actress Janine Garnier (Nicole Garcia), and manager René Ragueneau (Gérard Depardieu), then a quick account of each's childhood, education, and break with family to pursue a career.

René's textile company in Lille is merging and he encounters a rival in Léon Veestrate (Gérard Darrieu) for his job. Jean leaves his wife Arlette (Nelly Borgeaud) and children to move in with Janine and start a creative project.

Feeling inadequate next to Veestrate's modern methods, a threatened René develops stomach pains. His wife Thérèse (Marie Dubois) suggests inviting his competitor to dinner, but the party turns into a disaster. Jean is shocked to learn he's been summarily fired from his top-level position in radio broadcasting. When he discovers at a luncheon that his old friend and colleague Michel Aubert (Philippe Laudenbach) was instrumental in his dismissal he suffers a kidney attack. Summoned to Paris by Zambeaux (Pierre Arditi), the firm's director, René learns that Veestrate has replaced him, but he's offered a new position in Cholet. Thérèse refuses to relocate and René fears it may be a trap.

Arlette meets Janine, convinces her she's dying and implores her not to tell Jean but let him return for the few remaining months. . . . An unhappy Janine deliberately picks a quarrel with her lover to send him back to his "sick" wife.

Two years pass. Jean and Janine meet by accident on his isle in Brittany. She is now a designer in textiles; he is a successful politician. Janine is deeply upset to learn that Arlette is alive and well. Jean won't listen to her explanation and leaves. In Cholet, Zambeaux informs René of his failure as a production manager—he will be replaced. René, angry, storms off, then returns later to hear Janine's offer of a job selling gourmet products. Feeling patronized and rejected, he goes to his boardinghouse and tries to hang himself but he's caught in time.

Janine confronts Arlette who defends her great lie as a means of saving her marriage. Janine spots the polemical book Jean finally wrote. She pursues him at a hunt where he informs her that Arlette told him everything last night. She was marvellous, he tells her, but so was his wife. He says that what happened was for the best. Furious, Janine starts hitting the complacent, mediocre man.

COMMENTARY

At the 1980 Cannes Film Festival *Mon Oncle d'Amérique* won the Special Jury Prize and the International Critics Award. It also received the Grand Prix du Cinéma Français (1980), the Prix Méliès (1980), and was nominated for six Césars (1980): "Best Film," Alain Resnais for "Best Director," Nicole Garcia for "Best Actress," Jean Gruault for "Best Screenplay," Sacha Vierny for "Best Cinematography," and Jacques Saulnier for "Best Art Direction." Resnais' biggest commercial success in France, it grossed over $5,000,000. Critically and commercially successful in America, where it is also known as *My Uncle from America*, it was voted "Best Foreign Film" (1980) by the New York Film Critics and Jean Gruault received an "Oscar" nomination for best "Screenplay Written Directly for the Screen" (1980).

After learning that an administrator will replace him and feeling humiliated and rejected, René (Gérard Depardieu), back in his boardinghouse, turns to prayer for guidance during his crisis.

For a film with a decidedly pedagogical approach, *Mon Oncle d'Amérique* is above all compellingly visual. Gérard Depardieu commented on Resnais' brilliant and imaginative direction: "He makes his films as a savant, with a scientific precision in the setting up of the camera shots."

The film is carefully structured, without seeming contrived or doctrinaire, as it develops the parallel struggles of the three characters confronting crises with career, love, and illness. Prof. Laborit intervenes from time to time to suggest with modesty a "biological key" to our behavior.

Although some critics have found it totally pessimistic since it presents a mechanistic view of life, Resnais considers it "an ambiguous film," one which is a "provocation . . . ," and he adds, "this assumes, to whatever degree, hope that something is going to result from it." Laborit points out that until we are made aware of the ways by which the brain functions, we will continue to attempt to dominate others unless we can recognize these tendencies within ourselves and alter our acquired behavioral patterns.

The film's title refers to the long-held French fantasy that each has a distant relative who left for America where he made a fortune and would return home some beautiful "tomorrow" and resolve all problems. All three characters partake of this myth in varying degrees: there's a vestige of hope in René and Jean but not ultimately in a disillusioned Janine. Each character identifies with a mythological French film star. For Jean, Danielle Darrieux is an ideal woman; for Janine, Jean Marais is a dashing hero; for René, Jean Gabin is a model of strength. A total of twenty-nine clips from their old films punctuates the narrative and represent "some perfect examples of behavior," Resnais said, and influences which helped shape their lives.

Far from being casebook studies, the characters are individualized, vivid, and quite complex. Their capacity for self-deception is underscored by the film's alternate title "The Sleepwalkers" ("Les Somnambules"). Resnais treats them objectively without judging or special pleading.

Gérard Depardieu is outstanding and restrained in a role that represents off-beat casting. Nicole Garcia is a lovely, spirited, and elegant actress, a discovery. And Roger-Pierre is effective as a character described by the director as "an infant who cannot grow up."

Mon Oncle d'Amérique is an original, intelligent, fascinating, and provocatively dense film. This sad/funny depiction of the human comedy remains among the most satisfying achievements of a director whom critic Andrew Sarris characterized as "the cinema's most profound meditator on the human mind."

At the Villa Beauséjour, Janine (Nicole Garcia), right, confronts Jean's wife Arlette (Nelly Borgeaud), left, with her terrible lie but the woman defends her action to gain back her husband.

APPENDIX

Jean-Louis Barrault (*Children of Paradise*)

The preceding discussion of fifty titles from a country active in film production since Louis Lumière began shooting and exhibiting films in 1895 can merely suggest the vastness and eminence of the French film heritage.

In the following Appendix, to indicate still further the variety and achievement of France's cinema, I mention briefly an additional fifty significant films. In this collection the reader will find experimental, popular, influential, neglected as well as controversial selections, with special emphasis on those features which were honored by the Academy of Motion Picture Arts and Sciences in Hollywood.

Dita Parlo and Jean Dasté (*L'Atalante*).

L'INHUMAINE

CINÉGRAPHIC   1924

CREDITS

Screenplay: Marcel L'Herbier and Pierre MacOrlan; *Director:* Marcel L'Herbier; *Photographer:* George Specht; *Assistant Director:* Philippe Hériat; *Music:* Darius Milhaud; *Running Time:* 132 minutes; *New York Premiere:* March 14, 1926.

CAST

Claire Lescot: Georgette Leblanc; *Einar Norsen:* Jaque Catelain; *Innocent Girl:* Marcelle Pradot; *Djorah de Nopur:* Philippe Hériat; *Wladimir Kranine:* Léonid Walter de Malte; *Franck Mahler:* Fred Kellerman; *Dancers:* Ballets Suédois.

COMMENTARY

In 1923 Marcel L'Herbier (1890-1979), prominent director of the Impressionist movement in French silent cinema, brought together a group of modern artists to create an ambitious and avant-garde film, the fairy tale *L'Inhumaine* (shown briefly in New York as *The New Enchantment*). Building exteriors were designed by architect Robert Mallet-Stevens, the cubistic laboratory by Fernand Léger, the singer's Art Deco rooms by Alberto Cavalcanti, etc. "This was a synthesis—a deliberate one—of the French artistic movement of the 1920's," L'Herbier wrote.

Claire Lescot (Georgette Leblanc), a celebrated singer, charming but heartless (hence the title "the inhuman one"), is courted by several admirers including a young scientist, Einar Norsen (Jaque Catelain). Through a jealous maharajah (Philippe Hériat) Claire receives a fatal snake bite but Einar

The laboratory of the scientist Einar Norsen. A fascinating cubistic set by noted artist Fernand Léger.

restores her to life—and humanity—in his laboratory.

Although *L'Inhumaine,* released in 1924, was a failure, it's of interest today for its striking, innovative design and its brilliant use of rapid intercutting and visual experimentation.

UNDER THE ROOFS OF PARIS

(Sous les Toits de Paris)

SOCIÉTÉ DES FILMS SONORES TOBIS   1930

CREDITS

Screenplay and Direction: René Clair; *Photographers:* Georges Périnal and Georges Raulet; *Assistant Directors:* Georges Lacombe, Marcel Carné, and Jacques Houssin; *Editor:* René Le Hénaff; *Songs:* Raoul Moretti and René Nazelles; *Musical Direction:*

Albert the street singer (Albert Préjean) plies his trade assisted by Pola (Pola Illery).

Armand Bernard; *Running Time:* 96 minutes; *Paris Premiere:* January 2, 1930; *New York Premiere:* December 15, 1930; *16 mm. Rental Source:* Images.

CAST

Albert: Albert Préjean; *Pola:* Pola Illery; *Louis:* Edmond Gréville; *Fred:* Gaston Modot; *Drunkard:* Paul Olivier; *Bill:* Bill Bocket; *Neighborhood Woman:* Jane Pierson; *Thief:* Raymond Aimos; *François:* Thomy Bourdelle.

COMMENTARY

"While I was shooting one of my silent films," René Clair said, "I walked out of the studio one day and saw a crowd that turned out to have gathered around a street singer. The scene was so moving, so charming, so typically Parisian that I wanted to make a film on the subject."

Under the Roofs of Paris, shot as a silent film with sound dubbed in later, employed fluid camera-work, mime, an imaginative use of music, and minimal dialogue. Clair's innovative film about working class people was hailed as a triumph.

While the street singer Albert (Albert Préjean) is in jail on suspicion of theft, his Roumanian sweetheart Pola (Pola Illery) takes up with his best friend Louis (Edmond Gréville). Acquitted, Albert quarrels with Louis over Pola but relinquishes her when he realizes she prefers Louis. The three remain friends.

240

With Lazare Meerson's evocative sets René Clair recreated a Parisian worker's milieu with atmosphere, charm, and authenticity and discovered his favorite style.

LA MATERNELLE

STUDIOS PHOTOSONOR 1933

A solicitious Rose (Madeleine Renaud) brings the abandoned child Marie (Paulette Elambert) to her home.

CREDITS

Screenplay: Jean Benoît-Lévy and Marie Epstein, based on the Prix Goncourt novel by Léon Frapié (1904); *Directors:* Jean Benoît-Lévy and Marie Epstein; *Photographer:* Georges Asselin; *Music:* Edouard Flament; *Songs:* Alice Verlay; *Running Time:* 100 minutes; *New York Premiere:* October 14, 1935; *16 mm. Rental source:* M.O.M.A.

CAST

Rose: Madeleine Renaud; *Marie Coeuret:* Paulette Elambert; *Mme. Paulin:* Mady Berry; *Superintendent:* Alice Tissot; *Dr. Libois:* Henri Debain; *Mme. Coeuret:* Sylvette Fillacier; *The Professor:* Alex Bernard; *Singer:* Jany Delille; *Inspector:* Gaston Séverin; *Pantin:* Edmond van Daële.

COMMENTARY

Rose (Madeleine Renaud) goes to work as a children's maid in a day nursery in Montmartre. Among the neglected children is Marie (Paulette Elambert) abandoned by her prostitute mother (Sylvette Fillacier). The child forms a deep and jealous attachment to Rose and attempts suicide when she learns of her betrothal. Marie is rescued and there is a happy reconciliation.

The great Madeleine Renaud is radiant and unforgettable. Paulette Elambert, age 11, is poignant as an affection-starved waif. Mady Berry is outstanding as the head nurse.

Educational and documentary filmmaker Jean Benoît-Lévy (1888–1959) with Marie Epstein (1899–), (filmmaker Jean Epstein's sister) used nonprofessional children and took pains to make their 1933 release, La Maternelle* realistic, psychologically valid, and unsentimental. An early talkie, much of the film employs silent film techniques. Neither the 1925 version (Gaston Roudés) nor the 1948 treatment (Henri Diament-Berger) approaches the humanity and emotional appeal of this memorable film. "A truly sincere film will affect people of every class, every country, and even of every period"—Jean Benoît-Lévy.

*Also known for a time here as Children of Montmartre.

LES MISERABLES

PATHÉ-NATHAN   1933

CREDITS

Adaptation: André Lang and Raymond Bernard, based on the celebrated novel by Victor Hugo (1862); *Dialogue:* André Lang; *Director:* Raymond Bernard; *Photographer:* Jules Krüger; *Music:* Arthur Honneger; *Running Time:* 305 minutes (initial release); *Paris Premiere:* December 13, 1933; *New York Premiere:* October 27, 1936.

CAST

Jean Valjean, M. Madeleine, M. Fauchelevent: Harry Baur; *Javert:* Charles Vanel; *Bishop Myriel:* Henry Krauss; *Thénardier:* Charles Dullin; *Mme. Thénardier:* Marguerite Moreno; *Fantine:* Odette Florelle;

Cosette (as a Child): Gaby Triquet; *Marius:* Jean Servais; *Cosette (as an Adult):* Josseline Gaël; *Eponine (as an Adult):* Orane Demazis; *Enjolras:* Robert Vidalin; *Gavroche:* Emile Genevois; *Maboeuf:* Cailloux; *Gillenormand:* Max Dearly.

COMMENTARY

Raymond Bernard (1891–1977) made a version of epic proportions of Victor Hugo's classic *Les Misérables*. For the difficult and multifaceted role of Jean Valjean (by turns convict, industrialist, then self-sacrificing old man), he chose Harry Baur who conveyed perfectly the character's heroic stature.

It was initially released in three parts and shown simultaneously at three different theatres: *Tempête sous un Crane* (120 minutes), *Les Thénardiers* (90 minutes), and *Liberté, Liberté Chérie* (95 minutes). (The film was cut to 165 minutes in America). Bernard later reedited it to two parts: *Jean Valjean* (109 minutes) and *Cosette* (100 minutes).

Although there were three other French versions of this stirring human drama (Albert Capellani, 1912; Henri Fescourt, 1925; Jean-Paul Le Chanois, 1958), Bernard's treatment is the most impressive for its fidelity to the original, great acting and spectacle, and its remarkably skillful and fluid direction. Critic Jacques Salles wrote: "*Les Misérables* remains forever the last and most perfect of the great historical frescoes."

The exigencies of French film production curtailed future ambitious projects of this gifted director.*

*Mention should be made of Bernard's distinguished silent work, especially the spectacular *The Miracle of the Wolves (Le Miracle des Loups)* (1924).

While a guest in the Bishop's house, ex-convict Jean Valjean (Harry Baur) decides to steal his silverware.

CRIME AND PUNISHMENT

(Crime et Châtiment)

GÉNERAL PRODUCTIONS   1935

CREDITS

Adaptation: Pierre Chenal, Christian Stengel, and Wladimir Strijewski, based on the classic Fyodor Dostoevsky novel (1867); *Dialogue:* Marcel Aymé; *Director:* Pierre Chenal; *Photographers:* René Colas, Joseph-Louis Mundviller; *Editor:* André Galitzine; *Music:* Arthur Honegger; *Running Time:* 110 minutes; *Paris Premiere:* May 15, 1935; *New York Premiere:* November 12, 1935; *16 mm. Rental Source:* Audio Brandon.

CAST

Raskolnikov: Pierre Blanchar; *Porphyre:* Harry Baur; *Sonia:* Madeleine Ozeray; *Razoumikhine:* Alexandre Rignault; *Dounia:* Lucienne Le Marchand; *Mme. Raskolnikov:* Marcelle Géniat; *Catherine Ivanovna:* Sylvie; *Loujine:* Aimé Clariond; *Aliona Ivanovna:* Magdeleine Bérubet; *Nicolas:* Georges Douking; *Elisabeth:* Catherine Hessling; *Marmeladov:* Marcel Delaître; *Polia:* Paulette Elambert; *Nastassia:* Claire Gérard.

Police Inspector Porphyre (Harry Baur), on the right, plays an intricate game of cat and mouse with murder suspect Raskolnikov (Pierre Blanchar), on the left.

COMMENTARY

The French have a penchant for the brooding, psychologically penetrating works of the great Russian novelist, Dostoevsky. In 1935 Pierre Chenal (Pierre Cohen, 1903–) accepted the challenge to translate in cinematic terms the story of a young student who murders a greedy pawnbroker to prove to himself that he is above the law only to surrender after the torments of his conscience and the clever wiles of a police inspector.

Pierre Blanchar was outstanding as the tortured student and won the Coupe Volpi for "Best Actor" at the Venice International Exposition in 1935. Harry Baur, the most brilliant character actor of his time, was powerful as the inspector who suspects Raskolnikov's guilt but lacks proof. The expressionist sets of Aimé Bazin and Eugène Lourié contributed much to the film's stark atmosphere.

Although the novel had to be abridged, much of the work's tension was retained and projected through the excellent performances and careful direction of M. Chenal, who reached the height of his reputation with this much-acclaimed film.

MAYERLING

CONCORDEA PRODUCTION
CINÉMATOGRAPHIQUE/NÉRO FILM   1936

CREDITS

Adaptation: Irma von Cube, Joseph Kessel, based on the novel by Claude Anet [Jean Schopfer] *La Fin d'une Idylle* (1930), published in New York as *Idyll's End* (1930); *Dialogue:* Joseph Kessel; *Director:* Anatole Litvak; *Photographer:* Armand Thirard; *Assistant Director:* René Montis; *Editor:* Henri Rust; *Music:* Arthur Honegger with selections from Tchaikovsky, Weber, and Johann Strauss; *Songs:* H. May; *Lyrics:* Serge Veber; *Running Time:* 101 minutes. Version shown in U.S.: 96 minutes; *Paris Premiere:* February 12, 1936; *New York Premiere:* September 13, 1937; *16 mm. Rental Source:* Audio Brandon.

CAST

Archduke Rudolph of Austria: Charles Boyer; *Baroness Marie Vetsera:* Danielle Darrieux; *Countess Larisch:*

Suzy Prim; *Emperor Franz Joseph:* Jean Dax; *Empress Elizabeth:* Gabrielle Dorziat; *Count Taafe:* Jean Debucourt; *Baroness Vetsera (Hélène):* Marthe Régnier; *Stéphanie:* Yolande Laffron; *Chief of Police:* Vladimir Sokoloff; *Loschek, the Valet:* André Dubosc; *Marinka:* Gina Manès; *Szeps:* René Bergeron

COMMENTARY

An unhappily married prince, heir to the Austro-Hungarian Empire, meets and falls in love with a beautiful young woman. The Emperor moves to separate them so the doomed lovers apparently make a suicide pact and die in each other's arms in a snow-covered hunting-lodge at Mayerling on the dawn of January 30, 1889.

Such is the stuff of which romantic legends are made and Anatole Litvak (1902-1974) directed an elegant and irresistible *Mayerling* stressing the love interest rather than the political implications of the events. Charles Boyer as the Archduke Rudolph and the lovely ingénue Danielle Darrieux as Marie Vetsera incarnate the ill-fated lovers perfectly.

At the ballet each discovers the other in opposite loges. The camera then gracefully tracks and dissolves between the two. That nothing exists for each but the other is suggested.

Archduke Rudolph (Charles Boyer) is captivated by the young Marie Vetsera (Danielle Darrieux), whom he meets in Vienna's Prater.

Mayerling was an international success and received the New York Film Critics Award for "Best Foreign Film" (1937). All the remakes had diminishing effectiveness. The original is still definitive, one of the most powerful evocations of romantic love ever filmed.

Our narrator-memoirist (Sacha Guitry) has a droll reunion with an old friend, the Countess (Marguerite Moreno).

THE STORY OF A CHEAT

(Le Roman d'un Tricheur)

CINÉAS   1936

CREDITS

Screenplay: Sacha Guitry, based on his novel, *Mémoires d'un Tricheur* (1935); *Direction:* Sasha Guitry; *Photographer:* Marcel Lucien; *Editor:* Myriam; *Music:* Adolphe Borchard; *Running Time:* 100 minutes; *Paris Premiere:* September 19, 1936; *New York Premiere:* September 26, 1938.

CAST

The Cheat: Sacha Guitry; *Young Woman:* Jacqueline Delubac; *The Jewel Thief:* Rosine Deréan; *The Countess:* Marguerite Moreno; *Mme. Morlot, the Cousin:* Pauline Carton; *Waiter:* Gaston Dupray; *The Cheat as a Child:* Serge Grave; *The Cheat as a Young Man:* Pierre Assy; *Singer:* Fréhel; *M. Charbonnier:* Henri Pfeifer; *M. Morlot:* Pierre Labry; *Vautier:* Elmire Vautier.

COMMENTARY

The irrepressible Sacha Guitry (1885-1957), prolific playwright and prodigious actor, turned to film in the mid-1930's chiefly to conserve his own stage plays. He directed thirty films—even from a

243

wheelchair at the end! The cinema, he said, "does not have to pose social problems. It is a magic lantern. Irony and grace should not be excluded from it." The witty and original *Story of a Cheat* (1936) is considered his best film.

An aging adventurer (Sacha Guitry) sits at a café writing his memoirs. Guitry's off-screen voice presents a running commentary on his life. Caught stealing as a child, he was deprived of his supper. Since poisoned mushrooms were inadvertently served that night, our hero's made an orphan! Thus the pattern of his life as croupier, lover, gambler: every time he cheats, he prospers; whenever he tries honesty, he fails miserably.

The film is unique and innovative in being almost totally narrated. In this tour de force Guitry charms us with his remarkable presence, sly inversion of values, and nimble irony.

Guitry's clever films, once popular internationally, await rediscovery by another generation.

THE LIFE AND LOVES OF BEETHOVEN

(Un Grand Amour de Beethoven)

GÉNÉRAL PRODUCTIONS   1937

CREDITS

Adaptation, Scenario, and Direction: Abel Gance; *Dialogue:* Steve Passeur; *Photographers:* Robert Le Febvre and Marc Fossard; *Assistant Director:* Jean Arroy; *Editor:* Marguerite Beaugé; *Music:* Ludwig van

Beethoven, arranged by Louis Masson; *Running Time:* 135 minutes; *Paris Premiere:* January 16, 1937; *New York Premiere:* November 21, 1937; *16 mm. Rental Source:* Images.

CAST

Ludwig van Beethoven: Harry Baur; *Thérèse von Brunswick:* Annie Ducaux; *Giulietta Guicciardi:* Jany Holt; *Count Gallenberg:* Jean Debucourt; *Schuppanzigh:* Paul Pauley; *Count Guicciardi:* Lucien Rozenberg; *Countess Guicciardi:* Yolande Laffon; *Esther:* Jane Marken; *Smeskall:* Lucas Gridoux; *de Ries:* Roger Blin; *Karl:* Jean-Louis Barrault; *Steiner:* Marcel Dalio.

COMMENTARY

The Life and Loves of Beethoven represents another variation of Abel Gance's preoccupation with titans. Although Beethoven's biographers differ in identifying the "Immortal Beloved" *("Die Unsterbliche Geliebte"),* a phrase found posthumously in a letter by the composer, Gance ascribes it to Guilietta Guicciardi (Jany Holt) who realizes her love for Beethoven (Harry Baur) when it is too late.

In his episodic development of Beethoven's life from 1801 to his death, Gance took liberties with facts and the order of compositions but remained faithful to the great composer's spirit. The most striking sequence occurs at Heiligenstadt as Beethoven confronts the terrible onslaught of his deafness wandering amidst a world of birds, violinist, blacksmith, waterfall, bell tower and hearing nothing while Gance employs a brilliant use of montage and expressionistic sound.

Harry Baur is altogether convincing and remarkable. "To say that I am happy to have created this role," he said, "the word 'happy' would be a ridiculous phrase. I am dazzled."

UN CARNET DE BAL

PRODUCTIONS SIGMA   1937

CREDITS

Story: Julien Duvivier; *Adaptation:* Julien Duvivier, Jean Sarment, Pierre Wolff, Yves Mirande,

After his "immortal beloved" married another, Beethoven (Harry Baur) retires to a mill at Heiligenstadt.

Christine (Marie Bell) seeks to recapture her youth which is haunting her.

Bernard Zimmer; *Dialogue:* Bernard Zimmer, Henri Jeanson, Jean Sarment; *Director:* Julien Duvivier; *Photographers:* Michel Kelber, Philippe Agostini, and Pierre Levent; *Editor:* André Versein; *Music:* Maurice Jaubert; *Running Time:* 109 minutes; *Paris Premiere:* September 9, 1937; *New York Premiere:* March 25, 1938.

CAST

Christine Sugère: Marie Bell; *Mme. Audie:* Françoise Rosay; *Jo (Pierre Verdier):* Louis Jouvet; *Fr. Alain Regnault:* Harry Baur; *Eric Irvin:* Pierre-Richard Willm; *François Patusset:* Raimu; *Dr. Thierry:* Pierre Blanchar; *Fabien Coutissol:* Fernandel; *Jacques:* Robert Lynen; *Jo's Accomplice:* Roger Legris.

COMMENTARY

A recent widow (Marie Bell) finds the program of her first ball and decides to seek out the six men who had once danced with her. Her journey brings disenchantment as she discovers her beaux leading mediocre, even dubious, lives. She finds a purpose at the end when she chooses to help the son (Robert Lynen) of the man she loved but who is dead. Julien Duvivier's film of eight episodes (known for a time in America as *Life Dances On*) was awarded the Coupe Mussolini for "Best Foreign Film" at the Venice International Exposition in 1937, and was widely acclaimed and enormously popular. It inaugurated in France the vogue for the sketch film filled with stars. Duvivier did a version of it in Hollywood: *Lydia* (1941).

Although *Un Carnet de Bal* does not hold up, it is memorable at least as a showcase for much of the great French film talent of the 1930's (Baur, Jouvet, Raimu) and for Jaubert's haunting "Valse Grise."

LA BETE HUMAINE

PARIS FILMS PRODUCTION   1938

CREDITS

Screenplay: Jean Renoir, based on the Emile Zola novel (1890); *Director:* Jean Renoir; *Photographer:* Curt Courant, assisted by Claude Renoir (director's nephew); *Assistant Directors:* Claude Renoir (director's brother) and Suzanne de Troeye; *Editor:* Marguerite Renoir *(Railway Sequence:* Suzanne de Troeye); *Music:* Joseph Kosma; *Song:* "Le P'tit Coeur de Ninon" ("The Little Heart of Ninon"), an anonymous Italian song from 1920; *Running Time:* 105 minutes; *Paris Premiere:* December 23, 1938; *New York Premiere:* February 19, 1940; *16 mm. Rental Source:* Images.

CAST

Jacques Lantier: Jean Gabin; *Séverine:* Simone Simon; *Roubaud, Séverine's Husband:* Fernand Ledoux; *Pecqueux:* Julien Carette; *Flore:* Blanchette Brunoy; *Cabûche, the Poacher:* Jean Renoir; *Dauvergne's Son:* Gérard Landry; *Philomène:* Jenny Hélia; *Victoire:* Colette Régis; *Grandmorin:* Jacques Berlioz.

In Le Harve's railroad yard Séverine (Simone Simon) spots her husband making his rounds and urges her lover Lantier (Jean Gabin) to kill him.

COMMENTARY

In adapting *La Bête Humaine* Jean Renoir reduced the novel's plot and updated the 1869 setting to the present but remained faithful to Zola's naturalistic spirit and produced a powerful film noir.

Lantier (Jean Gabin), a locomotive engineer cursed with ungovernable compulsions through heredity, falls for Séverine (Simone Simon) whose jealous stationmaster husband Roubaud (Fernand Ledoux) had recently killed her godfather-lover. She pushes Lantier to murder Roubaud, but he cannot do it. Later, in a violent fit, he strangles her then throws himself off a moving train.

Gabin, who learned to operate a locomotive for the film (also known here as *The Human Beast),* is remarkable as another doomed hero. Simone Simon ("Her Séverine was unforgettable"—Renoir) and Fernand Ledoux are outstanding.

"*La Bête Humaine* strengthened my longing to achieve poetic realism," Renoir wrote. "The steel mass of the locomotive became in my imagination the flying carpet of oriental fable." The stunning opening train ride sequence bears this out. Fritz Lang directed a mediocre remake, *Human Desire* (1954).

LE CIEL EST A VOUS

LES FILMS RAOUL PLOQUIN FOR UFA   1944

CREDITS

Story: Albert Valentin; *Adaptation and Dialogue:* Charles Spaak; *Director:* Jean Grémillon; *Photographer:* Louis Page; *Assistant Directors:* Serge Vallin and Jacques Bost; *Editor:* Louisette Hautecoeur; *Music:* Roland Manuel; *Running Time:* 105 minutes; *Paris Premiere:* February 2, 1944; *New York Premiere:* August 29, 1957 (screening at the Museum of Modern Art); *16 mm. Rental Source:* Facsea.

CAST

Thérèse Gauthier: Madeleine Renaud; *Pierre Gauthier:* Charles Vanel; *Larcher:* Jean Debucourt; *Docteur Maulette:* Léonce Corné; *Marcel:* Albert Rémy; *Robert:* Robert Le Fort; *Jacqueline:* Anne-Marie Labaye; *M. Noblet:* Raoul Marco; *Mme. Brissard:* Raymonde Vernay; *Claude:* Michel François; *Lucienne Ivry:* Anne Vandenne; *Neighbor:* Renée Thorel.

COMMENTARY

The films of Jean Grémillon (1901-59) are little known abroad. His best feature, *Le Ciel Est à Vous* ("The Sky Is Yours"), awaiting discovery, was based on the exploit of Mme. Dupeyron who set a world record for women's distance flying in 1938.

First garage owner Pierre Gauthier (Charles Vanel) then his wife Thérèse (Madeline Renaud) catch aviation "fever." When he breaks his arm her ambition is aroused and without marital conflict they lovingly sacrifice everything to realize their dream of setting a record.

Madeleine Renaud and Charles Vanel are splendid. More than an aviation drama, a Resistance allegory or an early feminist work, it is a drama of man's spirit which, despite difficulties, can dare to reach out beyond the self's limitations and be triumphant. Besides the Gauthiers this describes Grémillon himself who faced such obstacles as the bombardment of his locale, Le Bourget Airport; the Nazi ban on French use of planes; etc., to produce a glowing, heartfelt film. "A true masterpiece"—Marcel Carné.

L'IDIOT

SOCIÉTÉ DES FILMS SACHA GORDINE   1946

CREDITS

Screenplay: Charles Spaak, based on the novel by Fyodor Dostoevsky (1874); *Director:* Georges Lampin; *Photographer:* Christian Matras; *Editor:* Léonide Azar; *Music:* Maurice Thiriet; *Running Time:* 95 minutes; *Paris Premiere:* June 7, 1946; *New York Premiere:* February 4, 1948; *16 mm. Rental Source:* Facsea.

Thérèse (Madeleine Renaud) and Pierre Gauthier (Charles Vanel) purchase a piano from M. Larcher (Jean Debucourt), left, for their daughter Jacqueline.

Prince Muichkine (Gérard Philipe) generously offers to marry Nastasia (Edwige Feuillère); however, it is Rogogine (Lucien Coëdel) who desires her the most.

CAST

Nastasia Philipovna: Edwige Feuillère; *Prince Muichkine:* Gérard Philipe; *General's Wife:* Marguerite Moreno; *Rogogine:* Lucien Coëdel; *Aglae:* Nathalie Nattier; *Totsky:* Jean Debucourt; *General Epantchine:* Maurice Chambreuil; *Gania:* Michel André; *General Ivolgin:* Félicien Tramel; *His Wife:* Sylvie

COMMENTARY

"My intention is to portray a truly beautiful soul," wrote Dostoevsky. *The Idiot,* his classic novel of a saintly young man confronting a corrupt universe, was given an authentic and respectful mounting by Russian-born Georges Lampin (1895-1979) which became his best remembered film. Although the long novel was somewhat condensed for the movie, its spirit was not betrayed.

The lovely Edwige Feuillère, the most prestigious actress of her time, played the doomed Nastasia, one of her best roles, a woman torn between love for the spiritual Prince Muichkine (Gérard Philipe) and bondage to the brutal Rogogine (Lucien Coëdel) who eventually kills her.

Gérard Philipe was brilliantly cast as the innocent and Christ-like Prince who ultimately collapses under the oppressive weight of the world's evil. He was absolutely convincing and impressive in this difficult role, his first important screen appearance.

Lavish sets by Léon Barsacq and striking photography by Christian Matras enhanced this powerful film which deserves to be remembered.

Nicolas (Raimu) attempts to kill his late wife's lover Michel (Aimé Clariond).

THE ETERNAL HUSBAND

(L'Homme au Chapeau Rond)

ALCINA   1946

CREDITS

Screenplay: Charles Spaak and Pierre Brive, based on Fyodor Dostoevsky's novella (1870); *Director:* Pierre Billon; *Photographer:* Nicolas Toporkoff; *Assistant Director:* Jacques de Casembroot; *Editor:* Germaine Artus; *Music:* Maurice Thiriet; *Running Time:* 90 minutes; *Paris Premiere:* June 19, 1946; *New York Premiere:* January 8, 1949.

CAST

Nicolas Pavlovitch: Raimu; *Michel:* Aimé Clariond;

Lisa: Lucy Valnor; *Marie:* Gisèle Casadesus; *The Father:* Louis Seigner; *The Mother:* Jane Marken; *A Neighbor:* Micheline Boudet; *Agathe:* Héléna Manson; *Mathilde:* Arlette Méry.

COMMENTARY:

A film of Dostoevsky's disturbing novella, *The Eternal Husband*, was skillfully directed by Pierre Billon (1906-1981). A widower, Nicolas (Raimu), discovering from her letters that his late wife had lovers and that his little daughter Lisa (Lucy Valnor) was actually fathered by Michel (Aimé Clariond), a dandy, decides to seek revenge through perverse means.

He haunts Michel, then after arousing in him strong feelings of parental responsibility callously turns his daughter over to him. The child, feeling rejected, dies. Michel suffers agony over Nicolas' cruel indifference to Lisa. Unable to kill his "rival," Nicholas wanders off into the night.

The Eternal Husband is a remarkable film of psychological density. Maurice Thiriet's brooding score, Nicolas Toporkoff's shadowy images, and Georges Wakhévitch's gloomy, atmospheric sets heighten the film's somber mood.

As the eternal husband Raimu gives a powerful, controlled performance in what was his last screen role. (He died in Paris on September 20, 1946.) Orson Welles said of Raimu: "This was the world's greatest actor."

GATES OF THE NIGHT

(Les Portes de la Nuit)

SOCIÉTÉ NOUVELLE PATHÉ CINÉMA   1946

CREDITS

Screenplay: Jacques Prévert, based on his ballet *Le Rendez-Vous* (1945) with music by Joseph Kosma; *Director:* Marcel Carné; *Photographer:* Philippe Agostini; *Assistant Directors:* Roger Blanc and Georges Baudoin; *Editor:* Jean Feyte; *Music:* Joseph Kosma; *Running Time:* 120 minutes; *Paris*

Premiere: December 3, 1946; *New York Premiere:* March 15, 1950

An enigmatic vagabond (Jean Vilar), on the right, brings together the lovers, Malou (Nathalie Nattier) and Diego (Yves Montand), during a fateful night.

CAST

Diego: Yves Montand; *Malou:* Nathalie Nattier; *Georges:* Pierre Brasseur; *Monsieur Sénéchal:* Saturnin Fabre; *Guy:* Serge Reggiani; *Raymond Lécuyer:* Raymond Bussières; *Monsieur Quinquina:* Julien Carette; *Vagabond:* Jean Vilar; *Claire Lécuyer:* Sylvia Bataille; *Madame Quinquina:* Mady Berry; *Etiennette:* Dany Robin; *Cri-Cri:* Christian Simon

COMMENTARY

Gates of the Night is set in Paris "during the hard winter following the Liberation." In the course of one night Diego (Yves Montand), a Resistance hero, is led by a mysterious vagabond (Jean Vilar), representing Destiny, to a meeting with Malou (Nathalie Nattier), the beloved he has been searching for. The drama also concerns her husband Georges (Pierre Brasseur) and her brother Guy (Serge Reggiani), a collaborationist who eventually commits suicide.

The admixture of such realistic details as Nazi collaborators and war profiteers with Prévert's symbolic mythology seemed dated and out of touch with current taste. Too, Marlene Dietrich and Jean Gabin had been replaced by Mlle. Nattier and a young Yves Montand who did not realize the possibilities of the script. The costly film flopped. This was the last completed project of the famed Marcel Carné–Jacques Prévert team*. The popular song "Autumn Leaves" comes from Kosma's beautiful score used in the original ballet. An ambitious though not unflawed work, *Gates of the Night* deserves recognition for its many poetic and striking effects and waits to be rediscovered.

The loner, M. Hire (Michel Simmon), offers protection and love to his neighbor, Alice (Viviane Romance).

PANIQUE

RÉGINA   1947

CREDITS

Adaptation: Charles Spaak and Julien Duvivier, based on the novel of Georges Simenon, *Les Fiançailles de M. Hire* (1933), translated as *Mr. Hire's Engagement* and published in London in a volume entitled *The Sacrifice* (1956); *Dialogue:* Charles

---

*A subsequent project, *La Fleur de l'Age* (1947), was abandoned; Prévert contributed dialogue (uncredited) to Carné's *La Marie du Port* (1950). After he died on April 11, 1977 Carné said: "Jacques Prévert is the one and only poet of the French cinema. He created a style, original and personal, reflecting the soul of the people. His humor and poetry succeeded in raising the banal to the summit of art."

Rescurer of the poor and the outcast, M. Vincent de Paul (Pierre Fresnay) cleans bandages at an overcrowded hospital.

Spaak; *Director:* Julien Duvivier; *Photographer:* Nicolas Hayer; *Editor:* Marthe Poncin; *Music:* Jacques Ibert; *Running Time:* 100 minutes; *Paris Premiere:* January 15, 1947; *New York Premiere:* November 26, 1947; *16 mm. Rental Source:* Images.

CAST

Alice: Viviane Romance; *M. Hire:* Michel Simon; *Alfred:* Paul Bernard; *Michelet:* Charles Dorat; *M. Fortin:* Lucas Gridoux; *Capoulade:* Max Dalban; *M. Breteuil:* Emile Drain; *M. Sauvage:* Guy Favières; *Inspector Marcelin:* Louis Florencie; *Cermanutti:* Marcel Pérès.

COMMENTARY

After murdering a woman in a Parisian suburb, Alfred (Paul Bernard) with the assistance of his mistress Alice (Viviane Romance) diverts suspicion to the neighborhood loner, M. Hire (Michel Simon), who is secretly in love with Alice. The couple manipulate a gradually hysterical populace to strike out at the unfortunate victim. M. Hire is killed trying to flee from their fury but leaves behind an incriminating photograph to trap the real killer.

Panique (known here for a time as *Panic*) was Duvivier's first post-war French film. A fine study of mob psychology, it's also an outstanding example of the film noir tradition, full of menacing shadows and evoking an overpowering sense of evil. Michel Simon was remarkable as the persecuted scapegoat with hints of a Jewish background.

"It says that people are not nice, that the crowd is imbecilic, that outsiders are always harmed," Duvivier said in 1946 of his bitter, disturbing film. "*Panique* is the most significant film of my career because it wished to say something." *Panique* was cited for "Special Mention" at the 1946 Venice Film Festival.

MONSIEUR VINCENT

U.G.C. (UNION GÉNÉRALE
CINÉMATOGRAPHIQUE)/E.D.I.C.
(EDITION ET DIFFUSION
CINÉMATOGRAPHIQUES)   1947

CREDITS

Story: Jean Bernard-Luc and Jean Anouilh; *Adaptation:* Jean Anouilh, Jean Bernard-Luc and Maurice Cloche; *Dialogue:* Jean Anouilh; *Director:* Maurice Cloche; *Photographer:* Claude Renoir; *Assistant Director:* Guy LeFranc; *Editor:* Jean Feyte; *Music:* Jean-Jacques Grünenwald; *Running Time:* 112 minutes; *Paris Premiere:* November 5, 1947; *New York Premiere:* December 20, 1948; *16 mm. Rental Source:* Audio Brandon.

CAST

Vincent de Paul: Pierre Fresnay; *Cardinal Richelieu:* Aimé Clariond; *Anne of Austria:* Germaine Dermoz; *Count de Gondi:* Jean Debucourt; *Countess de Gondi:* Lise Delamare; *Louise de Marillac:* Yvonne Godeau; *Mme. Groussault:* Gabrielle Dorziat; *Portail, the Assistant Priest:* Jean Carmet; *Consumtive:* Michel Bouquet.

COMMENTARY

A true labor of love, *Monsieur Vincent,* a moving biography of St. Vincent de Paul (canonized in 1737) directed by Maurice Cloche (1907–), was produced with money raised by national subscription. (Appeals were made throughout French parishes.)

Unsentimental and realistic, the film traces the life of a genuine saint motivated by an unbounded love of his fellow man whose dedicated mission was to help the poor and the outcasts of seventeenth century France.

Pierre Fresnay meets the difficult challenge of making his Vincent spiritual, human, and totally credible. It is a beautiful and memorable performance. Claude Renoir achieves some wonderful effects with his photography.

Though the film's impact is somewhat lessened by its episodic development of a forty-odd-year career, the remarkable life achievement of the saint is nonetheless forcefully and sincerely presented.

Pierre Fresnay was voted "Best Actor" at the Venice Film Festival (1947). *Monsieur Vincent* was awarded the Grand Prix du Cinéma Français (1947) and received a special "Oscar" for "most outstanding foreign language film released in the United States during 1948."

Michel (Jean Marais) restrains his hysterical mother (Yvonne de Bray) after she learns he loves a young lady—who unknown to them is the father's mistress.

LES PARENTS TERRIBLES

LES FILMS ARIANE   1948

CREDITS

Screenplay: Jean Cocteau from his play (1938); *Director:* Jean Cocteau; *Photographer:* Michel Kelber; *Assistant Director:* Raymond Leboursier; *Editor:* Jacqueline Sadoul; *Music:* Georges Auric; *Running Time:* 105 minutes; *Paris Premiere:* December 1, 1948; *New York Premiere:* April 22, 1950; *16 mm. Rental Source:* Audio Brandon

CAST

Michel: Jean Marais; *Yvonne-Sophie:* Yvonne de Bray; *Léo:* Gabrielle Dorziat; *Georges:* Marcel André; *Madeleine:* Josette Day; *Narrator in concluding scene:* Voice of Jean Cocteau.

COMMENTARY

In adapting his play to the screen, Jean Cocteau said he wanted to "record the acting of an incomparable cast; secondly, walk among them and look them straight in the face, instead of contemplating them at a distance on the stage; thirdly, peep through the key-hole and catch my wild beasts unawares with my telephoto lens."

Les Parents Terrible (here a.k.a. *The Storm Within*), a model cinematic adaptation, is considered by some critics as Cocteau's masterpiece although this writer feels he is more successful with myth and fantasy. A series of interconnecting triangles (Father-Son-Girl, Mother-Girl-Son, even Mother-Aunt-Father) create "overheated" melodramatic effects. Yvonne de Bray as the neurotic, domineering mother and Gabrielle Dorziat as the clear thinking Aunt Léo dominate the film. Cocteau's masterly camera shots and Georges Auric's moving score are impressive. The director brilliantly saved a wobbly concluding dolly shot by narrating: "And the gypsy caravan continued on its way." *Intimate Relations* (1953) was a mediocre and forgettable British treatment.

THE WALLS OF
MALAPAGA

(Au-delà des Grilles)

FRANCORIZ PRODUCTION/ALFREDO
GUARINI PRODUZIONE   1949

CREDITS

Scenario: Cesare Zavattini, Suso Cecchi d'Amico and Alfredo Guarini; *Adaptation and Dialogue:* Jean Aurenche and Pierre Bost; *Director:* René Clément; *Photographer:* Louis Page; *Assistant Directors:* Pierre Chevalier, Claude Clément, Alessandro Fersen, and Sergio Grieco; *Editor:* Mario Serandrei; *Music:* Roman Vlad; *Running Time:* 95 minutes; *Paris Premiere:* November 16, 1949; *New York Premiere:* March 20, 1950; *16 mm. Rental Source:* Audio Brandon.

CAST

Pierre: Jean Gabin; *Marta:* Isa Miranda; *Cecchina:* Vera Talchi; *Manfredini:* Andréa Cecchi; *Bosco:* Robert Dalban; *Maria:* Ave Ninchi; *Superintendent of Police:* Carlo Tamberlani.

COMMENTARY

In this French-Italian co-production, Pierre (Jean Gabin) is a stowaway who leaves his ship in Genoa to search for a dentist to stop his toothache. He is befriended by little Cecchina (Vera Talchi) and falls in love with Marta (Isa Miranda), her waitress mother. Their romance is short-lived for this fugitive from justice (who in France had killed his unfaithful mistress) is soon arrested.

This is the last appearance of the "myth of Jean Gabin": an implacable Fate not permitting the doomed hero happiness or freedom. Besides recalling the Prévert-Carné poetic realism of the 1930's, *The Walls of Malapaga* reflects the style of neo-realism as it depicts honestly and accurately the ravages of a war-torn Genoa where it was filmed. At the Cannes Film Festival, René Clément won an award for "Best Director" and Isa Miranda for "Best Actress" (1949). The film received an Honorary "Oscar" for "the most outstanding foreign language film released in the United States in 1950."

Pierre (Jean Gabin) gives up his chance of escape to return to Marta (Isa Miranda), who offers him love and a new life.

251

Alfred, the Young Man (Daniel Gélin) finds solace, albeit briefly, with Frau Breitkopf, the Married Woman (Danielle Darrieux).

LA RONDE

SOCIÉTÉ DES FILMS SACHA GORDINE   1950

CREDITS

Adaptation: Jacques Natanson and Max Ophüls, based on the play *Der Reigen* by Arthur Schnitzler (1896); *Dialogue:* Jacques Natanson; *Director:* Max Ophüls; *Photographer:* Christian Matras; *Assistant Directors:* Tony Aboyantz and Paul Feyder; *Editor:* Léonide Azar; *Music:* Oscar Straus; *Running Time:* 97 minutes; *Paris Premiere:* September 27, 1950; *New York Premiere:* March 16, 1954; *16 mm. Rental Source:* Janus.

CAST

Master of Ceremonies; Anton Walbrook; *Léocadie, the Prostitute:* Simone Signoret; *Franz, the Soldier:* Serge Reggiani; *Marie, the Chambermaid:* Simone Simon; *Alfred, the Young Man:* Daniel Gélin; *Emma Breitkopf, the Married Woman:* Danielle Darrieux; *Charles, her Husband (The Married Man):* Fernand Gravey; *The*

Grisette: Odette Joyeux; *Robert Kühlenkampf, the Poet:* Jean-Louis Barrault; *The Actress:* Isa Miranda; *The Count:* Gérard Philipe; *Professor Schüller:* Robert Vattier.

COMMENTARY

With an expensive production of Arthur Schnitzler's ground-breaking play, *La Ronde,* Max Ophüls entered the brilliant, final phase of his career. This roundelay of seduction and disillusionment in fin-de-siècle Vienna had its cynicism softened somewhat by the film's glittering cast, elegant style, and graceful direction.

A carrousel becomes a metaphor for love as a ring of revolving partners (prostitute–soldier, soldier–chambermaid, chambermaid–young man, etc.); inevitably, a certain amount of ennui sets in. The visually opulent *La Ronde* with its lovely Oscar Straus waltz enjoyed an enormous success. Banned in New York State as "immoral," the case went to the U.S. Supreme Court before it was allowed to be shown there, with some cuts, in 1954; a restored version appeared in 1969.

At the 1950 Venice Film Festival Jacques Natanson and Max Ophüls' script was voted "Best Screenplay" and Jean d'Eaubone won an award for "Best Décor." *La Ronde* received two "Oscar" nominations (1951), again for screenplay and "Art Direction—Set Direction (black-and-white)." The British Film Academy voted *La Ronde* "Best Film" of 1951.

THE RED INN

(*L'Auberge Rouge*)

MEMNON FILMS   1951

CREDITS

Story: Jean Aurenche; *Adaptation and Dialogue:* Jean Aurenche, Pierre Bost, and Claude Autant-Lara; *Director:* Claude Autant-Lara; *Photographer:* André Bac; *Assistant Directors:* Ghislaine Autant-Lara and Henri Carrier; *Editor:* Madeleine Gug; *Music:* René Cloërec; *Ballad:* Sung by Yves Montand; *Running Time:* 95 minutes; *Paris Premiere:* October 24, 1951;

CAST

Le Moine (The Monk): Fernandel; Marie Martin: Françoise Rosay; M. Martin: Julien Carette; Mathilde: Marie-Claire Olivia; Darwin: Jean-Roger Caussimon; Mlle. Elisa: Nane Germon; Rodolphe: Jacques Charron; Janou: Didier d'Yd; Fétiche: Lud Germain; Barbeuf: Grégoire Aslan.

COMMENTARY

Fleeing a snowstorm, into a remote country inn run by M. Martin (Carette) and his wife (Françoise Rosay) comes a group of travellers which includes a monk (Fernandel). In one of The Red Inn's hilarious scenes the monk improvises a confessional with a toasting grid and hears Mme. Martin matter-of-factly confess that she and her husband have been routinely murdering their guests for their riches.

Forbidden by his vows to reveal the secrets of the confessional, the hapless monk has his hands full trying to save his fellow travellers. His smug, facile piety is no match for the powerful evil he contends with, leading critic Raymond Durgnat to speculate "perhaps . . . the whole world is a red inn of which God is the landlord."

Claude Autant-Lara's droll, anticlerical "black comedy," banned in England, was a delicious vehicle for the great comedian Fernandel, possessor of one of the most expressive faces in cinema, who

The Innkeeper's Wife, Mme. Martin (Françoise Rosay), tends to her guest, the Monk (Fernandel), who has every reason to be apprehensive.

starred in a number of amusing and popular farces. Françoise Rosay was superb as usual.

Tossed a tulip and a nickname by Mme. Pompadour whom he had just rescued, Fanfan (Gérard Philipe) broods on the apparition of the King's daughter and ignores the obvious charms of Adeline (Gina Lollobrigida).

FANFAN THE TULIP

(Fanfan la Tulipe)

LES FILMS ARIANE / FILMSONOR
PRODUCTION (PARIS) / AMATO
PRODUZIONE (ROME)   1952

CREDITS

Story: René Wheeler and René Fallet; Adaptation: Christian-Jaque, Henri Jeanson, and René Wheeler; Dialogue: Henri Jeanson; Director: Christian-Jaque; Photographer: Christian Matras; Assistant Directors: Raymond Villette, M. Randome, André Fey; Editor: Jacques Desagneaux; Music: Georges Van Parys and Maurice Thiriet; Running Time: 102 minutes; Paris Premiere: March 21, 1952; New York Premiere: May 4, 1953.

CAST

Fanfan the Tulip: Gérard Philipe; Adeline: Gina Lollobrigida; Fier-A-Bras (NCO of the Cavalry): Noël

253

Roquefort; *Tranche (Samson):* Olivier Hussenot; *Louis XV:* Marcel Herrand; *Lebel:* Jean-Marc Tennberg; *Capt. La Houlette:* Jean Parédès; *Marshal of France d'Estrées:* Henri Rollan; *Sgt. La Franchise:* Nerio Bernardi; *La Pompadour:* Geneviève Page; *Henriette de France:* Sylvie Pelayo; *Mme. Samson:* Georgette Anys.

COMMENTARY

The witty, satirical swashbuckler, *Fanfan the Tulip*, was fashioned on the adventures of the legendary eighteenth-century French folkhero. Fanfan (Gérard Philipe) is saved from a shotgun—or, rather, pitchfork—wedding by enlisting in the French army during the Seven Years' War. After the *"chevalier flamboyant"* combats highwaymen, fights duels, undergoes a mock death sentence, raids a convent to rescue the heroine, evades pursuers, and inadvertently causes a confused enemy to surrender without firing a shot, our hero is made a captain and wins the hand of the ravishing Adeline (Gina Lollobrigida).

The versatile Gérard Philipe scored a triumph as the dashing, devil-may-care soldier and displayed athletic prowess along with a great comic sense. Popular and prolific director Christian-Jaque (Christian Maudet, 1904–) was voted "Best Director" at the 1952 Cannes Film Festival* for this film which became an international favorite.

A spoof on war, a lively tongue-in-cheek movie of much charm and delight, *Fanfan the Tulip* deserves to be remembered.

WE ARE ALL MURDERERS

(Nous Sommes Tous des Assassins)

U.G.C. (UNION GÉNÉRAL
CINÉMATOGRAPHIQUE)   1952

CREDITS

Story and Adaptation: Charles Spaak and André

*In addition *Fanfan the Tulip* received an Audience Award at the 1952 Berlin Film Festival.

Cayatte; *Dialogue:* Charles Spaak; *Director:* André Cayatte; *Photographer:* Jean-Serge Bourgoin; *Assistant Director:* Pierre Léaud; *Editor:* Paul Cayatte; *Music:* Raymond Legrand; *Running Time:* 115 minutes; *Paris Premiere:* May 21, 1952; *New York Premiere:* January 8, 1957.

The child-murderer Bauchet (Julien Verdier) is dragged before the chaplain (Louis Seigner) moments prior to his execution. Behind him stands his lawyer (Henri Crémieux), between the guards, and restraining him on the right is the head guard Léon (Paul Frankeur).

CAST

René Le Guen: Marcel Mouloudji; *Michel Le Guen:* Georges Poujouly; *Gino:* Raymond Pellegrin; *Dr. Dutoit:* Antoine Balpêtré; *Marcel Bauchet:* Julien Verdier; *Dr. Detouche:* Jean-Pierre Grenier; *Abbé Roussard, the Chaplain:* Louis Seigner; *Philippe Arnaud:* Claude Laydu; *M. Arnaud:* Henri Vilbert; *Mme. Arnaud:* Line Noro; *Léon, the Head Guard:* Paul Frankeur; *Gino's Mother:* Sylvie; *Malingre:* Marcel Pérès; *Lawyer:* Henri Crémieux.

COMMENTARY

Ex-lawyer André Cayatte (1909–) is a polemic filmmaker attacking social injustice. *We Are All Murderers* is an indictment against capital punishment. Awaiting execution in death row are: René (Marcel Mouloudji), an unbalanced cop slayer conditioned to be a killer in the Resistance; Gino

(Raymond Pellegrin), guilty of a Corsican vendetta; Dr. Dutoit (Antoine Balpêtré), accused of poisoning his wife; and Bauchet (Julien Verdier), murderer of his crying child who kept him from sleeping.

The execution ritual is shocking and harrowing. The prisoners are not told when they will die. During the night the guards remove their shoes, sneak up to the cell and rush in to bind the bewildered convict, then drag him for the chaplain's hasty blessing before being guillotined.

The film won a Special Jury Prize at the Cannes Film Festival (1952). Although its impact is weakened by its heavy-handed sermonizing, *We Are All Murderers* is a sincere and disturbing filmed thesis underscoring Cayatte's belief that "the death penalty is a senseless and criminal matter."

HOLIDAY FOR HENRIETTA

(La Fête à Henriette)

RÉGINA / FILMSONOR PRODUCTION   1952

CREDITS

Scenario: Julien Duvivier and Henri Jeanson; *Dialogue:* Henri Jeanson; *Director:* Julien Duvivier; *Photographer:* Roger Hubert; *Editor:* Marthe Poncin; *Music:* Georges Auric; *Running Time:* 118 minutes; *Paris Premiere:* December 17, 1952; *New York Premiere:* January 24, 1955.

CAST

Henriette: Dany Robin; *Rita Solar:* Hildegarde Neff; *Marcel/Maurice:* Michel Auclair; *First Author:* Louis Seigner; *Second Author:* Henri Crémieux; *Robert:* Michel Roux; *Adrien (the Detective):* Daniel Ivernel; *The Mother:* Paulette Dubost; *The Father:* Alexandre Rignault; *Arthur:* Julien Carette; *Nicole (Scriptgirl):* Micheline Francey; *Antoine (Man in Café):* Saturnin Fabre.

COMMENTARY

When their latest script is censored beyond redemption, two film writers set about improvising a story concerning Henriette (Dany Robin), a young Parisian dressmaker. The "noir" writer (Henri Cremieux) concocts lurid melodramatic episodes whereas the "rose" writer (Louis Seigner) fashions a sentimental tale of innocence and love. Their fantasies, set in Paris on Bastille Day, are dramatized before our eyes and eventually the "film" is written. However, an actor (Michel Auclair) informs them at the end that their story had already been filmed!

Before the soufflé sinks a bit, Duvivier has had a field day in *Holiday for Henrietta* twitting his contemporaries, satirizing cinematic clichés, displaying a brilliant and virtuoso use of the camera (the chase scenes with gangster Marcel/Maurice are clever and riotous), and creating a convincing love story to boot.

The expensive American remake *(Paris When It Sizzles,* 1964) was slick, strained, and lacked the zest and dazzling pyrotechniques of the original. Duvivier's crazy, witty spoof of movies is a film buff's delight and deserves to be better known.

The screenwriters have the gangster, now called Maurice (Michel Auclair), treat Henriette (Dany Robin) to champagne on her birthday.

THE GAME OF LOVE

(Le Blé en Herbe)

FRANCO-LONDON FILMS   1954

CREDITS

Screenplay: Jean Aurenche, Pierre Bost, Claude

Autant-Lara, based on the novel by Colette (1923), published in New York as *The Ripening Seed* (1955); *Director:* Claude Autant-Lara; *Photographer:* Robert Le Febvre; *Assistant Director:* Ghislaine Autant-Lara; *Editor:* Madeleine Gug; *Music:* René Cloërec; *Running Time:* 108 minutes; *Paris Premiere:* January 20, 1954; *New York Premiere:* December 14, 1954.

CAST

Madame Dalleray: Edwige Feuillère; *Vinca:* Nicole Berger; *Phil:* Pierre-Michel Beck; *Vinca's Father:* Charles Deschamps; *Phil's Mother:* Renée Devillers; *Vinca's Mother:* Hélène Tossy; *Vinca's Grandmother:* Julienne Paroli; *Movie Projectionist:* Louis de Funès; *Pianist:* Simone Duhart; *Policeman:* Robert Berri.

COMMENTARY

Colette's popular novel of a tense adolescent boy who is initiated into the mysteries of love and sex by an older woman during a summer vacation in Brittany was faithfully made into a successful film under the skillful direction of Claude Autant-Lara. Banned in Nice, denounced from pulpits, *The Game of Love* provided its director with another scandal and went on to win the Grand Prix du Cinéma Français (1954).

Banned in Chicago as "immoral and obscene," the film helped to challenge the constitutionality of American censorship laws, particularly the practice of prior censorship of films.

The fascinating and elegant Edwige Feuillère in one of her best screen roles is impressive as Mme. Dalleray who leads the young—and lucky—Phil (Pierre-Michel Beck) through a delicate rite of passage. Nicole Berger plays his girl friend Vinca whom he later seduces.

A bedridden Colette was shown the film shortly before her death and exclaimed afterwards: "The magic of the cinema has brought my characters before me."

DIABOLIQUE

(Les Diaboliques)

FILMSONOR PRODUCTION / VÉRA FILMS   1955

CREDITS

Screenplay: Henri-Georges Clouzot, Jérôme Géronimi, Frédéric Grendel, and René Masson, based on the novel *Celle Qui N'Etait Plus* by Pierre Boileau and Thomas Narcejac (1952), published in New York as *The Woman Who Was No More* (1954); *Director:* Henri-Georges Clouzot; *Photographer:* Armand Thirard; *Assistant Director:* Michel Romanoff; *Editor:* Madeleine Gug; *Music:* Georges Van Parys; *Running Time:* 115 minutes; *Paris Premiere:* January 29, 1955; *New York Premiere:* November 21, 1955; *16 mm. Rental Source:* Images.

CAST

Nicole Horner: Simone Signoret; *Christina Delasalle:* Véra Clouzot; *Michel Delasalle:* Paul Meurisse; *Inspector Fichet:* Charles Vanel; *Plantiveau, the Gardener:* Jean Brochard; *M. Herboux:* Noël Roquefort; *Mme. Herboux:* Thérèse Dorny; *M. Drain:* Pierre Larquey; *Dr. Loisy:* Georges Chamarat; *Prof. Bridoux:* Jacques Varennes; *M. Raymond:* Michel Serrault; *The Pupil Moinet:* Yves-Marc Maurin; *The Pupil Soudieu:* Georges Poujouly; *Hotel Valet:* Jean Temerson.

COMMENTARY

In *Diabolique* Nicole (Simone Signoret), the apparently ill-treated mistress of sadistic schoolmaster Michel Delasalle (Paul Meurisse), and Christina (Véra Clouzot), his frail and long-suffering wife, conspire to seek vengeance. Accordingly, he is drugged, drowned in a bathtub, and dropped in the school pool. Yet when the pool is drained soon after no body is found. Then Michel's face shows up at the window in a class photograph. . . .

Mme. Dalleray (Edwige Feuillère) shares a light moment with her young friend Phil (Pierre-Michel Beck).

At the end, when the "dead" man rises from a bathtub the tortured Christina has a fatal heart attack—the goal all along of the diabolical lovers, Michel and Nicole.

Famed director of suspense Henri-Georges Clouzot transposed a mystery novel (two lesbian lovers plot to kill one of the pair's commercial traveller husband) into a sensational melodrama abetted by chilling sound effects and Armand Thirard's murky photography. This memorable thriller won a Prix Louis Delluc (1954) and tied with de Sica's *Umberto D* for the New York Film Critics Award as "Best Foreign Film" (1955).

Nicole (Simone Signoret) coolly examines the drugged Michel (Paul Meurisse) preparatory to drowning him in the bathtub. His wife Christina (Véra Clouzot) watches in fear.

RIFIFI

(Du Rififi chez les Hommes)

INDUS FILM / SOCIÉTÉ NOUVELLE
PATHÉ
CINÉMA/PRIMA FILM   1955

CREDITS

Adaptation: René Wheeler, Jules Dassin, and Auguste Le Breton, from the latter's novel (1953); *Dialogue:* Auguste Le Breton; *Director:* Jules Dassin; *Photography:* Philippe Agostini; *Assistant Directors:* Patrice Dally, Jean-Jacques Vierne, and Bernard Declandre; *Editor:* Roger Dwyre; *Music:* Georges Auric; *Song:* "Rififi" by Philippe Gérard and

Jacques Laure; *Running Time:* 116 minutes; *Paris Premiere:* April 13, 1955; *New York Premiere:* June 5, 1956; *16 mm. Rental Source:* Budget.

CAST

Tony Stephanois: Jean Servais; *Jo:* Carl Mohner; *Mario:* Robert Manuel; *César:* Perlo Vita [Jules Dassin]; *Mado:* Marie Sabouret; *Louise:* Janine Darcey; *Ida:* Claude Sylvain; *Pierre Grutter:* Marcel Lupovici; *Louis Grutter:* Pierre Grasset; *Rémi Grutter:* Robert Hussein; *Viviane:* Magali Noël; *Tonio:* Dominique Maurin.

COMMENTARY

Hollywood director Jules Dassin (1912–), unofficially blacklisted during the McCarthy period, went to Europe and eventually made the low-budget, realistic melodrama *Rififi*.

A gang of thieves: Tony (Jean Servais), Jo (Carl Mohner), Mario (Robert Manuel), and César (Jules Dassin) painstakingly execute a Paris jewel robbery. A rival gang, the Grutter brothers, finds out and starts a ruthless manhunt and kidnapping which ends in a massacre.

The film's highlight is the robbery sequence—approximately twenty-eight minutes—without dialogue or music showing the quartet drilling through the store's ceiling, descending, extinguishing the alarm, and cracking the safe. It is a meticulous, brilliantly orchestrated, suspenseful set piece. The audience becomes co-conspirators watching craftsmen perform as skillfully as surgeons during an operation.

Dassin shared a "Best Director" prize at the

During the robbery, a kneeling Jo (Carl Mohner) eases the safe onto the floor aided by Tony (Jean Servais), Mario (Robert Manuel), and master safecracker César (Jules Dassin).

Cannes Film Festival (1955) for *Rififi* which was enormously successful and spawned spin-offs in various locales: Tokyo, Panama, Amsterdam; parodies: Mario Monicelli's *Big Deal on Madonna Street (I Soliti Ignoti)* 1958; and—alas—actual robberies by movie-attentive thieves.

LOLA MONTES

GAMMA FILMS / FLORDIA FILMS
(PARIS) / UNION FILM (MUNICH)   1955

CREDITS

Adaptation: Jacques Natanson, Annette Wademant, Max Ophüls, from an unpublished novel, *La Vie Extraordinaire de Lola Montès,* by Cecil Saint-Laurent; *Dialogue:* Jacques Natanson; *Director:* Max Ophüls; *Photographer:* Christian Matras (Eastmancolor, CinemaScope); *Assistant Directors:* Willy Picard, Tony Aboyantz, and Claude Pinoteau; *Editor:* Madeleine Gug (original version); *Music:* Georges Auric; *Running Time:* 110 minutes; *Paris Premiere:* December 23, 1955; *New York Premiere:* April 20, 1969 (restored version); *16 mm. Rental Source:* Audio-Brandon.

CAST

Lola Montès: Martine Carol; *Circus Master:* Peter Ustinov; *Ludwig I, King of Bavaria:* Anton Walbrook; *Lt. James:* Ivan Desny; *Franz Lizst:* Will Quadflieg; *Student:* Oskar Werner; *Mrs. Craigie:* Lisa Delamare; *Maurice:* Henri Guisol; *Joséphine:* Paulette Dubost; *James's Sister:* Héléna Manson.

COMMENTARY

Given an enormous budget, an extensive shooting schedule in both France and Germany, the use of Eastmancolor and CinemaScope for the first time, Max Ophüls directed what turned out to be his last film, *Lola Montès,* in 1955.

In the frame of a circus performance the movie traces the rise and fall of the famous nineteenth-century courtesan-dancer, Lola Montès (Martine Carol), who at one time was the lover of Lizst (Will Quadflieg), the mistress of Ludwig I, King of Bavaria (Anton Walbrook), etc.

Initially the film ran 140 minutes but the producers demanded thirty minutes be cut. When the film flopped they re-edited its complex pattern of flashbacks to a more traditional chronological development and deleted twenty more minutes—all to no avail. However, a reconstructed version was reissued in 1969 to critical acclaim.

In its fluid and graceful camerawork, its breathtaking slow dissolves, its stunning display of sheer cinematic virtuosity, *Lola Montès* is very much quintessential Ophüls and some consider it his masterpiece, but for many style alone cannot compensate for lackluster characterization and a central figure (Martine Carol) with little screen presence.

The scandalous Lola Montès (Martine Carol) and her circus master lover (Peter Ustinov) during a presentation of her enacted life story.

AND GOD CREATED WOMEN

(Et Dieu Créa la Femme)

IÉNA/U.C.I.L. (UNION CINÉMATOGRAPHIQUE LYONNAISE)/COCINOR   1956

CREDITS

Story: Roger Vadim and Raoul J. Lévy; *Adaptation,*

Although a shy Michel (Jean-Louis Trintignant) marries the tempestuous Juliette (Brigitte Bardot), much havoc will ensue before she becomes his faithful wife.

Dialogue, and Direction: Roger Vadim; *Photographer:* Armand Thirard (Eastmancolor and Cinema-Scope); *Assistant Directors:* Paul Feyder and Pierre Boursans; *Editor:* Victoria Mercanton; *Music:* Paul Misraki; *Running Time:* 95 minutes; *Paris Premiere:* November 28, 1956; *New York Premiere:* October 21, 1957; *16 mm. Rental Source:* Corinth.

CAST

Juliette Hardy: Brigitte Bardot; *Eric Carradine:* Curt Jurgens*; *Michel Tardieu:* Jean-Louis Trintignant; *Antoine Tardieu:* Christian Marquand; *Christian Tardieu:* Georges Poujouly; *M. Vigier-Lefranc:* Jean Tissier; *Mme. Morin:* Jane Marken; *Mme. Tardieu:* Marie Glory; *Lucienne:* Isabelle Corey: *René:* Jean Lefebvre; *Perri:* Philippe Grenier; *Mme. Vigier-Lefranc:* Jacqueline Ventura.

COMMENTARY

"And God Created Woman," the American advertisement ran, "but the devil invented Brigitte Bardot." This first feature of Roger Vadim (Roger Vadim Plemiannikov 1928–), shot in St. Tropez, grossed

*This actor, familiar to Americans, was known professionally in Europe as Curd Jürgens.

over twenty-five million dollars worldwide and launched the curvaceous Brigitte Bardot—termed variously "sex kitten" and "sex uncorked"—into international stardom.

Juliette (Brigitte Bardot), a sexually uninhibited eighteen-year-old orphan raised by the Tardieu family in St. Tropez, marries one son Michel (Jean-Louis Trintignant), seduces his elder brother Antoine (Christian Marquand), and flirts with wealthy tycoon Eric Carradine (Curt Jurgens). Eventually Michel manages to "tame" his wife. "She didn't have any sense of guilt on a moral or sexual level," Vadim said of Juliette's character. "I wanted to show that because it really existed but wasn't yet a social attitude. . . ." For once, a woman was portrayed with a normal sexual appetite without being treated as a nymphomaniac.

And God Created Woman attacked traditional mores, created a scandal, helped broaden the screen's depiction of sexual frankness, and encouraged producers to venture with other untried "New Wave" directors.

MY UNCLE

(Mon Oncle)

SPECTRA FILMS/GRAY FILMS/ALTER FILMS/CADY FILMS (PARIS) LA FILM DEL CENTAURO (ROME)   1958

CREDITS

Screenplay: Jacques Tati, with the collaboration of Jacques Lagrange and Jean L'Hote; *Director:*

M. Hulot (Jacques Tati) gives his nephew Gérard (Alain Bécourt) a lift home from school.

Jacques Tati; *Photographer:* Jean Bourgoin (Eastmancolor); *Assistant Directors:* Henri Marquet and Pierre Etaix; *Editor:* Suzanne Baron; *Music:* Alain Romans and Frank Barcellini; *Running Time:* 116 minutes; *Paris Premiere:* May 10, 1958; *New York Premiere:* November 3, 1958.

CAST

M. Hulot: Jacques Tati; *M. Arpel:* Jean-Pierre Zola; *Mme. Arpel:* Adrienne Servantie; *Gérard Arpel:* Alain Bécourt; *M. Pichard:* Lucien Frégis; *Neighbor:* Dominique Marie; *Landlord's Daughter:* Betty Schneider; *M. Walter:* J. F. Martial; *Sweeper:* André Dino; *Georgette, Arpels' Maid:* Yvonne Arnaud.

COMMENTARY

Five years after *Mr. Hulot's Holiday,* M. Hulot returned in color in *My Uncle.* Here his sister (Adrienne Servantie) and brother-in-law Arpel (Jean-Pierre Zola) attempt to program the nonconformist into a "solid" factory job and respectable marriage—with disastrous results.

Tati contrasts Hulot's relaxed lifestyle in his old-fashioned milieu with the Arpel's sterile existence in their ultra-modern, gadget-dominated house.

Whereas Hulot maintains his humanity—and is a mentor to his nephew Gérard (Alain Bécourt)—the Arpels have become, in effect, machines. An English version *(My Uncle, Mr. Hulot)* was shot simultaneously. *My Uncle* ("a . . . defense of the individual, seen in a basically optimistic way"—Tati) won a Special Jury Prize at the Cannes Film Festival (1958), the Prix Méliès (1958), and received the New York Film Critics Award for "Best Foreign Film" and an Academy Award for best "Foreign Language Film" (1958). Overlong and less funny than its predecessor, *My Uncle* was a "warm-up" for Tati's forthcoming, more ambitious satire on a mechanized world, *Playtime* (1967).

THE LOVERS

(Les Amants)

NOUVELLES EDITIONS DE FILMS   1958

CREDITS

Adaptation: Louis Malle and Louise de Vilmorin, based on the tale, *Point de Lendemain* (1777), by Vivant Denon; *Dialogue:* Louise de Vilmorin; *Director:* Louis Malle; *Photographer:* Henri Decaë (Dyaliscope); *Assistant Directors:* Alain Cavalier, François Leterrier; *Editor:* Léonide Azar; *Music:* Brahms: Sextet No. 1 in B Flat, Op. 18, additional music: Alain de Rosnay; *Running Time:* 90 minutes; *Paris Premiere:* November 5, 1958; *New York Premiere:* October 26, 1959; *16 mm. Rental Source:* New Yorker Films.

CAST

Jeanne Tournier: Jeanne Moreau; *Henri Tournier:* Alain Cuny; *Bernard Dubois-Lambert:* Jean-Marc Bory; *Maggy Thiébaut-Leroy:* Judith Magre; *Raoul Florès:* José-Luis de Villalonga; *Coudray:* Gaston Modot; *Catherine (Jeanne's Daughter):* Patricia Garcin; *Marcelot:* Claude Mansard; *Marthe:* Georgette Lobbe.

COMMENTARY

The Lovers concerns a woman who rejects conventional morality "for a higher morality of self-realization," Louis Malle wrote, when she found love, "the kind of love everybody has a right to dream about." Jeanne (Jeanne Moreau), an unfulfilled wife in Dijon, undergoes a lyrical awakening during the course of one evening with Bernard (Jean-Marc Bory), a young archeologist she's just met. Next morning she abandons husband (Alain Cuny) and child and goes off with him to an uncertain future.

Instead of traditionally tracking away when the lovers start kissing, Malle lingered and in close-up revealed Miss Moreau in physical ecstasy underscored by Brahms' exquisite music.

Awarded a Special Jury Prize at the 1958 Venice Film Festival, branded "diabolical" by Vatican's *L'Osservatore Romano,* found "obscene" by censors throughout America until the Supreme Court ruled otherwise, the controversial hit *The Lovers*

The new lovers, Jeanne (Jeanne Moreau) and Bernard (Jean-Marc Bory) drift slowly in the moonlight during "the cinema's first night of love"—François Truffaut.

made Jeanne Moreau an international star and led to the screen's franker treatment of sex.

Today, those "shocking" night scenes, beautifully photographed by Henri Decaë, seem very tender and delicate.

BLACK ORPHEUS

(Orfeu Negro)

DISPATFILM (PARIS) / GEMMA CINEMATOGRAFICA (ROME) / TUPAN FILMES (BRAZIL)   1959

CREDITS

Screenplay: Jacques Viot and Marcel Camus, based on the play *Orfeu da Conceição* (1956), by Vinícius de Moraes; *Director:* Marcel Camus; *Photographer:* Jean Bourgoin (Eastmancolor and CinemaScope); *Assistant Director:* Robert Mazoyer; *Editor:* Andrée Feix; *Music:* Antonio Carlos Jobim and Luis Bonfa; *Running Time:* 100 minutes; *Paris Premiere:* June 12, 1959; *New York Premiere:* December 21, 1959; *16 mm. Rental Source:* Janus.

CAST

Orpheus: Breno Mello; *Eurydice:* Marpessa Dawn; *Mira:* Lourdes de Oliveira; *Serafina:* Lea Garcia; *Death:* Adhémar da Silva; *Hermes:* Alexandro Constantino; *Chico:* Waldetar de Souza; *Benedito:* Jorge dos Santos; *Zeca:* Aurino Cassanio.

COMMENTARY

Thinking, as he said, that "a contemporary version of the timeless legend of Orpheus and Eurydice set against a colorful background of Carnival time in Rio would make a beautiful and exciting movie," Marcel Camus (1912-1982) recruited non-professional actors (Mello was a soccer player, Miss Dawn an American dancer) and staged a "mock carnival" in Brazil to create the vibrant *Black Orpheus.*

Eurydice (Marpessa Dawn), escaping a vengeful, rejected suitor, flees to Rio at Carnival time and meets Orpheus (Breno Mello), a streetcar conductor. They fall in love but her pursuer, disguised as Death (Adhémar da Silva), kills her. True to the myth, Orpheus enters Hades (here a morgue) and with the help of a Macumba rite regains her temporarily before the ultimate fated tragedy.

The lovers are convincing and the spectacular carnival, with its lively samba music, is simply irresistible. *Black Orpheus,* Camus' only important film, was awarded the Grand Prize at the 1959 Cannes Film Festival and an "Oscar" for best "Foreign Language Film" (1959).

At the Longchamp racetrack Michel (Martin Lassalle) is tempted to steal once more, and this leads to his arrest.

PICKPOCKET

AGNÈS DELAHAIE PRODUCTION CINÉMATOGRAPHIQUE   1959

CREDITS

Screenplay and Direction: Robert Bresson; *Photographer:* Léonce-Henry Burel; *Assistant Directors:* Michel Clément, Claude Clément, and Jacques Bal-

On the steep bluffs overlooking Rio de Janeiro, Orpheus (Breno Mello) is quickly drawn to Eurydice (Marpessa Dawn) after meeting her—the legendary lovers now reincarnated in a Brazilian setting.

lanche; *Editor:* Raymond Lamy; *Music:* Jean-Baptiste Lully; *Running Time:* 75 minutes; *Paris Premiere:* December 16, 1959; *New York Premiere:* May 21, 1963; *16 mm. Rental Source:* New Yorker Films.

CAST

Michel: Martin Lassalle; *Jeanne:* Marika Green; *Jacques:* Pierre Leymarie; *Police Inspector:* Jean Pelegri; *Tutor in Theft:* Kassagi; *Accomplice:* Pierre Etaix; *Michel's Mother:* Dolly Scal; *Detective:* César Gattegno.

COMMENTARY

Taking Dostoevsky's *Crime and Punishment* as a scheme, Robert Bresson created another original and highly idiosyncratic film, *Pickpocket*—initially *Incertitude*—which concerns Michel (Martin Lassalle), an isolated young man evading his humanity who is drawn into the pickpocket's trade not for profit but through some inner compulsion which he doesn't understand. Loneliness, suffering, and imprisonment follow until there's eventual redemption through the steadfast love of Jeanne (Marika Green). A professional was employed to coach Lassalle. The real drama, however, lies not in the surface events but in the internal struggle against grace and Michel's ultimate acceptance of it.

The montage scenes of Kassagi teaching Michel the craft of the pickpocket accompanied by the music of Lully are remarkable and the sequence of the thieves plying their trade at a train station is so stunning that it seems more choreographed than directed. Louis Malle wrote: "It is a film with deep inspiration, free, instinctive, burning, bewildering ... Everything is beautiful in this film, because *Pickpocket* is a film of lightning newness."

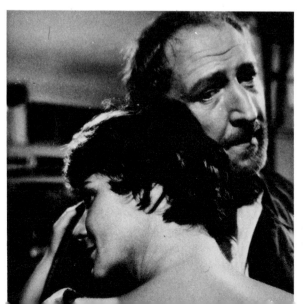

THE LONG ABSENCE

(Une Aussi Longue Absence)

PROCINEX PRODUCTIONS CINÉMATOGRAPHIQUE / LYRE SOCIÉTÉ CINÉMATOGRAPHIQUE (PARIS) / GALATEA (ROME)   1961

CREDITS

Screenplay: Marguerite Duras and Gérard Jarlot; *Director:* Henri Colpi; *Photographer:* Marcel Weiss; *Assistant Director:* Martin-Pierre Hubrecht; *Editor:* Jasmine Chasney; *Music:* Georges Delerue, with arias from Rossini and Donizetti; *Running Time:* 105 minutes; *Paris Premiere:* May 17, 1961; *New York Premiere:* November 15, 1962; *16 mm. Rental Source:* Facsea.

CAST

Thérèse Langlois: Alida Valli; *Tramp:* Georges Wilson; *Trucker:* Jacques Harden; *Client:* Charles Blavette; *Michel:* Amédée.

COMMENTARY

In the outskirts of Paris, a tramp (Georges Wilson), humming a Rossini aria, passes a café run by Thérèse (Alida Valli). Could this be her missing husband Albert, deported in the war sixteen years ago? Obsessively yet gently she tries to get the man to "remember," but he is amnesiac. Later while they dance she notices a deep scar in his skull, but this does not deter her quest.

"The principal theme," director Henri Colpi (1912–   ) said of his first feature, *The Long Absence,* "is the constancy of a love and the fundamental impossibility between two human beings to communicate."

A delicate, poignant film with two extraordinary performances by Alida Valli and Georges Wilson, abetted by Georges Delerue's moving score, *The Long Absence* won a Prix Louis Dellux (1960) and shared a Grand Prize with Buñuel's *Viridiana* at the 1961 Cannes Film Festival but was not a commercial success in this country. It is a beautiful, sensitive gem and deserves to be better known.

While dancing in her empty café with the man (Georges Wilson) she believes to be her missing husband, Thérèse (Alida Valli) is moved to tenderness.

A scene from the ballet *The Lovers of Téruel,* performed before spectators in a square, with the Duke of Téruel (Milko Sparemblek), center, hand raised, and Isabella (Ludmila Tchérina), being borne by soldiers.

THE LOVERS OF TERUEL

(Les Amants de Teruel)

SOCIÉTÉ MONARCH   1962

CREDITS

Story and Adaptation: Raymond Rouleau; *Dialogue:* René-Louis Lafforgue; *Director:* Raymond Rouleau; *Photographer:* Claude Renoir (Technicolor and Totalscope); *Assistant Directors:* Pierre Blondy and Jean Sayous; *Editor:* Marinette Cadix; *Music:* Mikis Theodorakis; *Choreography:* Milko Sparemblek; *Running Time:* 90 minutes; *Paris Premiere:* May 23, 1962; *New York Premiere:* December 14, 1962; *16 mm. Rental Source:* Walter Reade 16.

CAST

Isa: Ludmila Tchérina; *Manuel:* Milko Sparemblek; *Diego:* Milenko Banovitch; *Director:* René-Louis Lafforgue; *Grebilito:* Stevan Grebel; *Dwarf:* Ro-

berto; *Pablo:* Antoine Marin; *The Father:* Jean-Pierre Bras.

COMMENTARY

In the Paris outskirts a Gypsy dance theatre performs a ballet based on a seventeenth-century Spanish legend, "The Lovers of Téruel": Don Diego sets off with three years to prove himself worthy of marrying his beloved Isabella. Later, thinking him killed, she reluctantly consents to wed a cruel Duke. Diego returns, learns of her marriage, and kills himself. Insane with grief, Isabella takes her life. The real life drama runs parallel: Isa (Ludmila Tchérina), the troupe's star dancer, succumbs to the myth that she interprets. She longs for the return of her lover, the dancer Diego (Milenko Banovitch), while her current partner, the jealous Manuel (Milko Sparemblek), courts her. Diego reappears only to be murdered by Manuel. Isa goes mad and commits suicide.

The Lovers of Téruel, called "a voyage into phantasmagoria" by actor-director Raymond Rouleau (1904-1981), is a compelling, visually stunning dance-drama with gorgeous music by Mikis Theodorakis.* Originally a successful stage ballet, it proved a beautiful cinematic experiment and should be rediscovered by lovers of dance films.

THERESE DESQUEYROUX

FILMEL   1962

CREDITS

Adaptation: François Mauriac, Claude Mauriac, and Georges Franju, from the novel by François Mauriac (1927), published in New York as *Thérèse, A Portrait in Four Parts* (1947); *Dialogue:* François Mauriac; *Director:* Georges Franju; *Photographer:* Christian Matras; *Assistant Directors:* Georges Casati, Michel Worms, and Antoine Jacquet; *Editor:*

*The film was cited at the 1962 Cannes Film Festival "for the successful arrangement of special effects, color and sound in a discerning montage."

Gilbert Natot; *Music:* Maurice Jarre; *Running Time:* 109 minutes; *Paris Premiere:* September 21, 1962; *New York Premiere:* November 12, 1963; *16 mm. Rental Source:* Facsea.

CAST

Thérèse Desqueyroux: Emmanuèle Riva; *Bernard Desqueyroux:* Philippe Noiret; *Anne de la Trave:* Edith Scob; *Jean Azévédo:* Sami Frey; *Mme. de la Trave:* Renée Devillers; *M. de la Trave:* Richard Saint-Bris; *Jérome Larroque:* Lucien Nat; *Aunt Clara:* Hélène Dieudonné; *Balionte:* Jeanne Perez; *Duros:* Jacques Monod.

Tension mounts as Thérèse (Emmanuèle Riva) comes to realize how trapped she is in her unhappy marriage with the stolid and complacent Bernard (Philippe Noiret).

COMMENTARY

Georges Franju (1912–   ) co-founded the Cinémathèque Française in 1937 and directed important short documentaries and three features before making a faithful and psychologically penetrating adaptation of François Mauriac's celebrated novel, *Thérèse Desqueyroux,* which he updated from the twenties to the present.

Acquitted after being tried for attempting to poison her husband, the lonely Thérèsè (Emmanuèle Riva) reviews her empty marriage with the pompous Bernard (Philippe Noiret) and her stifling existence in Argelouse (Bordeaux countryside). Her hopes for a reconciliation are crushed as the implacable man condemns her to a torturous solitary confinement in her room. Later he permits

264

his debilitated wife to go to Paris, where she faces an uncertain future.

Emmanuèle Riva manages to arouse our sympathy for a character whom Franju called "a Bovary who strikes back" and "an enigma, a challenge." For her masterful performance Miss Riva was voted "Best Actress" at the 1962 Venice Film Festival. *Thérèse Desqueyroux* is a remarkable film, possibly Franju's finest achievement.

SUNDAYS AND CYBELE

(Les Dimanches de Ville-d'Avray)

TERRA FILMS / FIDES / ORSAY FILMS / LES FILMS DU TROCADÉRO   1962

CREDITS

Adaptation: Serge Bourguignon and Antoine Tudal, based on the novel by Bernard Eschasseriaux (1958); *Dialogue:* Serge Bourguignon and Bernard Eschasseriaux; *Director:* Serge Bourguignon; *Photographer:* Henri Decaë (Franscope); *Assistant Director:* Georges Lussan; *Editor:* Léonide Azar; *Music:* Maurice Jarre; *Running Time:* 110 minutes; *New York Premiere:* November 12, 1962; *Paris Premiere:* November 23, 1962; *16 mm. Rental Source:* Swank.

Pierre (Hardy Kruger) with Cybèle (Patricia Gozzi). "These two outsiders befriend one another, and each Sunday afternoon they explore a magic, secret child's world."—Serge Bourguignon.

CAST

Pierre: Hardy Kruger; *Françoise (Cybèle):* Patricia Gozzi; *Madeleine:* Nicole Courcel; *Carlos:* Daniel Ivernel; *Nurse:* André Oumansky; *Bernard:* Michel de Ré.

COMMENTARY

Pierre (Hardy Kruger), an amnesiac young man, suffers guilt about killing a girl when his plane crashed in the Indochina conflict. After seeing a man abandon his child (Patricia Gozzi) at an orphanage not far from Paris he pretends to be her father and each Sunday they go to the woods. She is twelve, precocious; their delicate friendship grows. Friends misconstrue the relationship and while the pair celebrate Christmas in the woods—as a gift she reveals her real name, Cybèle—police kill Pierre fearing he's about to harm her.

"I was fascinated by the contrast between a man who is very much a child and the child who is very much an adult," director Serge Bourguignon (1928–   ) said of his successful first feature, *Sundays and Cybèle.* In spite of some self-conscious "arty" shots, the film remains poignant and memorable with an enchanting performance by Patricia Gozzi and superb photography by Henri Decaë. *Sundays and Cybèle* won an "Oscar" for best "Foreign Language Film" of 1962.*

AU HASARD, BALTHAZAR

ARGOS FILM / PARC FILM / ATHOS FILMS (PARIS) / SVENSK-FILMINDUSTRI / SVENSK FILMINSTITUTET (STOCKHOLM)   1966

CREDITS

Screenplay and Direction: Robert Bresson; *Photographer:* Ghislain Cloquet; *Assistant Directors:* Jacques

---

*The following year it received two additional "Oscar" nominations: Serge Bourguignon and Antoine Tudal for "Writing (Screenplay—Based on Material from another Medium") and Maurice Jarre for "Scoring of Music—Adaptation or Treatment."

Kebadian and Sven Frostenson; *Editor:* Raymond Lamy; *Music:* Schubert's Sonata in A Major Op. Post. (D. 959), Second Movement; *Song:* Jean Wiener; *Running Time:* 95 minutes; *Paris Premiere:* May 25, 1966; *New York Premiere:* February 19, 1970; *16 mm. Rental Source:* New Line Cinema.

The donkey Balthazar receives affection from Marie (Anne Wiazemsky).

CAST

Marie: Anne Wiazemsky; *Gérard:* François Lafarge; *Marie's Father:* Philippe Asselin; *Marie's Mother:* Nathalie Joyaut; *Jacques:* Walter Green; *Arnold:* Jean-Claude Guilbert; *Grain Merchant:* Pierre Klossowski; *Baker:* François Sullerot; *Baker's Wife:* M. C. Frémont; *Notary:* Jean Remignard.

COMMENTARY

In *Au Hasard, Balthazar* Robert Bresson said he wished "to see an analogy between the different stages of the life of a donkey [Balthazar] and the life of a human being," and "to see the donkey suffering for all human vices."

In various episodes we see Balthazar proceed from children's pet to beast of burden under various abusive masters until he's fatally shot while being used to smuggle contraband. His life intersects with that of Marie (Anne Wiazemsky) and her seducer Gérard (François Lafarge) who subjects both to degradation and pain. The closing scene of this unsentimental film is remarkable: the donkey expires slowly in a field surrounded by sheep accompanied by Schubert's exquisite music. Balthazar is a witness to man's frailty and self-destructive impulses. "This film is really the world in an hour and a half"—Jean-Luc Godard. Showered with awards,* *Au Hazard, Balthazar* was referred to by Bresson as his "freest film . . . the one in which I have put the most of myself."

As their intimacy grows, Anne (Anouk Aimée) and Jean-Louis (Jean-Louis Trintignant) take their children and go out to a restaurant together for the first time.

A MAN AND A WOMAN

(Un Homme et une Femme)

LES FILMS 13   1966

CREDITS

Story: Claude Lelouch; *Adaptation and Dialogue:* Pierre Uytterhoeven and Claude Lelouch; *Director and Photographer:* Claude Lelouch (Eastmancolor

*Including a Special Jury Prize at the 1966 Venice Film Festival.

*Known here as *The Birds, the Bees and the Italians.*

and Sépia); *Assistant Director:* Claude Gorsky; *Editors:* Claude Lelouch and Claude Barrois; *Music:* Francis Lai; *Lyrics:* Pierre Barouh; *Song:* "Samba Saravah": *Music:* Baden Powell; *Lyrics:* Vinícius de Moraes; *Running Time:* 110 minutes; *Paris Premiere:* May 27, 1966; *New York Premiere:* July 12, 1966; *16 mm. Rental Source:* United Artists 16.

CAST

Anne Gauthier: Anouk Aimée; *Jean-Louis Duroc:* Jean-Louis Trintignant; *Pierre Gauthier:* Pierre Baròuh; *Valérie Duroc:* Valerie Lagrange; *Headmistress of Boarding School:* Simone Paris: *Antoine Duroc:* Antoine Sire; *Françoise Gauthier:* Souad Amidou; *Jean-Louis' Mistress:* Yane Barry; *Pump Attendant:* Paul Le Person; *Jean-Louis' Co-Driver:* Henri Chemin.

COMMENTARY

Anne (Anouk Aimée), a widow, and automobile racer Jean-Louis (Jean-Louis Trintignant), a widower, meet in Deauville where each has a child in boarding school. Anne's close bond to her late husband Pierre (Pierre Barouh) clouds their developing relationship, but the film ends on a hopeful note for the pair.

A Man and a Woman, the sixth feature of Claude Lelouch (1937–), dramatically weak but visually impressive, enhanced by beautiful photography and Francis Lai's popular score, was an enormous hit and launched the young director into international prominence. The film shared the Grand Prize at the 1966 Cannes Film Festival with Pietro Germi's *Signore e Signori.** Claude Lelouch was nominated for an "Oscar" for direction and Anouk Aimée for "Best Actress" (1966); *A Man and a Woman* won two "Oscars": Claude Lelouch and Pierre Uytterhoeven for best "Story and Screenplay (Written Directly for the Screen)" and for best "Foreign Language Film" of 1966. Miss Aimée was cited "Best Foreign Actress" by the British Society of Film and Television Arts (1967).

Instead of going off to the front to continue the madness of fighting, Pvt. Plumpick (Alan Bates), the "King of Hearts," decides to have himself committed and rejoin his gentle friends inside the asylum.

KING OF HEARTS

(Le Roi de Coeur)

SOCIÉTÉ DE FILDEBROC / LES
PRODUCTIONS ARTISTES ASSOCIÉS
(PARIS) / COMPANIA
CINEMATOGRAFICA MONTORO (ROME)   1966

CREDITS

Screenplay: Daniel Boulanger; *Director:* Philippe de Broca; *Photographer:* Pierre Lhomme (Color by Deluxe); *Assistant Directors:* Marc Monnet, Renzo Senato, and Marc Grunebaum; *Editor:* Françoise Javet; *Music:* Georges Delerue; *Running Time:* 102 minutes; *Paris Premiere:* December 21, 1966; *New York Premiere:* June 19, 1967; *16 mm. Rental Source:* United Artists 16.

CAST

Pvt. Charles Plumpick: Alan Bates; *"Gen. Geranium":* Pierre Brasseur; *"Duke de Trèfle":* Jean-Claude Brialy; *Coquelicot:* Geneviève Bujold; *Col. Alexander MacBibenbrook:* Adolfo Celi; *"Duchess":* Françoise Christophe; *"Monseigneur Marguerite":* Julien Guiomar; *"Mme. Eglantine":* Micheline Presle; *"M. Marcel":* Michel Serrault; *Lt. Hamburger:* Marc Dudicourt; *Col. Helmut von Krack:* Daniel Boulanger; *Albéric:* Pierre Palau.

COMMENTARY

From an account concerning French mental patients whose hospital was bombed and who, wandering around, donned American uniforms, only to be taken for soldiers by the Germans and fired upon, Philippe de Broca (1933–) created a charming farce (this "tragedy seen comically," he said) in *King of Hearts*.

During WWI retreating Germans plant timed explosives in a northern French town's square. The terror-stricken townspeople flee. Pvt. Plumpick (Alan Bates), of the advancing Scottish troops, is ordered to save the place. Hiding out briefly in the insane asylum, he calls himself the "King of Hearts." The inmates take over the empty town and become "prelate," "general", "brothel keeper," etc. Plumpick finally manages to defuse the charge but the two enemies confront and slaughter each other. Enroute to the front Plumpick opts to rejoin his tenderhearted but loony friends rather than continue with the insanity of war.

King of Hearts with Georges Delerue's memorable score mocks war successfully and became a counterculture hit in America during the Vietnam War.

During the war a very close friendship develops between young Claude (Alain Cohen) and Gramps (Michel Simon).

THE TWO OF US

(Le Vieil Homme et l'Enfant)

P.A.C. (PRODUCTION ARTISTIQUE
CINÉMATOGRAPHIQUE) / VALORIA
FILMS / RENN PRODUCTIONS   1967

CREDITS

Story, Dialogue, and Direction: Claude Berri; *Adaptation:* Claude Berri, Gérard Brach, and Michel Rivelin; *Photographer:* Jean Penzer; *Assistant Directors:* Pierre Grunstein, Claude Confortes, and Philippe Garnel; *Editors:* Sophie Coussein and Denis Charvein; *Music:* Georges Delerue; *Running Time:* 90 minutes; *Paris Premiere:* March 10, 1967; *New York Premiere:* February 19, 1968; *16 mm. Rental Source:* Cornith.

CAST

Gramps (Pépé): Michel Simon; *Claude:* Alain Cohen;

Granny (Mémé): Luce Fabiole; *Claude's Father:* Charles Denner; *Victor:* Roger Carel; *Maxime:* Paul Préboist; *Schoolteacher:* Jacqueline Rouillard.

COMMENTARY

The first feature of Claude Berri (Claude Langmann, 1934–   ), *The Two of Us,* was autobiographical. During WWII Claude (Alain Cohen), a mischievous and appealing eight-year-old Jewish boy, is sent to stay with a friend's grandparents for safekeeping in the Grenoble countryside. He feigns Catholicism and copes with an irascible but endearing Gramps (Michel Simon) who spouts Vichy propaganda, vegetarianism, and anti-Semitism. They become inseparable pals and part at the war's end.

Although this popular film wears thin for lack of dramatic or character development, the scenes of Simon and the boy playing together—enhanced by Georges Delerue's lyrical score—are charming. It is delightful to see the bright kid recognize the illogic behind the old man's prejudices and poke fun at such nonsense.

François Truffaut wrote that Berri's "comic and daring film moved me from beginning to end [and] . . . showed me that men are worth more than the ideas they hold. . . ."

Michel Simon was voted "Best Actor" at the 1967 Berlin Film Festival.

268   Roland (Jean Yanne) manages to escape from the burning wreck, while his wife Corinne (Mireille Darc) screams hysterically "Heeelllp! My Hermès bag!" Still indicates the mixture of horror and humor in this unusual film.

WEEKEND

COMACICO / LES FILMS COPERNIC / LIRA FILMS (PARIS) / ASCOT CINERAÏD (ROME)   1967

CREDITS

Screenplay and Direction: Jean-Luc Godard; *Photographer:* Raoul Coutard (Eastmancolor); *Assistant Director:* Claude Miller; *Editor:* Agnès Guillemot; *Music:* Antoine Duhamel, Mozart's Piano Sonata K576; *Song:* "Allô, Tu M'Entends" ("Hello, You Hear Me"), Guy Béart; *Running Time:* 95 minutes; *Paris Premiere:* December 29, 1967; *New York Premiere:* September 30, 1968; *16 mm. Rental Source:* New Yorker Films.

CAST

Corinne: Mireille Darc; *Roland:* Jean Yanne; *Leader of the F.L.S.O.:* Jean-Pierre Kalfon; *His Girlfriend:* Valérie Lagrange; *Saint-Just/Young Man in Phone Booth:* Jean-Pierre Léaud; *Member of the F.L.S.O.:* Yves Beneyton; *Pianist:* Paul Gégauff; *Joseph Balsamo:* Daniel Pommereulle; *Tom Thumb:* Yves Afonso; *Emily Brontë/Girl in Farmyard:* Blandine Jeanson; *Girl in Car Crash/Member of F.L.S.O.:* Juliet Berto; *Girl in Farmyard/Member of F.L.S.O.:* Anne Wiazemsky.

COMMENTARY

Enroute to visiting her parents, Corinne (Mireille Darc) and Roland (Jean Yanne)—a scheming, rapacious Parisian couple—experience a progression of violent, and often hilarious, encounters culminating in capture and his death by a band of cannibalistic Maoist guerillas.

Weekend ("A film found on a scrap heap"—Jean-Luc Godard) represents a bleak, apocalyptic landscape of smashed cars, aimlessness, nihilism, and unrelenting cruelty—our contemporary, materialistic culture depicted by Godard as a vision of Hell. Here the director moves from the personal angst of *Pierrot le Fou* to a preoccupation with radical politics. The most stunning sequence is near the beginning when a series of long tracking shots of stalled traffic finally reveal the shocking cause of the jam, a bloody multiple accident.

Typical of Godard's style, there are many cinematic and literary allusions and didactic addresses to the audience by the film's characters. Eventually the dazzling inventiveness, energy, and savage satire peter out, but *Weekend* remains a brilliant though markedly uneven film.

Although Maud (Françoise Fabian) wants a departing Jean-Louis (Jean-Louis Trintignant) to telephone, his interest lies elsewhere.

MY NIGHT AT MAUD'S

(Ma Nuit chez Maud)

LES FILMS DU LOSANGE /F.F.P. / SIMAR FILMS / LES FILMS DU CARROSSE / LES PRODUCTIONS DE LA GUÉVILLE / RENN PRODUCTIONS / LES FILMS DE LA PLÉÏADE / LES FILMS DES DEUX-MONDES   1969

CREDITS

Screenplay and Direction: Eric Rohmer; *Photographer:* Nestor Almendros; *Assistant Director:* Pierre Grimberg; *Editor:* Cécile Decugis; *Running Time:* 110 minutes; *Paris Premiere:* June 4, 1969; *New York Premiere:* March 22, 1970; *16 mm. Rental Source:* Corinth.

CAST

Jean-Louis: Jean-Louis Trintignant; *Maud:* Fran-

---

*Also known here as *My Night with Maud.*

çoise Fabian; *Françoise:* Marie-Christine Barrault; *Vidal:* Antoine Vitez; *Violinist at Concert:* Léonide Kogan; *Blonde Friend:* Anne Dubot; *Priest:* Guy Léger; *Marie, Maud's Daughter:* Marie Becker; *Student:* Marie-Claude Rauzier.

COMMENTARY

In Clermont-Ferrand, Vidal (Antoine Vitez), a Marxist friend, introduces Jean-Louis (Jean-Louis Trintignant), engineer and devout Catholic, to Maud (Françoise Fabian), an attractive divorcee. They spend the night discussing their conflicting philosophies. Snowbound, Jean-Louis stays over but declines Maud's sexual invitation. Later he marries the Catholic Françoise (Marie-Christine Barrault), closer to him temperamentally. Ironically, she had been the mistress of Maud's ex-husband.

*My Night at Maud's** is the third of the ambitious six "Moral Tales" ("*contes moraux*") which director Eric Rohmer (Jean Marie Maurice Scherer, 1920–) wrote and directed between 1962–72. They are not "moral" tales but films in which "a particular feeling is analyzed," said Rohmer, and whose reflective characters lucidly probe their feelings.

Intelligent, well-acted, *My Night at Maud's* won critical acclaim and was an international success. It received two "Oscar" nominations, for best "Foreign Language Film" (1969) and Eric Rohmer for best "Story and Screenplay Based on Factual Material or Material Not Previously Published or Produced" (1970), and won the New York Film Critics Award for "Best Screenwriting" (1970).

The beginning of an elegant dinner at the Sénéchal's: the Ambassador (Fernando Rey), (who is dreaming this scene), Mme. Thévenot (Delphine Seyrig), and servant Inès (Milena Vukotic), and M. Sénéchal (Jean-Pierre Cassel) before another interruption—this time by terrorists.

THE DISCREET CHARM OF THE BOURGEOISIE

(Le Charme Discret de la Bourgeoisie)

GREENWICH FILM PRODUCTION
(PARIS) / JET FILM (BARCELONA) / DEAN
FILM (ROME)   1972

CREDITS

Screenplay: Luis Buñuel and Jean-Claude Carrière; *Director:* Luis Buñuel; *Photographer:* Edmond Richard (Eastmancolor); *Assistant Directors:* Pierre Lary and Arnie Gelbart; *Editor:* Hélène Plémiannikov; *Running Time:* 105 minutes; *Paris Premiere:* September 15, 1972; *New York Premiere:* October 22, 1972; *16 mm. Rental Source:* Films Incorporated.

CAST

Raphaël Acosta, Ambassador of Miranda: Fernando Rey; *Simone Thévenot:* Delphine Seyrig; *Alice Sénéchal:* Stéphane Audran; *Henri Sénéchal:* Jean-Pierre Cassel; *Florence:* Bulle Ogier; *François Thévenot:* Paul Frankeur; *Bishop:* Julien Bertheau; *Colonel:* Claude Piéplu; *Minister:* Michel Piccoli; *Peasant:* Muni; *Inès, the Maid:* Milena Vukotic; *Dying Gardener:* George Douking; *Lt. Hubert de Rochecachin (Youth in Tearoom):* Bernard Musson; *Superintendent of Police:* François Maistre.

COMMENTARY

The Discreet Charm of the Bourgeoisie finds Luis Buñuel observing his *bêtes noires*—the bourgeoisie, church, and army—in a mellow, low-key, and droll manner. The Old Master said: "I now say with humor what I used to say with violence."

The attempts of the Ambassador of Miranda (Fernando Rey) to dine with his comfortable friends or make love to the wife (Delphine Seyrig) of one of them are constantly frustrated, sometimes hilariously so. Buñuel intersperses an episodic narration with bizarre, disturbing dreams to create another personal, Surrealistic film.

270

Beneath their facade of respectability these "charming" bourgeoisie are engaged in drug trafficking, political oppression, and corruption. However, immune to suffering, our imperturbable sextet manage to survive and endure. A recurring scene has the group strolling aimlessly along a country road.

Asked who were his favorite characters in the movie, Buñuel replied, "the cockroaches." This delightful entertainment received an "Oscar" nomination in the original screenplay category and won an Academy Award for best "Foreign Language Film" (1972).*

COUSIN, COUSINE

LES FILMS POMEREU/GAUMONT   1975

CREDITS

Story and Dialogue: Jean-Charles Tacchella; *Adaptation:* Jean-Charles Tacchella and Danièle Thompson; *Director:* Jean-Charles Tacchella; *Photographer:* Georges Lendi (Eastmancolor); *Assistant Director:* Jacques Fraenkel; *Editor:* Agnès Guillemot; *Music:* Gerard Anfosso; *Running Time:* 95 minutes; *Paris Premiere:* November 19, 1975; *New York Premiere:* July 25, 1976; *16 mm. Rental Source:* Cinema 5.

CAST

Marthe: Marie-Christine Barrault; *Ludovic:* Victor Lanoux; *Karine:* Marie-France Pisier; *Pascal:* Guy Marchand; *Bijou:* Ginette Garcin; *Diane:* Sybil Maas; *Sacy:* Jean Herbert; *Gobert:* Pierre Plessis; *Nelsa:* Catherine Verlor; *Thomas:* Hubert Gignoux.

COMMENTARY

An oppressed Marthe (Marie-Christine Barrault), wife of womanizing Pascal (Guy Marchand), meets nonconforming Ludovic (Victor Lanoux), husband of listless Karine (Marie-France Pisier), at a wedding. A zestful, liberating relationship—at first platonic, for they are cousins—blossoms. When they

*The British Society of Film and Television Arts voted Stéphane Audran "Best Actress" and Luis Buñel and Jean-Claude Carrière's script "Best Screenplay" (1973).

The special friendship between cousin Ludovic (Victor Lanoux) and cousine Marthe (Marie-Christine Barrault) gets more involved as the couple prepare for a rendez-vous.

decide to go off for a while, spouses, children, and relatives somehow manage to cope.

Director Jean-Charles Tacchella (1925–) said of his celebrational second feature, *Cousin, Cousine*: "I only had one aim in making this film: to recreate life in the way it fascinates me most—as absurdity, funniness, and fragility."

Cousin, Cousine, with its appealing cast and bouncy score, possessed great naturalness, charm, and vitality ("I like life to burst out on the screen"—Tacchella) and was a surprise hit here. It garnered a Prix Louis Delluc (1975) and received four César nominations (1975): best film, screenplay, actor, and supporting actress (which Marie-France Pisier won) and three "Oscar" nominations (1976): Marie-Christine Barrault for "Best Actress," Jean-Charles Tacchella and Danièle Thompson for "Writing (Screenplay Written Directly for the Screen)," and best "Foreign-Language Film."

NO TIME FOR BREAKFAST

(Docteur Françoise Gailland)

ACTION FILMS / FILMEDIS / S.F.P.
(SOCIÉTÉ FRANÇAIS DE PRODUCTION)   1976

CREDITS

Adaptation: André G. Brunelin and Jean-Louis Ber-

In spite of a hectic schedule, Dr. Françoise Gailland (Anne Girardot) finds time for an affair with Daniel (Jean-Pierre Cassel).

tucelli, based on the novel *Un Cri,* by Noëlle Loriot (1974); *Dialogue:* André G. Brunelin; *Director:* Jean-Louis Bertucelli; *Photographer:* Claude Renoir (Eastmancolor); *Assistant Director:* Franck Apprederis; *Editor:* François Ceppi; *Music:* Catherine Lara; *Running Time:* 100 minutes; *Paris Premiere:* January 14, 1976; *New York Premiere:* September 15, 1978; *16 mm. Rental Source:* Films, Inc.

CAST

Françoise Gailland: Annie Girardot; *Daniel Letessier:* Jean-Pierre Cassel; *Gérard Gailland:* François Périer; *Elisabeth Gailland:* Isabelle Huppert; *Julien Gailland:* William Coryn; *Geneviève Liénard:* Suzanne Flon; *Fabienne Cristelle:* Anouk Ferjac; *Régis Chabret:* Michel Subor; *Hélène Varese:* Joséphine Chaplin; *Jean Rivemale:* André Falcon.

COMMENTARY

Françoise Gailland (Annie Girardot) is a busy Parisian physician highly regarded by her staff and patients who attempts to manage a career, an unrewarding marriage to Gérard (François Périer), a pregnant teenage daughter (Isabelle Huppert) and neglected son (William Coryn), and a lover besides (Jean-Pierre Cassel). When she discovers she has cancer, she confronts her pending operation with courage and optimism.

In *No Time for Breakfast,* the popular fourth feature of Jean-Louis Bertucelli (1942–   ), we have a realistic portrait of a modern professional woman on the run. There's little plot but much absorbing characterization and a sense of the rhythm of contemporary life.

No Time for Breakfast is essentially a vehicle for the enormously popular Annie Girardot who won a César as "Best Actress" (1976) for her radiant performance. "She can do anything, this Annie Girardot," writes critic Hélène Demoriane. "For the past twenty years she has held us in her spell, she possesses us. Better than beautiful: true. Better than attractive: irresistible."

While the Great War rages in Europe, the ineffectual Sgt. Bosselet (Jean Carmet) oversees its mini-equivalent in French West Central Africa.

BLACK AND WHITE IN COLOR

(La Victoire en Chantant)

REGGANE FILMS / S.F.P. (SOCIÉTÉ FRANÇAISE DE PRODUCTION / F.R.3 (FRANCE RÉGIONS 3) (PARIS) / SMART FILM PRODUKTIONS (MUNICH) / S.I.C. (SOCIÉTÉ IVOIRIENNE DE CINÉMA) (ABIDJAN, IVORY COAST)   1976

CREDITS

Screenplay: Georges Conchon and Jean-Jacques Annaud; *Director:* Jean-Jacques Annaud; *Photographer:* Claude Agostini (Eastmancolor); *Assistant Directors:* Dominique Cheminal and Roger Fritz; *Editor:* Jean-Claude Huguet; *Music:* Pierre Bachelet; *Running Time:* 100 minutes; *Paris Premiere:* September 22, 1976; *New York Premiere:* May 8, 1977; *16 mm. Rental Source:* Corinth.

CAST

Sgt. Bosselet: Jean Carmet; *Paul Rechampot:* Jacques

272

Dufilho; *Marinette:* Catherine Rouvel; *Hubert Fresnoy:* Jacques Spiesser; *Maryvonne:* Dora Doll; *Caprice:* Maurice Barrier; *Jacques Rechampot:* Claude Legros; *Fr. Simon:* Jacques Monnet; *Fr. Jean de la Croix:* Peter Berling; *German Colonial:* Dieter Schidor.

COMMENTARY

Early in 1915 a tiny, remote French trading post in French West Central Africa still coexists peaceably with a nearby settlement consisting of a few German colonials. When Fort Coulais finally learns that the mother country has been at war with Germany for months, patriotic fervor mounts and on each side preparations for war are made, i.e., each side trains natives to fight the "enemy." Sgt. Bosselet (Jean Carmet) attacks the German post, but the assault is a fiasco. The idealistic young geographer Hubert Fresnoy (Jacques Spiesser) then takes command and we watch the former socialist evolve into an arrogant militarist.

Black and White in Color, the first feature of Jean-Jacques Annaud (1944–   ), shot in the Ivory Coast, is a satiric look at the vicissitudes of war. Through *reductio ad absurdum* the "Great War" in Europe becomes a ludicrous imbroglio in an obscure African outpost. Clever and witty, *Black and White in Color* was critically well-received and won an "Oscar" for best "Foreign Language Film" (1976).

MADAME ROSA

(La Vie devant Soi)

LIRA FILMS   1977

CREDITS

Screenplay: Moshe Mizrahi, based on the Prix Goncourt novel of Emile Ajar [Romain Gary] (1975), published in New York as *Momo* (1978); *Director:* Moshe Mizrahi; *Photographer:* Nestor Almendros (Eastmancolor); *Assistant Directors:* Tony Aboyantz and Emmanuel Fonlladosa; *Editor:* Sophie Coussein; *Music:* Philippe Sarde and Dabket Loubna; *Running Time:* 105 minutes; *Paris Premiere:* November 2, 1977; *New York Premiere:* March 19, 1978; *16 mm. Rental Source:* New Line Cinema.

CAST

Madame Rose: Simone Signoret; *Momo:* Samy Ben Youb; *Nadine:* Michal Bat Adam; *Mr. Hamil:* Gabriel Jabbour; *Mr. Charmette:* Bernard La Jarrige; *Docteur Katz:* Claude Dauphin; *Kadir Youssef:* Mohammed Zineth; *Maryse:* Genervièvre Fontanel; *Ramon:* Costa-Gavras; *Mme. Lola:* Stella Anicette.

COMMENTARY

Jewish, a survivor of Auschwitz, Madame Rosa (Simone Signoret) is an aging, former streetwalker who earns a living by looking after prostitutes' children in a multiracial quarter of Paris. She's especially attached to Momo (Samy Ben Youb), a young, attractive Arab boy she's raising as a Muslim. Momo returns her love by caring for her until her death.

Some twenty-five years after *Casque d'Or,* Simone Signoret is back in Belleville in the fourth feature by Moshe Mizrahi (1931–   ), *Madame Rosa.* "To accept being ten years older than you are," Miss Signoret commented, "wear the worst costumes . . . the least flattering make-up, be subjected to camera angles that make you look bigger if you're big, swollen up if you're puffy, it was a big dive for me." And well worth the risk, for Simone Signoret commands the screen with her unique presence and gives a performance which earned her a César for "Best Actress" (1977), while *Madame Rosa* won an "Oscar" for best "Foreign Language Film" (1977).

Portrait of Simone Signoret as the unforgettable Madame Rosa. "I never thought of anyone for the role of Madame Rosa other than Simone Signoret"—Moshe Mizrahi.

The loving friends, Alexa (Christine Murillo), left, and Fernand (Sami Frey), right, try to console an unhappy Louis (Mario Gonzalez), center.

POURQUOI PAS !

DIMAGE/S.N.D. (SOCIÉTÉ NOUVELLE DE DOUBLAGE)   1977

CREDITS

Screenplay and Direction: Coline Serreau; *Photographer:* Jean-François Robin (Eastmancolor); *Assistant Directors:* Patrick Dewolf and Georges Manulelis; *Editor:* Sophie Tatischeff; *Music:* Jean-Pierre Mas; *Running Time:* 93 minutes; *Paris Premiere:* December 21, 1977; *New York Premiere:* July 23, 1979; *l6 mm. Rental Source:* New Line Cinema.

CAST

Fernand: Sami Frey: *Louis:* Mario Gonzalez; *Alexa:* Christine Murillo; *Sylvie:* Nicole Jamet; *Inspector:* Michel Aumont; *Sylvie's Mother:* Mathé Souverbie; *Mme. Picaud:* Marie-Thérèse Saussure; *Roger:* Alain Salomon; *Louis' Father:* Jacques Rispal; *Roger's Colleague:* Bernard Crommbe.

COMMENTARY

Each from a disastrous, unfulfilled marriage, Alexa (Christine Murillo) and Fernand (Sami Frey), a carpenter, share a loving, intimate relationship with Louis, a jazz pianist, in a house in suburban Paris. The fragile equilibrium of the men's bisexual life style is upset when Fernand leaves and falls for Sylvie (Nicole Jamet), who has traditional values.

273

He brings her to the house where, after some conflict, she decides to join them to form a *ménage à quatre*.

Pourquoi Pas! (known here also as *Why Not?*), the first feature of Coline Serreau (1948–   ), is a compassionate and sensitive treatment of a delicate theme. Miss Serreau points out that her likable and unstereotyped characters "have found a way of life convenient for them—not necessarily for everyone. I'm only saying that we must have wider choices in our lives—they might be good choices and they might not."

Ostensibly realistic, *Pourquoi Pas!* is actually an unusual and provocative fable which was a critical success and a promising directorial début.

GET OUT YOUR HANDKERCHIEFS

(Preparez Vos Mouchoirs)

LES FILMS ARIANE/C.A.P.A.C.
(COMPAGNIE ARTISTIQUE DE
PRODUCTIONS ET D'ADAPTATIONS
CINÉMATOGRAPHIQUES)
(PARIS) / BELGA FILMS / SODEP
(BRUSSELS)   1978

CREDITS

Screenplay and Direction: Bertrand Blier; *Photographer:* Jean Penzer (Eastmancolor); *Assistant Director:* Jacques Fraenkel and Jean-Jacques Aublanc; *Editor:* Claudine Merlin; *Music:* George Delerue and selections from Mozart and Schubert; *Running Time:* 108 minutes; *Paris Premiere:* January 11, 1978; *New York Premiere:* December 17, 1978; *16 mm. Rental Source:* New Line Cinema.

CAST

Raoul: Gérard Depardieu; *Stéphane:* Patrick Dewaere; *Solange:* Carole Laure; *Neighbor:* Michel Serrault; *Christian Beloeil:* Riton; *Mme. Beloeil:* Eléonore Hirt; *M. Beloeil:* Jean Rougerie; *Passerby:* Sylvie Joly.

COMMENTARY

Another off-beat exploration of human relationships is the fourth feature of Bertrand Blier (1939–   ), *Get Out Your Handkerchiefs*. "It's the only subject that interests me," the director (son of actor Bernard Blier) said. "The relations between men and women are constantly evolving and it's interesting to show people leading the lifestyle of tomorrow."

Raoul (Gérard Depardieu) is obsessed with bringing his wife Solange (Carole Laure) out of her prolonged torpor. Thinking she needs a lover, he selects a candidate—Stéphane (Patrick Dewaere)—at a Paris restaurant. Stéphane gets heavily involved but Solange remains unresponsive. The men agree that she needs a baby, but again, they are unsuccessful. Ironically, at a summer camp she finds satisfaction with a precocious thirteen-year-old boy, Christian (Riton), who proceeds to get the happy woman pregnant.

Blier's original film is a consistently amusing and zany farce. Georges Delerue received a César for "Best Music" (1978) while *Get Out Your Handkerchiefs* won an "Oscar" for best "Foreign Language Film" (1978).

LA CAGE AUX FOLLES

LES PRODUCTIONS ARTISTES ASSOCIÉS
(PARIS) / DA MA PRODUZIONE SPA
(ROME)   1978

CREDITS

Screenplay: Francis Véber, Edouard Molinaro, Marcello Danon, and Jean Poiret, based on Jean

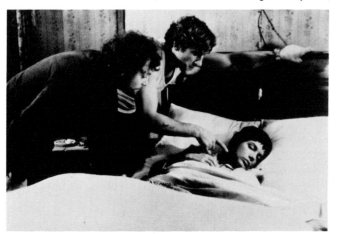

A solicitous Raoul (Gérard Depardieu), center, along with Stéphane (Patrick Dewaere), left, tends to his fragile wife Solange (Carole Laure), resting at a seaside hotel.

Poiret's play (1973); *Director:* Edouard Molinaro; *Photographer:* Armando Mannuzzi (Eastmancolor); *Assistant Directors:* Albino Cocco and Rafaèle Errige; *Editors:* Robert and Monique Isnardon; *Music:* Ennio Morricone; *Running Time:* 105 minutes; *Paris Premiere:* October 25, 1978; *New York Premiere:* May 13, 1979; *16 mm. Rental Source:* United Artists 16.

CAST

Albin ("Zaza"): Michel Serrault; *Renato:* Ugo Tognazzi; *Charrier:* Michel Galabru; *Simone:* Claire Maurier; *Laurent:* Remy Laurent; *Jacob:* Benny Luke; *Mme. Charrier:* Carmen Scarpitta; *Andrea:* Luisa Maneri.

COMMENTARY

Albin (Michel Serrault) and Renato (Ugo Tognazzi), long-time lovers, run a night-club, "La Cage aux Folles," in Saint-Tropez featuring drag shows with Albin as "Zaza." Renato's son Laurent (Remy Laurent) announces he's engaged but his fiancée's stuffy parents want to meet his parents. . .

Crazy complications ensue before the young couple make it to the altar.

Jean Poiret's smash play ran over seven years in Paris and was successfully filmed by prolific director Edouard Molinaro (1928–   ). Although it unfortunately perpetuates stereotypes of homosexuals as effeminate, *La Cage aux Folles* (also known as *Birds of a Feather*) is an outrageous, hilarious farce,

"Zaza" (Michel Serrault), Albin in drag, is greeted by the prospective father-in-law, M. Charrier (Michel Galabru), Deputy Secretary of the Union for Moral Order!

especially when the gay couple convert their flamboyant apartment into *"Nouveau Monastique."*

Michel Serrault won a César for "Best Actor" (1978); *La Cage aux Folles* received three "Oscar" nominations: Edouard Molinaro for direction; Francis Véber, Edouard Molinaro, Marcelle Danon, and Jean Poiret in the screenplay adaptation category; and Piero Tosi and Ambra Danon for "Costume Design" (1979). The hit earned over $17 million here, making it the biggest grossing foreign language film ever. It spawned a sequel, *La Cage aux Folles II* (1980); a third installment and a Broadway musical version are in the offing.

SELECTED BIBLIOGRAPHY

Additional titles in English not mentioned in the text:

GENERAL WORKS

Armes, Roy. *French Cinema Since 1946.* Vol. One: *The Great Tradition.* Enl. Ed. 1970. Vol. Two: *The Personal Style.* Enl. Ed. 1970. A. S. Barnes & Co.

Bazin, André. *What Is Cinema?* Vol. I, 1967. Vol. II. 1971. University of California Press.

———. *French Cinema of the Occupation and Resistance.* Frederick Ungar. 1981.

Monaco, James. *The New Wave.* Oxford University Press. 1976.

Sadoul, Georges. *French Film.* Arno Press. 1972.

Truffaut, François. *The Films in My Life.* Simon and Schuster. 1978.

SCRIPTS

Grove Press publishes *Day for Night, The 400 Blows, Hiroshima Mon Amour,* and *Last Year at Marienbad.*

New York University Press publishes a bilingual edition of *Beauty and the Beast.* 1970.

Frederick Ungar distributes the following Lorrimer Classic Screenplays: *Belle de Jour, Children of Paradise, La Grande Illusion, Le Jour se Lève, Jules and Jim, A Man and a Woman, A Nous la Liberté / Entre'acte, Pierrot le Fou, Rules of the Game, Weekend / Wind from the East,* and *Zéro de Conduite / L'Atalante.* Another Lorrimer title, *Masterworks of the French Cinema,* contains: *The Italian Straw Hat, Grand Illusion, La Ronde,* and *The Wages of Fear.*

Cocteau, Jean. *Three Screenplays: The Eternal Return, Orpheus,* and *Beauty and the Beast.* Grossman Publishers. 1972.

Dreyer, Carl. *Four Screenplays* (inc. *The Passion of Joan of Arc*). Indiana University Press. 1970.

STUDIES OF DIRECTORS

Ayfre, Amedée *et al. The Films of Robert Bresson.* Praeger. 1970.

McGerr, Celia. *René Clair.* Twayne. 1980.

Gilson, René. *Jean Cocteau.* Crown Publishers, Inc. 1969.

Kramer, Steven Philip and James Michael Welsh. *Abel Gance.* Twayne. 1978.

Roud, Richard. *Jean-Luc Godard.* Indiana University Press. Revised Edition. 1970.

Nogueira, Rui. *Melville.* The Viking Press. 1972.

Bazin, André. *Jean Renoir.* Simon and Schuster. 1973.

Sesonske, Alexander. *Jean Renoir, the French Films, 1924-1939.* Harvard University Press. 1980.

Monaco, James. *Alain Resnais.* Oxford University Press. 1979.

Insdorf, Annette. *François Truffaut.* William Morrow and Company, Inc. 1979.

Sallès Gomès, P. E. *Jean Vigo.* University of California Press. 1971.

FILM

Armand Panigel's excellent thirteen-part documentary film, *The History of the French Cinema by Those Who Made It,* is available for 16mm. rental from FACSEA.

FILM RENTAL
INFORMATION
(16 mm.)

Audio Brandon Films

34 MacQuesten Pkwy. S.
Mount Vernon NY 10550

Budget Films

4590 Santa Monica Blvd.
Los Angeles CA 90029

Cinema 5

595 Madison Avenue
New York NY 10022

Corinth Films

410 E. 62nd St.
New York NY 10021

Em Gee Film Library

16024 Ventura Blvd. Suite 21
Encino CA 91436

Facsea

972 Fifth Ave.
New York NY 10021

Films Incorporated

4420 Oakton St.
Stokie IL 60076

Hurlock Cine-World

13 Arcadia Rd.
Old Greenwich CT 06870

The Images Film Archive

300 Phillips Park Road
Mamaroneck NY 10543

Janus Films

Suite 400
119 W. 57th St.
New York NY 10019

M.O.M.A. (Museum of Modern Art)
Department of Film

11 W. 53rd St.
New York NY 10019

New Line Cinema

575 Eighth Avenue
New York N.Y. 10018

New Yorker Films

16 W. 61st St.
New York NY 10023

Swank Motion Pictures

201 S. Jefferson Ave.
St. Louis MO 63166

United Artists 16

729 Seventh Ave.
New York NY 10019

Walter Reade 16

241 E. 34th St.
New York NY 10016

Arletty (*Children of Paradise*)

(Overleaf)

The Boulevard du Temple at carnival time (the conclusion to *Children of Paradise*).